China's Economic Dialectic

China's Economic Dialectic

The Original Aspiration of Reform

Cheng Enfu

INTERNATIONAL PUBLISHERS, New York

ISBN 10: 0-7178-0887-4   ISBN-13 978-07178-0887-8
Typeset by Amnet Systems, Chennai, India

Table of Contents

Foreword

John Bellamy Foster

China's record of accelerated economic growth and continuous industrial revolution over the last four decades has no historical precedent. Between 1978 and 2015, while the wealthy capitalist economies at the center of the world system stagnated in economic terms (with average growth rates per decade falling below 3 percent), China saw a thirty-fold increase in its real Gross Domestic Product (GDP).[1] In 1978, the per capita income in China was only one-third that of sub-Saharan Africa, with more than 800 million of the Chinese population, in 1981, living on less than $1.25 a day, in what was a predominantly agrarian country.[2] By 2018, China's per capita income had climbed to the world's median-income level, and today it has eliminated absolute poverty within its borders.[3] China is now the earth's leading industrial powerhouse and the foremost global exporter of manufactured goods. Since 2014, it has been a net exporter of capital.[4] It dominates some of the world's most technologically advanced industries. As Yi Wen, economist, and vice president of the Federal Reserve Board of St. Louis, has noted, 'China compressed the roughly 150 to 200 (or more) years of revolutionary economic changes experienced by England in 1700-1900 and the United States in 1760-1920 and Japan in 1850-1960 into one single generation'.[5]

None of this, however, captures the full extent of the Chinese achievement, which constitutes the greatest U-Turn in the history of the world economy. To understand this, it is necessary to go back to the dawn of the industrial era. In 1800, China accounted for 33.3 percent of total world industrial potential. By 1900, as a result of the Industrial Revolution in the West, which was fed by colonialism and slavery (including the imposition of unequal treaties on China via Western 'gunboat diplomacy'), the Chinese share of world industrial potential had dropped to 6.3 percent. By 1953, it had dropped still further to as little as 2.3 percent.[6] 'At no time between the 1840's and 1949', W.W. Rostow wrote in *The World Economy* in 1978, 'were the Chinese free to concentrate wholeheartedly on the tasks of economic and social modernisation', while from 1949-1978, 'the pace of industrial expansion' was 'relatively rapid'.[7] The turning point, in 1949, was, of course, the Chinese Revolution, which, following a century of colonial-capitalist intrusions, allowed China to control its own destiny once again.

In two roughly thirty-year periods, the first associated with the name of Mao Zedong (1949-1977), the second mainly with Deng Xiaoping (1978-2008), China went from the initial revolutionary construction of a centrally planned, collectivised socialist economy in a peasant society (during which its progress was impeded by the Cold War launched by the United States), to a period of opening up, market reform, and reinsertion into the world economy. Beginning in 1978, it privatised much of its economy while nevertheless maintaining a large state sector. In 2001, China became a member of the World Trade Organisation, and in the eyes of many was on the way to becoming a leading, second-tier capitalist economy. The Great Financial Crisis of 2008, beginning in the United States and spreading to the global economy was a watershed. China saw a massive decline in the external demand for its goods. Yet, it was able to pull itself out of the crisis with remarkable speed. Nevertheless, the veil was suddenly torn away from the so-called Washington Consensus, exposing the misguided views of those advocating neoliberal restructuring, and causing Beijing to place renewed emphasis on safeguarding the strategic role of its state-owned enterprises.[8]

In Xi Jinping's New Era, beginning in 2012, China, having emerged as an economic superpower, has shifted its core emphasis back to fulfilling its 'original aspirations' of promoting a socialist 'common prosperity'. The New Era has stressed combatting corruption, the creation of greater equality so as to ensure that the benefits of growth go to the entire population, and the development of an 'ecological civilisation', along with rural revitalisation. This dramatic shift has been accompanied by a turn toward the Global South with the launching of the Belt and Road Initiative spanning the globe. China is now moving rapidly toward fulfilling its second-centennial goal — following the achievement in 2021 of its first-centennial goal of a 'moderately well-off' society — in which it is to become, by 2049, a 'prosperous, strong, democratic, culturally advanced, and harmonious' society: a modern *socialism with Chinese characteristics*.[9]

How is China's Great U-Turn to be explained? What were the means of carrying it out? Why is it unstoppable?[10] Orthodox, neoclassical economics, within their limited frame of analysis, which measures everything by the yardstick of a capitalist system conceived as a universal, insurmountable reality, have no real answers to these questions. All hegemonic-Western attempts to analyse China, in terms of the dominant categories of capitalist economics, have failed, including ludicrous endeavors to delimit the Chinese political economy, variously, as neoliberal, Keynesian, social democratic, welfare capitalist, or state capitalist. The nature of China's political order (commonly dismissed in the West as simply an 'authoritarian regime'), along with its economic system, have been little understood, since not fitting into the well-worn ideological categories that define the dominant liberal world view. Widely accepted convictions, emanating from the Washington Consensus, that China would fall into the middle-income trap or fall prey to corruption emanating from its domestic capitalist class have thus far proven false.[11] Likewise, the widespread expectation in the West in late 2019 and early 2020 that the People's Republic of China would be overcome by the spread of COVID-19, turned out to be wrong. Rather, China, demonstrating the strength of its polity, was able to rely on the self-mobilisation of its population, utilising the model of people's revolutionary war, with the result that, as of September 2021, China has suffered three deaths per million from COVID-19, as compared with 2,140 deaths per million in the United States.[12]

The truth is that China, under the leadership of the Communist Party of China (CPC), while rapidly absorbing ideas and technology from the West, has been guided strategically all along by Marxian political-economic theory and a dialectical and historical materialism with Chinese characteristics, giving it an advantage in terms of theory and practice over all previous paths of development. China has, in fact, invented a new mode of economic and social development, setting aside many of the so-called 'free market' nostrums of conventional capitalist economics and avoiding the pitfalls of monopoly-finance capital. To understand this, it is necessary to learn from Marxism with Chinese characteristics.

All historical periods of great social ferment give rise to revolutionary new ideas and to the new thinkers in whom these ideas are embodied. Commenting on the Renaissance, Frederick Engels observed that the rediscovery of the Greek civilisation lying under the Roman ruins, resulted, in the early modern era, in a whole new flowering of science and culture. The result was the emergence of 'giants in power of thought, passion and character, in universality and learning', who became the world-historical intellectual figures of their time.[13] In its current flowering, during the New Era, China is seeing such a renaissance, rooted in its long revolution, leading to the emergence of new intellectual 'giants', embodying the spirit of the times.

Cheng Enfu, the principal author of this book, certainly rates as one such world-historical thinker, associated with the current renewal in the New Era of Marxist political economy in China. He is a former academic president of the Institute of Marxist Studies and of Western Economic Studies in the Chinese Academy of Social Sciences (CASS), and is currently director of the Research Center of Economic and Social Development at CASS. He is also director of the World Association for Political Economy and president of the Chinese Forum on Innovation in Marxism. He edits two international journals, published in Britain: *International Critical Thought* and *World Review of Political Economy*, as well as two Chinese journals: *Research in Political Economy* and the *Journal of Economics of the Shanghai School*. Among his many economic and political works is his masterpiece, *Creation of Value by Living Labour*, coauthored with Wang Guijin and Zhu Kui.[14]

In *China's Economic Dialectic*, written by Cheng with the assistance of a number of colleagues, including Ding Xiaoqin, we encounter a study that captures the inner logic of China's political economy, while addressing issues of strategy and policy at every level.[15] This work, therefore, illuminates the full significance of 'socialism with Chinese characteristics', with respect to the mode of economic regulation. Central to the Chinese socialist market system, still governed by five-year plans, is the large role of state and collective property, and the continuing strategic dominance of the state sector over the private sector — while leaving room for the latter to prosper and help guide economic development within the parameters set by the state and under the leadership of the CPC. The critical needs of the economy and society are understood as changing in various eras, representing different 'principal contradictions'.[16] In the early Revolutionary Era, the principal contradiction was creating a basis for collective property, and for Chinese independence in the world at large. In the Reform Era, the chief need was rapid economic growth and industrialisation. In the New Era, the emphasis is on building a strong, 'autocentric' Chinese economy, relying on increased internal innovation, a dual circulation strategy (encompassing outward and inward growth, urban and rural codevelopment), greater equality, and the reinstitution of the *mass line* as a means of popular protagonism.[17] The balance between the state and private sectors is again changing, with increased stress on the strategic role of state ownership and a growing emphasis on a more equitable distribution according to labour. These and many other issues, related to the Chinese economy, are discussed in this work.

If China can be seen as entering a New Era in the Xi period, focused on fulfilling the 'original aspirations' of the Chinese Revolution, Cheng's research in this book can be viewed as that of an organic intellectual, in the Gramscian sense, who resisted earlier tendencies and played a formative role in a new turn toward innovative Marxism within the academy. Much of the analysis here was written when the field of economics within the Chinese academy (as opposed to the party and state) was almost completely dominated by neoliberal analysis. His work thus represents an early dialectical synthesis pointing to China's current phase.

For Western Marxists, what is likely to be most astonishing is the many-sided approach to Marxism displayed throughout this work. This reflects a strong emphasis on cultivating an open Marxism, drawing on different views and debates, and various movement vernaculars, in the continuing world struggle for socialism.[18] Here we see the emergence of a unified critical perspective in line with Marx and Engels's original conception of a historical-materialist *Wissenschaft*, a term usually translated into English as 'science', but, in fact, standing for something far wider: a system of knowledge, learning, and science, rooted in dialectical and materialist inquiries.[19] Chinese Marxism, with the work of Cheng Enfu standing as one example, can thus be viewed today as offering a new, creative 'historical-materialist *Wissenschaft*' with Chinese characteristics for the twenty-first century.

John Bellamy Foster

Eugene, OR
September 2021

Notes

1. Yi Wen, 'The Making of an Economic Superpower: Unlocking China's Secret of Rapid Industrialization', Federal Reserve Board of St Louis, Economic Research, Working Paper Series, (August 2015), 2, https://research.stlouisfed.org/wp/more/2015-006; John Bellamy Foster and Robert W. McChesney, *The Endless Crisis* (New York: Monthly Review Press, 2012), 4, John Ross, *China's Great Road* (Glasgow: Praxis Press, 2021), 13, 178.

2. Yi Wen, 'China's Rapid Rise: From Backward Agrarian Society to Industrial Powerhouse in Just 35 Years', Federal Reserve Board of St. Louis, April 11, 2016, https://www.stlouisfed.org/publications/regional-economist/april-2016/chinas-rapid-rise-from-backward-agrarian-society-to-industrial-powerhouse-in-just-35-years; John Ross, *China's Great Road*, 23.

3. Yi Wen, 'Income and Living Standards Across China', Federal Reserve Bank of St. Louis (January 8, 2018).

4. Yi Wen, 'The Making of an Economic Superpower', 114.

5. Yi Wen, 'The Making of an Economic Superpower', 9.

6. David Christian, *Maps of Time* (Berkeley: University of California Press, 2004), 406-09; Paul Bairoch, 'The Main Trends in National Economic Disparities Since the Industrial Revolution', in Bairoch and Maurice Lévy-Leboyer, eds., *Disparities in Economic Development Since the Industrial Revolution* (New York: St. Martin's Press, 1981), 7-8. See also Yi Wen, 'China's Rapid Rise', Figure 1. The Chinese percentage of world industrial potential rose from 2.3 in 1953 to 3.9 in 1973, as a result of the industrialisation in the Mao period. Christian *Maps of Time*, 408.

7. W.W. Rostow, *The World Economy: History and Prospect* (Austin: University of Texas Press, 1978), 522, 536. Rostow's statement that China's industrial growth had been 'relatively rapid since 1949' — an observation that he backed up with extensive statistics — has added significance given the 1978 date of his book, since he was referring to the successful industrial growth path of the Chinese economy during its first thirty years following the revolution, *prior to the reform period.*

8. Lowell Dittmer, "Transformation of the Chinese Political Economy in the New Era," in Dittmer, ed. *China's Political Economy in the Xi Jinping Epoch* (Singapore: World Scientific Publishing, 2021), 3-40.

9. Xi Jinping, *The Governance of China*, vol. 2 (Beijing: Foreign Languages Press, 2017), 15. The first centennial marked the hundredth-year anniversary of the formation of the Chinese Communist Party.

10. In 2004, the *New York Times* declared that nothing other than 'Mao's resurrection or nuclear cataclysm' was likely to arrest China's economic course. By 'Mao's resurrection' was meant a return to the original aspirations of the Chinese Revolution. Given that the New Era in China promises precisely this kind of revolutionary rejuvenation aimed at a socialism with Chinese characteristics, making China in fact even more unstoppable, the world-hegemonic order led by the United States is now threatening China with 'nuclear cataclysm' with the launching of a New Cold War on China. See Ted C. Fishman, 'The Chinese Century', *New York Times*, July 4, 2004; John Bellamy Foster, 'The New Cold War on China', *Monthly Review* 73, no. 3 (July-August 2021): 1-20.

11. With respect to the view that China would almost inevitably be caught in the 'middle-income transition' trap see Michael Spence, *The Next Convergence* (New York: Farrar Strauss and Giroux, 2011), 195-98. On the corruption trap, former U.S. Treasury Secretary Larry Summers wrote (with Lant Pritchett) as recently as 2014: 'We suggest that salient characteristics of China — high levels of state control and corruption along with high measures of authoritarian rule — make a discontinuous decline in growth even more likely than general experience [the normal regression to the mean in economic growth] would suggest'. Lant Pritchett and Lawrence H. Summers, 'Asiaphoria Meets Regression to the Mean', National Bureau

of Economic Research, Working Paper, no. 20573 (October 2014), 2 (abstract), https://www.nber.org/system/files/working_papers/w20573/w20573. pdf. What Spence and Summers failed to understand is that, in the case of China, historic trends (including the middle-income trap and the corruption trap) do not necessarily apply in the same way, given that it is a partially planned, state-regulated socialist-market economy. Thus, the current 'dual circulation' strategy aimed at the development of internal markets, and the goal of a socialist 'common prosperity', are both directed at transforming economic and social institutions to avoid these two classic traps of capitalist development.

12. On the role of the model of people's revolutionary war in combatting the SARS-Cov-2 virus see Wang Hui, 'Revolutionary Personality and the Philosophy of Victory: Commemorating Lenin's 150th Birthday', Reading the Chinese Dream (blog), April 21, 2020, https://www.readingthechinadream. com/wang-hui-revolutionary-personality.html.

13. Frederick Engels, *Dialectics of Nature* (Moscow Progress Publishers, 1972 printing), 21.

14. Cheng Enfu, Wang Guijin, and Zhu Kui, *The Creation of Value by Living Labour* (Istanbul: Canut, 2019).

15. A précis of Cheng's views on China's economic 'miracle', summarizing much of the argument in this book was provided in Cheng Enfu and Ding Xiaoqin, 'A Theory of China's 'Miracle': Eight Principles of Contemporary Chinese Political Economy', *Monthly Review* 68, no. 8 (January 2017): 46-57.

16. Mao Tse-Tung (Zedong), *Selected Works*, vol.1 (Peking: Foreign Languages Press, 1967), 346.

17. On 'autocentric' development see Samir Amin, *Unequal Development* (New York: Monthly Review Press, 1976), 76-78, 191-97. On 'dual circulation' see Xi, *The Governance of China*, vol. 3, 20; 'What We Know About China's 'Dual Circulation' Economic Strategy', *Reuters*, September 15, 2020.

18. In relation to open Marxism see: the preface to this book; Cheng Enfu and Wang Zhongbao, 'Enriching and Developing Marxism in the Twenty-First Century in Various Aspects: Six Definitions of Marxism', *International Critical Thought* 8, no. 2 (2018): 1-16; and John Bellamy Foster, 'Marx's Open-Ended Dialectic', *Monthly Review* 70, no. 1 (May 2018): 1-16. Cheng's approach to revolution in the Global South, and his understanding of the need for different strategies and revolutionary vernaculars, builds on Lenin's theory of imperialism and its continuing relevance in the contemporary phase of global monopoly-finance capital. See Cheng Enfu and Lu Baolin, 'Five Characteristics of Neoimperialism: Building on Lenin's Theory of Imperialism in the Twenty-First Century', *Monthly Review* 73, no. 1 (May 2021): 22-58. On the concept of vernacular revolutionary movements see Teodor Shanin, *Late Marx and the 'Russian Road'* (New York: Monthly Review Press, 1983), 243-79.

19. Joseph Fracchia, 'Dialectic Itineraries', *History and Theory* 38, no. 2 (May 1999): 194.

Acknowledgements

Just as Marx stated in *Capital* that 'collaboration produces new productive forces', I have cooperated for many years with my graduate students, with post-doctoral researchers, and with visiting scholars in writing academic articles. This has been necessary since my academic research has continuously led me to formulate fresh ideas, and I have not been able to spare the time to complete articles by myself. In addition, my students have shown much eagerness to cooperate, as they seek to enter the academic frontiers and obtain research results as soon as possible. While all the articles selected and edited for this book conform to my ideas and thoughts, some were therefore co-written with my students and colleagues. In the case of these articles, I made some revisions to the drafts and created the final version. My collaborators also performed copious amounts of research and offered thoughtful interpretations, which is evidence of a typical win-win cooperation. In the order of the chapters, the co-authors are Chai Qiaoyan, Gao Jiankun, Zhou Zhitai, Tan Jinsong, Ding Xiaoqin, Hu Jingchun, Hou Hehong, Liu Wei, Zhou Zhaoguang, Wang Cui, Sun Yexia, Lian Shu, Li Bingyan, and Zhu Bingyuan. In addition, Lecturer Zhang Yang put a great deal of effort into sorting out the materials in this book. I would like to express my heartfelt gratitude for the efforts these people have contributed.

Moreover, Jin Bidong and other staff members of the National Development and Reform Commission have put a great deal of energy into the publication of this book. I would like to express my sincerest gratitude to them!

Any comments or suggestions related to this book are welcome.

Cheng Enfu
August 2018

China's Economic Dialectic

Introduction: Ten Views on Marxism Formed during the Chinese Revolution and Their Development at Home and Abroad

By Cheng Enfu

For many years, I have called for an organic combination of academic research in the field of Marxism with the exploration of new methods for applying its principles, while actively spreading Marxist ideas. It follows that I must take the lead in practicing Marxism. As an academic researcher, I have successively been editor-in-chief of *The History of Marxist Economic Thought* (Volumes on Classics, China, the Soviet Union, Japan, Europe, and the United States), etc. I have published many papers including *Theoretical Research on 60 Years of Marxism in China* and *On Promoting the Academic Principle of the Modernization of Chinese Economics*. A prominent thread in my works has been analysis of the relationship between Marxism, Western scholarship, and studies of ancient Chinese civilisation, specifically, in texts such as *On the Four Major Theoretical Assumptions of Modern Marxist Political Economy* and *The Theory of Classification and Innovation in Marxist Economics*, etc. In the area of applying Marxist ideas and enacting the recommendations of think tanks, I have been the editor-in-chief of publications discussing the new population strategy, the new pension strategy, the new opening-up strategy, and so forth. I have also published papers entitled *How to Build an Accounting System for Gross Domestic Welfare* and *On a State-Led System for the Protection of Enterprise Employees' Rights and Interests*, as well as the commentary *On Some Issues of Income Distribution*, and so on. As a representative at three sessions of the National People's Congress (NPC), I submitted several policy recommendations in writing to each annual session. In the field of Marxist theory, I have been editor-in-chief of such works as *The New Development of Marxism in Contemporary China* and *Research Series on the System of Socialism with Chinese Characteristics* (in five volumes, dealing with the economy, politics, culture, society, and the environment). I have also published works including *On Promoting Socialism with Chinese Characteristics and Continuing to Emancipate the Mind* and *Social Democracy and How it Differs from Socialism with Chinese Characteristics.*

In the current period, I am progressively implementing a personal academic plan. While concentrating on innovations in economic theory, I have also turned to the study of Marxism in the fields of philosophy, political science, and international relations. I have summarised my thinking here into ten viewpoints of Marxism, which are expounded briefly as follows.

1. The Definition of Marxism

In my view, the definition of Marxism and the exposition of its basic content found in most textbooks and works in the academic world is correct, but not sufficiently so that it can fully resolve all doubts. Therefore, I will begin by expanding the definition of Marxism into four levels (Cheng and Hu 2010), and later into six levels (Wang and Cheng 2017), in order to enrich and develop 21st century Marxism in a range of its aspects.

First, it is necessary to define Marxism from the perspective of its origins, since Marxism as a theoretical system was initiated by Marx and Engels and since then, has gradually been developed and improved by their successors. Some scholars disagree with the proposition that Marxism should be developed on the basis of two main bodies functioning respectively as political leader and scholar; coupled with two main platforms presented in political and academic circles; and giving rise to the two 'Marxisms' represented by the guiding thought of the Communist Party and by academic thought. The above-mentioned scholars believe that Marxism is an inseparable indissoluble body of thought, and thus reject the notion that political and academic Marxists exist separately and need to establish a positive interaction with each other. In my opinion, this view is clearly archaic and one-sided. The reason lies in the fact that while the theoretical system of Marxism is an organic whole, objectively it is studied and developed both by leaders of the Communist Party and by scholars of Marxism. The two groups, of course, have similarities and differences in their methods and characteristics, as well as in the content of their research and in the development of their ideas.

Second, Marxism, from an academic perspective, is a system of ideas concerned with the laws of nature, society, and the development of thought. Public opinion in some quarters mistakenly believes that Marxism is exclusively a revolutionary theory and ideology. In my view, the ideas of Marxism, like non-Marxist theories dealing with the same topics, are both ideological and academic, though with essential differences from non-Marxist theories in standpoint and method. Further, Marxism is not only a general academic system of thought, but more important, the most scientific of all academic systems.

Third, Marxism is the ideological guiding system of socialist revolution and construction, as well as of the transition to a communist society. Certain sectors of public opinion believe mistakenly that Marxism is out of date or useless or has undergone no theoretical improvement. In *Das Kapital* alone, however, Marx expounded numerous times on socialism and the communist economy and elaborated on a series of issues such as the forms of ownership, development in proportion, economic planning, reproduction, necessary labour and surplus labour, the distribution system, funds of all kinds, land and agriculture, the all-round development and education of the human individual, the family, and so on. The theories of socialism with Chinese characteristics inherit and develop these ideas comprehensively and systematically, play an extremely important guiding role, and have enormous social effects. The political economy of socialism with Chinese characteristics needs to establish an innovative theoretical system that does not place capital at its centre, but people, and that makes free united labour its core concept.

Fourth, and from the perspective of people's well-being, Marxism is a system of principles and ideas whose focus is on improving people's livelihood and on realizing their free and comprehensive development. Some elements of public opinion mistakenly hold that Marxism is a 'lofty and superior' theory that has nothing to do with such issues as entrepreneurship and employment, with income distribution and housing, with social security and welfare, or with marriage and family. The truth is quite different: all classical Marxist writers, Communist Party leaders, and Marxist scholars have attached great importance to and have elaborated on the issues of people's livelihood and well-being. All have engaged in a large number of theoretical and policy discussions that today's Marxists have inherited and kept up to date. We must pay close attention to people's livelihood, to their happiness and human development, and take a down-to-earth approach to developing the Marxist principles and policies of common prosperity, of sharing benefits, and of common happiness.

Fifth, and from the perspective of values, Marxism is a cultural-ideological system that stresses faith and values. There is a strain

of public opinion that mistakenly holds that only religious followers have beliefs and values in life. But generally speaking, I regard
faith as a belief in and respect for a certain doctrine, religion, or other
set of principles that people embrace as their own code of conduct.
There are three types of belief that are compatible with basic values: primitive belief, where people believe in totems, taboos, myths,
and witches, religious belief, in which people follow the teaching
of founders and believe in religious doctrines that they themselves
help to shape, and finally, a third category that consists of secular
doctrines. In modern times, various theoretical systems or doctrines
have attracted many believers; these systems include Western 'universal values', constitutional views, neoliberalism, etc., and also
adherence to Marxism and communism. However, it is only Marxist beliefs concerning life and basic values that are scientific and
advanced, and that therefore should be and eventually will be realised throughout the world.

Sixth, and from the perspective of international relations, Marxism is an international ideological system that is founded on a belief
in the need for peaceful development throughout the world, and
for the promotion of a world community with a shared future for
humankind. It is sometimes believed, mistakenly, that Marxism only
advocates violent revolution. Marx, in fact, considered that peaceful
and violent revolutionary measures represent two ways of dealing
with problems of domestic and international relations, and that they
should be used flexibly in different situations. Peaceful means should
be the first choice, and permanent peace is the ideal goal pursued by
progressive human beings. In the area of international relations, we
need to create a 'new internationalist' school of Marxism.

2. The Holistic Theory of Marxism

In my view, the importance of studying Marxism reflects urgent
needs in the areas both of theory and of reality. From the theoretical point of view, strengthening the study of Marxism as a whole
represents an urgent need if we are to correct the shortcomings of
previous studies of isolated topics and to deepen our understanding
of Marxism. In the past, the study of Marxism was scattered across
fields that included Marxist philosophy, political economy, scientific
socialism, and others. Conducting this study on the basis of the subject areas where Marxism was applied had its advantages. However,
it tended to result in a fragmented understanding of Marxism, which
affected people's overall grasp of the topic. Meanwhile, strengthening the study of Marxism as a whole also represents an urgent

need if we are to eliminate the fragmentation and dismemberment of Marxism and to respond to anti-Marxist trends of thought. To strengthen the study of Marxism as a whole, it is helpful for people to grasp the fundamental spirit that runs through all the theoretical components and historical periods of Marxism, to understand the 'pulse' of Marxism, and to respond to all kinds of anti-Marxism with effective counter-arguments.

Over the past decade, with the implementation of the research and elaboration project of Marxist theory and the establishment of Marxist theory as a high-level discipline, research on the integrity of Marxism has made rapid progress. Many scholars have conducted in-depth discussions, from a range of perspectives, on the propositions, connotations, essence, research paths, and related issues involved in the study of the integrity of Marxism and have achieved important results. However, I believe that on the whole, the achievements of holistic research in the area of Marxism, during the recent period, have not been ideal. Attempting to summarise the experiences and lessons of previous research in the field of holistic Marxism, I acted as chief researcher in the innovative project 'Marxism in a holistic perspective,' sponsored by the Chinese Academy of Social Sciences. In this capacity, I put forward a new research concept: that of carrying out all-round research into holistic Marxism from a total of fourteen perspectives.

The first of these perspectives has involved carrying out the research needed to reach a definition: that is, to define and expound Marxism in an innovative fashion drawing on six key aspects of the creator of Marxism, its academic significance, its social function, the well-being of the people, value conceptions, and international communication. The second perspective is focused on synthetic research, that is, on four aspects of Marxism: its theoretical characteristics, social ideals, political stances, and theoretical qualities. The third perspective researches the unity of Marxism, that is, dialectical unity incorporating the categories of standpoint, viewpoint, and method. The fourth perspective concerns hierarchical research, that is, research into three key aspects: the general principle, specific judgment, and method of reasoning, while also examining the internal level and mutual relations. The fifth perspective is that of developmental research, that is, research from the angle of the complete history of the development of Marxism. The sixth involves study of the three features, that is, change according to the times, Sinicisation, and popularisation. The seventh focuses on practical research, that is, studying the theoretical integrity of Marxism on the basis of its practical integrity. The eighth perspective is concerned with the study of interactivity, that is, proceeding from the ideas put forward by leaders and scholars and from the interactive development of these ideas. The ninth consists of disruptive research, that is, proceeding from critical and constructive elaboration and from the interaction of multiple aspects. The tenth perspective is that of classification research, which is required mainly to clarify the so-called 'four whats': what are the basic principles that must be adhered to over the long term; what are the theoretical judgments that need to be developed; what are the dogmatic understandings that must be rectified; and what are the wrong views that must be rejected? The eleventh concerns subject research, that is, research conducted from the perspective of the overall taxonomic relationship of the seven secondary disciplines covered by the first-level discipline of Marxism. The twelfth is research on the topic of division, that is, the contributions made by philosophy, economics, politics, cultural studies, sociology, ecology, institutional science, anthropology and other disciplines, and the mutual relations between them. The thirteenth perspective is that of applicability research, that is, research that elaborates the methods, theories, and policies of Marxism, and their mutual relations. Fourteenth is the study of national characteristics, involving analysis and expatiation on the academic and political theories that distinguish capitalist countries from socialist states such as China, Vietnam, Laos, Cuba, and North Korea.

I have therefore stressed that the teaching and research in university schools of Marxism and the publishing in journals of academic Marxism should not be confined to just three components of Marxism, the 'narrow Marxism' of popular media accounts. Instead, I have argued that these schools and journals, together with other academic institutions, should establish an integrated, synthetic system of 'comprehensive Marxism' that combines sophisticated academic studies with the broad dissemination of Marxist ideas and with effective policy.

3. The Sinicisation of Marxism

How should we evaluate the initial theoretical achievements of the Sinicisation of Marxism, and its practical accomplishments? In an article during the 1990s, which took issue with the ideas of the neoliberal economist Professor Steven N. S. Cheung (Wuchang Zhang) from the University of Hong Kong, I was an early critic of historically nihilistic views on the economic development of post-revolutionary China. Later, on the occasion of the 20th anniversary of the reform and opening-up, and of the 60th and 70th anniversaries of the People's Republic of China, I wrote articles emphasising that Mao Zedong Thought had guided China to tremendous achievements of economic and social development, specifically, the 'first miracle'.

During the period of almost thirty years from 1949 to 1978, before the reform and opening-up, China completed its basic heavy and chemical industrialisation, set up a national economic system that, at least at a preliminary stage, included complete categories and basic self-sufficiency relying on an 'inner loop', created an independent defence complex that included the production of missiles, satellites, and nuclear weapons, and achieved an average annual GNP growth rate of more than 6% over this period. China, during these years, caught up with and surpassed the majority of the world's countries in the speed of its economic growth, and indeed, was among the countries with the fastest economic development over the period. Important indicators, such as the scale of the productive forces, overall national strength, popular living standards, and so forth, increased dramatically compared with the period before the founding of the New China, and the gap with the main developed countries was narrowed. The Hong Kong, Macao and Taiwan regions of China achieved some successes in their economic development during this period, but none of these achievements can be compared with the 'first miracle' represented by the development in mainland China of industry, science, technology, and the entire national economic system. Moreover, those gains were achieved despite such factors as the blockade of China's economy by the imperialist countries, the falling-out with the Soviet Union, the providing of aid to foreign countries, excessively 'left-wing' domestic policies, and a sharp increase in the population. Therefore, the 'Resolution on Certain Historical Issues of the Party since the Founding of the People's Republic of China,' drafted under the leadership of Deng Xiaoping, and the new Constitution adopted by the National People's Congress in March 2018, were both correct in fully affirming those achievements. It therefore follows that the turn to constructing a socialist market economy was not undertaken because of any failure of the socialist planned economy. What it instead involved was a de-prioritisation of the planned economy, at the same time as the market elements of the economy were continued and expanded. If the socialist market economy is properly run, it can record greater achievements than the traditional planned economy.

A popular saying among today's Chinese population states that Mao Zedong made us stand up, Deng Xiaoping made us rich, and that Xi Jinping has made us strong. Another saying is that Mao

Zedong's 'version 1.0' of socialism was poor, that Deng Xiaoping's 'version 2.0' of socialism was rich, and that since the 18th National Congress of the Communist Party of China, the 'version 3.0' of socialism has been strong. There is some truth in these statements, but in my opinion, none are fully accurate. Properly speaking, the old China was extremely poor, but in the New China since 1949, beginning with the Mao Zedong era, China has not only stood up, but also become steadily richer and stronger. This is a continuous process in which, as the Chinese expression has it, 'the waves at the back push the waves at the front'. The statistics on the prosperity of the people and the country's strength over the past seventy years do not support the suggestion that this prosperity and strength are unrelated, nor do they support the argument that China during the Mao era did not gradually increase in its wealth and strength. Xi Jinping is thus quite right to stress that the political bottom line and principle of China's development is that the past two thirty-year periods (before and after the beginning of the policy of reform and opening-up) should not be viewed as negating each other.

In fact, the two periods before and after the reform and opening-up are both integral parts of the seventy-year history of the New China, and both make up the history of the new socialist China as a whole. It should be said that the development that occurred before the reform and opening-up laid the economic, political, and cultural foundations for today's development, and made major progress toward it. This is the case even though the development since the beginning of reform and opening-up has been even greater. However, a number of works written in China and abroad, since the reform and opening-up, have responded to the necessity for the main policies followed during the first thirty years of the People's Republic of China, and the great achievements registered during this period, by demonstrating an attitude of historical nihilism. Adopting a one-sided approach, speaking only of mistakes and shortcomings, and even engaging in basic denial, these works have distorted the inheritance from the past and the relationship between the development that occurred before the reform and opening-up and that which has occurred since. This is very harmful to our scientific understanding of how the gradual historical development of prosperity in the People's Republic of China occurred, and thus presents an obstacle to objectively summarising the relevant historical experience and lessons and grasping the laws of scientific development. Our actual experience demonstrates that China has been 'steadily moving toward prosperity and strength' since 1949 (Xi 2017). The theory of socialism with Chinese characteristics has guided China in recording greater economic achievements, specifically, the 'second miracle'.

Deng Xiaoping Theory, the important concepts summed up as the 'Three Represents',[1] the Scientific Outlook on Development,[2] and Xi Jinping Thought on Socialism with Chinese Characteristics for a New Era jointly constitute the system of theories of socialism with Chinese characteristics. This represents another theoretical advance along the road to adapting Marxism to China's conditions, an advance that has helped to guide and lead China's reform and opening-up as it continues to register remarkable achievements.

As an important group among Marx's successors, we Marxist scholars should continue to actively enrich and develop Marxism in China, striving to better promote contemporary Chinese Marxism as the guiding ideology in the major basic disciplines of philosophy and the social sciences. At the same time, we should actively promote the new image of Chinese Marxism as a benign interaction between the faith of the 'scholar for the people'[3] and academic ideas under the guidance of Xi Jinping Thought.

We should draw lessons from the history of the period before the reform and opening-up, when it was believed that only leaders could develop Marxism, while the task of scholars was to interpret and defend it. Since the reform and opening-up, many new Marxist terms

---

1. The 'Three Represents' or 'the important thought of Three Represents' is a guiding socio-political theory within China credited to Jiang Zemin, which was ratified by the Chinese Communist Party (CCP) at the Sixteenth Party Congress in 2002. The Three Represents define the role of the CCP, and stress that the Party must always represent the requirements for developing China's advanced productive forces, the orientation of China's advanced culture, and the fundamental interests of the overwhelming majority of the Chinese people.

2. The 'Scientific Outlook on Development' is one of the guiding socio-economic principles of the Communist Party of China and incorporates scientific socialism, sustainable development, social welfare, a humanistic society, increased democracy, and, ultimately, the creation of a Socialist Harmonious Society. The theory was credited to Hu Jintao, ratified into the Communist Party of China's constitution at the 17th Party Congress in October 2007.

3. Xi Jinping: Speech at the Symposium on the Work of Philosophy and Social Sciences. http://www.xinhuanet.com/politics/2016-05/18/c_11188 91128.htm

and theories developed by Party leaders have been continuously absorbed by Marxist scholars, and many new terms and theories devised by scholars have also been continuously absorbed by leaders and employed in Party documents.

We should gradually establish and make clear the mechanism of benign interaction between political (official) Marxism and academic Marxism. Only when socialist countries truly implement the 'freedom of both speech and argument' policy and allow the extensive development of every school of thought that appears within Marxism, can outstanding Marxist figures emerge in the social sciences. An important sign of the true flourishing of academia is the formation of numerous schools of thought. Many Marxist ideas are first mentioned in Party documents, but they may not be the first to attract notice among academics. Therefore, political Marxism cannot be used to replace academic Marxism. This is an important point of view of mine, which I first mentioned in a speech draft published in the *Wenhui* newspaper on 11 April 2004. Drawn from the experience of the international communist movement and the governing party in managing the social sciences, this viewpoint has been widely circulated and endorsed in academic circles. We should draw lessons from the relationship between Western officials and academic circles. Officials enhance their capacities by selecting and integrating certain theories and policies from academic circles; both sides can also discuss and criticise each other to truly clarify what is right and what is wrong. If this course is not followed, Marxist academics in China will be reluctant to do anything, scarcely daring to think or speak, and will therefore enjoy little academic status. At the same time, non-Marxist scholars will be able to speak freely, and to expand their influence in society. This pattern now needs to change. Non-Marxist learning should be able to exist and develop properly, but it cannot occupy the mainstream position.

4. The Policy Orientation of Marxism

I have always taken the view that Marxist scholars should seek to organically combine the academic study of Marxism with propagating theory and investigating policy. They should not confine their educational and publicity work to Marxist theory while largely ignoring academic research and innovation in more general areas of Marxism, and especially, should not neglect to explore areas of policy closely related to Marxist theory, while making innovative contributions. Accordingly, I attach great importance to the use of Marxist theory to study the policies associated with reform and opening-up and development and would like to put forward some new policy proposals.

As a first example, I propose a new economic accounting indicator, 'Gross Domestic Product of Welfare' (hereafter, GDPW). For a long time, GDP has been the primary indicator used to measure China's national economy. China has focused excessively on the pursuit of economic growth, and hence there is a great practical need to introduce this new indicator and to examine the level of national welfare embodied in economic growth. GDPW, unlike GDP, encompasses the total value of the welfare created by the production and business activities of all resident units in a country (or region) during a certain period. As an alternative concept of modernisation, it is the aggregate of the positive and negative utility produced by the three systems of economy, nature, and society, and essentially reflects the sum of objective welfare. As an indicator measuring the welfare created by people's productive activities, it effectively supplements and corrects the defects and deficiencies found in GDP and is more comprehensive than measures such as Sustainable Economic Welfare (Cheng and Cao 2009).

As a second example, let us consider another new social indicator that I have proposed, the so-called 'happiness index'. In China and abroad, various 'happiness indices' have been reported from time to time, but some of the data and rankings are obviously not consistent with the subjective feelings of the public. In view of this, it is of great theoretical and practical importance to analyse the advantages and disadvantages of the existing 'happiness indices' at home and abroad, and to establish a happiness index that is scientific from the standpoint and method of Marxism. The newly designed 'happiness index' indicator system (known formally as the 'happiness and well-being index') is a synthesis of objective and subjective measures of happiness and sense of well-being based on objective indices and supplemented by subjective measurements. Compared with existing indicator systems in China and abroad, it is more scientific and allows better comparisons. Two levels of micro and macro indicators, corresponding to the research level of the 'happiness index', have also been constructed. Of these, the micro-level indicator system is known as the 'individual or family' indicator system of the 'happiness index', while its macro-level counterpart is termed the 'social or national' system (Wang and Cheng 2013). At the time when these indices were devised, a large company decided they represented a lucrative potential investment and sought to buy the copyright. However, I did not agree, preferring to safeguard the innovation rights of Marxist scholars.

As a third example of a policy proposal, a 'new pension strategy' has been put forward with linkages to government agencies, institutions, and enterprises. Accompanied by a booklet entitled 'A Pilot Plan for Reform of the Pension Insurance System for Institution Employees' (hereafter referred to as Plan 08), this was published and distributed in 2008. The urban pension insurance system reform, with government agencies, institutions, and enterprises as the three main participating organisations, has become an important link in the broader scheme of pension insurance reforms. However, Plan 08 suffers from innate deficiencies and poor implementation, so that the reform of the urban pension insurance system in China has hit a bottleneck. At the time when Plan 08 was first announced, I began subjecting it to an in-depth study, and eventually put forward a preliminary plan for the reform of the urban pension insurance system with linkages to government agencies, institutions, and enterprises (hereafter referred to as the linkage scheme). In this scheme, based on my analysis of the 'new pension strategy', I set out the background to my criticisms, their basic purpose, and the improvement measures I proposed. The target model for China's pension insurance should be a unified urban and rural basic pension system, with the government contributing a portion of the urban workers' wages to the pension system and with the possibility of adding supplementary insurance. Under the scheme, farmers are provided with the same basic pension insurance, and supplementary pension insurance can be added in different districts.

During the National People's Congress and the Chinese Political Consultative Conference in 2009, I was one of twenty people who put forward written opinions on Plan 08. A vice-premier in charge of the area submitted my new strategy for internal reference and sent it to the relevant departments for study. In 2010, I convoked the first ever Think Tank Forum on China's Economic and Social Development to address the topic of pension reform. At this forum, I put forward my new pension strategy, inviting heads of government departments to attend and join in the discussion. Ultimately, the government authorities ceased implementing Plan 08.

In addition, I have successively put forward and argued in favour of the 'new opening strategy', 'new housing strategy', 'new population strategy', 'new State-Owned Enterprise (SOE) strategy', 'new private enterprise strategy', 'new land strategy', 'new culture strategy', 'new distribution strategy', 'new consumption strategy', 'new finance strategy', 'anti-inflation strategy', and so on.

5. The Internationalisation of Marxism

In 2010, I wrote that for many years an unhealthy state has existed in China in the research field of Marxist theory, with the concepts of the 'Sinicisation of Marxism' and 'internationalisation of Chinese Marxism' kept separate and isolated (Cheng and Hu 2010). In 2019, I wrote another article stressing the importance of constructing a 'Chinese discourse' in global Marxist studies and of continuing to lead developments in this area. We should realise that 'Marxism and its Sinicized theories are the soul and core of soft power' (Cheng and Li 2019). It is necessary to reinforce international communication in this field, and to enhance the interactive exchange of the research results of Chinese Marxist theories.

Future research on Marxist theories in China, as it adapts to the need to update Marxism for the 21st century, should stress the exchange of ideas with foreign Marxist scholars, turning the contribution of Chinese concepts to the debate and the acceptance of Marxist concepts from outside into a unified process. We should strengthen communication and cooperation with our foreign counterparts in the field of Marxist theoretical research, learning from one another. In this way, we can expand our international vision of the all-round development of research in the field of Marxist theory. We need to actively introduce and explain the latest achievements of Marxist academic studies in China to the outside world through translating and publishing Chinese works, building our contacts with foreign media and calling international conferences. We should participate voluntarily in international research that discusses vexed questions and difficulties in the area of Marxist studies. We must strive to build an international voice for China in research on Marxist theory, enhance the international influence of the research on Marxist theory in China, and play an active role in leading future trends in international Marxist thought.

In my view, Marxists of all countries should expand their exchanges, cooperation, and mutual learning. They should not limit their studies to their own countries, but at the same time, should not recklessly denounce each other or engage in sharp debates that have the potential to affect inter-academic and inter-party relations. Even when important issues of Marxist or non-Marxist theories are involved, the stress should be on internal discussions and debates rather than on open debates between parties. This is because the main task of the communist party of every country is to lead the revolution and carry out socialist construction in its own country.

Generally speaking, theoretical activity will be richer and will yield better lessons in the communist party of a country that is growing stronger and that has more remarkable achievements in the fields of revolution and construction. Here, the lessons of history are worth summarising. The Sino-Soviet debate led to a deterioration of the relations between the two parties and countries and to a split in the international communist movement, with the divisions then being utilised by the United States and other Western countries to attack Marxism, socialism, and the communist movement as a whole. The lessons of this experience were painful, and still need to be subject to reflection.

To have theoretical differences is completely normal, and practice can demonstrate whether these theories and foci are correct or not, whether they amount to innovative Marxism, 'revisionism', or dogmatism. When I gave a speech at an international symposium held by the Marx Memorial Library in Britain in 2012, I specifically elaborated on the historical lessons and practical problems mentioned above.

In addition, and on the basis of research by Marxist scholars and theorists of the communist parties in major countries (with whom I have been in long-term communication), I wrote and published an article in 2012 in which I argued: 'To a large extent, the future of world socialism depends on the level of effective joint work by the contemporary proletariat'. In order to realise the call 'Proletarians of all Countries, Unite!' proposed by Marx in the Manifesto of the Communist Party, we need at this stage to strengthen our joint work in more forms and ways, while emphasising that Marxists and the Left should pay attention to a number of important strategic and tactical issues (Cheng 2012). During 2012, based on these points of view and on in-depth studies carried out by various schools of international relations, I continually put forward the 'new internationalism' theory of class and international relations, as well as further expounding the Marxist theory of internationalisation. This theory not only proposes a new type of cooperation between the working class, political parties, and scholars, but also prefigures a new type of cooperation between China and the rest of the world, one that aims to strengthen the power of the international working class, to maintain common global security against the new imperialist hegemony, and to promote the shaping of a community of shared future for mankind. A global academic group named the World Association for Political Economy was founded in 2005, along with two journals published in the UK, *World Review of Political Economy* and *International Critical Thought*, both of which are important international theoretical platforms for implementing the above academic concepts. At the same time, I am the chief editor of ten works in a series titled *Translations of Foreign Classics of Modern Political Economy* and have published books and articles together with colleagues in ten countries, including the United States, Japan, Russia, Italy, Canada, Vietnam, etc., as an element in two-way academic exchanges between China and foreign countries.

6. View of Social System in Marxism

I have played a role in the process of development that has seen the formation and successive improvement of the theory of three stages of socialism (referring solely to the economic system). In October 1987, the Thirteenth National Congress of the CPC systematically discussed the theory of the primary stage of socialism for the first time. In less than two months, I wrote a contribution to this discussion, setting forward my view that the main economic characteristics of the primary stage of socialism are 'different from the characteristics of the transition from capitalism to socialism', and also 'different from the characteristics of the intermediate or advanced stage of socialism' (Cheng and Xu 1987). In 1988, my article formally elaborating the three stages of socialism from the perspective of the economic system (Cheng and Zhou 1988) was published in the *Fudan Journal* (social sciences edition). Other publications followed: a monograph in 1991 entitled 'Theory of The Three Stages of Socialism', in 1992, the paper 'Thoughts on the Three Stages of Socialist Development', in 1998, a paper entitled 'The Reconstruction and Improvement of the Primary Stage of the Basic Socialist Economic Form', in 2008 the paper 'Implementing the Concept of Scientific Development so as to Gain a Deep Understanding of the Theory of the Primary Stage of Socialism', and in 2018, two papers, 'Learn Well and Use Well the Political Economy of Socialism with Chinese Characteristics to Achieve a Clear Direction in the Reform of SOEs', and 'Several Theoretical Innovations by the Synthesis School of New Marxist Economics since the Reform and Opening-Up'. Through such publications, the theory has gradually been developed.

In the light of such considerations as the level of development of productivity, the degree of modernisation and the corresponding living standards, the relations of production and the ownership of the means of production, and the social mechanism underlying the operation of the economy, I maintain that the ultimate function and indirect or ultimate assessment of productivity, as well as the direct function and assessment of the means of production, can be observed on the basis of different historical socio-economic forms or of different stages of development within the same socio-economic form. This is in accordance with Marx's general thinking on socio-economic forms and development stages. I thus consider that three stages of socialism come into being as a result of the partial qualitative changes to the relations of production and the economic system that are caused by increases in productivity (this view is compatible with the conclusion that different stages of socialist development can be distinguished mainly, and directly, on the basis of changes to GDP and living standards). Thus, the primary stage of the socialist economic system = a variety of public ownership as the main body (with private ownership as the auxiliary body) + market-oriented distribution according to one's work as the main body (with distribution according to capital as the auxiliary body) + the market economy led by national plans. The intermediate stage = a variety of public ownership + a variety of commodity distribution according to work + a planned economy with the state as the main body (and with market regulation as the auxiliary body). The advanced stage = sole public ownership by the whole people + distribution of products according to one's need + a completely planned economy; communism = sole public ownership by the whole people + distribution of products according to one's need as the main body (with the few new consumption goods that are in short supply distributed according to one's work) + a completely planned economy; and the modern capitalist economic system = private ownership as the main body + distribution according to one's capital as the main body + a state-directed market economy.

This new theory defines different social and developmental stages objectively, meaning that it can reveal in coherent fashion the essential relationship between the primary stage of socialism and the lofty institutional goal of communism, and explain that the primary stage of socialism is the primary form of scientific socialism.

7. The Differentiation of Marxist Principles

After a decade spent implementing the Project of Studying and Developing Marxist Theory by the CPC Central Committee, a national conference on propaganda and ideological work was held on 19 July 2013. This concentrated on finding answers to the questions: what are the basic principles of Marxism? What needs to be insisted on over a long period? What are the theoretical judgments that need to be enriched and developed by combining the various elements of the new reality? What are the dogmatic ideas concerning

Marxism that need to be broken with? What are the mistaken ideas that have become attached to the name of Marxism, and that need to be cleared away by approaching Marxism with a scientific attitude? Together with the researcher Bin Yu, I immediately wrote an article entitled 'On Research into Marxist Scientific Integrity from the Perspective of the 'four whats', later published in the *Journal of Academic Research*. This article set out my thoughts on the scientific integrity of Marxism from the perspective of the 'four whats' put forward by the CPC Central Committee, as well as from the points of view of a number of other theoretical approaches, and also responded scientifically to a number of issues that the 'four whats' had raised. The article has been quoted and downloaded repeatedly, since it is based on the classical spirit of Marxism, addresses a number of problems that have caused controversy in theoretical circles, and provides a combination of critical and innovative elaboration.

Since the basic tenets of Marxism are scientific, long-term, and effective, they must be followed over a prolonged period; indeed, there is no basic tenet that does not need to be adhered to in long-term fashion. These tenets, however, do not necessarily mean that specific claims, reflecting the special circumstances of a particular place and time, should be regarded as having long-term validity. In view of the argument that the principles of Marxism cannot be subject to innovation but can only be applied, I emphasise that the basic principles of Marxism can be enriched, expanded, and modified through the development of practice or deepening of theoretical understanding. It is possible, for example, to develop Marx's labour theory of value, theory of surplus value, theory of reproduction, etc., just as it is possible to develop Lenin's theories of imperialism, the state, and revolution. Equally, it is possible to introduce innovations to the theory of the primary stage of socialism, to the theory of the socialist market economy, and so forth. Of course, a mistaken understanding of Marxism often leads to revisionism, dogmatism, pragmatism, and other undesirable tendencies, so it is necessary to get rid of dogmatic habits of thought when these affect the study of Marxism as a whole. For example, a dogmatic understanding of the 'two nevers'[4] can negate or belittle the 'two inevitabilities' of 'the inevitable victory of socialism'

---

4. In the Preface to the Critique of Political Economy, Marx stated that (1) social formation, whatever it is, will never perish until all the productive forces it can accommodate have been brought into play; and (2) new and higher relations of production will never emerge until the conditions of its material existence have matured in the womb of the old society.

and 'the inevitable demise of capitalism', and even prompt the argument that in revolutionary terms, the successful revolutions in China and the Soviet Union were 'premature babies'.

I have always stressed that the study of the scientific nature and integrity of Marxism cannot be undertaken without clarifying some erroneous views. Among these views, for example, is the belief that Marx's reference to 'rebuilding individual ownership' called for rebuilding personal ownership of the means of production and labour, and that the joint-stock system and the rural household contract system are forms of its realisation. If this is believed, then it follows that Marx's political economy is less rigorous in its mathematical and quantitative analysis than economic works of the past and present. If this is accepted, then it must also be accepted that Marx's economic works are works of economic philosophy rather than of economics, that Marx's theory of economic cycles and crises is out of date, that socialist public ownership cannot combine effectively with the market economy system, that distribution according to one's work cannot be implemented under the conditions of a socialist market economy, and so on. These erroneous views, which are popular in Chinese and foreign theoretical circles, must be cleared up one by one.

In his article 'Strategic Issues in China's Revolutionary War', Mao Zedong stated vividly: 'The naked eye is not enough, we must have the aid of the telescope and the microscope. The Marxist method is our telescope and microscope in political and military matters' (Mao 1965a, 222). Extending Mao Zedong's metaphor, I believe that for the purposes of theoretical and practical analysis, Marxism is a telescope through which we can clearly see the trends according to which reality develops, and a microscope through which we can see its crucial details. It is a set of night-vision goggles through which we can see light and hope in the darkness, a set of diving goggles through which we can see things at a deeper level, a fluoroscope through which we can see into the nature of matter beyond the level of appearances, and a megaloscope through which we can make sense of blurred images. Marxism is a reflector through which we can see the truth behind things, a polygonal mirror that enables us to see the diversity and unity of opposites, an asymptotic mirror that allows us to see things near and far with multiple focal points, and a monster-revealing mirror in which, if we have sharp eyes, we can see mistakes clearly. In short, with the help of the ten mirrors or ten facets of the changeable mirror of Marxism, we can truly and completely distinguish the complexities of reality, contrary to the various distorting mirror (magic mirror) theories that distort the nature of things.

8. Innovation in Marxism

At the beginning of 1994, I wrote, in a brief article entitled 'The 21st Century: Reconstructing Chinese Economics' (Cheng 1994), that the Chinese economics of the development stage, together with the further prospects for China's economy, had attracted general attention and stirred widespread debate. In 2000, I proposed the formula 'Marxist concepts as the body and Western learning for their use'. In 2009, I wrote an article proposing basic policy directions and principles for promoting the modernisation of Chinese economics. I believe that the approach I set out in this text, 'Marxist concepts as the body and Western learning for their use, Chinese learning as the root, the world situation as the mirror, national conditions as the basis, and comprehensive innovation', is broadly suited to the whole field of philosophy and the social sciences. The formula 'Marxist concepts as the body and Western learning for their use' is a borrowed expression but is innovative in content; it derives from the expression 'Chinese learning for the body and Western learning for the use' proposed by Zhang Zhidong, a state official who advocated westernisation under the late Qing dynasty.

The phrase 'Marxist concepts' refers to the system of Marxist ideas as developed both in China and abroad. As applied in the field of economics, 'Marxist concepts' refer to the extremely rich tradition of Marxist economic thought. This tradition, elaborated under the guidance of historical materialism and materialist dialectics, includes *Das Kapital*, written by Marx in the mid-19th century, and also incorporates the economic methods and theories that Marx inherited, enriched, and expanded. The 'body', in the philosophical terminology of ancient China, refers to the elements that are 'fundamental and intrinsic'. Emphasising that the modernisation of Chinese economics must proceed on the basis of 'Marxist concepts as the body' means insisting that Marxist ideas should represent the fundamental and dominant content of modern Chinese economics.

Stressing that Marxist concepts must make up the body means insisting that attempts to employ 'Western learning' as the body are inappropriate. 'Western learning', in this case, refers to Western economic ideas and methods, excepting those of Western Marxist economics, and essentially designates the mainstream Western economic tradition. For us to refrain from using 'Western learning as the body', however, does not mean we should avoid employing

'Western learning for the use'. In this case, of course, 'Western learning for the use' does not signify 'use' in the sense of 'Western learning as the body', but refers to a discriminating application of Western knowledge, developing some elements and discarding others, subject to the general premise of 'Marxist concepts as the body'. While insisting on the consistent application of Marxist concepts, and on the distinction between 'for the body' and 'for the use', it is necessary to put forward 'Western learning for the use'. This is consistent with the spirit, embraced by Mao Zedong, of 'foreign learning for Chinese use'; as employed by Mao, this approach meant critically referencing and utilising knowledge from abroad, rather than adopting it indiscriminately as in the sense of 'the body consistent with the use'.

In a broad sense, 'Chinese learning' refers to the knowledge system of social sciences and natural sciences in ancient and modern China, while 'Chinese learning' in a narrow sense refers to the knowledge system of ancient and modern Chinese social sciences alone or of ancient and modern Chinese natural sciences alone. The economic aspects of Chinese learning include research on the economic ideas in ancient China, and on the place of these ideas in the ancient knowledge system, as well as investigation of their modern-day resonances. The 'Chinese learning as the root' thus involves attaching importance to the place held by China's ancient and modern economic thought in the country's current process of economic modernisation and taking this thought as the foundation. Just as Mao Zedong once stressed, 'We should sum up our history from Confucius to Sun Yat-sen and take over this valuable legacy'. (Mao 1965b, 209). Our historical experience is of great ideological value for forming the modern system of economics with Chinese characteristics, in a Chinese manner, and in the Chinese style.

The term 'world situation' in the phrase 'world situation as a guide'' has diverse and profound meanings. From the economic point of view, it refers to the history, current situation, and development trend of all countries and of the overall world economy. The origin and development of today's 'world economic situation', and the accompanying positive and negative experiences and lessons, have important practical sources that cannot be ignored as we seek to modernise Chinese economic science.

The founding of a modern, scientific school of economics with Chinese characteristics, formed in a Chinese manner and in the Chinese style, can only be accomplished if it is based on China's national conditions. These conditions are determined by complex factors such as social forms, cultural traditions, and the natural environment, as well as by the level of the productive forces, and also include various 'coloured layers' made up of provincial conditions, city conditions, county conditions, and the differences between the conditions in urban areas and the countryside. The contemporary social and economic practice of the Chinese people is evolving amid this reality, and as the economic practice of the broad masses of the people is being updated, the diversity in the economic conditions and levels of development within the country is becoming apparent. Only by relying on the economic practice of the broad masses can we achieve the 'national conditions for the foundation', which represent the main realistic source of scientific innovation in the process of China's economic modernisation.

The above axioms, 'Marxist concepts as the body', 'Western learning for the use', 'Chinese learning as the root', 'the world situation as the guide', and 'national conditions as the foundation' will finally be put into practice and will end up as elements of the 'comprehensive innovation' taking place in the course of China's economic modernisation. In the historical materialist view, the 'comprehensive innovation' that occurs as the modernisation of Chinese economics goes ahead is the process of analysing and synthesising, through the use of materialist dialectics, of the economic facts and ideological materials provided by the three knowledge systems of (1) 'Marxist concepts,', (2) 'Western learning' and (3) 'traditional Chinese learning'. 'Comprehensive innovation' means actively absorbing and correctly dealing with the relationship between the three knowledge systems, as well as the relationship between theoretical analysis and synthesis and the testing of concepts in practice.

9. The Development of Different Schools of Marxism

In my opinion, it is only when socialist countries truly implement a policy of 'letting a hundred flowers bloom and letting a hundred different schools of thought contend' and allow the vigorous development of various schools of thought within Marxism, that they will be able to produce true masters of Marxist social science. An important sign of the true flourishing of academic life is the formation of numerous schools of thought. Many Marxist ideas are mentioned first in Party documents, but these ideas are not necessarily the first to attract notice in academic circles. Therefore, political Marxism cannot be used to replace academic Marxism. This is an important position that I hold; it has been drawn from the experience of the international communist movement and its governing parties in developing and applying the social sciences and has been widely circulated and endorsed in academic circles. I have already mentioned this in a speech draft published by the *Wenhui* newspaper on 11 April 2004. We should draw lessons from the relationship between Western officials and academic circles. Officials in the West build their careers by selecting and integrating theories and policies first conceived by academics. Both sides can also discuss and criticise each other in order to truly clarify what is right and what is wrong. If this is not the case in China, Marxist academics here will do nothing, will not dare to think or speak, and therefore will gain no academic status, at the same time as non-Marxist scholars are able to speak freely and expand their influence in society.

In Shanghai in 1995, I joined with other scholars in organising the first China Shanghai School Economic Forum; during the more than twenty-five years since then, the forum has been held in many universities and the Chinese Academy of Social Sciences. Established in 2001, the Research Center of Economics of Shanghai School (renamed the Institute Economics of Shanghai School in 2019) of Shanghai University of Finance and Economics is a key scientific research base in the university. The *Journal of Economics of Shanghai School*, founded in 2003, has long been selected as part of the core journal collection of Nanjing University due to its great academic influence. In the first half of 2020, the new journal *Chinese Journal of Political Economy* was approved by the state for publication.

What is the Economics of Shanghai School? It is indeed easy for people to fall into the misconception that this school studies Shanghai, or economic doctrines that all the scholars in Shanghai agree on. In fact, the Economics of Shanghai School has merely taken the name of the region where it emerged; this was done mainly for the sake of simplicity, and there are many precedents for it in academic history. Membership in the school is open; its personnel are not regionally limited; and it is only the initiating scholars who mainly have their origins in Shanghai. There are now many scholars who join voluntarily in the economic research and development of ideas carried on by the Shanghai School (in 2003, under the leadership of Professor Bingyan Li and Professor Ganqiang He, the 'Nanjing Institute of Economics of Shanghai School' was established, with about twenty symposiums held over ten years).

From a theoretical perspective, the Shanghai School is the Synthesis School of New Marxist Economics (in 2019, the Research Center of Synthesis School of New Marxist Economics was set up in Guangxi University for Nationalities), a school within the field of Sinicized Marxism. Theoretically, the school is based on

Marxist economics, and integrates the rational thinking of ancient and modern China and foreign countries. It seeks to incorporate the synthesis, reference, and use of various methods of the social sciences and natural sciences, and on this basis, to innovate comprehensively, constructing a new paradigm that surpasses both Marxist and mainstream Western economics. Its academic style stresses openness to all (it sets out to 'admit all rivers flowing into the sea'), in order to bring forth the new and explore the truth. Over the years, a series of original theoretical viewpoints have been put forward. One of these has to do with the relationship between fairness and efficiency, where we present a theory of their 'mutual promotion and complementary change'. The 'four main material/bodily form' concepts applicable to the socialist market economy, and constituting the economic formulae of the primary stage of socialism with Chinese characteristics include: (1) public ownership as the main material form co-existing with other ownership types, (2) distribution according to work as the main material form co-existing with other factor distribution types, (3) state-led multi-structure market reform as a third material form coexisting with limited planning, and (4) the self-reliant national opening-up as the main material form co-existing with opening-up in all directions. Other original viewpoints include 'new monism of living labour value', 'high performance of market-oriented public ownership', 'a new system of state-owned asset management classified on the basis of one government, two departments and three layers', the 'three stages of socialism', and the 'contemporary basic global economic contradictions'. The Economics of Shanghai School has formed its own unique system of academic theory, consisting of systematic economic methods, basic assumptions, basic principles, and policy propositions (Cheng 2004).

In recent years, with the expansion of its field of concern from the economic to the non-economic area, the Synthesis School of New Marxist Economics has evolved into the Synthesis School of New Marx, and has also put forward the concept of 'makers of history in a broad sense' (Cheng and Zhan 2016) in the field of philosophy, 'three views of scientific socialism' and 'the future of world socialism' (Cheng 2012) in the field of scientific socialism, 'new perception of the Communist International and Chinese revolution' (Cheng and Yang 2020) and 'three major causes for the dramatic changes in the Soviet Union' (Cheng and Ding 2011) in the field of history, and 'nine types of interest groups' (Cheng and Zhan 2015) in the field of sociology.

10. The Role of Marxist Scholars and the View of Academic Research in Marxism

A particular strand of public opinion once argued that Marxism was 'attractive but useless', that it was 'outdated', and that it was unsuited to the socialist market economy. Studying, researching, and reflecting on Marxism since my early years, I have always believed that Marxist principles, methods, and systems represent scientific knowledge or academic truth, and that truth possesses absoluteness and relativity, so that it needs effective, determined dissemination, and an insistence on scientific development.

Various elements of public opinion also hold that the study of Marxism is only appropriate for members of the communist party members, and that it should not be part of the national education system. In my opinion, Marxism, like other major social science theories, has academic and ideological value, and that accordingly, it should be included in the national education systems of all countries. However, bourgeois academics are afraid of the truth of Marxism, so they pursue only academic closed-mindedness and dogmatism. Not only should all Marxists discuss Marxism and believe in Marxism, but scholars of humanities and social sciences should incorporate faith in Marxism in their writing, and highly civilised modern people should demonstrate belief in Marxism in their activities. This is the same principle as the one that holds, 'the people have faith, the country has strength, and then the nation has hope.' The ideological root of the major problems in the world, such as the constant wars and the polarisation between rich and poor, is not that too few people believe in Christianity or Islam (ironically, the American presidents who have constantly waged wars and pursued hegemony and so on have believed in Christianity), but that too few people believe in Marxism. If the people of the world (and especially the 'elites' of all countries) truly believed in Marxism, the world would enjoy peaceful development and common prosperity, and humankind would build a community with a shared future.

Certain elements within public opinion also believe it would be sufficient if Marxist scholars simply did a good job in the area of publicity and education work. I take a broader view: Marxist scholars should act as strategic social scientists for the working class. They should be guards on the field of Marxism, defending the truth, warriors for innovation, counsellors advising on national work, fighters who dare to struggle, and guides who lead the way. I am not in favour of eclecticism and unprincipled harmony. Instead, I emphasise the unity of knowledge and action. This is how it was in the past with revolutionary leaders and exemplary scholars. Engels once admonished Marx's son-in-law Paul Lafargue: 'When one is an economist, "a man of science", one does not have an ideal, one elaborates scientific results, and when one is, to boot, a party man, one struggles to put them into practice' (Engels 2010, 183). Mao Zedong once wrote an inscription praising Ai Siqi as 'a scholar, a warrior, and a sincere man'. President Xi Jinping has criticised 'enlightened gentlemen' who care only about their own reputations and fine feathers and has called for a new era in which such people would 'dare to fight and be good at fighting'[5]

Some currents within public opinion consider that in today's academic world there is no concern with value or class but only with empirical research. Or else, they contend that Marxist scholars need to be leader-oriented instead of classics-oriented. When the Shanghai School of Economics was founded, I drew up the requirements for the school's style of study, stating that it should be 'rigorous but not rigid', and that the mind should be liberated but not lacking in self-discipline. Throughout ancient and modern times in China and abroad, it has been relatively easy to be classics-oriented, and to avoid being oriented toward any particular leader or toward the people. By contrast, being oriented toward practice is difficult. The reason is not hard to understand. In the face of mistaken 'Left' tendencies as well as while combating the Right, Marxist scholars should be prepared to stand against the trend and should not be followers or be concerned solely about style. Nevertheless, it is not easy for them to display the bold spirit needed to take on responsibility.

As a scholar born in the 1950s, I have experienced both the edification and tempering of the Mao Zedong era, and the innovation and new perspectives of the reform and opening-up era. I thus possess the personality traits, spiritual scope, and work style of the two periods, and I am trying to carry on with coordinating my knowledge of Marxism with practice by promoting strengths, avoiding weaknesses, and pursuing excellence. On my future academic road, I will not only continue the academic work that combines the motherland and me but will also expand the academic work that combines the world and me, while speeding up the pace of academic outreach and giving play to my function as an academic ambassador. On the basis

---

5. See Xi Jinping's speech at http://dangjian.people.com.cn/n1/2019/0904/c117092-31335067.html.

of the world and the motherland and me, the academic dream of promoting the effective union of Marxist scholars all over the world will be realised.

References

Chen, S. 2011. 'Divisions within the Current World Socialist Movement: A Case Study of the Debate between the Greek Communist Party and CPUSA Chairman Sam Weber.' [In Chinese.] *Scientific Socialism*, no. 5: 151–154.

Cheng, E. 1994. 'The 21st Century: Reconstructing Chinese Economics.' [In Chinese.] *Social Sciences Weekly*, April 7.

Cheng, E. 2004. 'An Original and Flourishing School to Promote the Development of Chinese Academics.' [In Chinese.] *Exploration and Dispute*, no. 11: 5–7.

Cheng, E. 2012. 'The Future of World Socialism Depends on the Effective Joint Action of International Proletariat.' *Social Sciences Abroad*, no. 5: 13–16.

Cheng, E., and J. Ding. 2011. 'A Systematic Analysis of the Main Causes of the Dramatic Changes in the Soviet Union.' [In Chinese.] *Social Sciences in China*, no. 6: 207–217.

Cheng, E., and L. Cao. 2009. 'How to Establish an Accounting System for the Gross Domestic Product of Welfare.' [In Chinese.] *Economic Review*, no. 3 1–8.

Cheng, E., and L. Hu. 2010. 'Sixty Years of Research on Marxist Theories in China.' [In Chinese.] *Studies on Marxism*, no. 1: 11–22.

Cheng, E., and L. Li. 2019. 'Marxism and its Sinicized Theory Are the Soul and Core of Soft Power.' [In Chinese.] *Marxist Cultural Studies*, no. 1: 15–28.

Cheng, E., and H. Xu. 1987. 'Economic Characteristics and Reform in the Primary Stage of Socialism.' [In Chinese.] *Ganjiang Economy*, no. 12: 26–28.

Cheng, E., and J. Yang. 2020. 'The Chinese Revolution and the Communist International.' *Third World Quarterly* 41 (8): 1338–1352.

Cheng, E., and Z. Zhan. 2015. 'Analysis of Current Interest Groups in China.' [In Chinese.] *Research on Mao Zedong and Deng Xiaoping Theory*, no. 10: 42–49.

Cheng, E., and Z. Zhan. 2016. 'A New Historical Materialist Interpretation of the Role of Historical Figures as 'Makers of History in a Broad Sense.''' [In Chinese.] *Philosophical Research*, no. 10: 17–21.

Cheng, E., and H. Zhou. 1988. 'On the Basic Signs for Different Social and Economic Forms and Social Development Stages.' [In Chinese.] *Fudan Journal*, no. 1: 15–20.

Engels, F. 2010. 'Engels to Paul Lafargue. About 11 August 1884.' In *Marx and Engels Collected Works*, vol. 36, 179–183.' Electronic Edition. Lawrence & Wishart.

Mao, Z. 1965a. 'Problems of Strategy in China's Revolutionary War.' In *Selected Works of Mao Zedong*, vol. 1, 179–254. Beijing: Foreign Languages Press.

Mao, Z. 1965b. 'The Role of the Chinese Communist Party in the National War.' *Selected Works of Mao Zedong*, vol. 2, 195–212. Beijing: Foreign Languages Press.

Wang, Y., and E. Cheng. 2013. 'Happiness Index from Marxist Perspective.' [In Chinese.] *Academic Monthly*, no. 4: 68–75.

Wang, Z. and E. Cheng. 2017. 'Enriching and Developing Marxism in the 21st Century at Multiple Levels.' [In Chinese.] *Research on Mao Zedong and Deng Xiaoping Theory*, no. 9: 53–61.

Xi, J. 2017. 'Secure a Decisive Victory in Building a Moderately Prosperous Society in All Respects and Strive for the Great Success of Socialism with Chinese Characteristics for a New Era.' [In Chinese.] *People's Daily*, October 18.

Chapter *1*

China's Modern Economic System

Building a modern economic system is the strategic goal of China's development. This requires a transformation in the mode of economic development, both by optimising the overall economic structure, and modifying the driving forces of economic growth. This unique transition to a modern economic system characterised by high-quality development with Chinese characteristics has profound historical roots and is associated with what might be thought of as a *timely inevit*ability.

* * *

Section I Characteristics and Connotations of China's Economic System

1. Distinguishing between the Dual Meanings of Its Economic Model

China's tremendous achievements in economic and social development have attracted worldwide attention. In 2008, China's total GDP (gross domestic product) leapt to third place in the world, trailing only the United States and Japan. The total combined value of exports and imports climbed to third place as well, behind only the United States and Germany. Notable was the fact that foreign exchange reserves ranked first globally. Specifically, China's economy has continued to grow rapidly for thirty consecutive years since the beginning of Reform and Opening Up; with an average annual GDP growth rate of 9.6%, China has led the world in terms of the speed and duration of its economic ascent. In 2008, China's gross national income per capita reached 3,292 U.S. dollars, signifying that in global terms the country had attained middle-income status. In 2007, when the Global Financial Crisis swept the world, developed countries and many developing countries as well were hit hard financially, and subsequently fell into recession. China, however, was able to maintain strong economic growth; its annual GDP growth rate in 2009 was expected to exceed 8%. In 2009, China marked its 30th anniversary of Reform and Opening Up, which coincided with the 60th anniversary of the founding of the People's Republic of China. These events prompted Chinese and foreign scholars to devote particularly close attention to the *China Model of Economic and Social Development*, and to take part in a range of intensive discussions. In engaging in this dialogue, the experts sought to refine and summarise China's paths of economic and social development, along with the experience it had acquired and the patterns that would help it construct a bridge from the past financial system to the future economy, while also providing greater context for the rest of the world.

The methodology of singling out various models of economic development has and extensive history. Once the economic development of a country or region has registered significant achievements, or has taken on characteristic features, a corresponding model will be proposed. For example, the *Rhine Model* (or *Social Democratic Model*) emphasises the role of government and a welfare society; it is represented by Germany, Switzerland, Norway, Sweden, etc. The *Anglo-Saxon Model* (or *Liberal Capitalist Model*) highlights free, competitive market economies and is represented by the United States and the United Kingdom. The *East Asian Model*, represented by Japan, South Korea, etc., emphasises government-led market economies. The *Latin American Model* stresses the *Washington Consensus* and is characterised by economic privatisation, non-regulation, and

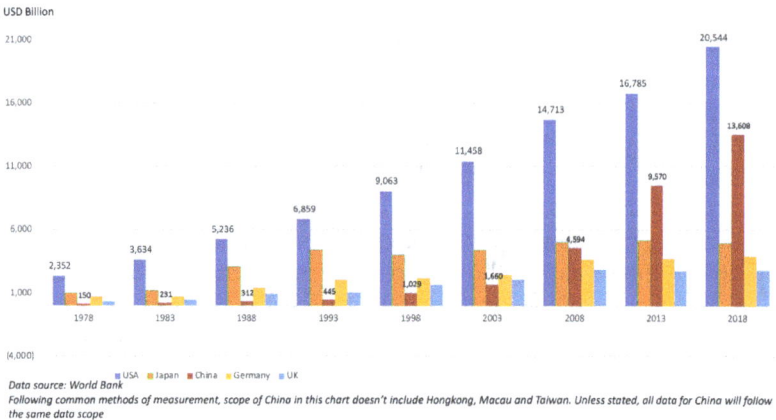

USD Billion

Data source: World Bank

Following common methods of measurement, scope of China in this chart doesn't include Hongkong, Macau and Taiwan. Unless stated, all data for China will follow the same data scope

Chart 1 1978-2018 GDP China and Top 5 (Ranked by 2008 facts)

USD Billion

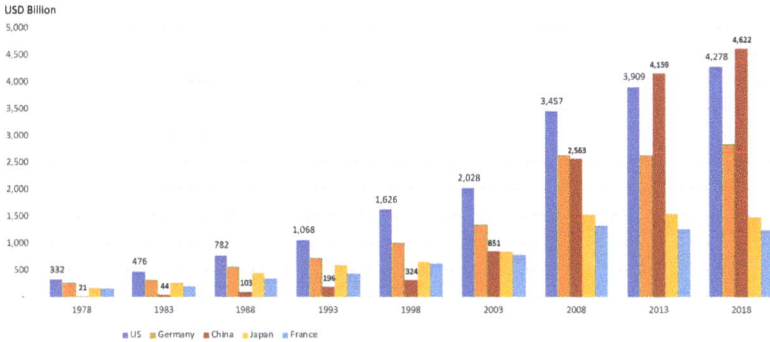

Data source: WTO
1. Commercial service exports& imports are not combined because only 1980- 2013 data are available. In order to have an apple- apple comparison within time series, data in the chart above only refer to merchandise exports and imports
2. Germany's data before 1990 doesn't include German Democratic Republic's export- import

Chart 2 1978-2018 Total Merchandise Export-Import Value China and Top 5 (Ranked by 2008 Facts)

USD

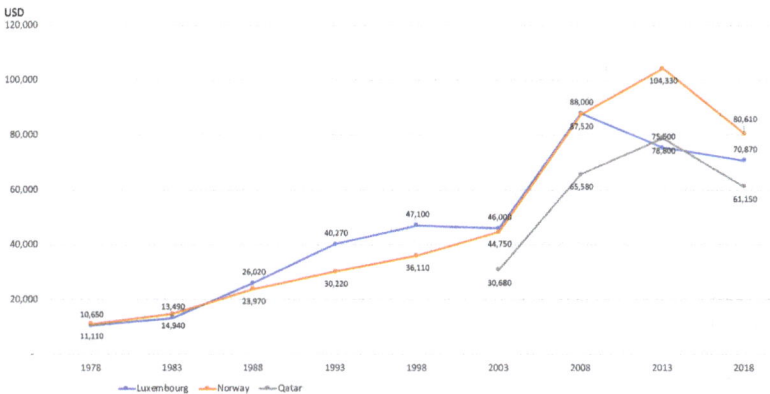

Data source: World Bank; data of Qatar from 1978-2001 is not available

Chart 3 Comparative Example of 3 High GNI per Capita Countries

liberalisation. It is also known as the *Latin American Trap* because of the inability to develop a self-sustaining economic system and has been represented by Mexico, Argentina, and others. The *Radical Transformation Model* (or *Shock Therapy*) emphasises rapid economic privatisation, non-regulation, and economic liberalisation, and has also failed wherever it has been applied; historically, it has been represented by post-Soviet Russia in the 1990s and by other nations. The *Soviet Model* emphasises the use of centralised economic planning to attain great achievements. Initiated during the *Stalin Period*, it has also been termed the *Stalin Model*, and was represented by the Soviet Union. The *Socialist-Oriented Market Economy Model*, emphasising the

USD
16,000

14,000

12,000

10,000

8,000

6,000

4,000

2,000

14,250   14,020

9,780   10,270

9,180
9,460

7,360   8,840

5,000   6,770

4,490

3,100

2,400   2,090
1,590

700   1,160
1,590   130   250   370   700   1,280
200   230   330   420   800
1978   1983   1988   1993   1998   2003   2008   2013   2018

—▲—Equatorial Guinea   —■—Mexico   —◆—China

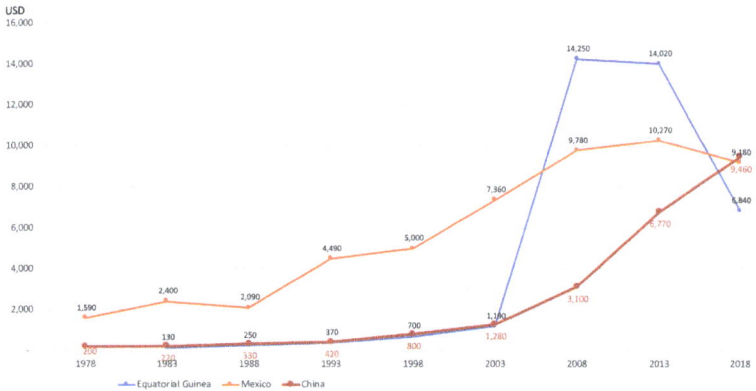

Data source: World Bank; data of Equatorial Guinea from 1978-1981 is not available

Chart 4 Comparative Example of 3 Mid GNI per Capita Countries

use of the market economy and also known as the *Vietnam Model*, is represented by Vietnam.

Although different development models exhibit their own characteristics, they also share some similarities. For example, both the *Social Democratic Model* and the *Liberal Capitalist Model* are implemented by developed capitalist countries; both rely heavily on the private ownership of capital, with the former having a more developed welfare state. The *Latin American Model* and the *Radical Transformation Model* are both associated with developing capitalist countries, and closely mimic the *Liberal Capitalist Model* but in a context of relative economic dependency. Collectively the forms most closely related to the *Liberal Capitalist Model* are sometimes referred to today as *Neoliberal Models, particularly if taking more extreme market-dominated forms.* The *East Asian Model* borrows, to some extent, from the *Social Democratic Model,* as well as from the distinct Japanese Model of organised monopolistic capital. The *Soviet Model, Vietnam Model, China Model,* and even the *Cuba Model* are all development models from socialist countries based primarily on the public ownership of capital. However, the *Soviet Model* and *Cuba Model* highlight the role of planning, while the *Vietnam Model* and *China Model* incline toward greater reliance on the market, even though retaining strong planning sectors.

2. The Characteristics and Connotations of China's Economic System

The distinctive institutional features of the *China Model* can be expressed in terms of economic development that distinguish it from other models, and may be seen as consisting of *Four Main Types* of economic development. These are: (1) a public ownership-based multiple property rights system, (2) a labour-based multi-factor distribution system, (3) a state-led multi-structure market system, and (4) a self-supporting multi-faceted open system.

The public ownership-based multiple property rights system has the following key characteristic: a non-public sector of the economy, featuring both Chinese and foreign ownership, has been developed subject to the premise that public ownership, including the qualitative and quantitative advantages possessed by public assets, plays a dominant role. Within the dynamic development of various forms of ownership, China attaches importance to maintaining a subject-subsidiary (dominant-auxiliary) ownership structure with regard to public and non-public ownership. The purpose of maintaining this ownership structure is not simply to control the rise of the non-public economy, but to consolidate, develop, and strengthen the public economy while giving moderate encouragement to the non-public economy. The structure is thus intended to maintain the basic, dominant role of the public economy and the leading and controlling role of the state-owned economy. This basic, dominant position of the public economy is not only reflected in the advantages possessed by the state-owned sector in terms of the quantity and quality of total social assets, but more importantly, its advantages in terms of the quantity and quality of operating assets.

In the United States and other countries that accept private ownership as the subject of property, assets such as certain lands and mineral resources, the armed forces, government office buildings, public educational and public medical institutions, police forces, prisons, and fiscal revenue are state-owned and occupy the majority of the total social assets. State-owned operating assets, however, account for a very small portion of total operating assets. In contrast, China's state-owned capital, collective capital, and other public capital account for the majority of the country's operating assets. Within the state-owned economy, the various service, construction, and regulation functions of core industries, the guiding role of science and technology, and the overall profit-making determinants of society, are seen as integral parts of the national economy insofar as they respectively account for employed workers, capital, GDP, and tax revenues. Based principally on public ownership, China's property rights structure is characterised by a system of distribution according to work, a state-led structure of economic regulation, and access based on principles of self-reliance.

Within the labour-based, multi-factor distribution system, distribution according to work is predominant, and multi-factor owners are able to participate in distribution based on property rights. This system is further characterised by economic fairness and efficiency, displaying the same trends and equal relationships. The property rights system, within which public ownership is predominant, provides an appropriate prerequisite for a distribution system in which distribution according to work is its main form. Distribution according to work guarantees a virtuous circle of production, consumption, and sustainable economic development. Countries such as the United States, where private ownership is the main form of property, base their economies on the private allocation of capital. Typically, the income gap in these countries is not determined as much by the gap in wage income, but by the gap in property income that arises from unequal ownership of property. As Samuelson and Nordhaus put it, 'The difference in income is mainly caused by the amount of wealth. Compared with the difference in property, the difference in wages and personal ability is negligible. This class difference hasn't disappeared. Today, working-class parents often cannot afford to send their children to a business school or medical school. These children are excluded from well-paid occupations.'[6] High efficiency is inseparable from equitable distribution based on a reasonable public ownership economic system.

The injustice of capitalism is manifested above all in the private property system and in distribution according to capital and its derivatives. In contrast, the weaknesses of traditional (or Soviet-style) socialism are manifested principally in the rigidity of the system and in distribution based on egalitarianism and its derivatives. As a result, China's reforms have moved in the direction of a market-based system of distribution according to work. Within this system, income gaps of reasonable size, based on remuneration formed by market competition, have served to maximise human potential and to optimise the allocation of labour resources on the scale of society as a whole. Compared with distribution according to capital, distribution according to work is fairer and more efficient. China implements a social distribution structure summed up in the phrase 'getting rich first – common prosperity', with distribution according to work in the dominant position. Not only is it emphasised that capital, land, technology, information, and other production factors can be employed in distribution by virtue of ownership, but also highlights the mechanism and principle of the

6. Paul Samuelson, William Nordhaus. *Economics* [M]. Gao Hongye, et al. translated. Beijing: China Development Press, 1992: 1252-1253

market-oriented distribution according to work. This illustrates a basic distribution pattern suitable for the contemporary development of productivity and the market economy.

A key characteristic of this labour-based, multi-factor distribution system is that it emphasises the basic role of fairness and efficiency in the initial distribution, and the subsidiary role of fairness and efficiency in the process of redistribution and adjustment of state finance and taxation. With distribution currently carried out using multiple factors, China needs to focus on increasing the proportion of labour remuneration in the initial distribution, on increasing the incomes of low and middle-income earners, and on gradually raising the minimum wage standard. A further core issue is the need to make constant improvements to the normal wage growth and payment guarantee mechanisms for enterprise employees, and to continuously upgrade social security and other welfare standards for urban and rural residents. The state-led, multi-structure market system refers to the development of a multi-structure market system that gives play to market mechanisms in the basic allocation of resources, while at the same time assigning a leading role to state regulation on the basis of integrity, low cost, democracy, and efficiency. China has established and steadily improved: (1) a market object structure that features various commodities and production factors as exchange objects, (2) a market subject structure with various market entities or parties involved in exchange activities, (3) a market space structure based on the place and scope of the activities of various market subjects and objects, and (4) a market time structure characterised by the continuity and sequence of the starting and ending points of exchange. China has formed a buyer-oriented market system with a complete structure, appropriate hierarchy, and flexible mechanisms. While maintaining the basic role of the market in regulating the allocation of resources, the country has given due attention to the regulatory role of the national planning system and fiscal and monetary policies. It has maintained the stability, balance, and sustainability of the macro economy with a view to the unification and maximisation of overall interests. Under the premises of integrity, low cost, democracy, and efficiency, the dominant position of a 'small but strong government' has been established. It is essential to use the optimal function of market regulation to prevent 'state regulation failure,' and to employ the optimal state regulation to correct 'market regulation failure.' These beneficial regulations have achieved a 'basic-dominant' dual regulation mechanism able to form a 'dual strength' pattern featuring both a strong market and a strong government. The result has been that the role and functioning of China's economic regulation have proven greater and stronger than those of capitalist countries.

The self-supporting, multi-faceted, open system in China has created a powerful nexus between the introduction of foreign technologies and capital, the self-reliant development of independent intellectual property rights, and the efficient use of domestic capital to forge economic relationships with domestic and foreign partners. The effect, based on domestic demand and combined with foreign demand, has been to promote the transition from an extensive open model that pursues the achievement of quantity to a more intensive quality-focused open model centred on the attainment of benefits. In its process of opening up to the outside world, China has not only emphasised the active use of foreign capital, technology, and talent, but also placed stress on independence and self-reliance. It advocates 'relying mainly on our own efforts while making external assistance subsidiary,' and makes it the basic guideline of modernisation and fostering of open markets.

On the basis of its independence and reliance on its own strength, China has gradually realised a multi-directional opening toward both developed and developing countries, as well as a two-way opening between the Mainland and Hong Kong, Macao, and Taiwan. This approach has brought about multi-level openings in the areas of primary, secondary, and tertiary industry, along with access to a wide variety of goods and services, capital, and technology. It has also helped to open up markets in various fields in the eastern, central, and western regions. China attaches importance to carefully designing and adjusting strategies and policies for introducing capital, technology, and talent. These strategies are implemented through combining comparative advantages with competitive advantages, through stressing the enhancement of the degree of independent innovation and vigorously developing national enterprise groups and China-based multinational corporations. Typically, these groups and organisations control holdings, technologies (especially core technologies), and brands, especially famous brands. It is these technologies and brands that highlight the cultivation and utilisation of intellectual property advantages. The goal is to create a world factory in China rather than a world processing factory, and to this end, a concerted effort is made to introduce goods and services, capital, and technology. At the same time, the Chinese people will work hard to go global, participating in international cooperation and competition, while introducing goods and services, capital, and technology.

This will be done with a view to transforming China from a merely large trading country to a genuinely strong trading country, and from a country with a large economy to an economic powerhouse.

3. The Process and Nature of China's Economic System Reform

The above-mentioned characteristics of China's economic system show clearly that the *China Model of Economic Development* is a model of a socialist economy with distinctive Chinese characteristics. As China is the largest country in the developing world, the *China Model of Economic Development* has obviously been created for use in a large developing country. China has utilised the *China Model* as its preferred option for making the transition from a socialist planned economy to a socialist market economy. In short, the *China Institutional Model of Economic Development* is the transformation model with Chinese characteristics of the world's largest developing socialist country.

For further analysis, a comparison has been made with the reform and transformation of the economic system in Russia and other countries. We shall first take a look at the difference in goals and positioning. The aim of China's economic reform and transformation has been to establish a socialist market economy, while Russia and other countries have tried to establish capitalist market economies, resulting in different institutional characteristics. Countries such as Russia have changed to a mixed form of private property rights, to polarised forms of distribution based on capital allocation, to neoliberal (Yeltsin-era) or Keynesian (Putin-era) patterns of market regulation, and to an open economic pattern that is dependent on the West.

Broadly speaking, the processes and paths chosen in China and Russia have been markedly different. China took a methodical approach to reforming its economic system and paced the transformation deliberately, while Russia and other countries have adopted more radical tactics. China's economic system reform and transformation measures have been advanced incrementally, by means of trial and error and adopting a method of piloting first and then scaling up. Meanwhile, Russia and other countries have implemented a 'one step in place' sequence, slowly correcting their errors after the fact. China tends to construct first and then to destruct, while Russia and other countries follow the reverse principle. The Chinese method combines mandatory change with inducements, while Russia and other countries employ a mandatory and imperative approach. The *China Model of Economic Development* has been a socialist development model with obvious advantages and has also provided a model of development and transition for less developed countries. As a natural progression, it has also provided a reference for socialist countries, developing countries, and countries in transition. The success of the *China Model* has also had a certain universal significance. As numerous foreign experts and scholars have pointed out, it can logically be used as a reference for developed countries.

Usually, the characteristics of different development models that receive the most attention are those that distinguish them from each other. Even when examining the same development model, however, Chinese and foreign scholars have often come to different conclusions owing to their different viewpoints and perspectives. Scholars in China, too, hold different views on China's economic development model. For example, some scholars have argued that the reform and development of China's economic system has followed the *Neoliberal Model*. These researchers appear to conclude that the country's transition from a traditional, highly centralised planned economic system to a socialist market economy has gained from some of the general theories on the market economy favored by Western economics, including its neoliberal variety. In practice, a shift has occurred from the past position of over-emphasising national and collective interests to an appropriate emphasis on local and individual interests, and from an almost pure public economy to a moderate reduction in the proportion of the public economy and the creation of multiple forms of public ownership. The aim has become to encourage, support, and guide the development of the non-public economy, including the operations of individual, private, and foreign capital. As a result, these scholars mistakenly argue that China's policy of reform and opening up follows the logic of mainstream Western economics and its policy propositions.

In fact, if mainstream Western thinking in this case were to be followed, China would not be able to uphold and improve its basic economic system, in which public ownership constitutes the main body while distribution according to work represents the core. If the central logic of neoliberal economics were to be followed, and a radical market economy implemented, it would also be impossible to maintain and improve the regulatory system of the socialist state, and thus to optimise the level of regulation. Further, it would be impossible to make continuous improvements, on a basis of self-reliance, to the necessary combination of independence from the outside world and openness to it. Nor would it be possible to bring about gradual changes to the mode of foreign economic development. Obviously, the argument that China's economic development is proceeding in line with the *Neoliberal Model* – an argument that for the most part is merely declarative in nature – fails to capture the main characteristics of this development. The proposition that China's economic reform and development is 'guided by Western theories' is not realistic, and this mistaken theorising can only serve to mislead the reform and development efforts concerned.

It should not be hard to discern that the tremendous achievements China has realised during its thirty years of reform and opening up are not the result of following Western mainstream economics, or of implementing the policies that derive from it. Moreover, problems such as the gradually widening gap in income and wealth, the destructive exploitation and wasteful use of resources, severe environmental pollution, loss of public assets, poor working conditions in some private companies, and the prevalence of corruption, are precisely the results of the influence of mainstream Western economic theories and policies represented by neoliberal economics. The one-sided pursuit of profit maximisation advocated by mainstream Western economics has led to companies not paying attention to resource conservation, deliberately discharging pollutants, minimising wages and working conditions, and even producing and selling counterfeit or shoddy goods. These maleficent practices seriously harm people's lives and health. The *Selfish Economists Theory*, advocated by Western mainstream economics, emphasises the unbridled pursuit of personal interests, which leads to the dishonesty of economic players, profits at public expense, bribery, smuggling and trafficking, and even violent crime. The reason for the excessively widening gap in income and wealth lies in the property rights and initial distribution systems of Chinese and foreign private enterprises; it has resulted in self-aggrandising behavior by senior managers in state-owned enterprises, and inappropriate actions by competent authorities.

Here is a key theoretical and policy challenge worth analysing and highlighting. Modifications to the layout, structure, and productive activity of public enterprises, especially state-owned enterprises, and even the bankruptcy of some state-owned enterprises, are required if the public economy is to be expanded and more fully developed. It cannot be said that the public economy is inefficient, just as the bankruptcy of some privately-owned enterprises does not directly prove that privately-owned enterprises are inefficient. The great advances China has made in the past thirty years of reform and opening up are the result of the common development of multi-economic sectors, with public ownership playing the dominant role. This fully reflects the overall benefits of the public economy, both macro and micro, internal and external. The dominant position of the public economy, and the leadership and control exercised by the state-owned sector, guarantee the dominant position of distribution according to work and a virtuous cycle of production and consumption; they thereby ensure the effective, rapid, and sustainable development of the national economy in the long term.

In contrast, a market economy based on capitalist private ownership is polarised according to the distribution of capital, as the mainstay, and the distribution of income. It is inevitable that there will be insufficient consumption and corresponding overproduction, so the economy will be constantly interrupted by economic crises. These phenomena make no contribution to long-term, sustainable, and rapid development. If the reform and development of China's economic system follows the *Neoliberal Model*, the system will not escape the failure experienced by the *Latin American Model*. Nor will it avoid financial and economic crises. The fact that China has not experienced a financial or economic crisis, is affected by Western financial and economic crises only to varying degrees and can maintain a growth rate of more than 8%, shows the superiority of the *China Model*, and that the model applied in China does not correspond to the *Neoliberal Model* of economic system reform and development.

Other studies contend that China's system of economic reform and development follows the *Social Democratic Model* adopted by Sweden, that is, principally a market economy with a larger, but secondary, welfare state role. This view focuses mainly on the development of China's non-public economy, while largely ignoring the dominant public economy and the leading and controlling role played by the state-owned sector. It sees only the premise of China allowing some people to become rich before others, remaining blind to the core premise represented by distribution according to work. Nor does it take into account China's goal of eliminating exploitation and polarisation so as to achieve common prosperity, seeing only the commonalities of the socialist and capitalist market economies. It disregards the essential difference in the nature of the two. That difference arises from the fact that in the socialist market economy or mixed economy public ownership holds the dominant position; by contrast, the capitalist market economy or mixed economy is based on the dominant position of private ownership. The *Social Democratic Model* recognises the welfare guarantee system as a mechanism through which capitalism eases the contradiction between capital and labour and improves the living conditions of the working class but fails to discern that welfare capitalism represents an improved set of ideas and policies that is set in place by the class struggle between employers and employees, rather than an economic system that fundamentally alters the exploitative nature of capitalist employment. The view that China has followed the *Social Democratic Model* in China's reform and development treats these processes one-sidedly, concluding mistakenly that China's economic development has followed and will continue to follow the *Social Democratic Model*. This, however, is not the case.

It should be noted that the reform and development of China's economic system has always proceeded under the guidance of *Marxist Economic Theory*, while adhering to the principles of socialism. The system in China has always endeavoured to reform those links and aspects of socialist productive relations that have not proved suited to the development of the social productive forces. It has done this by taking foreign management experience and advanced technology as its reference. Reform, however, has not involved changing the nature of the socialist system, and development does not mean copying foreign development models. To establish and improve the socialist market economy system, China has combined the basic socialist system with the market economy to make full use of the advantages of both, and this has been an important reason behind China's tremendous achievements. Through reform, China has overturned the idea, expounded by Western capitalist economics, that only capitalist private ownership can be combined with the market economy.

The implementation of a socialist market economic system, that combines the basic socialist system with the market economy, is a great initiative in the historical development of scientific socialism, and a major theoretical innovation to Marxist political economy. If the ideas and practices underlying China's economic development are described as the *China Model*, this model is beyond a doubt thoroughly consistent with socialist development. Because of its Chinese context and features, it may be referred to as the economic development model of socialism with Chinese characteristics. The development model of socialism with Chinese characteristics alludes to the political development model, cultural development model, and social development model of socialism with Chinese characteristics, corresponding to political development, cultural development, and social development respectively. These are collectively referred to as *the development model of socialism with Chinese characteristics*. Considering the salient features of this model, that is, the combination of public capital with the market economy, it is obvious why the *China Model* of economic development can also be called the socialist market economy model with Chinese characteristics.

References

[1] Liu Guoguang. *China's Performance and its Relationship with Socialism with Chinese Characteristics in the Current World Economic Crisis* [J]. *Social Sciences in Chinese*, 2009 (5).

[2] Zhang Yu. *Definition and Significance of the China Model* [J]. *China Review of Political Economy*, 2009 (1).

[3] Li Bingyan, Xiang Gang. *China Miracle and China Model - Great Achievements and Basic Experience of the 3-decade Economic Reform in China* [J]. *Journal of Jiangsu University of Science and Technology: Social science edition*, 2009(1).

[4] Cheng Enfu, Gu Hailiang. *Journal of Economics of Shanghai School: Volume 22-23* [M]. *Shanghai: Shanghai University of Finance and Economics Press*, 2008.

(Originally published in *Economic Perspectives*, Issue 12, 2009)

*   *   *

Section II *Four Key Words* for Accelerating the Improvement of the Socialist Market Economic System

1. The First Key Word Is Public Ownership

The report of the 18th National Congress of the Communist Party of China clearly states: 'We should speed up improvements to the socialist market economy. We should improve the basic economic system in which public ownership is the mainstay of the economy and economic entities of diverse ownership develop together, and we should improve the system of income distribution in which distribution according to work is the main form that coexists with other forms of distribution. We should leverage to a greater extent and in a wider scope the basic role of the market in allocating resources, improve the system of macro-regulation, and perfect the open economy.[7] This

---

7. Full text of the report from the 18th National Congress of the Communist Party of China: (English version) http://www.china-embassy.org/eng/zt/18th_CPC_National_Congress_Eng/t992917.htm

scientifically defines the connotation and direction of acceleration of social improvement from the four levels of property rights, distribution, regulation, and opening. China should combine the spirit of the 18th National Congress of the Party and carry out profound theoretical and realistic elabouration and innovation of these four levels or keywords based on changing national and world conditions.

Broadly defined, property rights are conceptually similar to ownership. The system in which public ownership plays a dominant role and diverse forms of ownership develop together is the basic economic system that must be adhered to and perfected during the initial stage of socialism. A socialist market economy system is derived from the principles of economics, economic attributes, and economic types. When the term *market socialism* was defined in the *Palgrave Dictionary of Economics* (U.S.), it was believed that resource allocation or economic operation was primarily a market mechanism, and public ownership was the main form. This interpretation makes sense. On the contrary, if private ownership is dominant and multiple forms of ownership develop side by side, it is then considered to be a capitalist market economic system or basic economic system; typically referred to as *market capitalism*. This is the mainstream consensus of modern political economists and of western comparative economic system experts.

The question is, how to improve the basic economic system of primary socialism? The report of the 18th National Congress of the Communist Party of China (NCCPC) emphasised: 'We should unwaveringly consolidate and develop the public sector of the economy; allow public ownership to take diverse forms; deepen reform of state-owned enterprises; improve the mechanisms for managing all types of state assets; and invest more of state capital in major industries and key fields that comprise the lifeline of the economy and are vital to national security. We should thus steadily enhance the vitality of the state-owned sector of the economy and its capacity to leverage and influence the economy. At the same time, we must unswervingly encourage, support and guide the development of the non-public sector, and ensure that economic entities under all forms of ownership have equal access to factors of production in accordance with the law, compete on a level playing field and are protected by the law as equals.[8]

The traditional socialist planned economic system and the contemporary capitalist market economic system have shown that if either public ownership or private ownership plays the dominant

---

8. Ibid

role, it is difficult to achieve the potential efficiency and fairness that the development of science and technology can provide. The cyclical economic recessions and other crises that occur in Western countries every few years also show that the non-public market economy is always subject to endogenous, unsustainable dysfunction. Therefore, in order to improve the ownership structure of the whole society in which public ownership is dominant and private ownership is auxiliary, it is essential to enhance the symbiosis and complementarity of the two ownerships under market competition and state orientation. It is necessary to unswervingly consolidate and develop the public sector and support and develop the non-public sector, while avoiding the situation in which the public economy advances while the non-public economy retreats, and vice-versa. Meanwhile, in the face of the grim situation in which Western transnational monopoly capital is gradually coming to control many areas of our economy, it is imperative to strengthen cooperation between the public and non-public sectors of the economy; rather than generating internal frictions, China must respond to the fierce competition of foreign monopoly capital at home and abroad.

2. The Second Keyword Is Distribution

Since property relations and the property system determine distribution relations and the distribution system, the right to income is one of the rights that are categorised under general property rights. It follows that the subject of public ownership decides or derives the subject of distribution according to work. At the primary stage of socialism, the distribution system is based on distribution according to work, which coexists with other subsidiary distribution methods. Leaving aside the natural economy and the individual economy, the basic form of distribution under the modern enterprise system is market-based distribution according to work or distribution according to capital. The so-called multiple distribution methods or distribution according to the property rights of production factors can essentially be broken down into distribution according to work or capital. Distribution according to business ability belongs to distribution according to work, while distribution according to land elements belongs to distribution according to capital. Income obtained by enterprise personnel for the invention of technology belongs to distribution according to work, and income obtained after being converted into shares is classified as distribution according to capital. What is apparent is the need to improve the distribution system in which distribution according to work is dominant and distribution according to capital is auxiliary.

The question is: *How does China improve the primary socialist distribution system*? The report to the 18th NCCPC emphasised the need to *safeguard social fairness and justice* and to *strive for common prosperity*. Common prosperity is the fundamental principle of socialism with Chinese characteristics. At present, the root cause and primary source of the large disparity in residents' wealth and income distribution is the non-public economy, together with the large proportion of distribution according to capital determined by it. The report to the 18th NCCPC therefore stated: 'We should adhere to the basic socialist economic system and the socialist income distribution system. We should adjust the pattern of national income distribution, tighten its regulation by secondary distribution and work hard to narrow income gaps so that all the people can share in more fruits of development in a fair way and move steadily toward common prosperity.'[9] The report continued: 'To ensure that the people share in the fruits of development, we must deepen reform of the income distribution system, and increase individual income in step with economic development and work remuneration in step with improvement in labour productivity, and we should raise the share of individual income in the distribution of national income and increase the share of work remuneration in primary distribution.'[10]

In addition, doubling China's 2010 GDP and per capita income for both urban and rural residents will require us to implement a general policy of reform and development in distribution. Specifically, *a proper balance must be struck between efficiency and fairness in both primary and secondary distribution, with particular emphasis on fairness in secondary distribution*. This is due, economically, to the fact that equality or fairness is not conceptually equal to the mathematical average. The true relationship between economic fairness and efficiency is not a substitutional relationship, a 'zero-sum' in which gains for one are losses for the other, but a mutually promotional relationship that changes in the same direction. The fairer the rules, rights, and opportunities, the greater the efficiency, and vice versa. At present, in order to effectively solve the problem of large gaps in the distribution of wealth and income among enterprise personnel, the *Four-link*

9. Ibid
10. Ibid

Method and reform policy, that the author has emphasised for many years, should be adopted. That is, the income of ordinary employees must be linked to labour productivity, to the profit rate of the enterprise, to the income of the executives, and to local price changes so as to promote harmonious distribution.

3. The Third Keyword Is Regulation

Giving full play to the basic role of the market in resource allocation can be referred to as *basing allocation on market regulation*. Its opposite is state regulation, which primarily includes regulation by the National People's Congress (the legislature) and regulation by the government, involving both macro and micro regulation. As Samuelson said, 'The market is brainless and heartless, and it requires the state to play a role'. Stiglitz's 'Economics of Government', Krugman's 'Return to Keynesian Theory', and many other western works have fully explained the necessity and feasibility of a dual-functional regulation system. China has been a late-developing country that will implement large-scale development. China must not only avoid an absence or vacuum of policies and mechanisms in the reform, but also *continuously enhance the vitality, control, and influence of the state-owned economy*, and draw lessons from the useful government-led experiences of the *Four Asian Tigers* and other relevant countries. China must therefore take full advantage of the important role of the state in ensuring the rapid and stable development of the national economy. At the primary stage of socialism, China should build an efficient and effective state regulatory system on the basis of integrity, low costs, democracy, and efficiency. It is important to create a dual regulatory mechanism with complementary functions based on market regulation and state regulation, and China should eliminate the cyclical economic crises and other dilemmas brought about by the excessive implementation of market regulation and market-oriented reforms in Western countries.

Another pertinent question is: *How does China improve the primary socialist regulation system*? The report to the 18th NCCPC emphasised that 'The underlying issue we face in economic structural reform is how to strike a balance between the role of the government and that of the market. We should follow, more closely, the rules of the market and have government play a substantial role. We should improve the modern market system and strengthen institutional procedures for setting macro-regulation targets and employing policy tools'. Accelerating the improvement of the object structure, main structure, space structure, and time structure of various markets such as commodities, technology, capital, land, housing, and manpower, and setting in motion their well-coupled functions, are important components of a comprehensively deep reform. At the same time, China must focus on deepening the reform of the fiscal and taxation systems and establish a mechanism for the appropriate sharing of revenues from the transfer of public resources. China must deepen the reform of the financial system, improve the modern financial system that promotes macroeconomic stability and supports the development of the real economy, accelerate the transformation of economic development methods, and intensify reform in the areas of science and technology, education, culture, and the health system. Additionally, China must enhance scientific and technological innovation and national soft power, while improving national health provisions. China must heighten the reform of the urban-rural integration system and solve the problems faced by agriculture, rural areas, and rural residents.

4. The Fourth Keyword Is Opening-up

An essential requirement of the market economy and economic globalisation is for the national economy to be opened internally and externally. This factor optimises resource allocation, promotes complementary advantages, and stimulates economic development. Openness and protectionism are contradictory, and both of them have positive and negative effects, which can be moderate or excessive. Developed countries and countries that gained a lot from opening up, paid great attention to independent innovation, self-development, and economic security before they opened up their economies and stressed the long-term benefit of opening-up to benefit the people. The report to the 18th NCCPC therefore sought to promote all-around improvements to China's open economy, stating: 'In response to new developments in economic globalisation, we must implement a more proactive opening up strategy and improve the open economy so that it promotes mutual benefit and is diversified, balanced, secure and efficient'.[11] It can be seen that a self-supporting, universally open system requires managing the relationship between attracting investments, technology and wisdom on the one hand, and on the other, applying a thoughtful strategy for making efficient use of domestic capital and wisdom and developing independent intellectual property rights. Meanwhile, it is necessary to

---

11. Ibid

promote a foreign economic exchange relationship where China's domestic requirements are primary and external requirements are auxiliary. The transformation must be realised from an extensive open model that pursues quantity to a lean open model that pursues benefits. The effect will be to complete China's transformation from a large producing and trading country to a trading and economic powerhouse.

Yet another question is: How can the open system of primary socialism be improved? The report to the 18th NCCPC provided the following focus: 'We should move faster to change the way the external-oriented economy grows, and make China's open economy become better structured, expand in scope and yield greater returns. We should make innovations in the mode of opening up. '[12] Indeed, with the world economic structure seeing profound changes, and leaders calmly facing the current problems of foreign economic development, an urgent new direction is now required if China is to plan strategically for the long-term development of foreign economic relations, to establish new thinking, and to adopt new ideas, strategies, and initiatives in accelerating the transformation of foreign economic development methods.

To this end, and with the availability of China's large capital surplus, the country should first, in an appropriate way, control its dependence on foreign capital, and then improve the benefits of coordinating the use of Chinese and foreign capital. Second, in order to build an innovative country, it must correspondingly reduce the country's dependence on foreign technology and promote independent innovation. Third, confronted with the need for greater global ecological and environmental protection and with the shortage of resources, our dependence on external sources should be suitably reduced and the efficiency of resource and energy allocation should be improved. Fourth, China should set out to circumvent the disadvantages that result from an export-oriented economy, through limiting our dependence on foreign trade and increasing the role of consumption in driving growth. Fifth, so as to confront the challenge posed by the United States in overprinting the U.S. dollar and undertaking several rounds of quantitative easing policies, China must properly control its foreign exchange reserves, and actively increase the use of foreign exchange. On the basis of consolidation and improvement of a general open market system oriented toward self-reliance, and with the guidance provided by the *Scientific*

---

12. Ibid

Outlook on Development, these five controls and enhancements will allow China to present a low-loss, highly-efficient, lean and open economy to the outside world. It is therefore necessary to coordinate the relationship between economic development and an open economy, while placing greater emphasis on autonomous development, high-end competition, economic security, national rights, and benefits for the livelihoods of the population. In this way, it is possible to promote the sound, rapid, and healthy development of China's national economy.

*   *   *

Section III This New Era Will Accelerate the Process of Increasing the People's Wealth and the Country's Prosperity under the *New Normal* of China's Economy

The *Two Centenary Goals* strategic plan will accelerate the process of increasing the people's wealth and the country's prosperity. It will promote the steady progress of China toward prosperity and strength. The fundamental reason that the prosperity for both people and countries in the West is hindered is the various antagonistic contradictions of capitalism. The result is that the 'new *normal*' of China's economy is sharply differentiated from the economies of Western countries. This section elabourates on the current levels of prosperity in China and Western countries, as well as on the actual performance, institutional characteristics, and theoretical approaches that characterise the different *new normal* situations of different economies. It will also address the concept that China now stands at the *quasi-centre* of the world economic system's *centre-periphery*.

1. The Two Centenary Goals *Strategic Plan Accelerates the Process of Increasing the People's Wealth and the Prosperity of the Entire Country*

Rooted in the heritage of Marxist-Leninist theory, synthesised in the course of its application to China's specific conditions, the thinking of socialism with Chinese characteristics for a new era is reflected most prominently in the combining of the strategic guiding role of state planning in economic and social development with the decisive role played by market allocation of general resources. In the administration of state affairs, the biggest difference between the

Communist Party of China (hereinafter referred to as *CPC*) as a ruling party equipped with long-term strategic planning and the western *two-without* (without a party constitution, without party members) ruling parties is that the CPC is based on the people-centric development concept of strengthening the people's wealth and the country's prosperity. This concept combines, in natural fashion, the socialist system with the system of the market economy. It not only *takes full advantage of the strategic guiding role of state development planning*, but also makes full use of the decisive role of market allocation of general economic resources (general economic resources exclude those in the fields of education, culture, health, social security, housing, mineral resources, and transportation, along with other important non-material or material resources). This is clearly reflected in the *Two Centenary Goals* strategic plan and its implementation.

Specifically, the CPC, following its reform and opening up of the economy, made strategic arrangements for carrying out China's socialist modernisation, and put forward the *three-step* strategic goal. These measures were designed to achieve the two goals of guaranteeing the people's basic living needs and of securing the premise that the people, on the whole, live a moderately well-off life. On this basis, the 18th NCCPC established the *Two Centenary Goals*. These goals amount to a plan to build a comprehensive, moderately prosperous society by the time of the CPC's centenary and through the struggle of the next three decades to achieve modernisation and build China into a socialist modern country.

The report adopted by the 19th NCCPC states that from now until 2020 China must follow the requirements of constructing a moderately prosperous society in a broad way; respond to the constant evolution of the principal contradiction in Chinese society; and implement the *Five-Sphere Integrated Plan* and the *Four-Pronged Comprehensive Strategy.* These plans and strategies will create a moderately prosperous society that will earn the people's approval and stand the test of time. We have drawn up a dual-stage developmental plan that will be implemented from 2020 to the middle of the 21st century. In the first stage, set for 2020 to 2035, we will build on the foundation created by our moderately prosperous society. It will require a further fifteen years of hard work to ensure that socialist modernisation is fundamentally realised. This solid foundation will advance the schedule of modernisation proposed in the 18th NCCPC's report by fifteen years. The second stage, planned for 2035 to the middle of the 21st century, with the envisioned modernisation in place, calls for a further fifteen years of effort to

develop China into a great, modern, socialist country that is prosperous, strong, democratic, culturally advanced, harmonious, and
beautiful.'[13]

As the above-mentioned medium and long-term strategic plans,
designed to strengthen people's wealth and the country's prosperity,
played a leading role in the socialist market economy, China made
full use of the advantages of the market economy as well as the superiority of the socialist system. These measures have been devised so
as to effectively counter the disadvantages that under capitalism
arise from the contradiction between the organised nature of production in the enterprises of the capitalist market economy, and the
anarchic or disordered state of the social economy as a whole. Achieving a dual, organic combination in which state regulation plays the
leading role while market regulation acts as the foundation the two
are complementary to each other and makes it possible to fulfil the

13. Winning to build a moderately prosperous society across the
board and seizing the great victory of socialism with Chinese characteristics in the new era [N]. People's Daily, 2017-10-28. http://www.gov.cn/
zhuanti/2017-10/27/content_5234876.htm

objective requirements that allow the law of planned development of socialism to register its outstanding performance.

As General Secretary Xi Jinping has pointed out:

> *Developing a market economy under socialism is a great initiative of the Party. One of the key factors in the great success of China's economic development is that we not only employ every form of leverage to realise the advantages of the market economy, but also to bring to bear the superiority of the socialist system. We are developing our market economy under the leadership of the CPC and the socialist system, and consequently, we shall never forget socialism. The reason we call it a socialist market economy is that we shall adhere to the superiority of our system and effectively guard against the disadvantages of the capitalist market economy. We should adhere to the dialectics of our system, which dictate that everything has two aspects. We shall continue to concentrate our efforts on combining the basic socialist system and the market economy, while bringing into service the advantages of both. We shall not only provide an effective market, but also build a promising government, so as to overcome worldwide economic problems in practice.* [14]

That is to say, the practice of the socialist market economy with Chinese characteristics indicates that in view of *the opposition between the organised production in individual factories and the anarchic production in society as a whole* that characterises capitalist market economies, we must combine the strategic guiding role of state planning, recognising the decisive role of market allocation, with general economic resources successfully based on the superiority of the socialist system. In this way, we can effectively guard against the disadvantages of the capitalist market economy and tackle the worldwide economic problem of not only providing an *effective market* but also of becoming a *promising government*. We must achieve a strong record in both market and government functions and accelerate the process of increasing the people's wealth and the country's prosperity under the economic *new normal* in this new era.

---

14. According to People's Daily, this is from Speech at the Twenty-eighth Collective Study of the Political Bureau of the Eighteenth Central Committee (November 23, 2015).
    http://cpc.people.com.cn/xuexi/n1/2019/0128/c385476-30592929.html

2. China's Steady, Innovative Progress Toward Prosperity and Strength

It has been said that Mao Zedong made us stand up, Deng Xiaoping made us rich, and Xi Jinping made us strong. It has also been said that the aim of Mao Zedong's Socialism 1.0 was to allow us to rise from being a *poor and barely functioning* state; that the task of Deng Xiaoping's Socialism 2.0 was to make people rich; and that Socialism 3.0, since the 18th NCCPC, has sought to make us strong. None of these statements, in fact, are accurate. Precisely speaking, China was poor and barely functioning before the founding of the People's Republic of China, but since the founding of the *new* China, i.e., since the era of Mao Zedong, China has not only stood up, but also gradually become rich and strong. The process has been one of continuous improvement, of accelerating progress. The statistics relating to the increase in the people's wealth and the country's prosperity over the past seventy years of the new China neither validate the argument that separates popular wealth from the country's prosperity, nor support the contention that the country failed to advance gradually toward prosperity and strength during the Mao Zedong era. In view of this, General Secretary Xi Jinping is correct concerning the political bottom line and principle that the two thirty-year periods of construction and development since the founding of China cannot negate each other.

Common knowledge tells us that the birth of the new China has truly opened the door to a great rejuvenation of the Chinese nation. Despite all the setbacks and distractions, China has still attained brilliant economic achievements like no other country in the history of the world. Before the reform and opening up, China completed its heavy and chemical industrialisation over about thirty years from 1949 to 1978. It established a national economic system in which all the basic categories were present and achieved fundamental self-sufficiency in internal circulation. It armed itself with missiles, satellites, and nuclear weapons. In its pace of economic development, it caught up with and surpassed the vast majority of countries in the world, with an average annual Gross National Product (GNP) growth rate of over 6%. This important statistic places China among the fastest developing countries in the world during the period concerned. Social productivity, comprehensive national strength, and people's living standards improved greatly compared with the situation before the founding of the People's Republic of China. A number of major economic gaps between China and the major developed countries have been rapidly narrowed. Consequently, the *Resolution on Certain Questions in the History of Our Party Since the Founding of the People's Republic of China,* drafted under the leadership of Deng Xiaoping, was correct when it noted: 'Great achievements have been made in industrial construction, while an independent and relatively complete industrial system and national economic system have been established'.[15] The Resolution went on to say 'Agricultural production conditions have changed dramatically, and peoples living standards are greatly improved... In 1980, grain production nearly doubled and cotton production more than doubled compared with 1952. Despite the rapid growth of population (to nearly a billion), we still rely on our own strength to basically ensure the people's needs for food and clothing. Urban and rural commerce and foreign trade have grown dramatically... In 1980, the average per capita consumption level in urban and rural areas (excluding price factors) was nearly double that of 1952, and education, science, culture, health, and sports have all made great progress'.[16]

In the past forty years since the reform and opening up, China's national economy has taken off at an exceptional pace. Average annual GDP growth has been about 9%, much higher than the average growth of about 3% in the world economy during the same period. This ranked China first in the world during that period, with growth rates well above those of Germany, Japan, the United States, and other countries during their respective *golden ages* when they experienced rapid ascent. At present, China's national economic and

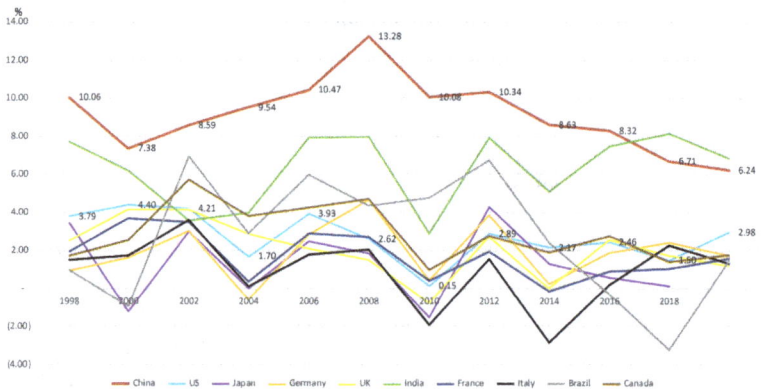

Data source: World Bank; only select time series that China's data are available

Chart 5 China GNI (GNP) Growth between 1996 to 2018 Compared with Top 9 Biggest Economies

15. http://www.people.com.cn/item/20years/newfiles/b1040.html
16. Ibid

'0000 tons

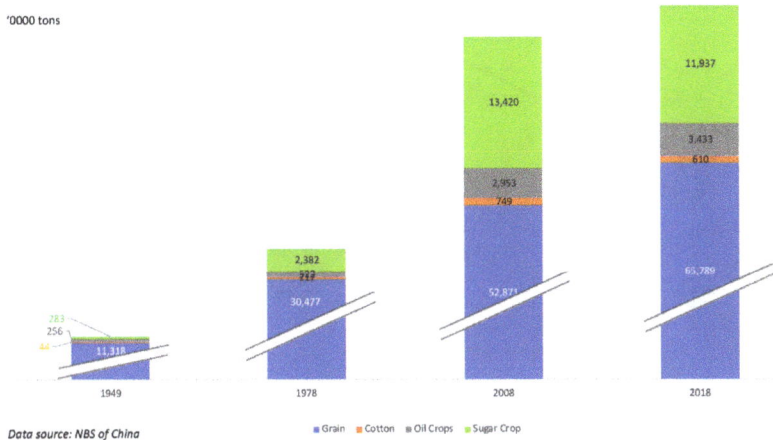

Data source: NBS of China

■ Grain ■ Cotton ■ Oil Crops ■ Sugar Crop

Chart 6 Grain, Cotton and Other Key Agricultural Products Production of China 1949-2018

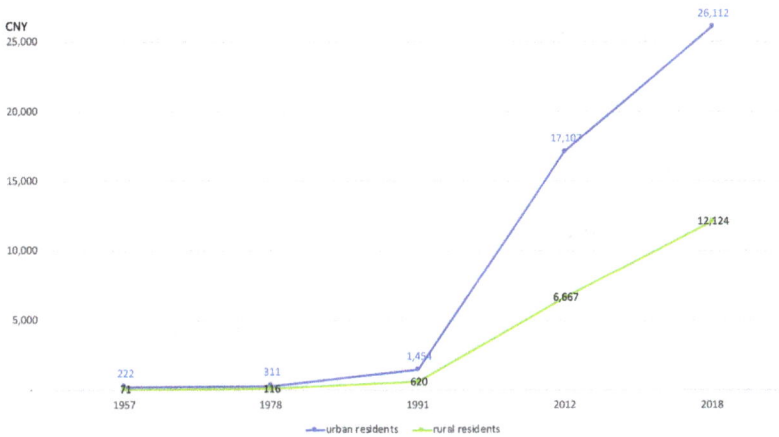

Data source: NBS of China

Chart 7 1957-2018 Average per Capita Consumption Level for Urban and Rural in China

total foreign trade volume ranks second in the world, and its foreign exchange reserves are the world's largest. *Shenzhou* manned space-craft have been successfully launched, as have the Chang'e Lunar Exploration Program, high-speed rail, the Tianhe supercomputer, the Beidou Satellite Navigation System, and other famous techno-logical achievements These achievements have served as powerful evidence of the *China miracle*. They have become a sign that China leads the world in terms of comprehensive strength and international

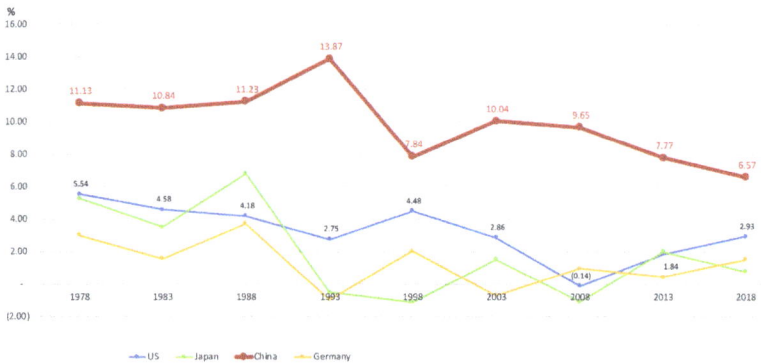

Data source: World Bank

Chart 8 GDP Growth Comparison among China, US, Japan & Germany

standing. In addition, China's annual per capita GDP has reached over 8,000 U.S. dollars, and its people are nearing an historic leap from having adequate food and clothing to enjoying a moderately prosperous life in all important aspects. Meanwhile, China has made remarkable achievements in democratic politics, culture, social construction, and so forth.

The periods before and after the reform and opening up are both integral parts of the new China's nearly seventy-year history. Both are indicative of the history of the new socialist China as a whole. The years before the adoption of the policy of reform and opening up saw the laying, so to speak, of the material and cultural foundations for the development that followed the reform and opening up. Creating these preconditions for reform and opening up represented a great achievement in its own right. Nevertheless, some studies of today's Chinese society, in seeking to demonstrate the necessity for the reform and opening up and its outstanding achievements, have adopted a nihilistic historical attitude toward the development that occurred during those initial thirty years, or in a one-sided fashion, have focused only on its mistakes and deficiencies. A number of scholars, misinterpreting events and ignoring important elements within them, have even denied these accomplishments. They have distorted the inheritance from the first decades of socialist construction and misrepresented the developmental relations between the two periods before and after the reform and opening up. This has undermined our understanding of the process of historical development, which took place under scientific guidance provided by Chinese Marxism, leading to the new China's prosperity and growing strength. To reap the benefits, China must be able to objectively summarise the historical experience and lessons, while grasping the relevant laws of development.

The report to the 19th NCCPC provided an accurate account of this when it stated:

> *Socialism with Chinese characteristics entering a new era means the Chinese nation, which since modern times began had endured so much for so long, has achieved a tremendous transformation: it has stood up, grown rich, and is becoming strong; it has come to embrace the brilliant prospects of rejuvenation. Our party united the people and led them in completing socialist revolution, establishing socialism as China's basic system, and advancing socialist construction. This completed the broadest and most profound social transformation in the history of the Chinese nation. It created the fundamental political conditions and the institutional foundation for achieving all development and progress in China today. Thus, was made a great transition: The Chinese nation reversed its fate from the continuous decline of modern times to steady progress toward prosperity and strength![17]*

3. Empirical Data Supporting the Strengthening of the Country, Enrichment of the People, and the **Quasi-Centre** Concept of the World Economy

A relatively recent saying held that the new China, since its founding and especially since the reform and opening up, had gradually become rich and strong; but that while it was widely acknowledged that *the country was strong, its people remained poor*. Professor Liu Guoguang, a famous economist and former vice-president of the Chinese Academy of Social Sciences, once specifically criticised this false idea in one of his articles. The Chinese like to make comparisons, which is often a good thing. They compare their industries with those of the United States, Germany, and Japan. They compare their agriculture with that of Israel and Holland, their military strength with that of the United States, and their natural environment with that of Australia and New Zealand. China compares its people's standard of living with that of Denmark and Norway, and their

---

17. http://www.xinhuanet.com/english/special/2017-11/03/c_13672
5942.htm

soccer with that of Germany, etc. On the basis of these comparisons, it seems that China is not the most advanced in every single respect. These comparisons are possible, but they are not comprehensive or scientific. A specific comparison may help motivate China to forge ahead, but if the supposition that China is not capable of anything or is not particularly advanced in any respect is made, then one-sided conclusions may be drawn. Actually, a comprehensive vertical comparison can be made between the old and new China, before and after 1949, in terms of the country's strengthening and the peoples' enrichment. In addition, horizontal comparisons can be made between China and other countries such as India, which before its independence shared similar national conditions with China, at least in a general way. Comparisons can also be made between China and the United States, Sweden, and other countries in terms of the rate of development of various important indicators. The conclusions that flow from the comparisons are obvious.

First, let us examine GDP measured at purchasing power parity. According to statistics from the World Bank Database, China's economic aggregate in 2016 reached 21.4 trillion U.S. dollars, which surpassed the 18.6 trillion U.S. dollars recorded by the United States and India's 8.7 trillion U.S. dollars. Research proves that purchasing power parity is the most scientific way of making such measurements and comparisons. Purchasing power parity refers to the ratio between the purchasing power per unit of currency and the exchange rate between two currencies. For example, the Chinese people might need to pay RMB forty in China and ten U.S. dollars in the United States to buy a basket of goods of the same quantity and quality. For this basket of goods, the purchasing power parity of RMB to a U.S. dollar is 4:1, that is, the purchasing power of RMB 4 is equivalent to 1 U.S. dollar. According to the exchange rate comparison, China is now second in the world, behind only the United States, in terms of its economic aggregate. However, the exchange rate fluctuates greatly, resulting in a less objective comparison. According to the figures for per capita GDP at purchasing power parity calculated by the International Monetary Fund in 2016, China's per capita GDP was 15,424 U.S. dollars, while India's was 6,658 U.S. dollars. Compared with developed countries or some developing countries, China's per capita GDP is still relatively small due to its large population base. If China's total population begins to decline, the per capita GDP figure will better reflect the achievements made in strengthening the country and enriching its people, as well as in economic and social development.

Another key indicator is the wealth index. In 2016, China's family wealth per capita was 169,000 RMB, of which the net value of real estate accounted for 66% (69% in urban households and 55% in rural households). As demonstrated in the China Family Wealth Survey Report, 2017, (prepared and released by the China Economic Trend Research Institute, the Economic Daily), the proportion of household automobiles in movable property was relatively high. In addition, according to the *Global Wealth Report 2016* released by the Credit Suisse Research Institute, the average wealth of Chinese

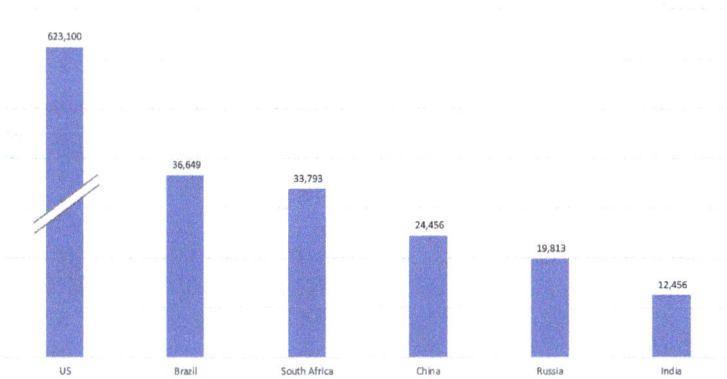

Data source: Global Wealth Report 2016, China Family Wealth Survey Report, OECD.org, Euromonitor
Argentina's data is not available

Chart 9 Family Wealth per Capita in 2016 (USD)

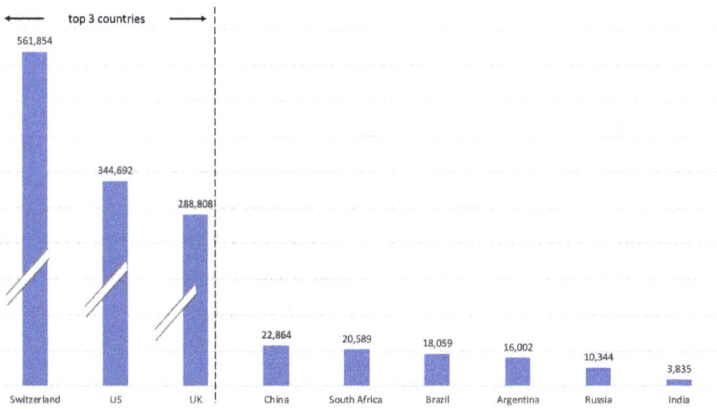

Data source: Global Wealth Report 2016

Chart 10 Average Wealth per Adult in 2016 (USD)

adults in 2016 was 22,864 U.S. dollars (RMB 158,000), which was at a medium-low level.[18]

It can be seen from the above data (some figures will be discussed below) that since the founding of the new China, the country has developed its economy and enriched its people at a fast pace by international standards. This pace has been even more rapid since the reform and opening up. The situation in India, however, with its similar national conditions to China, is relatively far behind.

The author has twice visited India for conferences and surveys and has also had discussions with Indian professors of economics and leaders of the Communist Party to gain a fuller picture. He has come to the following conclusion: if the Communist Party of India does not win power and form a socialist government, and if China does not revert to capitalist rule, it will be impossible for India to catch up with China economically. At present, there is a growing consensus that India, as 'the world's largest democracy', but with a weaker economy than China's, is likely to catch up with China within a few years. But this is, in fact, impossible, due to the different development pathways and systems of the two countries. It is only in terms of total population that India can be expected to surpass China. In the late 1940s, India had almost the same GDP per capita as China, better natural and geographic conditions, and more than twice the cultivated land per capita. But compared with China both during the Mao Zedong years and in the era of reform and opening up, India was weaker in terms of prosperity and strength and lagged behind by fifteen to twenty years.

In the report to the 19th NCCPC, General Secretary Xi Jinping stressed that 'It will be an era that sees China moving closer to centre stage and making greater contributions to mankind.'[19] These sentiments echo the conclusion that China is closer to the centre of the world stage than ever before, something that I think is most obvious in our economy. As everyone knows, Samir Amin, a world-famous left-wing economist, proposed and demonstrated the theory of *Centre and Periphery* within the world economic system in his masterpiece *Accumulation on a World Scale: A Critique of the Theory of Underdevelopment* (1970). Raúl Prebisch, a famous Argentine economist, also published his book *Capitalism of Periphery: Crisis and Transformation* (1990). The question may be posed: is today's China still a peripheral

---

18.   http://www.ce.cn/xwzx/gnsz/gdxw/201705/24/t20170524_2314 7241.shtml

19.   http://www.xinhuanet.com/english/special/2017-11/03/c_1367 25942.htm

country attached to developed countries? The United States and other G7 members are the centre of the contemporary world economy, but China neither depends on them nor acts as a peripheral country. It is perhaps more necessary than ever to propose a new concept, that of the *quasi-centre country*. China's economic might, its scientific and technological prowess, and the international cooperation on the Belt and Road Initiative, their participation in BRICS (Brazil, Russia, India, China, South Africa), the Asian Infrastructure Investment Bank (AIIB), and the Shanghai Cooperation Organisation (SCO) that the country has initiated, could be important signs pointing in this direction. In any case, China needs to continue moving forward from being a *quasi-centre* of the world economy to becoming the *absolute centre*. However, in the face of doubts from the West, including Latin American countries, China has been criticised for its investment and energy cooperation in Latin America and Africa. Suspicions exist that China may be developing a new *centre-periphery* attachment relationship. It should be made clear, however, that China is moving towards the *centre* of the world economic stage in a way that is different from the Western countries that make up today's centre. China will not follow the old path through which possession of leading-edge technology is used to exploit the labour forces of other countries. The *central* position that China pursues is actually geared to promoting the improvement of community with a shared future and shared interests on the basis of its own development. China will not only catch up with the countries that traditionally have been at the *centre* of the global economy and of world science and technology, thus gaining access to opportunities for equal cooperation with developed countries, but it will also conduct helpful cooperation on an equal basis with countries that traditionally have been at the *periphery*. China will offer these countries a superior model for development and progress, while leading the world in jointly establishing a new international economic order, shaping international economic security, and driving fair economic globalisation.

China will put in place theories and strategies aimed at a transition from its current *quasi-central* to its future *central* position. First, it will develop the theory and strategy of intellectual property advantage, and accelerate the improvement of the system of science and technology built by an innovation-oriented society, (it is not enough to rely solely on the new structural economic thinking and on strategies based on the theory of comparative advantage). Second, China will pursue a theoretical and strategic approach aimed at transforming finance from being *virtual* in character to being *real*, that is, integrated fully with the real economy, and will accelerate the internationalisation of the RMB financial system. It will establish the developmental theory and strategy of improving quality and enhancing efficiency and accelerate the highly coordinated industrial system involving both the domestic and international economies. Lastly, it will pursue a theoretical and strategic approach of guiding fair economic globalisation and will accelerate the rise of a new international economic order and institutional system of common economic security.

4. The Root Cause That Hinders the West in Strengthening Its Countries and Enriching Their Peoples Lies in the Various Antagonistic Contradictions of Capitalism.

Facing various economic crises and a *new economic normal*, the West has been greatly hindered in strengthening its countries and enriching their peoples, goals that are more in line with humanity and the creation of a community with a shared future for humankind. This lack of progress is among the inevitable results of the development of a capitalist market system, including its various contradictions. In 2008, the financial, production, and management crisis in the West was extremely serious, and the harm caused was no less than that which resulted from the Great Depression of the 1930s. Compared with the eras of Marx and Lenin, the basic contradiction of the capitalist economy in today's world is the contradiction between the continuous socialisation and globalisation of the world economy, with its combination of private, collective, and state ownership of the forces of production, and the anarchy and disorder that prevail in national economies and the world economy. This basic economic contradiction, operating on an expanded global scale, has led to the subprime mortgage crisis, the global financial crisis, the production and management crisis, the fiscal crisis, and the persistently depressed *economic new normal*. The effects on Western countries have come about as a result of the following five specific contradictions and intermediate links, which have caused various institutional maladies in the areas of economic, social, and political development.

First, private monopoly and its enterprise management model are prone to the pursuit by senior management of short-term profit maximisation to reap the highest possible personal incomes. This model increasingly accepts risky financial instruments, such as subprime mortgages, which are in contradiction with normal enterprise operation and management. This creates the preconditions for various crises and for the emergence of a *new economic normal* at the micro level of enterprises. In essence, the decentralised ownership structure of individual equity based on corporate capital ownership lays a micro foundation for the control of enterprises by financial capital in the form of corporate shareholders. In such an ownership structure, the enterprise functions as an agent with two levels of corporate shareholders and managers. Specifically, corporate shareholders are agents who engage in capital operations on behalf of the owners of private capital; they are not the ultimate owners themselves. The ultimate owners are the corporate shareholders, and the ultimate principals, are still the owners of private capital. Professional managers are the actual organisers and controllers of business operations and management activities.

In the highly decentralised ownership structures of large modern capitalist enterprises, the relationship between the local interests of agents and the overall risks of the enterprises at the levels of corporate shareholders and managers represents a unity of opposites. The unity between the agent's personal interests and the enterprise's overall risk is mainly reflected in the long-term development of the enterprise, belonging to the secondary aspect of the contradiction. In the long run, under conditions of low overall risk, enterprises can obtain relatively stable and sustainable development benefits. Proxies, including corporate shareholders and managers, can also obtain more stable benefits from the development of enterprises. However, due to the highly decentralised individual equity, proxies, including corporate shareholders and managers, cannot be effectively supervised and restricted; they are thus more prone to pursuing benefit maximisation in the short term, ignoring the long-term benefits and overall risks of enterprises.

Second, a private monopoly operating within a market economy is prone to forming a pattern of relative overproduction and of imbalance between the real economy and virtual economy. The effect is to trigger various crises and a *new economic normal* at the level of economic structure. Social reproduction and the operation of the national economy must follow the principle of distributing social labour proportionately (a.k.a. the *proportion principle*). This principle requires that the aggregate social labour, which is manifested as staff, funds, and properties, will be distributed in social production and the national economy in proportion according to needs. Put simply, in the contradictory movement of production and demand, the output and demand of social production must maintain a dynamic comprehensive balance within the structure of use value, so as to maximise production results with minimum labour consumption under given conditions. Within the entire national economy, the structural balance of various industries and economic fields must be preserved. The proportion principle is the general principle of social reproduction and economic operation.

In the contemporary capitalist market economy represented by the United States, the prevalence of neoliberalism, which advocates relaxing the state's economic regulations and financial supervision, dictates that the proportion principle will mainly be realised through the combined action of the law of market regulation, or the law of value, and the law of private surplus value. For example, the contradictory movement between the virtual economy and the real economy objectively requires that the development speed and level of the virtual economy must be compatible with the real economy. If the development of the virtual economy lags behind the real economy, the development of the real economy will be hindered. If the development of the virtual economy is too far ahead of the real economy, risks to economic operations will continuously accumulate, and in the absence of financial supervision, this will eventually lead to financial and economic crises. The financial and economic crisis that broke out in 2008 in Western countries was the inevitable result of a virtual economy seriously divorced from the real economy under the conditions of financial liberalisation.

Third, private monopoly groups and financial oligarchies are prone to opposing state supervision and regulation. Meanwhile, capitalist countries promote the creation in their economies of private monopolies, resulting in a dual failure both of markets and of state regulations. These harmful phenomena contribute to various crises and to the dilemma of the *new economic normal* in resource allocation or economic regulation. State regulation (a.k.a. planned regulation) is a way to realise the proportion principle in socialised mass production and the national economy regulated by each state. Marx held that in a society based on joint production, 'Society must allocate its own time reasonably in order to achieve production that meets all the needs of the society. Therefore, the saving of time and the planned distribution of labour time among different production departments remain the first law of economy on the basis of joint production'.[20] However, at the stage of state monopoly capitalism and during the primary stage of socialism, due to the existence of the state, overall planning and comprehensive regulation of social production and the national economy can only be undertaken by the state. State regulation (a.k.a. planned regulation) represents a basic contradiction of the commodity economy, that is, of the objective

---

20. Marx, Engels. The complete works of Marx and Engels: Volume 46 [M]. Beijing: People's Publishing House, 1972: p. 120.

economic law of the contradictory movement between the labour of private individuals or local labour and social labour as it appears in large-scale socialised production regulated by the state. The connotation of state regulation is that the state employs the means of state power, such as the economy, law, administration, persuasion, etc. The state consciously makes use of the objective law of the development of socialised mass production, develops an overall advanced plan for social production and the national economy according to the actual operation and development situation of social production and the national economy, and adjusts the distribution of aggregate social labour in all production departments and the whole national economy in a rational and scientific way. In the contemporary capitalist market economy, however, where state regulation (a.k.a. planned regulation) cannot work, the way in which the proportion principle has objectively come to be realised is through economic crisis.

Fourth, the combination of private monopoly with a market economy is prone to creating polarisation between rich and poor in terms of social wealth and income distribution. This gives rise to a contradiction between the unlimited expansion of production and a relative reduction in demand by the masses, who are less able to pay for the goods. The masses are forced into excessive consumption using credit, including subprime lending, to make a living and are left heavily in debt. These conditions lead to a range of crises and define the situation of the new economic normal at the level of distribution and consumption. In a capitalist market economy, the combined action of the law of private surplus value and the law of market regulation (a.k.a. the law of value) aggravates the polarisation between rich and poor. The class of private capital owners, which accounts for a small minority of the population, controls most of the wealth of society, while wage workers and their family members, who make up the overwhelming majority of the population, are only able to access a very small part of the social wealth. In a contemporary capitalist economy, the development of mass consumer credit and of financial derivatives aimed at increasing deficit spending are unable to alleviate the contradiction between the trend of unlimited expansion of production and the relative reduction in the workers' demand and their ability to pay. This however also increases the overall risks involved in economic operations. In order to alleviate the above contradiction, the financial monopoly capital of the United States is committed to developing consumer credit and various associated financial derivatives. This strategy promotes debt-funded spending among ordinary residents. However, the bubbles of imaginary demand that underlie such *Debt-Based Economic*

Models will burst at a certain point as rising interest rates and other economic developments cause debtors to default, leading to inevitable financial payment crises and economic crises.

Fifth, private monopolism and a considerable reduction by governments of the tax revenues exacted from private enterprises, along with large increases in military expenditures, failure to reduce government overheads, and the use of tax revenues collected from citizens to bail out large private enterprises, will inevitably lead to increased financial deficits, rising government debt, and fiscal restraints on public welfare and state education. These various maladies cause a range of crises and constitute the *new economic normal* at the level of national finance. After the Reagan administration came into power in the 1980s, the trend of tax rate increases reversed, and the richest class enjoyed bigger cuts in taxes on payrolls, stock options, interest payments, and capital income. Since then, the rates of federal tax paid by low-income groups and the middle class in the United States have generally been on the rise, while those paid by the richest 5% of the population have declined significantly. The federal tax rate applied to the richest 0.01% of the population in 1990 was less than half their rate in 1960.

On 13 December 2017, the U.S. Congress adopted a further tax cut bill that cut the corporate tax rate from 35% to 21% and the top personal income tax rate from 39.6% to 37%. Many economists and independent analysts in the United States responded by pointing out that the tax reform enacted by the Republican administration clearly favored large enterprises and the rich. According to a study by the tax policy centre of a Washington think tank, high-income families would benefit most from this tax cut, whether in terms of absolute value or of the proportion of income paid as tax. In addition, the Congressional Budget Office estimated that abolishing the compulsory purchase of health insurance would save the federal government 300 billion U.S. dollars, which would then be available to finance tax cuts for enterprises and the rich. The effect would have been that as many as thirteen million Americans would have lost their health insurance. There was little sign that the tax cut program would bring sustained economic growth, and it promised to further widen the gap between rich and poor, worsening the fiscal situation of the U.S. government. Meanwhile, the U.S. military budget in 2019 was $732 billion U.S. dollars, a more than 5% increase from the previous year. Total official military spending by the U.S. that year amounted to around 3.5% of GDP.

Major western countries have delayed strengthening their economies and enriching their people due to the contradictions and crises

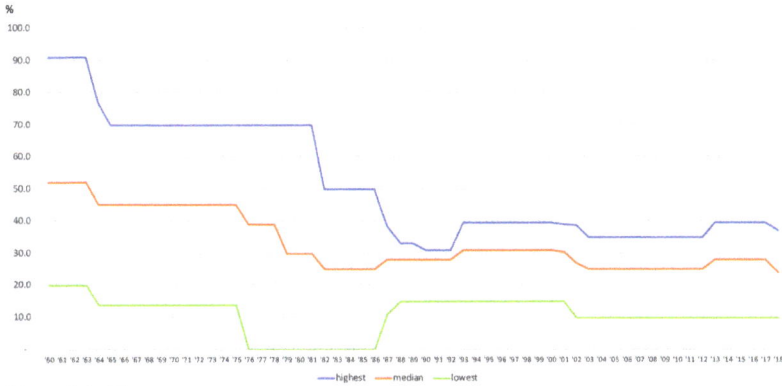

Data source: Taxfoundation.org

Chart 11 U.S. Federal Tax Rate - Highest, Median & Lowest Rates

noted above. Many western scholars and experts use the term *new economic normal* to describe the status quo as they look forward pessimistically to the future economy. After responding rapidly to the impacts of these crises, however, China has turned them into opportunities to deliberately advance toward a new normal of vigorous economic development. The *new economic normal* of western capitalism is different from that of socialism with Chinese characteristics in terms of actual performance, institutional characteristics, and policy concepts.

5. The Different Actual Performance, Institutional Characteristics, and Theoretical Policies of the Two Economic New Normals

(I) Different Status Quos of the Two Economic New Normals

First, we shall compare the growth rates. According to the World Bank's statistics from 2008 to 2016 (at constant prices), the average GDP growth rate in the United States was 1.3% (according to BEA statistics, the GDP growth rate in Q1 of 2017 was 1.4%). The corresponding rate in Japan was 0.4%, and that in the EU was 0.6%. After more than thirty years of high-speed growth, the annual GDP growth rate in China was 7.2% from 2013 to 2016, indicative of a smooth transformation from high-speed growth to medium-to-high speed growth.[21] According to the report entitled *2018 World Economic Situation and Prospects* released by the United Nations, China's

---

21. http://www.gov.cn/xinwen/2017-12/13/content_5246583.htm

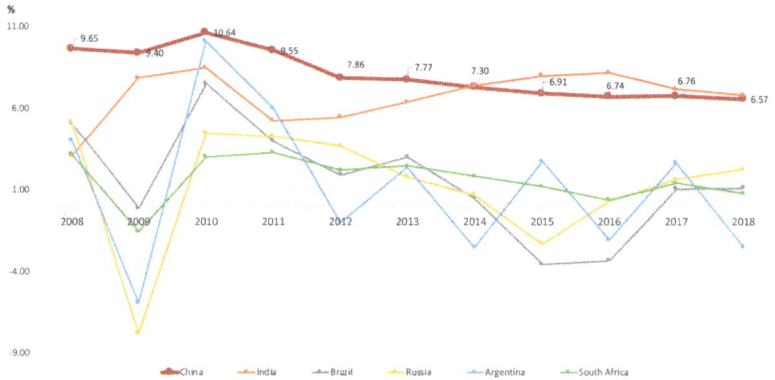

Data source: World Bank

Chart 12 Comparative GDP Growth between Countries

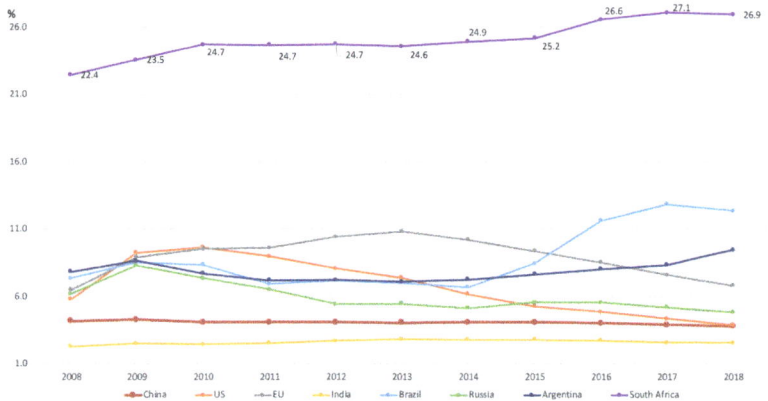

Data source: IMF, Statista

Chart 13 Average Unemployment Rate between Countries 2008-2018

contribution to global economic growth in 2017 was approximately one-third.[16]

Second, we shall make a comparison of unemployment. According to statistics of the International Monetary Fund, the average unemployment rate in the United States from 2008 to 2015 was 7.56%, and the estimated rate in 2016 was 4.85%. The average unemployment rate in the EU from 2008 to 2015 was 9.47%, and the estimated rate in 2016 was 8.53%. In recent years, the urban unemployment rate in China was slightly more than 4%, and China's *employment performance* ranks first among sixty-three major economies in the world as referenced in the *2017 World Competitiveness Report* released by the International Institute for Management Development based in Lausanne, Switzerland.[22]

Third, we shall compare government debt levels. The United States and other capitalist countries bail out private monopoly enterprises, utilising huge amounts of public funds; this forces a continuing rise in government debt. The proportion of U.S. government debt to GDP rose from 61.8% in 2006 to 106.1% in 2016. The debt of the Eurozone rose from 67.4% to 89.3%, while that of the Japanese government amounted to more than 250% of GDP in 2016. By the end of 2016, the debt balance of the central and local governments in China totaled RMB 27.3 trillion, and the government debt ratio was 36.7%, much lower than that of the United States, Europe, Japan, and other countries.

Fourth, we shall explore a comparison of real economies. According to the statistics of the Organisation for Economic Co-operation and Development (hereinafter referred to as *OECD*), in the United States the average sum of the value added in real industries such as agriculture, forestry, animal husbandry and fisheries, industry (including the energy industry), the construction industry, entity service activities (distribution trade, maintenance, transportation, accommodation, and food), and the information and communication industry accounted for 44.5% of total added value from 2008 to 2014. The related figure for Japan was 53%, and that for the EU was 51.3%. However, the figure for China (the value added by the information and communication industry was not even included) was 73.17% from 2008 to 2013. It can be seen that the system of financial capital represents the economic lifeline of western countries, and the excessively finance-oriented transition *from the real to the virtual* leads to depression in the real economy.

Fifth, we shall survey a comparison of income consumption. According to OECD statistics, the average ratio of household debt to disposable income in the United States from 2008 to 2014 was 130.18%. The corresponding figure for Japan was 122.5% from 2008 to 2013. For the 1% of the super-rich in Western countries, wealth and incomes have risen sharply, but the debts owed by ordinary households have generally increased, resulting in a consolidation of class divisions. In the United States the richest 1% of households own one-third of the nation's net household worth, and the 9% of households directly below them, another third. In terms of income, the proportion accruing to the top 1% has risen from 9% in 1978 to 20% in recent

---

22.   http://www.ce.cn/xwzx/gnsz/gdxw/201706/05/t20170605_2342 1431.shtmls

years. The Occupy Wall Street movement, which after its rise in 2011 affected about 80 capitalist countries, pushed for a change in the inequities represented by the *Gap between Rich and Poor* (the 1% vs. the 99%). This is completely different from the situation in China, where recent years have seen targeted poverty alleviation within a definite time, and rapid growth in the number of middle-income families. In China the great majority of urban and rural households own their dwellings, and median net household assets (taking into account debt) are much higher than the figure in the United States. In 2013, 2014, and 2015, the per capita consumption expenditure of urban residents in China accounted for 69%, 69%, and 70% of per capita disposable income, while that of rural residents accounted for 81%, 80%, and 79%, respectively. This clearly shows that economic growth and development have generally kept pace with the income growth of urban and rural residents.

Sixth is a comparative assessment of welfare and security. To varying degrees, Western countries in recent years have cut their spending on education, healthcare, pensions, and other welfare and social security provisions. Funding for public colleges in the United States has been reduced, and the Republican Party healthcare bill, which would slash taxes and federal spending for healthcare, promises to increase the number of Americans without health insurance. Germany, Portugal, the Netherlands, and other countries have also reduced their spending on healthcare. In March 2016 a protest movement in Paris triggered by changes to the labour code evolved into the 'Nuit Debout' protests in more than seventy cities across France. The movement even spread to neighboring countries and to non-European countries such as Canada. The aim was to block anti-worker 'reform' measures including cuts to social security and social welfare. These moves have been in sharp contrast to China's massive increases in education funding, continuous raises in minimum wage levels, steadily improving medical insurance in urban and rural areas, and preferential treatment for the elderly.

(II) Different Institutional Characteristics and Theoretical Policies of the Two New Economic Normals

There are many important differences between the economic systems, economic theories, and policy thinking of neoliberal capitalism and socialism with Chinese characteristics. First, the former advocates full privatisation of public facilities, education, and state-owned enterprises concerned with the national economy and people's livelihoods. The latter stresses the need for an economic system in which public ownership is the mainstay, state-owned enterprises play a leading role, and economic entities of diverse ownership develop together. These features require state-owned enterprises to become stronger, better, and bigger in the process of developing mixed ownership. It is also important to actively develop a collective and cooperative economy, leading and taking advantage of the non-public economy, which has an important role to play. This role is especially important in the case of small private companies and micro-businesses. In this way, socialism with Chinese characteristics is able to optimise the dual economic performance of public and private enterprises. It is thus apparent that viewpoints that attach importance only to the significant role played by the non-public sector of the economy, while ignoring or belittling the dominant role of the state-owned and collective sectors, are not conducive to improving overall social and economic performance and fairness.

Second, neoliberal capitalism advocates full marketisation and deregulates the economy and finance to an excessive degree. The government no longer provides active and effective regulation over a macro economy. In contrast, socialism with Chinese characteristics stresses the importance of the state playing a more decisive role in the market with respect to the allocation of general resources, and the important role of the state in macro-control and micro-regulation. These measures achieve the dual regulatory functions of the market and the government with the focus on improving quality and efficiency. It can thus be seen that market-only and pan-marketisation viewpoints, which require that all material, cultural, educational, scientific and technological, medical, housing, and service resources must be determined by the market (enterprises) are not conducive to the overall coordination of the multiple interests of individuals, enterprises and the state, or to the objectives of planned economic and social development.

Third, neoliberal capitalism advocates full liberalisation, upholds economic globalisation and liberalisation with dollar hegemony as the fulcrum, and opposes the establishment of a new international economic order. Meanwhile, socialism with Chinese characteristics emphasises the building of a community with a shared future for humankind and a community of shared interests for all countries. It guides the international community to jointly shape a new international economic order and common economic security, so as to usher in a new economic globalisation that will promote win-win cooperation with the Belt and Road Initiative as its model. It is obvious that a pattern that involved opening up the economy to the outside world based on pure economic integration and economic transition would not be conducive to implementing the new ideas and strategies of participating in global economic governance, leading economic globalisation and moving closer to the centre of the world economic stage.

Fourth, neoliberal capitalism advocates welfare personalisation, and squeezes the social well-being of citizens in order to reduce the tax taken from private monopoly enterprises at the same time as it increases military spending. Meanwhile, much of the burden of social welfare is loaded onto citizens and their families. Socialism with Chinese characteristics emphasises the people-centric development idea and constantly improves all the people's social welfare level and quality of life, so as to achieve the inclusive development of economic, social, income, and welfare growth. Viewpoints that criticise the steady improvements to social welfare and social security implemented by the government and enterprises do not aid in the progressive establishment of a high-level social welfare system and a welfare state.

Fifth, neoliberal capitalism actively seeks a polarisation of society between rich and poor. It weakens the power of trade unions through the joint efforts of monopoly enterprises and the government, while emboldening the representatives of capital to tightly restrict any increases in labour income. At the same time, it reduces the taxes on monopoly enterprises, so as to further widen the gap in the distribution of wealth and income. By contrast, socialism with Chinese characteristics promotes a system of basic distribution in which the main form is distribution according to work, and in which diversified modes of distribution coexist. In applying its new developmental strategy, it actively promotes innovative ideas for overcoming poverty and achieving prosperity, for acquiring common prosperity, and for sharing the outcomes, so as to ensure the improvement of people's livelihoods. Viewpoints that reject distribution according to work as the mainstay of development, and that favor polarisation between rich and poor over shared prosperity, are not conducive to promoting common prosperity, common enjoyment, and common happiness.

In summary, even setting aside the Great Depression from 1929 to 1933, Western countries have witnessed economic recessions or economic crises every few years or decades since World War II and even since the end of the Cold War. These debilitating events include *stagflation* in the 1970s, and the global financial crisis in the first decade of this century. The indication here is that neither the neoliberal economy nor the social democratic economy have worked on the level of strengthening the countries concerned and enriching their people, that is, of providing the essential requirements for the masses at home and abroad. By contrast, the socialist economy with Chinese characteristics, as a new model of human economic civilisation, has made a powerful positive showing. Marxism-Leninism and its synthesised political-economic theory and policy have effectively boosted China's people-centric goal of strengthening the country and enriching the population, while building a community of shared interests for mankind!

* * *

Section IV Basic Framework and Implementation Strategy of the Modern Economic System

Since the policy of reform and opening up was introduced, China's economy and society have achieved unprecedented, comprehensive development, and the country's accomplishments have attracted worldwide attention. Based on the actual progress of the Party and countless social programs, the 19th NCCPC arrived at the conclusion that *socialism with Chinese characteristics* has entered a new era and has made it possible to *apply a new vision of development while building a modern economic system*.[23] This has represented a major strategic initiative that the Party has implemented while remaining mindful of the new characteristics, major contradictions, and future development goals of the country in this new era. On 30 January 2018, the Political Bureau of the CPC Central Committee held its Third Collective Learning Meeting, with the theme, *Building a Modern Economic System*. General Secretary Xi Jinping put forward the objectives, content, and key points of the modern economic system before an attentive audience. He pointed out that building a modern economic system is an important, yet arduous task. The present work will now examine more closely the spirit of Xi Jinping's speech, and will explain the importance, the basic framework, and the strategic measures involved in building a modern economic system as set forward in the report of 19th CPC National Congress.[24]

---

23.   http://www.xinhuanet.com/english/special/2017-11/03/c_13672
5942.htm
24. Ibid

1. The Vital importance of Building a Modern Economic System

Building a modern economic system is an important endeavour for realising the *Two Centenary Goals*. The 19th NCCPC's report redefined these goals in the following manner: after securing a decisive victory in building a society that is moderately prosperous in all its aspects, between 2020 and 2035, China will build on the foundation created by this moderately prosperous society. It will take fifteen years of hard work and determination to realise modern socialism. Over the years, from 2035 to the middle of the 21st century China will strive to shape the country into a modern socialist country that is prosperous, democratic, culturally advanced, harmonious, and beautiful. The premise for achieving these grand aspirations is the comprehensive development of all the undertakings involved. Economic development is the most important undertaking, since it is needed to provide the basic material foundation for every other kind of development. Constructing a modern economic system that meets the requirements of this new era will act as a strong guarantee for economic and social stability and the realisation of even greater goals.

Building a modern economic system is an inevitable choice now that the basic social contradictions in our country are changing. The report of the 19th NCCPC illustrated how the principal contradiction in our society has evolved, becoming the contradiction between the people's growing need for a better life and unbalanced and inadequate development. In the future, as this major contradiction evolves further, the direction of China's economic and social development will change significantly. Unbalanced and inadequate economic development has restricted people's growing need for a better life. Only by conscientiously implementing the plan set forth by the 19th CPC National Congress on the establishment of a modern economic system can China fundamentally solve this major social contradiction in the new era. Guided by developmental philosophy and policy thinking focused on innovation that is coordinated, green, and open and sharing, China will shape an economic system that is thoroughly modern in terms of its industrial system, market system, income distribution system, urban and rural regional development system, green development system, comprehensive opening-up system, and dual adjustment system. The economic system will feature vigorous development of the real economy, deeper supply side structural reform, a more optimised industrial structure, a strengthened leading role for innovation, improvement of the socialist market economy system, and so forth. Together, these efforts are capable of achieving the full and balanced development of the national economy, of meeting people's growing need for a better life to the fullest extent, and of effectively solving the major social contradictions of the new era.

Building a modern economic system is the only way to meet the new requirement for high-quality development of the national economy. The basic needs of *socialism with Chinese characteristics* as it enters a new era require China's economy to change from the previous extensive mode of development, which stressed speed and scale, to an intensive stage of development that pursues high quality and efficiency. Only by addressing three key points of transformation, specifically, the mode of development, optimisation of the economic structure, and transformation of development power, can China solve the deep-rooted structural problems of the past economic system and further improve the productivity of various elements in our economy. On this basis, China needs to further protect the environment, address weak links in areas related to people's wellbeing, stimulate society's creativity and the vitality of its development, orient reforms consistently in the direction of socialism, and promote the ability of China's economy to achieve higher quality, greater efficiency, and more equitable, sustainable development. Accelerating the creation of a modern economic system will drive forward the transformation of the economic development mode, promote the continuous improvement of quality and efficiency, and meet the new requirements of economic development in the new era.

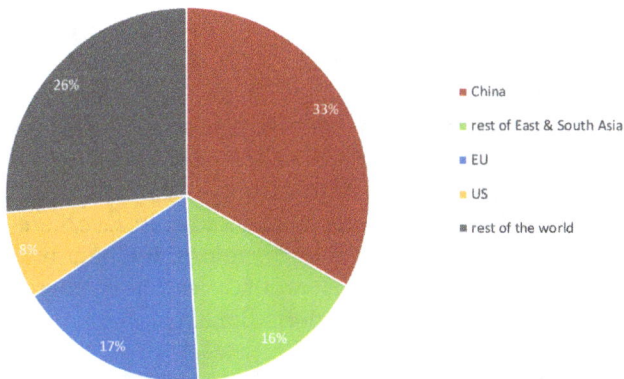

Data source: World Economic Situation and Prospects 2018; World Bank

Chart 15 Major Contributors to Economic Growth in 2017

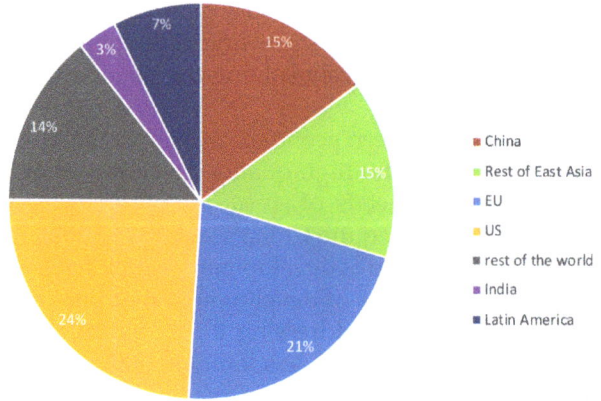

Data source: World Economic Situation and Prospects 2018; World Bank

Chart 16 Economic Volume by Country in 2017

The construction of a modern economic system is lending China powerful support as it takes the initiative in international competition. The impact of the Western financial crisis persists, and global economic recovery has been weak. The achievements of socialist China and the speed of its economic development are more prominent in the world. China's influence on the world economy is also increasing. According to the *World Economic Situation and Prospects 2018* report released by the United Nations, China accounted for one-third of global economic growth in 2017, and the country's economic aggregate accounted for 15% of the world total. Averaged over the past five years, China's annual contribution rate to world economic growth reached 30.2%.[25] It should also be noted that the pressure exerted by the *Re-Industrialisation Policy* of developed countries, such as the United States, Japan and various European nations, and the *Rapid Industrialisation Policy* of emerging market economies took a toll on China's economic growth. With the narrow-minded protectionism of the Trump Administration's *America First* policies, China's economy will inevitably face fiercer competition in the international market. Therefore, if China wants to adapt to changing times, take a just and fair lead in economic globalisation, and gain the initiative in international competition, it needs, as soon

---

25. https://www.un.org/development/desa/dpad/publication/%
e4%b8%96%e7%95%8c%e7%bb%8f%e6%b5%8e%e5%bd%a2%e5%8a%
bf%e4%b8%8e%e5%b1%95%e6%9c%9b-2018%ef%bc%9a%e6%8f%90%
e8%a6%81/

as possible, to build a modern economic system that includes a high-end industrial system, an orderly market system, coordinated urban and rural regional systems, a green development system, an independent system of opening up, and a highly efficient system of regulation.

2. The Basic Framework of the Modern Economic System

After setting forward the task of building a modern economic system, Xi Jinping's speech to the 19th CPC National Congress on 30 January 2018 clearly defined the connotations and basic framework of a modern economic system, including 'six systems and one institution'. These seven components not only have their respective functions and divisions of labour, but they are also interrelated. They make up a unified and organic whole and provide a general program for China's future economic construction. We will elabourate on this in further detail.

(I) An Industrial System of Coordinated, Innovation-Led Development

The report of the 19th NCCPC affirmed clearly that *innovation is the primary driving force behind development, providing the strategic underpinning for building a modernised economy,* and that *efforts should be made to accelerate the building of an industrial system that promotes coordinated development of the real economy with technological innovation, modern finance, and human resources.* As Xi Jinping further pointed out, 'We need to build an industrial system led by innovation and developed in coordination, so as to continuously increase the contribution of scientific and technological innovation in the development of the real economy. We must continuously enhance the ability of modern finance to serve the real economy, and continuously optimise the role of human resources in supporting the development of the real economy'.[26]

At present, the lack of innovation and coordination in China's industrial system is widespread. These shortcomings are primarily

---

26. Xi Jinping stressed at the third collective study of the Political Bureau of the CPC Central Committee: a deep understanding of the importance of building a modernised economic system to promote China's economic development with new vitality to a new level [N]. People's Daily, 2018-02-01 (1)

http://www.gov.cn/xinwen/2018-01/31/content_5262618.htm

manifested in the following aspects. First, the manufacturing industry, as the heart of the real economy, has lacked international competitiveness, has been positioned at the middle-to-low end of international industrial and value chains, and has been deficient in core competitiveness and high-tech products. Second, China's industrial system suffers from deficiencies that include a lack of innovation, insufficient investment in research and development and creative talent, difficulties in transforming scientific and technological innovation achievements into real-world solutions, low transformation rates, and an inability to provide strong support to the real economy. Third, the situation of *off real to virtual* in finance is serious. Financial resources are mismatched; the ability to serve the real economy is poor; the financing mode of the real economy is limited; loans are difficult to apply for; the leverage ratio is high, and in terms of financial security, the basis for developing the real economy is weak. Finally, there are structural contradictions between the supply and demand of talented workforce members. Most notably, every type of creative and entrepreneurial talent within the real economy is in short supply. Shortages of scientific and technological talent in research and development, shortages of skilled technicians in manufacturing, and shortages of management talent in marketing are prevalent.

If China wants to accelerate the construction of an industrial system led by innovation and featuring coordinated development, it must focus on a number of key tasks.

First, China must use supply-side structural reforms to adjust the existing industrial system. These reforms should include coordinating the industrial layout, promoting the transformation and upgrading of traditional industries, solving the problem of incompatibility between the supply structure and demand structure in the real economy, minimising low-quality and ineffective supply, and shifting the focus of economic development from expanding quantity and scale to developing high quality and high efficiency. China needs to anticipate the future trend of industrial development and changes in market demand, accelerate the development of advanced manufacturing industry, especially high-end manufacturing industry, cultivate and develop strategic industries, and consolidate the foundations of the real economy. China must broaden medium and high-end consumption, develop modern supply chains and human resource services, create new economic growth points and new driving forces, and seize opportunities for the future development of the global industrial and value chains.

Second, China must promote innovation and lead the high-end development of the industrial system. This includes providing an efficient policy support system for innovation, improving relevant laws and regulations on intellectual property protection, formulating an incentive mechanism to guide enterprises and individuals to invest in research and development, and forming an innovation system of markets, enterprises, and scientific research institutes that integrate new products and methods at a profound level. China must prioritise increased investment in innovative funds and innovative personnel training. The government should take the lead in utilising investments in applied basic research, especially cutting-edge technologies, key common technologies, and disruptive new technologies. Enterprises and individuals should be encouraged to invest in innovation, to broaden innovation platforms and carriers, to provide various specific services for innovation and research and development, and to integrate and share innovation and research and development information.

Third, it is necessary to improve the operations of the financial service industry and real economy. China should accelerate reform of the financial system, encourage the integration of finance with the real economy, and guide financial capital to concentrate on the sectors of the real economy that have development potential. By continuously broadening the financial channels of the real economy, innovating the means of financing in the realm of the real economy, and expanding various businesses, etc., China seeks to solve the difficulties of financing the real economy. To improve the level of financial services to the real economy, it is necessary to raise the level of support for various enterprises through innovative credit evaluation methods, innovative credit guarantee systems, and innovative mortgage loans.

Fourth, strengthening the role of human resources as the primary mechanism for improving the industrial system is necessary. By intensifying education reform and expanding the training of scientific personnel, China will cultivate the talent needed for basic and high-level research. Through improving vocational education, it will be possible to develop applied technical talent with a strong sense of utility and pertinence, so as to provide high-quality human resources for the construction of a modern industrial system. Through reform of the distribution system, China will adjust the gap between different industries and regions, guaranteeing that premium talent is available to the entire industrial system and the real economy.

(II) A Unified and Open Market System With Orderly Competition

The 19th NCCPC advanced the concept that reform of the economic system must concentrate on improving the property rights system and ensuring the market-based allocation of factors of production, so that property rights act as effective incentives, various factors flow freely, prices will be more flexible, and competition fair and orderly; business survival is determined by competition. Xi Jinping further stressed the need to 'build a unified, open, and orderly market system'.[27]

At present, China's market system is not perfect, and the allocation of resources is still affected by government monopoly, administrative examination and approval, price control, and other factors.

Moreover, there are some deficiencies. Specifically, the main problems lie in three areas. First, the market system is not transparent enough, and there are problems such as a defective pricing mechanism, unsound information disclosure regulations, unclear setting of market supervision rules, etc. These inadequacies create a certain space for rent-seeking and allow market transaction costs to become too high. Second, the pricing mechanism is insufficient. Due to state monopolies, price controls, or other governmental interventions in the market, the price transmission mechanism of some products or services is faulty. This problem results in market rules not playing a decisive role in the allocation of factors, and prices do not fully reflect the supply and demand situation and the scarcity of resources. Third, market access and exit policies are inadequate. Some hidden rules and local policies still exist that impede the integrated market and fair competition. Under these conditions, market players of the same level cannot always enter the market conveniently. Meanwhile, there is no market exit mechanism for selecting the superior and eliminating the inferior; the enterprise bankruptcy system does not work effectively, and the market cannot determine whether an enterprise exits or not.

To establish a unified, open, and orderly market system, multiple tasks must be addressed.

The first is to improve the transparency and fairness of the market system. If sound market laws and regulations are established, the smooth and rapid circulation of goods or services can be guaranteed. Adequate market regulations eliminate regional blockades and market segmentation and end the imbalance between urban and rural areas. It is necessary to standardise transaction behavior,

---

27. Ibid

establish a transparent, fair, and efficient market order, and reduce transaction costs. In areas that are prone to breeding corruption, China should clarify competition rules, increase the transparency of procedures, strengthen laws and regulations on information disclosure, vigorously improve the transparency of the market system, promote market informatisation, and protect the legitimate rights and interests of market participants. It is necessary to strengthen the construction of the market supervision system, clarify the rights and responsibilities of market participants, regulate the powers of law enforcers, and avoid problems such as power rent-seeking or excessive market transaction costs arising from unclear regulatory rules.

The second task is to further improve the pricing mechanism for various commodities, especially resource-based products, so that prices reflect the true supply and demand of products and the scarcity of resources. Appropriate measures here will allow China to take advantage of the market regulation mechanism and will promote the free circulation of commodities. China should make additional improvements to the market trading system, adjust the government's methods of macro-control, strive to achieve appropriate regulatory goals with the assistance of the market, establish a sound market trading system, and unleash goods and services that are not included in the negative list. It is necessary to give enterprises the right of independent pricing, so that the prices of goods and services are determined through the interaction of the law of value, the law of supply and demand, and the law of competition. Mechanisms should be created for the smooth transmission of prices and ensure that prices reflect the real cost of production, operation costs, and efficiency of enterprises.

The third task is to establish unified market access standards and exit policies. First, industry access must be opened. Industries that are not on the list of those restricted or prohibited by the government and industries that abide by the law should be opened to private capital. China should implement identical access standards in the same region and break down market blockades, local protectionism, and administrative monopolies. Various laws and regulations should be publicly and equitably improved as soon as possible, realising the equal use of production factors and various resources by state-owned and private capital. The government should participate impartially in various forms and instances of market competition and provide them with equal supervision and legal protection. It is necessary to accelerate market-oriented reforms, abolish various obstacles that affect the establishment of a unified market, formulate laws and regulations that promote fair competition, and stimulate the enthusiasm and vitality of various market participants. It is critical to improve the market exit mechanism, improve the corporate bankruptcy system, and adhere to the principle of corporate autonomy. The struggle for existence should be determined by market competition.

(III) An Income Distribution System Reflecting Efficiency and Promoting Fairness

Income distribution affects the vital interests of hundreds of millions of people and their personal enthusiasm for work. An irrational income distribution system is the root cause of many social problems. Xi Jinping stated this as follows in the report of the 19th NCCPC: 'It is necessary to build an income distribution system that reflects efficiency and promotes fairness, that realises reasonable income distribution, social equity and justice, and common prosperity for all people, that promotes equalisation of basic public services, and that gradually narrows the income distribution gap'.[28] As adopted by the 19th NCCPC, the important principle on which the income distribution system must be constructed is the following: 'We will adhere to the principle of distribution according to work while improving the system and mechanism for distribution based on factors of production, so as to make income distribution fairer and more orderly. We will encourage people to earn their money through hard work and legal means. We will expand the size of the middle-income group, increase the incomes of low-income people, adjust excessive income, and ban illegal income'.[29]

At present, due to the large-scale development of the non-public economy, the government's failure to achieve a timely adjustment of various kinds of unreasonable income distribution, the imperfect social security mechanism, structural unemployment, and other factors, the income gap has gradually expanded, thus leading to many other problems. First, the gap between urban and rural regional development is still wide, as are the inequalities in the distribution of income among residents. The income growth of urban and rural

---

28. Xi Jinping stressed at the third collective study of the Political Bureau of the CPC Central Committee: a deep understanding of the importance of building a modernised economic system to promote China's economic development with new vitality to a new level [N]. *People's Daily*, 2018-02-01 (1)

http://www.gov.cn/xinwen/2018-01/31/content_5262618.htm
29. Ibid

residents is not keeping pace with economic growth, especially the income growth rate of rural residents that is too slow to allow them to participate fully in sharing the dividends from economic development. Second, the laws and regulations on income distribution remain flawed. There are notable problems of invisible income and illegal income. Income distribution cannot act as a thoroughly positive incentive mechanism, and the interaction between distribution fairness and economic efficiency is not sufficiently harmonious. Third, the reform of the income distribution system is progressing too slowly. A situation persists in which people with low incomes have difficult lives and when they need to consume, they cannot afford to do so. Meanwhile, the marginal propensity of consumption for people with high incomes is too low; they have the ability to consume, but their impact on demand-driven economic growth is limited.

In order to improve the income distribution system so that it serves the mutual promotion of efficiency and fairness, measures must be taken in the following areas. First, China should establish a unified, open, and orderly market system in accordance with the law. Importance must be attached to the different roles of the market and government in income distribution, with a view to providing equal public services for urban and rural workers, ensuring equal distribution rules and opportunities. Income distribution barriers must be reduced between urban and rural areas, industries, and fields of employment. Equal payment for equal work and providing a fair and just platform for all workers must be realised. At the same time, the market should recognise the income gap caused by the differing talents and endowments of individuals. As a result of the income differences caused by the diverse quantities, states, levels, and opportunities of factor possession, appropriate adjustments must be made by introducing relevant tax and fiscal policies, further improving the transfer payment system, and promoting the right of different workers to enjoy equal basic public services.

Second, to correct the income differences caused by a less than reasonable system and imperfect rules, it is necessary to intensify reform and institutional construction, construct a rational and standardised policy system, and avoid the formation of grey incomes. Where grey incomes already exist, it is possible to amend the situation through appropriate redistribution measures. In the case of illegal incomes, the government must spare no effort to enforce the law and eliminate the conditions that allowed abuses to arise. Once illegal incomes are identified, it is necessary to resolutely ban them and fight the associated criminality in accordance with the law.

Third, the income distribution system must be completely redesigned. Through taxation and fiscal expenditure, the results of primary distribution should be adjusted at the redistribution stage, so as to serve the goal of common prosperity. The personal income tax system should be further improved; horizontal equity and vertical equity should be considered at the same time to ensure that taxes benefit low-income people without compromising the motivation of high-income people. Also, the government should refine the consumption tax and adjust the taxation link and scope of the consumption tax, alleviate the tax burden of the low income earners, promote property related tax reform, reinforce the regulation of property taxation, learn from foreign experience, and implement the exit tax as soon as possible.

(IV) A System of Urban and Rural Regional Development That Highlights Advantages and Coordinates Linkages

The report of the 19th NCCPC clearly announced the *Rural Revitalisation Strategy* and the *Coordinated Regional Development Strategy*. General Secretary Xi Jinping pointed out, 'We should actively promote the coordinated development of urban and rural areas, optimise the spatial layout of the modern economic system and establish an urban and rural regional development system that highlights advantages and coordinates linkages. Only through a gradual narrowing of the development gap between urban and rural areas and through balanced development involving the population, economy, resources, and environment can all components of the economy and society interact productively. Only in this way can the integrated development of both urban and rural areas be realised, thus promoting the balance and overall strength of China's economic development'.[30]

At present, the gap between urban and rural areas in the country remains huge; the degree of coordinated development between urban and rural areas is insufficient; and there are still many obstacles to the coordinated development between these areas. Due to natural conditions, population, history, and other factors, the spatial layout of the modern economic system is irrational. The

---

30. Xi Jinping stressed at the third collective study of the Political Bureau of the CPC Central Committee: a deep understanding of the importance of building a modernised economic system to promote China's economic development with new vitality to a new level [N]. *People's Daily*, 2018-02-01 (1)

http://www.gov.cn/xinwen/2018-01/31/content_5262618.htm

Beijing-Tianjin-Hebei region, Yangtze River Economic Belt, and Guangdong-Hong Kong-Macao Greater Bay Area are all densely populated areas. Although they cover a relatively small proportion of the whole country, they account for a massive proportion of the national economy. For example, the Beijing-Tianjin-Hebei region contributes 8% of the GNP while making up a mere 2.3% of China's total land area. The Yangtze River Economic Belt, with 21% of the country's land area, contributes 40% of GNP. Second, and as has been mentioned, the gap between urban and rural areas is still large; the linkage between urban and rural areas is inadequate; and regional development lacks the needed coordination. The system supply needed for implementing rural revitalisation is deficient; the available human resources are inadequate; and a gap persists in the available funds. The harsh natural conditions in some poverty-stricken areas have brought sharply deteriorating economic and social conditions. This has made the elimination of poverty problematic. The economic foundation in most rural areas is no more than basic, and together with this, the lack of infrastructure and basic public services make reviving and modernising the countryside a gigantic task. A lack of appropriate platforms slows the combined development of urban and rural areas, and without the supporting and driving role such platforms might play, expanding the scope of change has proven difficult.

To establish an urban/rural regional development system that constructs and coordinates the networks essential for progress, it is necessary to focus on the following tasks. First, the establishment of a development system that identifies and highlights specific advantages must rest upon a strategically optimised spatial layout of the modern economic system. Utilising the macro-planning of the Beijing-Tianjin-Hebei region, it is possible to continuously explore and cultivate new momentum for innovation and development. Progress in this area will enable China to create the most optimal layout and spatial structure of the city in the most logical way. The coordinated development of the Beijing-Tianjin-Hebei complex will promote the development of the whole region and then create a number of world-class urban agglomerations. It is imperative to promote the development of the Yangtze River Economic Belt, expand the economic growth seen in the eastern coastal areas to the central and western regions, and promote the orderly flow of economic factors along the golden waterway. Further, it is essential to promote the development of the Guangdong-Hong Kong-Macao Greater Bay Area, so that it becomes an important engine of China's regional economic progress as well as a leader in advanced scientific and technological innovation, forming a large-scale urban belt able to lead not only national, but global economic development.

Second, with a greater focus on rural development strategy, it is necessary to accelerate rural revitalisation through top-level design, promoting the coordinated development of urban and rural areas. Accelerating the integrated development of rural and urban areas with rural revitalisation as the focus will also require the construction of an institutional mechanism and policy system. The establishment of an urban and rural regional development system that utilises advantages and coordinates connections is necessary. To fulfil this task, China could implement the strategy of rural revitalisation, improve the property rights system and the market allocation of factors, and then strengthen the institutional basis for rural revitalisation. The role of the market should be maximised in the allocation of resources through optimising policies related to human capital, so as to fully coordinate talent and technologies. This is the best way to solve the problem of insufficient support for talented people who will be instrumental in rural revitalisation. Through fiscal, financial, and social multi-participation policies in conjunction with other approaches, diversified funds should be made available for rural revitalisation so as to solve the funding gap issue. In this way, the existing dual structure of urban and rural areas can be broken. Coordinated regional development can narrow the gap between backward and developed areas by promoting strategies and policies for economic development in afflicted regions, stimulating the flow of various economic factors throughout the country, and facilitating the spatial balance of population, economy, resources, and environment. These actions will boost China's economy and allow new, continuing progress. Beginning with a focus on the overall situation, China can establish coherent and unified regional policies and specifically targeted urban and rural development policies with precise functions and coherent levels of action. Through such mechanisms, the integration of urban, rural, and regional development will be strengthened. It is important to further improve the mechanism of coordinated development of regional urban and rural areas, including the positioning and cooperation mechanism of urban and rural areas and regions, the achievement sharing mechanism, the ecological protection mechanism, and the benefit compensation mechanism, so as to realise overall urban and rural development and regional development and cooperation. It is essential to nurture experimental areas, demonstration areas, and other platforms in order to create new momentum for regional economic development, as well as further improvement of various development platforms.

(V) A Green Development System That Economises with Resources and Remains Environmentally Friendly

As the report of the 19th NCCPC pointed out, we will step up efforts to establish a legal and policy framework that promotes green production and consumption, and promotes a sound economic structure that facilitates green, low-carbon, and circular development.[31] General Secretary Xi Jinping also proposed in his report that 'A green development system that saves resources and is environmentally friendly should be engineered to realise green, circular, and low-carbon development. This system should be constructed so as to foster harmonious coexistence between humanity and nature. It should adhere to the concept that *clear waters and lush mountains are invaluable assets* and should be formed in line with a new pattern of modernisation of harmonious development between human beings and nature'.[32] The green development system is a system of socialist ecological civilisation. Green development is an efficient, sustainable, and harmonious development mode. Green development has been closely linked to the development characteristics of socialism with Chinese characteristics entering a new era. Only by practicing green development can the country ease the restriction of resources and environmental factors. China must take a dynamic and favorable position in the international community so that China remains competitive in the long run.

At present, China faces many challenges in establishing a green development system that is environmentally friendly and makes only modest demands on economic resources. In the first place, insufficient attention has been paid in the past to resource conservation and environmental protection. In terms of personal consumption, extravagance and waste persist, and a significant social consensus has not yet formed around the need to embrace a green lifestyle. Second, the systems and mechanisms to ensure the construction of a green development system are lacking. From the point of view of a top-level design, China lacks the strong value orientation and corresponding system required to protect resources and the environment.

---

31. http://www.xinhuanet.com/english/special/2017-11/03/c_136725942.htm

32. Xi Jinping stressed at the third collective study of the Political Bureau of the CPC Central Committee: a deep understanding of the importance of building a modernised economic system to promote China's economic development with new vitality to a new level [N]. People's Daily, 2018-02-01 (1)

http://www.gov.cn/xinwen/2018-01/31/content_5262618.htm

The legal and regulatory system that is meant to protect the environment is not sufficiently robust; the system of environmental evaluation is not perfect; and the performance evaluation system of the Party and government departments often ignores or fails to provide the evaluation of green development. Third, rapid urbanisation and industrialisation inevitably consume large amounts of resources. The traditional industrial structure and economic development mode often follows the outdated developmental pathway of *high input, high energy consumption, high pollution, and low income*, which invariably causes a waste of resources and damage to the environment.

To establish a resource-saving, environmentally friendly, green development system, the following measures must be implemented. First, it is critical to guide people to attach importance to saving resources and protecting the environment. China needs to instill in its society the concepts, central to ecological civilisation, of saving resources, of cherishing the natural environment and respecting the laws of nature, of establishing the social custom of thrift and an awareness of the rational and efficient use of resources, of publicising the knowledge and ideas of popular science with a view to saving resources while protecting the environment, and of popularising the concepts of thrift and environmental protection. Energetically publicising, guiding, and encouraging the concept of a green, low-carbon life is important to changing the public's attitude so that China can minimise the waste of resources and other adverse effects on the environment caused by personal behaviors and form a new pattern of sustainable development in which people and nature coexist harmoniously. The green development system and the incorporation of ecological education into the national education system should be widely promoted. A vital need exists to educate people from all walks of life, especially governments and leaders at all levels, to realise the importance of ecological/environmental work, and to fashion the concept of green development into a common pursuit and conscious behavior for the whole of society.

Second, China should continuously improve the system and mechanisms for constructing a green development system. Applying top-level legal experience, the government should improve the relevant legislation, because a comprehensive system of laws will not only help solve the problems of resources and the environment but can also effectively regulate behavior in this area. It is important to constantly update and improve the system for the evaluation of green development, avoid sacrificing our natural environment for economic gain in the name of *progress*, and link economic with ecological development. In particular, the performance evaluation system for governmental departments must be improved. Green development and protection of the natural environment should be important criteria for evaluating the performance of leading government officials and should be key indicators in establishing a lifelong accountability system for these cadres. Such steps will ensure that when government officials consider questions of economic development, they are made fully aware of the importance of conserving resources and protecting the environment.

Third, supply-side reform must be enhanced. All economic behavior should be based on the premise of protecting the environment and ecological health. The original industrial development process, which left the real economy with low scientific and technological content, high resource consumption, severe environmental pollution, and unsustainable development patterns, needs to be transformed into a resource-saving and environmentally friendly process that will ensure industrial development with good environmental benefits. Relying fully on scientific and technological innovation and progress to improve the output efficiency of resources, and to reduce the consumption of resources in the fields of production and circulation is critical. It is necessary also to advocate recycling, in the processes of production and consumption, of means of production and means of living. China should encourage the development of an environmental protection economy, a low-carbon economy, and a circular, recycling economy. Economic benefits will be gained from industrial activities that save resources and protect the environment. It is necessary and important to develop environmental protection activities or environmental protection industries into new economic growth points, creating new economic profits, enabling environmental protection to generate economic benefits, and attracting more enterprises and individuals to engage in environmental protection.

(VI) A Diversified, Balanced, Safe and Efficient Open System

The report of the 19th NCCPC explicitly proposed to *make up new ground in pursuing the opening up of China on all fronts.*[33] Xi Jinping stated: 'Efforts should be made to develop an open economy, to improve the international competitiveness of the modern economic system, to make better use of global resources and markets, and to continue to actively promote international exchange and

33. http://www.xinhuanet.com/english/special/2017-11/03/c_136725 942.htm

cooperation under the framework of the *Belt and Road Initiative'*.[34] These important statements and strategic arrangements accurately express the new situation that China finds itself in as it enters this new era. They reflect the urgent requirements of economic global-isation for the development of productive forces and scientific and technological progress. They are the only way to realise economic prosperity, and to define the new national direction, goals, and methods needed to bring about the comprehensive opening up of China.

So far, China has not formed a balanced, safe, efficient or compre-hensive system for its opening up to the world. The problems lie in the following areas. First, the form and structure of China's opening up are effectively singular, and most of the country's foreign trade is concentrated in industries with the advantages of low-end fac-tors. As a result of China's foreign trade structure being more or less singular, the traditional mode of production can no longer adapt to the current situation of international competition. Although China is a big trading country, its export products are still typically pri-mary products or low value-added products. Its pricing power in the international market is relatively weak. With the rise of factor costs and environmental protection costs, it has become increasingly difficult for China to adapt the traditional mode of production to the new conditions of international competition, and this has become a threat to the development of the real economy. Second, China lacks a sound economic system able to ensure the safety and stability of the comprehensive *opening up*. As the scope of the opening up has expanded some existing systems and mechanisms have not been strong enough to ensure the smooth operation of the country's mac-roeconomy or to stabilise its financial markets. The existing foreign trade pattern has tended to exacerbate the unbalanced character of the domestic economic development. Meanwhile, misaligned for-eign investment access barriers, insufficient experience in handling overseas investment, incomplete protection of overseas investment interests, frequent trade frictions and disputes over unsatisfactory handling results still linger.

---

34. Xi Jinping stressed at the third collective study of the Political Bureau of the CPC Central Committee: a deep understanding of the importance of building a modernised economic system to promote China's economic development with new vitality to a new level [N]. *People's Daily*, 2018-02-01 (1)

http://www.gov.cn/xinwen/2018-01/31/content_5262618.htm

In order to ensure the establishment of a diversified, balanced, safe, efficient, comprehensive, and open system, effective measures must be taken. First, China must continuously optimise the trade structure, firmly grasp the main line of supply-side structural reform, vigorously develop high-quality and high-efficiency industries, turn quality advantages and the novel output of emerging industries into new advantages for China's foreign trade, and ensure the retention of existing market share in foreign trade. It is imperative to continuously expand the role of high-tech industries represented by equipment manufacturing as the leading export industry, carry through the shift from traditional manufacturing to advanced modern manufacturing and high-tech industries, and improve China's position in the global industrial chain and value chain.

Second, China must continuously improve the layout of foreign trade and cultivate new modes of trade. In the composition of its export industries, attention and encouragement should be given to adding high-end production factors such as technology, knowledge, information, and intelligence, so as to consolidate China's existing advantages in the information industry while striving to become the author of foreign trade rules. Through increasing the factor cost advantages of the export industries and increasing the weight within them of China's achievements in scientific and technological innovation, new demand points and growth points should be created for traditional industries. This will have the benefit of enhancing the position of China's industries in international competition and consolidating the foundations of a modern economic system.

Third, it is critical to continuously adjust the foreign economic system and its mechanisms, removing drawbacks so as to provide a stable economic environment for the comprehensive opening of China, meanwhile, providing a fair and competitive business environment for domestic and foreign enterprises. Setting in place good policy mechanisms is necessary to improving the management of overseas investment. China should actively guide and encourage enterprises to invest abroad efficiently and ensure the profitability of investment.

(VII) An Economic System That Gives Full Play to the Role of the Market and the Government

The report of the 19th NCCPC declared that *efforts should be made to establish an economic system with an effective market mechanism, dynamic micro-entities, and sound macro-regulation.*[35] Xi Jinping proposed to establish 'An economic system that gives full play to the role of the market and in which the government performs its functions better'.[36] Improving the dual system in which regulation is provided both by the market and by government will pay dividends in terms of system reform and will promote the construction of the entire modern economic system.

Although China has established a socialist market economic system, the need remains to navigate between two extremes in dealing with the relationship between government and the market. First, excessive pursuit of marketisation has resulted in the absence of the government and has weakened the regulatory effect of the government's *visible hand* on the macro and micro economies. Completely free market competition can easily lead to inefficient economic phenomena such as market failure. When too much emphasis is placed on market competition, the market pays more attention to short-term efficiency; people with talent and other endowments rely on their own resource advantages to obtain more and more wealth and income. Meanwhile, people from vulnerable groups are increasingly unable to change their situation, and this results in a widening gap in income and wealth. Excessive market competition often leads to structural imbalances, setting up cyclical phenomena in investment and consumption; as a result, these categories become either seriously insufficient or seriously excessive. Second, undemocratic government regulation, on the other hand, leads to improper management. *Top leaders have the final say,* bureaucracy, formalism, face-saving projects, and false reports of achievements become commonplace. As the famous American economist Joseph E. Stiglitz has commented, 'China's environmental pollution, food safety, and other problems are relatively serious, indicating that the role of the government has not yet been well played'.

In order to reform the system and mechanisms of the relationship between the market and government, China must do the following.

---

35.   http://www.xinhuanet.com/english/special/2017-11/03/c_13672 5942.htm

36. Xi Jinping stressed at the third collective study of the Political Bureau of the CPC Central Committee: a deep understanding of the importance of building a modernised economic system to promote China's economic development with new vitality to a new level [N]. People's Daily, 2018-02-01 (1)

http://www.gov.cn/xinwen/2018-01/31/content_5262618.htm

First, it must adhere unwaveringly to the socialist nature and type of market economy reform. China must organically unify the basic socialist economic system with the dual adjustment of the resource allocation system. It must improve the market economy system that combines the effectiveness of the market mechanism in seeking benefits and avoiding disadvantages, orderly innovation by the micro-entities, and the high efficiency brought about by timely government adjustment.

Second, it is necessary to improve the property rights system and the market-oriented allocation of general factors. The institutional barriers that restrict the vitality and motivation of development must be broken down. On the basis of the principle that public ownership is the anchor, the state-owned system plays the leading role, and that the various forms of ownership develop together, a decisive role must be assigned to the *invisible hand* in the allocation of general resources, at the same time recognising the leading role of governments at all levels. China should give full play to the role of government at all levels in macro, meso, and micro regulation, streamline government agencies, make better use of personnel, and further develop government functions. The government must be diligent in performing public services, in strengthening market supervision, in maintaining market order, and in creating a fair, competitive market and institutional environment.

Third, China needs a unified, open, and integrated market system. Eliminating unreasonable administrative or institutional segmentation and rooting out discrimination, unfair competition, and unequal treatment except as stipulated by laws and regulations so as to ensure trouble-free market access is imperative. It is critical to ensure full competition among enterprises and enable consumers to have free market choices and independent consumption.

Fourth, importance must be attached to the functions of economic legislation and economic supervision carried out by the people's congresses at all levels. It is necessary to ensure spontaneous adjustment by the *invisible hand* of the market and conscious adjustment by the *visible hand* of the government (in a broad sense, the government includes the National People's Congress). Full play must be given to the internal self-discipline function of the *invisible hand* of ethics (including economic ethics and honesty) and the basic institutional function of the *primary hand* of property rights (since the allocation of rights to property resources determines the social and economic nature), so as to promote the overall coordinated development of high quality and high performance in the economy and society.

3. The Construction of a Modern Economic System Requires a Number of Strategic Measures

(I) To Resolutely Implement a People-Centred Development Strategy

The concept of *people-centred development* makes up the fundamental difference between the socialist development view with Chinese characteristics and the Western view of development. People-centred development is fundamental to building a modern socialist economic system, and also provides the characteristic strategic focus of Xi Jinping's *Thoughts on Socialist Economy with Chinese Characteristics for a new era*.

Some believe that this concept is too abstract to be widely grasped and properly implemented; that it often encourages a one-sided pursuit of GDP growth and other political achievements; and that it may prompt deviations from the original aspirations of the Communist Party. They believe that the concept threatens to distract the Party from its fundamental purpose of exercising power in the interests of the people, leading potentially to a failure to satisfy the yearning of the people for a better life, and to a failure to establish a modern socialist economic system. As stated in the report of the 19th NCCPC, the guiding ideology running through the whole process is *people-centred development thought*, which fully reflects the CPC's ruling concept of always keeping the people in mind and of being people-centred in all Party activities and functions. This is the fundamental policy approach through which the CPC can solve the major socialist contradictions, realising economic and social innovation and development in the new era.[37] The construction of a modern economic system will solve the contradiction between the growing demand of the people for a better life and the currently inadequate and unbalanced state of development. The goal is to achieve a greater enrichment of social material and spiritual civilisation, and to realise the common prosperity and enjoyment of all the people. The construction of a modern economic system takes material and economic forms, but its essence is the people. The object of service is still the people, and in the final analysis, is the modernisation of the people's whole being. Only through consistently taking *people-centred development thought* as the starting point for the Party's work, and through implementing the new development ideas and policies of *Innovation, Coordination, Green Consciousness, Sharing, and the Opening Up*

---

37.   http://www.xinhuanet.com/english/special/2017-11/03/c_13672 5942.htm

of China can the goal of a comprehensively prosperous society and a powerful country be realised.

(II) To Continue to Implement the Development Strategy of Deepening Supply-Side Structural Reform

To build a modern economic system, China must firmly grasp the main task of supply-side structural reform. As China's economic development enters a *new normal* situation, the traditional demographic dividend is growing weaker, the momentum of development is decaying, constraints on resources and the environment are intensifying, and great changes are taking place in the consumption structure, product structure, enterprise organisation structure, and production factor structure. These structural problems are exerting great downward pressure on China's economy. The problems cannot be solved simply by expanding aggregate demand. Instead, it is necessary to adapt to the demands of the new situation, carry out supply-side reforms, solve structural contradictions, and remove institutional obstacles. Only then can China liberate and develop productive forces and rebuild various balances under the *new normal* of the economy. The fundamental path of supply-side structural reform must be to push forward the adjustment of the supply structure so as to enhance the quantity, quality, and structure of production factors, enterprises, and products and to improve the quality and efficiency of the supply system. Measures should also be taken to reform the mechanisms that inhibit the refinement of the supply structure, to fully mobilise the enthusiasm and creativity of the broad masses of the people, to enhance the endogenous power of micro-entities, and to continuously promote the modernisation of the industrial structure, while better meeting demand and promoting sustained and healthy economic and social development.

Some also believe that supply-side structural reform has basically been completed and need not be developed further. But according to the spirit of the Central Economic Work Conference on 20 December 2017, completing the task of supply-side structural reform will require more efforts to be put into *eliminating, cultivating*, and *reducing. Eliminating* means eradicating ineffective supply and *zombie enterprises,* while promoting the elimination of excess production capacity. *Cultivating* means vigorously developing new momentum, strengthening scientific and technological innovation, promoting the optimisation and advance of traditional industries, fostering a range of leading enterprises with innovative abilities, and pursuing in-depth military/civilian integration. *Reducing*, as defined here, means energetically limiting real economic costs and institutional transaction costs and investigating the fees charged to enterprises, so as to rectify those levied arbitrarily, furthering the reform of electricity, oil and gas, railway and other industries, and reducing the costs of energy consumption and logistics.

To magnify supply-side structural reform, it is necessary to further reduce low-end and ineffective supply; do away with excessive capacity, unessential inventories and unneeded leverage, expand medium and high-end effective supply, strengthen weak links and guarantee people's livelihoods, accelerate the development of new technologies, new products and new industries, and create new impetus for economic growth. To further combine supply-side and demand-side management, China should not only broaden supply-side reform so that it can adapt to changes in demand, but also act in line with macroeconomic policies to stimulate the role of demand in promoting the economy.

(III) To Vigorously Implement the Development Strategy of Strengthening the Real Economy

The central government has made clear that in order to build a modern economy, China must develop the real sector and prioritise its development. The real economy provides the basis of a country's material well-being and acts as the foundation for a modern economic system. It underlies the country's future core competitiveness and determines its long-term economic growth. Consolidating China's real economy is thus a prime task.

Some people, however, take the attitude that making money and raising GDP through the virtual economy is easy and quick, while scoring quick achievements in one's official career by promoting the real economy is necessarily difficult. This is an obviously false theory that lacks any pragmatic spirit, and it must be eliminated. At present, it is imperative to develop the real sector. To this end, first, China must formulate relevant policies, to work hard to create a sound institutional environment for the real economy, to promote the concentration of resource elements within it, to tilt government policies and measures toward it, and to guide its development. Second, it is necessary to make improving the quality of the supply system the primary thrust of development in the real economy, combining this with supply-side structural reforms, accelerating the optimisation of the supply structure, eliminating backward production capacity, cultivating potential markets with a view to setting excess production capacity to work, and enhancing globalisation so as to export excess capital, with a focus on reinforcing China's advantage in terms of economic quality. Third, China should strengthen the leading role played by innovation, basic research, and applied research. China should lead innovative and forward-looking research, while cultivating new, original, and revolutionising technological methods. China should promote the coordinated development of the real economy, scientific and technological innovation, and human resources, and should lead the development of the real economy with scientific and technological innovation. Fourth, investment capital should be channelled into the real economy; market-oriented reforms must be accelerated; entrepreneurship must be protected and stimulated; and more social capital must be invested in the real economy. Fifth, an appropriate balance must be struck between the virtual economy and the real economy. On the one hand, it is critical to avoid the situation in which financial capital *breaks away from the real economy and leans towards the virtual economy.* China should try to promote sustainable development in the real economy through leveraging financial capital to ensure that financial capital serves the real economy. On the other hand, it is important to develop multilevel capital markets, promoting the construction of a powerful financial apparatus.

(IV) To Accelerate the Implementation of a Development Strategy Driven by Scientific and Technological Innovation

To accelerate the implementation of an innovation-driven development strategy requires reinforcing the construction of the national innovation system, enhancing strategic scientific and technological strength, promoting the in-depth integration of scientific and technological innovation and economic and social development, and buttressing the innovation-driven and innovation-led development model. Some hold the position that the reform of production relations and systems has always been more important than the reform of productive forces and technologies. Adherents of this viewpoint maintain that if the system is well devised, growth of the productive forces and technological innovation will follow automatically. This is a misinterpretation of the dialectics of economic science, since production relations and productivity and system and technology are independent variables with their own actions and reactions, and are not automatic, irreversible variables.

To build a modern economic system, China in fact needs to achieve advances in the following areas. First, it is important to use innovation to promote supply-side structural reform, consolidating the foundation of the real economy, and improving productivity through making new technological breakthroughs. Innovation must further be utilised to reduce enterprise costs, to promote industrial refinements and transformations, to improve the level and quality of enterprise development, and to provide factor quality and allocation efficiency. Second, promoting innovation and entrepreneurship, speeding-up the emergence of new industries, and creating new employment opportunities through innovation and entrepreneurship, thus revitalising the real economy must be a priority. China must enhance the status of the international division of labour, break the constraints of resources and the environment, and make sustainable economic and social development a reality. Third, it is necessary to strengthen the building of a national innovation system. Policies should be formulated that can guide talent and investment in the direction of promoting basic research, applied basic research, and strategic scientific and technological innovation research with long investment cycles and high risks and disruptive features, making it possible to achieve breakthroughs in major projects. Fourth, China needs to establish a sound innovation policy system, give clear direction to the market, encourage innovation research to move in step with market demand, stimulate and support enterprise-led innovation, foster in-depth integration of the work of industry, universities, and research institutes, and encourage and guide the commercialisation of innovation achievements. Fifth, the implementation of more active, open, and effective talent policies and innovative cultural policies are needed. China should cultivate mass entrepreneurship and innovation, strengthen intellectual property protection policies, and encourage inventive talents and high-level innovation teams to meet international standards. Sixth, wherever existing concepts, policies, and systems are not conducive to rapid economic development, they should be challenged and replaced through the application of concept innovation, policy innovation, and system innovation, so that the combination of concepts, policies, systems, and practices becomes more closely aligned with the trend of practical development. These measures will promote smoother, faster, and more effective economic development.

(V) To Vigorously Promote the Development Strategy of Military/ Civilian Coordination in Urban and Rural Areas

The modern economic system is an organic whole, and rural revitalisation is thus an essential premise for the modernisation of China's economic system. Through realising coordinated regional development, the spatial layout of the modern economic system can be optimised to provide important support for the building of a modernised economic system. The coordinated development of urban and rural areas should focus on a rural revitalisation strategy and promote the coordinated development of regions. Some believe villages necessarily lag behind cities; regional development is always unbalanced; and military/civilian economic integration is difficult to achieve. These disproportions and imbalances exist in any modern society and there is no need to rush to change them. This, however, is a misconception, and one that is divorced from China's true national conditions. Since the economic gap between urban and rural areas in the country is too large, and the degree of military/civilian economic integration is not high, the need is urgent for these entities to integrate and coordinate their development in a timely manner.

To implement the strategy of coordinated development between urban and rural areas in a meaningful fashion, rural revitalisation must be realised first. This is a fundamental method to improve the weak links of economic development and solve the problems relating to agriculture, rural areas, and the agrarian population. First, the key to implementing rural revitalisation lies above all in the Party. The CPC's leadership must be upheld and improved in dealing with the three rural issues noted above. It is necessary to further develop the leadership system for rural work under the unified direction of the Party committee, improve the direction and coordination provided by the government, and enhance the overall coordination of the rural work departments of the Party committee. Improving the construction of relevant supporting systems, ensuring that these systems operate throughout the whole process of rural revitalisation, steadily enhancing the property rights system, continuously improving the market-oriented allocation of factors, and providing institutional support for rural revitalisation by promoting innovation in various systems and mechanisms is very important. Second, China must prioritise human capital above all other factors, pool the strength of the entire society, formulate relevant policies, attract capable people to work in rural areas, and strengthen talent incentive strategies. Human talents should be regarded as the fundamental factor involved in rural revitalisation. Finally, it is critical to focus on industrial prosperity, improve the quality of agricultural development, foster new momentum for rural development, form a three-in-one investment pattern of financial priority guarantees, financial priority incentives, and active social participation, so as to provide guarantees for the investment of rural revitalisation funds.

The strategy for the coordinated development of urban and rural areas represents a huge and complicated social undertaking. It is necessary to optimise the spatial distribution of the modern economic system through coordinated development of urban and rural areas, to implement the strategy of coordinated regional development, to promote the coordinated development of the Beijing-Tianjin-Hebei Region and of the Yangtze River Economic Belt, and to accelerate the promotion of economic development strategies and policies in the central and western regions along with other less developed regions. China must coordinate and promote the development of the Guangdong-Hong Kong-Macao Greater Bay Area, gradually narrow the economic development gaps between different regions, and build a coordinated urban and rural regional development system that utilises the inherent advantages of both cities and the countryside. Promoting a coordinated development strategy is necessary, involving urban and rural areas and narrowing the development gap between them. In addition, it is important to promote the sound interaction of economic and social components nationwide, accounting for the spatial balance of the population, the economy, resources, and the environment, so as to continuously make new progress in achieving high-quality development.

China must plan thoughtfully to carry out the tasks of implementing an effective military/civilian integration strategy, of building infrastructure, and of promoting resource sharing. China needs to develop a national defence science and technology industry and advanced military hardware. In the area of military/civilian science and technology, China must coordinate actions and foster collaoburative innovation. The challenges to be addressed include the two-way training and exchange of military and civilian personnel, the comprehensive development of social services and military logistics, the modernisation of national defence mobilisation, and the in-depth military/civilian integration in emerging fields. Therefore, it is necessary to learn from the valuable experience of foreign countries, accelerate the integrated formation of military/civilian development bodies and management systems, effectively engage operational and policy systems, promote military/civilian integration in key areas so as to make substantial progress, and form an all-factor, multi-field, high-efficiency pattern of military/civilian integration. As a first step, constructing an integrated national strategic system with the appropriate capabilities is required.

(VI) To Actively Implement the Development Strategy Leading Economic Globalisation

China's modern economic system is, in essence, an open system. Adapted to the country's national conditions, it simultaneously implements strategic measures aimed at providing leadership for economic globalisation. It is thus well fitted to shaping the modern world economic system. Some believe that China has not yet taken a place at the *centre* of this system, maintaining that the country is still in a *peripheral* or *dependent* position, able only to participate in, accept, and obey international rules and practices. However, this is an outdated view that does not account for the latest world situation and China's national conditions. Decades ago, few people in the world would have imagined that China would perform a magnificent feat of development, vaulting from *periphery* to *centre* in the space of forty years. China now finds itself closer to the centre of the world economic stage than ever before; it may be said that the country is playing the role of a *quasi-centre*. This view can be demonstrated in a number of ways: China's economy is growing rapidly; its total economic aggregate is already second in the world in terms of exchange rate and first in terms of purchasing power parity; while the volume of its import and export trade globally fluctuates between first and second. China has also emerged as the *top engine* of world economic growth, making the largest single national contribution. The Chinese Renminbi (RMB) has even become an international reserve currency.

In the future, China must boldly lead global economic development, playing the foremost role in the construction of a modern world economic system. First, it is very necessary to continue to implement China's two-way opening up that gives equal emphasis to introducing things from abroad into China and bringing things from China to other countries and to *going global*. China should continue to expand their foreign investment, especially foreign aid investment in Latin America and Africa. Chinese must continue to seek out mergers and acquisitions in developed countries such as the United States and Europe and take advantage of opportunities for international cooperation through the Belt and Road Initiative. It is of great importance to China to bolster financial institutions such as the BRICS Development Bank and the Asian Infrastructure Investment Bank (AIIB), so as to lead global economic development and build a community of interests for all countries, featuring a shared future for humankind.

Second, to promote the comprehensive opening up, it is necessary to broaden the scope of this new pattern, expanding its scale and improving its quality, so as to build a safe and efficient economic system, featuring a multitude of balances that can allow us to participate in a high-level internationally competitive world. The concept of diversified balance refers to the equilibrium provided by a wide variety of imports, exports, and investment sources, as well as to the diversification and balance of business entities, and goods and services that is an inherent requirement of an open economic system. Making China's economic system safe and efficient requires grasping the initiative to be found in the country's economic development, while adapting to economic globalisation, opening up to the outside world, and avoiding potential risks brought about by opening up. At the same time, China should proactively make use of the open market to promote the transformation of *production and the market* from the limited advantages of low-end factors to the new advantages of high-end factors. A multi-balanced, safe, and efficient open system will enable China to obtain more international resources and markets, to expand into a wider international space, to enhance the *extracorporeal* circulation of its economy, to gain a greater *right to be heard* for the vast number of developing countries, including China, in the future of economic globalisation, and to change those rules of the current economic globalisation that are unreasonable and unfair. In short, this open system represents a strategic move aimed at adapting to the construction of a modern economic system and must be consistently and proactively advanced so as to steadily improve China's position and voice in global economic governance. This open system will allow China, consciously and progressively, to change their position from that of a bystander and follower to a participant and leader. It will transform their standing from that of a supporting actor in a minor role in economic globalisation to that of a responsible, leading participant in global economic governance.

References

[1] Liu Zhibin. *Building a Modern Economic System: The General Program of Economic Construction in the New Era* [J]. *Journal of Shandong University: Philosophy and Social Sciences Edition*, 2018 (1).

[2] Wu Guoyou. *Building a Modern Economic System: New Ideas and Highlights of Changing the Mode of Economic Development in the Report on the 19th NCCPC* [J]. *Journal of Beijing Jiaotong University: Social Sciences Edition*, 2018 (1).

[3] Liu Wei. *The Modern Economic System is an Organic Unity of the Development and Opening of China* [J]. *Economic Research*, 2017 (11).

[4] Chi Fulin. Viewing the Construction of the Modern Economic System from Three Dimensions [J]. *China Economic Report*, 2017 (12).

[5] Wang Xiaodong. *Building a Unified and Open Market System with Orderly Competition* [EB/OL]. [February 5, 2015]. http://www.sohu.com/a/221042118_118570.

[6] Shi Jianxun. *How to Lay out the Construction of a Modern Economic System* [EB/OL]. [January 30, 2018]. http://www.sohu.com/a/219780688_115725.

(Originally published in *Review of Economic Research*, No.7, 2018, with Chai Qiaoyan as the second author)

* * *

Section V To Develop a Modernised Economy to Achieve High-Quality Development

Xi Jinping has pointed out that developing a modernised economy is not only the strategic goal of China's development, but also an urgent requirement for the transformation of the economic growth model, for the structural improvement of the economy, and for the shift to new economic growth drivers. Basing itself on the achievements of China's rapid economic growth since the reform and opening up, and proceeding from the three perspectives, namely the transformation of the country's growth model, its structural improvement, and its shift to new growth drivers, this section analyses the inevitability and importance of China's development of a modernised economy and of its turn to high-quality development. Accounting for the internal structure and development trend of the modernised economy, this section also systematically demonstrates a series of important relationships that need to be handled properly to expedite that development.

1. The Main Achievements of Rapid Growth Since the Beginning of China's Reform and Opening Up

Although China's economy has experienced certain fluctuations over the forty years since the policy of reform and opening up was introduced, a rapid growth trend has generally been maintained for more than thirty years. The country has thus *created an economic miracle, with rapid economic growth of longer duration than that of any other country* since the end of WWII. At constant prices, China's

GDP in 2016 was 32.306 times the 1978 figure. Just as notable, GNI in 2016 was 32.176 times that in 1978. Although China's population increased from 962.59 million in 1978 to 1,390.08 million in 2017, per capita GDP in 2016 was 22.402 times its 1978 mark. From 1979 to 2016, the average annual growth of China's GNI was 9.6%. According to preliminary statistics, China's 2017 GDP increased by 6.9% over the 2016 figure, while per capita GDP increased by 6.3%, and GNI by 7.0%.[38] These data show that China's economic growth rate during the past forty years has indeed been an historic miracle of sustained and rapid economic growth. (See charts below)

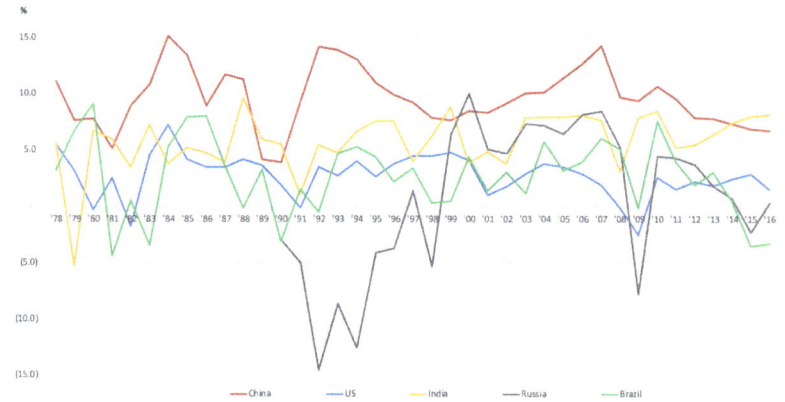

Data source: World Bank

Chart 17 GDP Growth 1978-2016

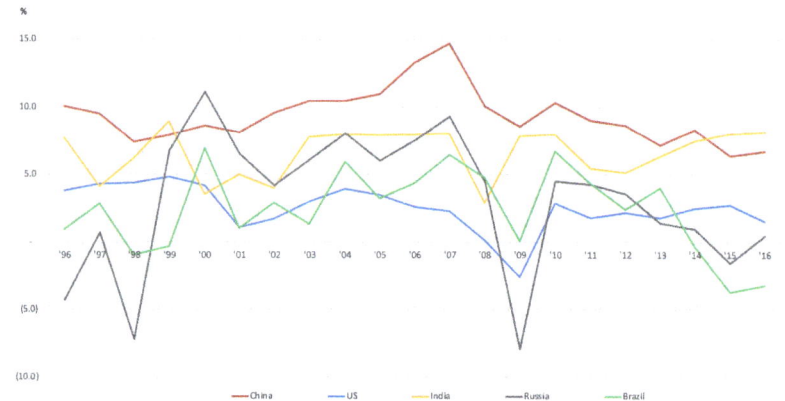

Data source: World Bank

Chart 18 China GNI Growth 1996-2016

38. http://www.stats.gov.cn/tjsj/ndsj/2017/indexch.htm

The scale of foreign trade in both goods and services has increased dramatically. The total value of exported goods increased from RMB 16.76 billion in 1978 to RMB 15,332.1 billion in 2017, and the total value of imported goods increased from RMB 18.74 billion in 1978 to a 2017 figure of RMB 12,460.2 billion. In the area of service trade, the total value of exports increased from USD 2.6 billion in 1982 to USD 208.3 billion in 2016, with a corresponding preliminary statistical value in 2017 of RMB 1,540.7 billion. The total value of service imports rose from USD 1.9 billion in 1982 to USD 449.2 billion in

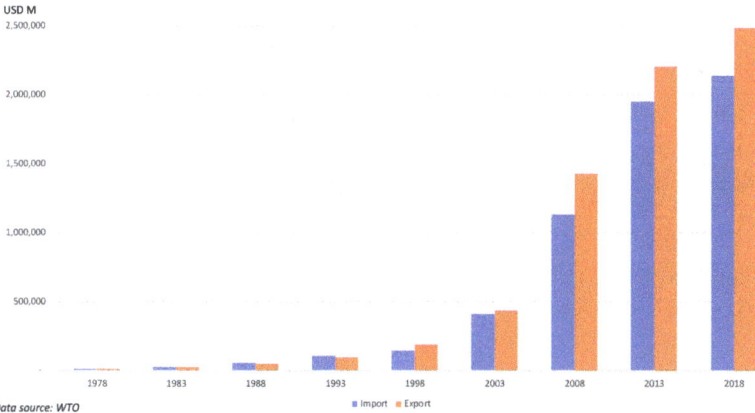

Data source: WTO

Chart 19 China Goods Trade- Export Value and Import Value

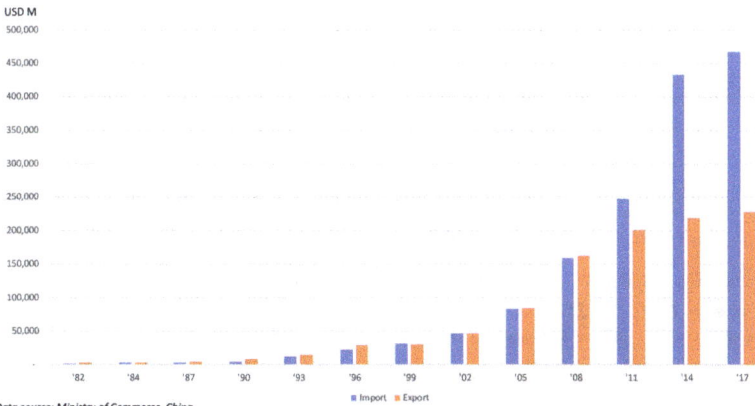

Data source: Ministry of Commerce, China

Chart 20 China Service Trade- Export Value and Import Value

2016, with a preliminary statistical value of RMB 3,158.4 billion in 2017.[39]

In terms of industrial structure, the proportional relationship between the three main areas of industry gradually improved. Measured as a proportion of GDP, the output value of primary industry decreased steadily from 27.7% in 1978 to 7.9% in 2017. The corresponding figure for secondary industry declined gradually from 47.7% in 1978 to 40.5% in 2017, while that for tertiary industry rose from 24.6% in 1978 to 51.6% in 2017. Employment in primary industry relative to total employment fell from 70.5% in 1978 to 27.7% in 2016, while the corresponding figure for secondary industry increased from 17.3% in 1978 to 28.8% in 2016, and that for tertiary industry, from 12.2% in 1978 to 43.5% in 2016.[40]

The construction of major infrastructure has made enormous progress. The density of the rail network rose from 53.9km/10,000km² in 1978 to 129.2km/10,000km² in 2016, while that of the road network increased from 927km/10,000km² in 1978 to 4,892km/10,000km² in 2016. In the area of posts and telecommunications, the changes have been even more dramatic; telephone coverage (including mobile phones) increased from 0.4% in 1978 to

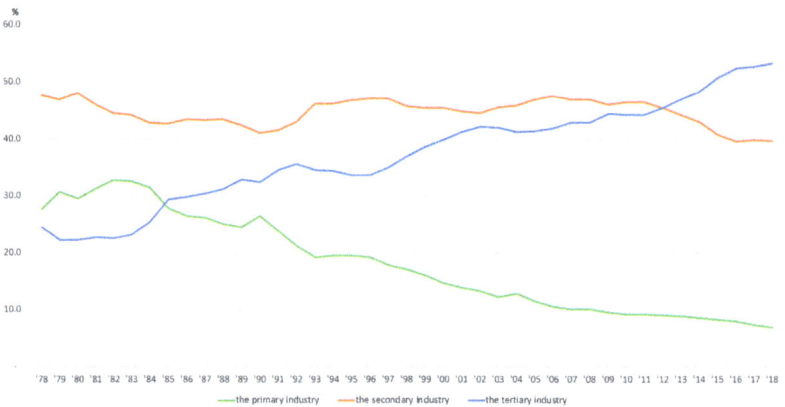

Data source: NBS of China; 2017's data are bit different with that of in article because NBS made adjustment by end of the year

Chart 21 Output Value of Primary, Secondary and Tertiary Industry between 1978-2018

39. http://www.stats.gov.cn/tjsj/zxfb/201802/t20180228_1585631.html
40. http://www.stats.gov.cn/tjsj/zxfb/201802/t20180228_1585631.html

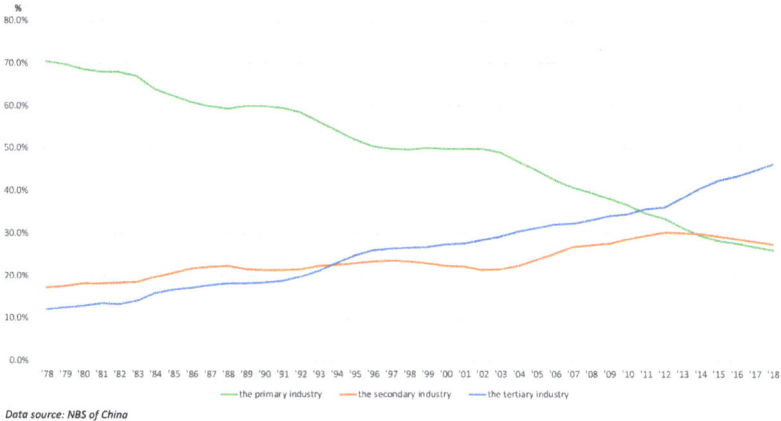

Chart 22 Proportion of Employment in Primary, Secondary and Tertiary

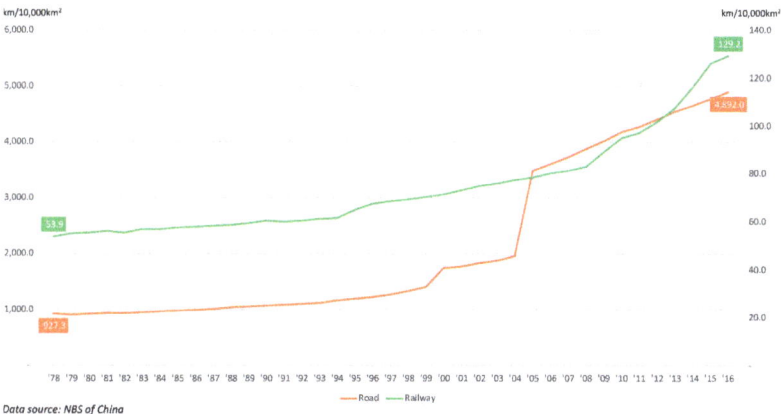

Chart 23 Density of Railway and Road per km2 1978-2016

110.5% in 2016, and mobile phone coverage increased from 6.7% in 2000 to 102.5% in 2017.[41]

Major quality of life indicators have meanwhile improved drastically. The average life expectancy of the population increased from 67.77 years in 1980 to 76.34 years in 2015, with the figure for males rising over this period from 66.28 to 73.64 years, and for females, from 69.27 to 79.43 years. The rural poverty headcount ratio (2010

41. http://www.stats.gov.cn/tjsj/ndsj/2017/indexch.htm
and http://www.stats.gov.cn/tjsj/zxfb/201802/t20180228_1585631.html

standard) decreased from 97.5% in 1978 to 49.8% in 2000, and to 3.1% in 2017. Household consumption by both urban and rural residents has maintained a high growth rate. In 2016, the per capita consumption level of all residents was 18.161 times that of 1978; for urban residents, the 2016 figure was 10.609 times that of 1978, and for rural residents, 12.549 times. According to preliminary statistics, nationwide per capita consumption expenditure increased by 5.4% in 2017 after adjusting for inflation. The per capita consumption expenditure of urban residents increased by 4.1%, and that of rural residents by 6.8%.

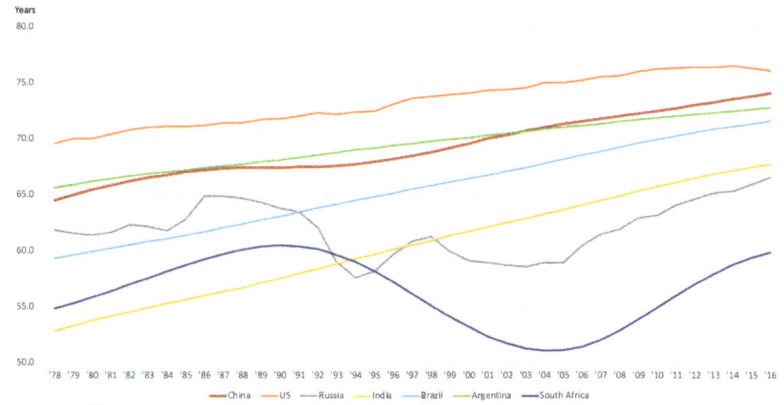

Data source: World Bank

Chart 24 Life Expectancy Comparison- Male

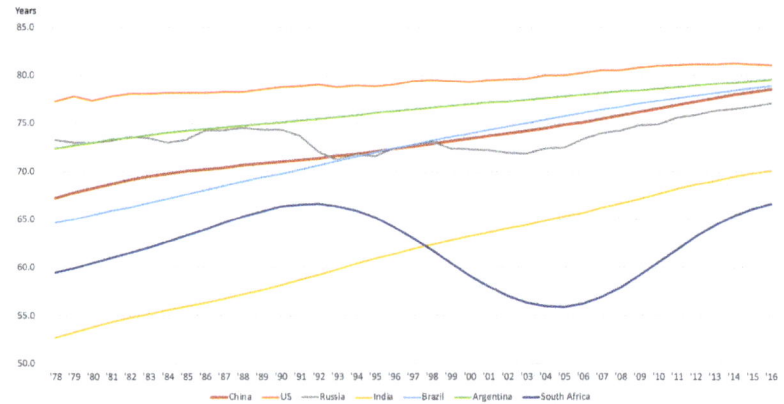

Data source: World Bank

Chart 25 Life Expectancy Comparison- Female

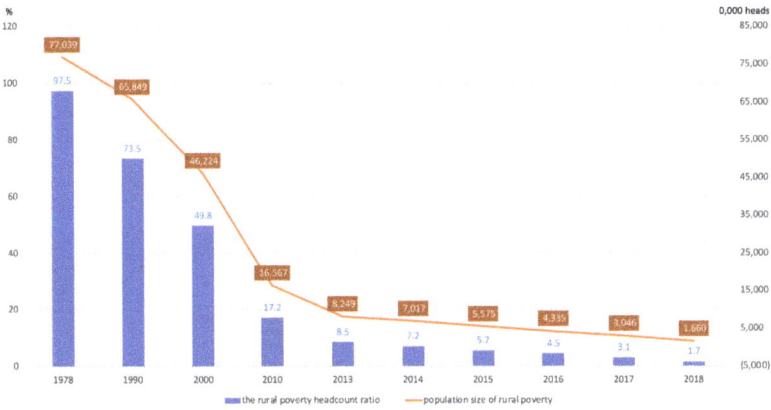

Data source: NBS of China

Chart 26 The Rural Poverty Headcount Ratio in China 1978-2018

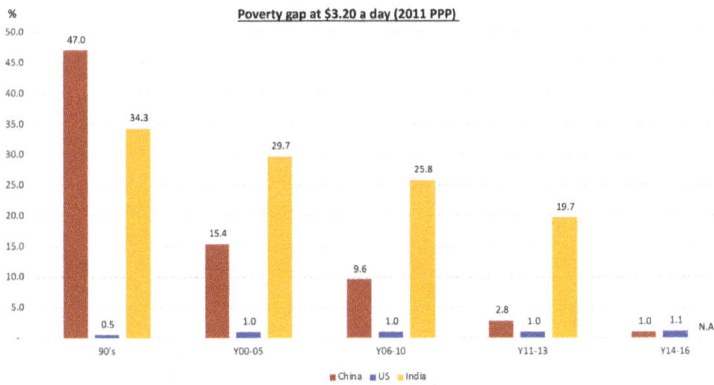

Data source: World Bank

Chart 27 The Poverty Headcount Ratio Comparison

Note: No country comparison because China's data is released by NBS (National Bureau of Statistics) which aligned with the data in this article. But data from World bank for China have big gaps. Please refer to the chart below,

Note: There isn't any data for Latin America and Africa from the World Bank.

In the areas of science, education, culture, and health, the great progress that has been made is demonstrated by the changes to major indicators of scale and quality. Spending on science and technology research and development increased as a proportion of GDP from 0.89% in 2000 to 2.12% in 2017. The proportion of the

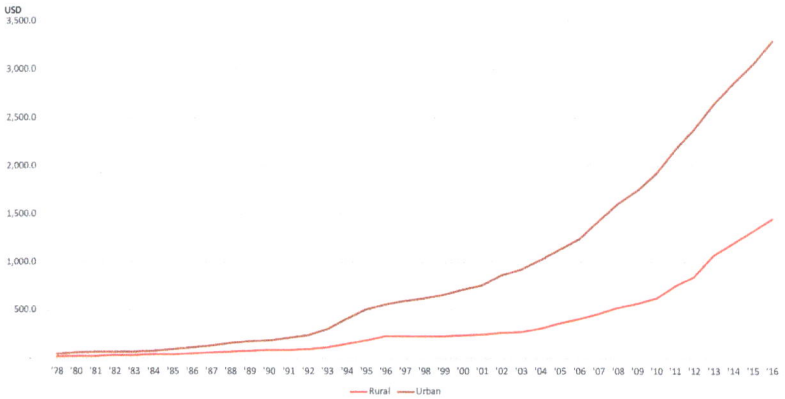

Data source: NBS of China

Chart 28 Rural and Urban Consumption Expenditure per Capita in China

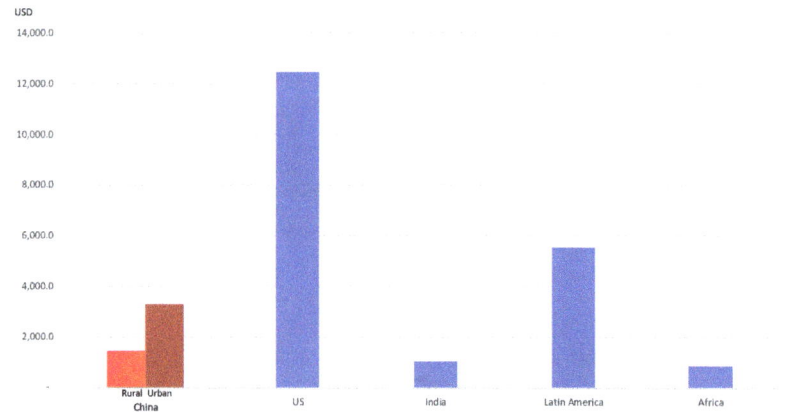

Data source: NBS of China, CEIC, World Bank

Chart 29 Consumption Expenditure per Capita Comparison in 2016

population receiving radio broadcasts rose from 77.4% in 1994 to 98.7% in 2017, while over the same period television coverage of the population increased from 83.3% in 1994 to 99.1% in 2017. In 1978, forty-six feature films were produced, while in 2017 a total of 798 feature films appeared, along with 172 scientific and educational films, documentaries, animated films, and special films. The number of books published grew from 14,987 in 1978 to 499,884 in 2016, and that of periodicals, from 930 in 1978 to 10,084 in 2016.[42] Since the 18th NCCPC, the guiding position of Marxism in the field of ideology

42. http://www.stats.gov.cn/tjsj/ndsj/2017/indexch.htm

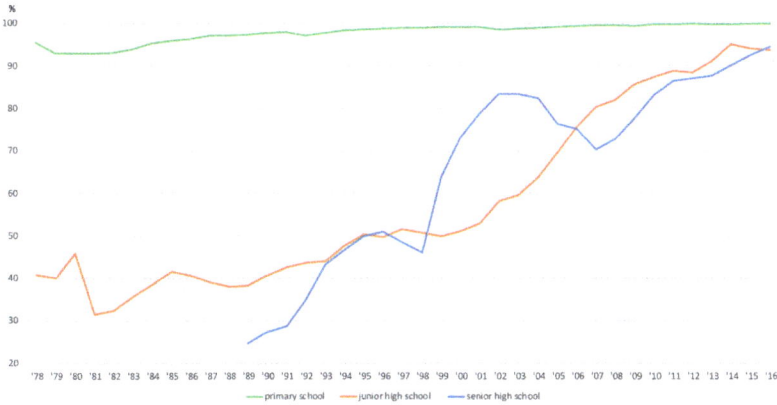

Data source: NBS of China, enrollment rate of senior high school is not available during 1978-1988

Chart 30 Education: Net Enrollment Rate in China

has been clearly evident, and core socialist values have been widely promoted, as has China's rich traditional culture. In general, cultural programs and cultural industries have undergone continuous and sound development, with literary works burgeoning.

A similarly robust expansion has been seen in the education sector. The net enrollment rate of primary school-age children increased from 95.5% in 1978 to 99.9% in 2016, while the junior high school enrollment rate rose from 87.7% in 1978 to 98.7% in 2016. The high school enrollment rate skyrocketed from 40.9% in 1978 to 93.7% in 2016, and the rate of high school seniors entering universities climbed from 73.2% in 2000 to 94.5% in 2016. Improvements in health care have also been impressive. The number of practicing (assistant) doctors per 10,000 persons jumped from 10.8 in 1978 to 23.1 in 2016, and the utilisation rate of sickbeds in medical institutions showed a marked increase from 60.8% in 2000 to 85.4% in 2015 and 85.3% in 2016.[43]

The above data show that in the forty years since China's reform and opening up began, the rapid economic growth has laid a solid material foundation for improving both the country's economic strength and people's lives.

2. The Inevitability and Importance of Transitioning to a Stage of High-Quality Development

In the forty years since the policy of reform and opening up was introduced, China has achieved rapid economic growth, but has also encountered new challenges and obstacles. These have imposed

---

43. http://www.stats.gov.cn/tjsj/ndsj/2017/indexch.htm

restrictions on economic growth. Inevitably, the whole national economy has had to transform its growth model, enact structural improvements, and shift toward new economic growth drivers, in a bid to achieve high-quality development.

(I) The Inevitability and Importance of Transforming the Economic Growth Model

In light of the restrictive conditions that came to bear on China's economy during the rapid growth stage, the country will inevitably need to shift from an extensive model of growth that emphasises scale and speed to a more intensive one, emphasising quality and efficiency.

During the stage of rapid economic growth, China has mainly applied an extensive model that emphasises scale and speed. According to this model, the central way to achieve growth is through the expansion of simple, labour-intensive industries. However, the products of these industries are located at the mid-to-low end of global value and industry chains. In the long term, this extensive growth model is unsustainable. First of all, it rests on an unsustainably low cost of labour. Emphasising scale and speed relies on quantitative expansion based on price competition. Under this model, China's main competitive advantage derives from the low price of its goods, reflecting low labour costs. In the long term, however, low labour costs will inevitably weaken the country's effective purchasing power, placing limitations on growth and even creating excess

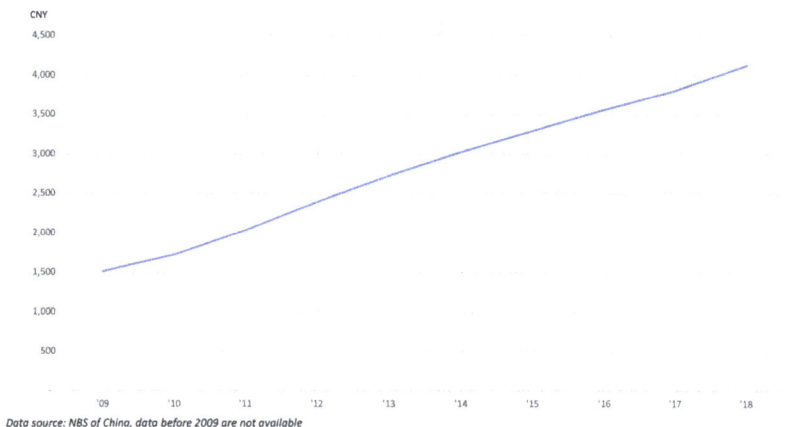

Data source: NBS of China, data before 2009 are not available

Chart 31 Average Monthly Wage of Employees in the Urban Private Sectors in China

productive capacity at the mid to low-end links of the industry chain. In 2009, for example, the total figure for employees in urban private enterprises together with self-employed individuals reached 97.889 million, while the average annual wage of employees in the urban private sector that year was only demand. On the other hand, the gradual increase of labour costs means that China's economy will face the risk of foreign investment moving to countries where labour is cheaper.

In this model of economic growth, the full-load or overload use of energy, resources, and ecology will not be sustainable. In terms of value, product margins under the extensive growth model, with its emphasis on scale and speed, are low due to the limited value that is added to the mid to low-end products; the main way in which high profits can be obtained is through the extensive expansion of simple labour-intensive, mid to low-end industries. In terms of utilisation value, this model will inevitably lead to a huge consumption of energy resources and serious degradation of the environment under the conditions of low utilisation efficiency. China's total energy consumption increased from 987.03 million tons of standard coal in 1990 to 4.49 billion tons in 2017. Energy imports grew from 13.1 million tons of standard coal (13.3% of total energy consumption) in 1990 to 897.3 million tons (20.6% of total energy consumption) in 2016. In terms of resources and the environment, the total amount of wastewater discharge in China increased gradually from 48,240.94 million tons in 2004 to 73,532.2683 million tons in 2015, and then fell slightly to 71,109.5388 million tons in 2016. Emissions of sulfur dioxide, the main pollutant in exhaust gases, reached as high as 22.549 million tons in 2004. Although this figure has declined gradually since then, it remained at or above the level of 20.439 million tons until 2013. In 2016 it dropped to 11,028,643.04 tons. But in some areas, air quality has remained at a poor level for far too long. Among the cities that put great emphasis on environmental protection, many still had fewer than 200 days of air quality at or above Grade II in 2016. Baoding, with the lowest index value, only reached 155 days. Monitoring in 2017 of 338 cities at prefecture level or above showed some 70.7% failing to meet air quality standards. The above data show that after years of applying the extensive growth model emphasising scale and speed, the impact of China's economic growth on energy, resources, and the environment has reached or approached the upper limit of natural carrying capacity.[44]

---

44. http://www.stats.gov.cn/tjsj/zxfb/201802/t20180228_1585631.html

Million tons

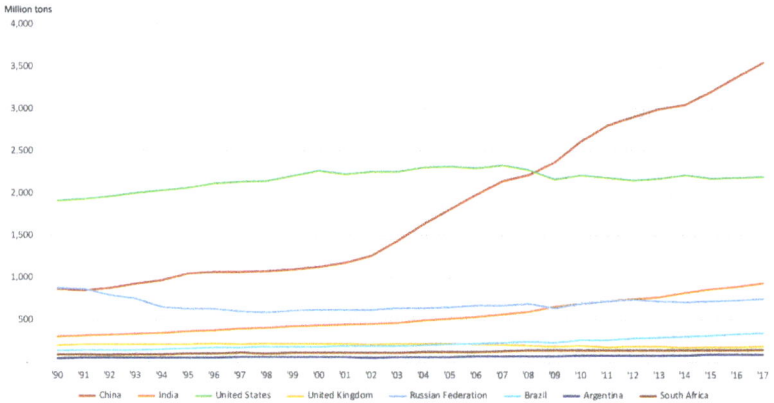

Data source: World Bank

Chart 32 Total Energy Consumption (Oil Equivalent)

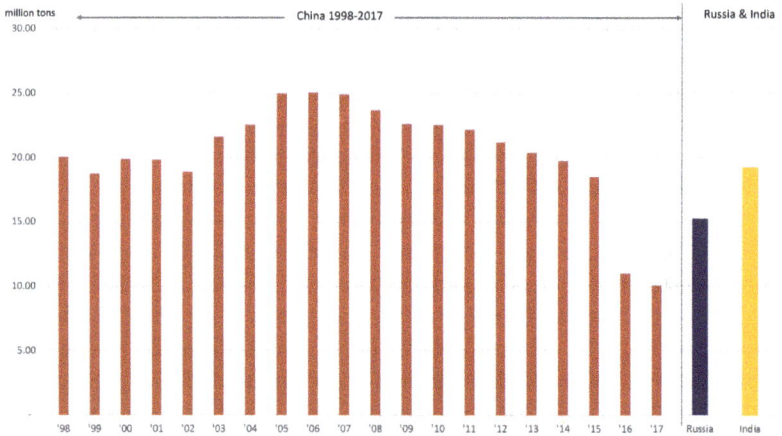

Data source: NBS of China, China State Council

Chart 33 So2 Emission

During the stage of rapid economic growth in China, the disadvantages of the extensive growth model must inevitably force a shift to an intensive growth model emphasising quality and efficiency.

(II) The Inevitability and Importance of Improving the Structure of the Economy

In light of the restrictions created by the rapid growth stage of China's economy, the country's economic structure requires in-depth adjustment, moving from quantitative increase and capacity expansion to an emphasis on stock adjustment and incremental optimisation.

In particular, the irrational industrial structure formed by the extensive model, with its emphasis on scale and speed, needs to be improved. Over the long term, the repeated expansion of high-profit but relatively low-technology industries has resulted in serious overcapacity. This overcapacity, at odds with the gradual upgrading of the consumption structure, has caused unsalable products to pile up in the industrial value chain. The enterprises affected by this problem often experience reduced profits, losses, or even bankruptcy. Meanwhile, infrastructure connectivity, environmental protection, basic pillars of industry, and various emerging strategic industries suffer underinvestment due to the long cycle of capital recovery, low short-term profit rates, and high investment risk.

Where the demand structure is concerned, the situation in which economic growth relies heavily on external demand needs to be changed. Before the global financial and economic crisis broke out in 2008, China's economic growth depended largely on external needs. Between 2004 and 2008, the contribution of net exports of goods and services to GDP growth had been at a high level, reaching an index value of 22.2% in 2005. After the financial and economic crisis broke out in Western countries, the power of foreign demand to drive economic growth in China remained greatly weakened due to the continued depression in major world economies. Except in 2012, 2014, and 2017, the contribution made by net exports of goods and services to China's GDP growth was negative during the period from 2009 to 2016.[45]

Meanwhile, an urgent need exists to narrow the large gap between the well-off and the poor in the distribution of income. For wealth overall, the Gini coefficients in 2015 and 2016 were 0.462 and 0.465. The urban to rural income ratio (the income of rural residents is represented here as 1) has remained relatively high; it was, respectively 2.57, 2.79, 2.73, 2.72, and 2.71 for the years 1978, 2000, 2015, 2016, and 2017. The income gap is reflected directly as a large gap in consumption levels. From 1978 to 2000, the urban/rural consumption level ratio increased gradually from 2.9 to 3.7, dropping later to 2.7 in 2016 and 2.23 in 2017.[46] These later figures were still regarded as high.

The dire need to address the imbalances of the economy between urban and rural areas is also apparent in urban and rural structures. Depending on economic development levels, different regions of China vary greatly in the average consumption levels of residents. In Shanghai and Beijing these reached RMB 49,617 and RMB 48,883

45. http://www.stats.gov.cn/tjsj/ndsj/2017/indexch.htm
46. Ibid

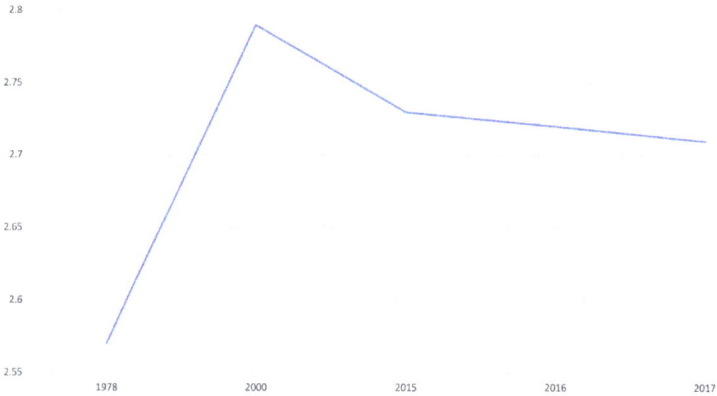

Chart 34 Urban-Rural Income Ratio

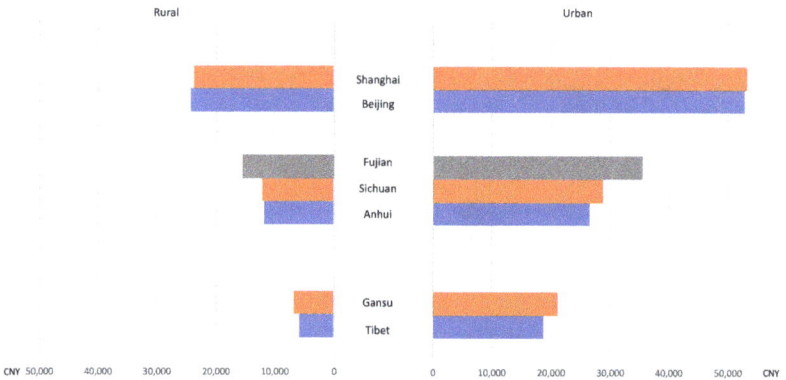

Chart 35 Top 2, Middle 3 and Bottom Two Rural-Urban Consumption Level

respectively in 2016, the top two figures in China. In Shanghai, the average consumption level for urban residents was RMB 53,240, while that for rural residents was RMB 23,660. In Beijing, the average consumption level for urban residents was RMB 52,721, while that for rural residents was RMB 24,285. For Gansu and Tibet, the levels were RMB 13,086 and RMB 9,743, the two lowest in China. The urban level in Gansu was RMB 21,128, while the rural level was RMB 6,781. In Tibet, the urban level was RMB 18,775, while the rural level was RMB 5,952.[47]

---

47. Ibid

(III) The Inevitability and Importance of Shifting to New Growth Drivers

When the restrictive conditions formed during the rapid growth stage of China's economy are accounted for, it becomes clear that traditional drivers of China's economic development such as factor and investment will inevitably shift to new ones, especially innovation.

The disadvantages of the traditional growth drivers such as factor and investment have gradually emerged during the stage of rapid economic growth. For an extensive growth model that emphasises scale and speed, the essence of factor-driven growth is the competitive advantage of commodity prices arising from low labour costs, while that of investment-driven growth lies in the repeated low-level expansion of a few high-profit industries. As the extensive growth model that features scale and speed has progressed, factor-driven growth has weakened. The total figure for employees of urban private enterprises and the self-employed jumped from 97.889 million in 2009 to 207.104 million in 2016, and the average salary of employees in urban private enterprises during the same period increased from RMB 18,199 in 2009 to RMB 42,833 in 2016. The increased labour costs must result in the shrinkage, or even disappearance, of profits in price competition. Also, investment-driven economic growth under such an extensive growth model will gradually weaken due to surplus capacity.

During the stage of rapid economic growth, the inevitability and importance of an innovation driver becomes increasingly evident. First, technical innovation directly influences the commercial profits of industries and enterprises. In contemporary global competition, knowledge and Intellectual Property Rights (IPR) monopolies based on core technological innovation in key areas are important sources of international monopoly profits. Under the extensive growth model emphasising scale and speed, products from numerous industries in China are at the mid-to-low end of the global value chain and industry chain. Weak technical innovation means that it is difficult for products from these industries to form strongly competitive self-owned brands with important influence. This directly limits added value and profit margins. Second, core technological innovation in key areas directly influences national security. *Core technologies are important instruments of the state.* For example, the ownership of core chip technology is directly related to the commanding heights and initiatives of national information security. Currently, no substantive breakthrough has been achieved by China in vital core technologies such as smartphone chips, and with the increasing trade protectionism and blockading of technologies practiced by the USA and other developed countries, industrial security and overall national security will face great challenges.

It can be seen that the new situations and problems that are emerging during the stage of high-speed growth will promote the transformation of China's mode of economic growth, optimise its economic structure, and transform its growth momentum with a focus on improving quality and efficiency. Such advances will allow China to turn transformations and achievements into high-quality development; the primary method is accelerating the construction of a modern economic system.

3. To Accelerate the Construction of a Modern Economic System and Promote High-Quality Development

Promoting high-quality development with the construction of a modern economic system requires that a series of important relationships in the core subsystem be properly handled in accordance with the inherent structural characteristics of the economic system. As Xi Jinping has pointed out, the modernised economic system is an organic whole composed of the interrelationships and internal connections of all links, levels, and fields in social and economic activities. To build a modern economic system, China must adhere to the principle of regarding people as the centre, implementing the new development concepts of innovation, coordination, greenness, openness, and sharing, while correctly understanding and handling a series of important relationships.

(I) The Industrial System: The Relationship between Independent Innovation and the Introduction of Foreign Technologies as Well as the Relationship between the Real Economy and Financial Development Must Be Handled Properly

At the industrial level, promoting high-quality development and the construction of a modern economic system requires focusing on the construction of an industrial system guided by innovation and coordinated development. To promote dynamic optimisation of the industrial structure in a high-quality manner, China must focus on the relationship between independent innovation and development based on the introduction of foreign technologies as well as the relationship between the real economy and financial development.

Correctly handling the relationship between independent innovation and development based on the introduction of foreign technologies and methods is central to clearing the bottlenecks that impede economic growth. In the industrial development of developing countries, independent innovation and the introduction of technologies exist in dialectical relationships that are both opposite and unified. The unification of independent innovation with development based on introduced technologies is reflected in the interactive relationship between the degree of independent innovation and the quality of development that follows the introduction of foreign technologies and methods; that is, the higher the degree of independent innovation within an industry, the greater the ability of the industry to introduce high-quality foreign technologies. At the stage when independent innovation is at a low level, the industries can only introduce non-core technologies that do not possess independent intellectual property rights. They engage mainly in low value-added production at peripheral levels, as elements within the low-end links of the global value chain. Their share in the total profits of industrial chains is extremely meager.

The contradiction between independent innovation and development based on introduced technologies and methods is embodied in the reverse interaction between independent innovation capacity and the extent of development based on introduced elements. This indicates that, at the initial development stage of a burgeoning industry in a developing country, independent innovation capacity can only be improved when the extent of development based on introduced technologies and methods is low. If a developing country overemphasises the comparative advantages that flow from its low labour costs at this stage (New Structural Economics exaggerate the comparative advantages that result from resource endowments), leading to excessive introduction of some weak industries, these industries will be controlled by foreign capital and technologies. The opportunity for development through independent innovative ability will have been lost, and the country will find itself caught in a *comparative advantage trap*.

In the construction of a modern industrial system, coping properly with the relationship between independent innovation and development based on introduced technologies requires insisting on theories and strategies that stress the advantages of independent intellectual property rights, on the development of industry along a path of independent innovation, supplemented by development on the basis of introduced technologies, and on systematic improvement of the capacity for independent innovation in key core technologies across a range of industries. For example, agricultural production capacity and quality should be systematically enhanced through modern seed growing, through better production equipment, through improved technical services, and through the application by farmers of modern technologies and scientific methods. Industrial development should centre on major technological innovations, and efforts should be made to achieve breakthroughs while mastering core technologies. On top of that, high-end, information-based, service-oriented, and green industrial production should be systematically promoted from the perspectives of innovation in platform construction, talent cultivation, incentive reinforcement, and achievement transformation. In developing service industries, the latest technologies should be used to facilitate modernisation and to continuously improve service quality and capability.

Properly handling the relationship between the real economy and financial development is vital if bottlenecks in the economic structure are to be removed. In the industrial development of a developing country, the relationship between the real economy and financial development is dialectical, at once opposite and unified. The unification lies in the obverse interaction between them. Financial development can help develop the real economy by providing secure, adequate, efficient capital support with a reliable structure, while development of the real economy will provide capital for financial development and support for currency stability and risk prevention.

A contradiction is found in the reverse interaction when its elements do not fit together. If financial development lags behind the real economy, the functioning of the former with relation to the latter will be weakened, and no strong financial support will be provided for the development of the real economy. If finance overdevelops independently of the real economy, financial bubbles will arise repeatedly, and if regulation is absent or inadequate, will result eventually in financial disorder and crisis. For the real economy, the result is likely to be serious damage.

To properly manage the relationship between the real economy and financial development in building a modern industrial system, China should eliminate the *financial deepening* and *financial repression* of neoliberalism. Finance must serve the real economy, promoting benign interactions between the real economy and financial development. The abilities of finance in this area need to evolve continuously, making it more scientific, accurate, and systematic in serving the real economy and in providing strong capital support for the latter's modernisation. The prevention and resolution of financial disorders and risks should be taken as a baseline. Foreign capital should be prevented from acquiring ownership in and monopoly control over the equity structure of key financial institutions. The financial system should be modernised through the introduction of a complete set of innovative supervision technologies, strengthening the supervision systems, and allowing the systematic improvement of supervision capability, as well as through other changes.

(II) The Market System: Properly Handling the Relationship between Effective Competition and a Moderate degree of Monopoly

At the market level, China will promote high-quality development by establishing a modernised economy. With a focus on building a unified and open market system featuring orderly competition, China will effectively manage the relationship between effective competition and a moderate degree of monopoly, in a bid to *accelerate the establishment of a modern market system with independent management of enterprises and fair competition between them, with freedom of choice and independent consumption for consumers, and with free mobility and equal exchange of goods and factors.*

In the modern market system, the relationship between effective competition and moderate monopoly is a dialectical relationship that is both opposite and unified. The unification of effective competition and moderate monopoly lies in the interaction between fair competition and moderate monopoly. In a modern market, effective competition is reflected in the fairness of competition rules. Modern global competition in specific business fields leads to a faster concentration of production and capital in particular enterprises. The scope of businesses is broader, and the extent of concentration is higher, thus giving rise to a larger-scale monopoly. As Lenin said, 'Free competition gives rise to the concentration of production, which, in turn, at a certain stage of development, leads to monopoly'.[48] Meanwhile, market competition is much fiercer than ever before because of the scale and power of monopolistic enterprises when they compete in the modern market, and therefore, effective competition under fair competition rules must be pushed forward. Marx pointed out that

---

48. Lenin. Imperialism is the highest stage of capitalism [M] // *Selected works of Lenin: Volume 2*. Beijing: People's Publishing House, 2012: p. 588.

'Monopoly can maintain itself only by continuously engaging in competition'.[49]

The contradiction between effective competition and moderate monopoly manifests itself in the conduct of monopolistic enterprises when they abuse their positions for monopoly profits. As a result, effective competition in the market is damaged and weakened. In the historical development of the modern market economy, monopolistic conduct, such as monopoly agreements and the abuse of dominant market positions has largely destroyed the fairness of market competition rules, and also redistributed social wealth to the benefit of monopolistic enterprises. This has resulted in a serious polarisation between rich and poor. In major economies worldwide, such monopolistic conduct needs to be limited and restrained.

To deal properly with the relationship between effective competition and moderate monopoly in the creation of a modern market system, China needs to maintain the fairness of market competition rules, and to comprehensively promote the construction of a unified and open market system with orderly competition. One necessary step is to improve the market supervision system so as to achieve fair and orderly competition between major market players in fields other than those on the negative list for market access, while safeguarding the legitimate interests of these market players, including of monopolistic enterprises. A further step involves proactively developing legislative and juridical practices aimed at curbing illegitimate monopolies. Monopolistic conduct that hampers competition or aids in the appropriation of monopoly profits needs to be scientifically, accurately, and effectively restricted or eliminated. For the modernised economy of socialism with Chinese characteristics, a combination of government capital with larger, stronger, and better state-owned enterprises is required. These should make up a category of modern monopolies that operate in an effective competition pattern, complementing other enterprises under different forms of ownership.

(III) Urban and Rural Regional: Dealing Properly with the Relationship between Coordinated Development and Self-Development

At the urban and rural regional levels, China needs to promote high-quality development by developing a modernised economy.

---

49. Marx, Engels. *Selected Works of Marx and Engels: Volume 1* [M]. 3 ed. Beijing: People's Publishing House, 2012: 256.

In building urban and rural regional development systems that utilise their particular advantages and coordinate their activity, China will focus our attention on managing the relationship between coordinated development and self-development, with the aim of promoting the coordinated development of urban and rural regional regions and developing an efficient, organically integrated economy.

In China's urban and rural regional development, the relationship between coordinated development and self-development is dialectical in nature, its elements both opposite and unified. The unity between coordinated development and self-development is reflected mainly in the intrinsic consistency between respective developments and the overall coordinated development of urban and rural regions. The respective developments of urban and rural regions themselves are important subsystems for the overall development of urban and rural regions. Examining the coordinated development of urban and rural regions, there is a strong case for utilising the overall advantages and synergies of urban and rural regions. Through this, the subsystems of urban and rural regions also achieve better development. At the same time, the overall advantages and synergies of urban and rural regions can reach a high level only if the advantages of each subsystem of the urban and rural regions are fully exploited.

The contradiction between the coordinated development of urban and rural areas and regions and their own self-development is reflected mainly in the likelihood that the one-sided pursuit of its own development by each subsystem of the urban and rural regions will lead to a range of externalities such as environmental damage, excessive resource development, and an irrational economic space layout. The result is likely to be a failure to realise the full benefits of the overall advantages and synergies of urban and rural regions. These conditions limit overall efficiency to a low level. In constructing the modern urban and rural regional system, China should seek to optimise the relationship between coordinated development and self-development by proactively promoting the positive interaction and integrated development of various subsystems in urban and rural regions under a scientific top-level design and a systematic overall plan. At the regional level, it is necessary to coordinate the economic development strategies of various regions from an overall perspective, and to systematically promote the organic integration of regional economic development strategies through methods such as the construction of inter-regional infrastructure network systems, the connecting of economic management systems, the collabourative protection of the environment, and the overall planning of regional opening-up strategies. At the urban and rural level, it is necessary to promote the integration of urban and rural development with the strategy of rural revitalisation. This requires the interconnection and integration of modern infrastructure network systems between urban and rural areas to eliminate the major differences in basic public services. These services include compulsory education, medical care, and elderly care. Education programs coordinated between urban and rural areas need to be employed to improve agricultural skills and to train rural migrant workers. China will continue to improve mechanisms, institutions, and policy systems for the integration of urban and rural development in many areas, such as the organic integration of urban and rural culture.

(IV) The Green Development System: Coping Properly with the Relationship between Humanity and Nature in Economic Development

At the level of green development, in order to promote high-quality development by building modern economic systems, China should focus on the construction of a resource saving and environmentally friendly green development system and fashioning an appropriate relationship between humanity and nature in the field of economic development. In this way, China could also *realise recycling, low-carbon, green development, as well as harmony between nature and the human population.*

Throughout the history of economic development, the relationship between humanity and nature has been a dialectical relationship that is both opposite and unified. The unity of humanity and nature in economic development represents the principal aspect of the contradiction, an aspect reflected mainly in *the formation by humanity and nature of a community of life.* Originating in nature, human beings belong to nature, rely on nature, and are a product of the long-term development of nature. Since the birth of our species, human beings have always been among the living organisms that are part of nature, and can only survive and develop by relying on natural resources. One aspect of this is that human economic activities require a continuous supply of resources obtained either directly or indirectly from nature. Another aspect is that as humans create the means of their material subsistence, natural resources have continuously entered the field of material production as labour objects and labour tools. They have thus become *inorganic bodies* of humankind.

The contradiction between humanity and nature in economic development is mainly reflected in the fact that under certain conditions of productivity, human economic activities are limited by nature. The natural resources available for human economic activities are finite and exist within a certain timeframe and geographical area. When human beings overexploit these resources, the related economic development will be unsustainable due to resource depletion. Because the ecological carrying capacity of nature to human economic activities is very limited for a certain period of time and geographical area, if human economic activities unilaterally pursue the economic benefits of microcosmic subjects beyond the ecological carrying capacity of nature, such activities will inevitably damage the resilience and stability of the ecological environment. Accordingly, nature will retaliate against the entire human species. As President Xi Jinping has pointed out, 'Any harm we inflict on nature will eventually return to haunt us'.[50]

To properly manage the relationship between humanity and nature when constructing a system of green economic development, China must always follow the laws of nature, population, and economics and systematically promote harmony between humanity and nature. The aim should be to realise a virtuous circle of sustainable development in the areas of population, resources, and the environment. The formulation of population policies should not be based solely on the fertility rate, but also on the supply and demand for labour in society. The total newborn population figures in 2013, 2014, 2015, 2016, and 2017 were 6.68 million, 7.1 million, 6.8 million, 8.09 million, and 7.37 million, respectively. China's total labour supply has exceeded demand, as reflected in the country's unemployment statistics. Each year, the addition to the population is about 7 million people. Therefore, even if the total fertility rate is low, an unfettered birth rate should not be encouraged. Otherwise, it will be difficult to achieve efficient use of resources, a high-quality living environment, or improvements in the realisation of people's human potential. At the conceptual level it is necessary to firmly establish, throughout the whole of society, the green development concept that *clear waters and lush mountains are invaluable assets*. Understanding of green life concepts, of green production concepts, and of job performance in the area of green development can be systematically strengthened through scientific, accurate, and comprehensive training and education, and through lobbying of various groups. At the scientific

---

50. Winning to build a moderately prosperous society across the board and seizing the great victory of socialism with Chinese characteristics in the new era - Report at the 19th National Congress of the Communist Party of China [N]. *People's Daily*, 2017-10-28 (1)

http://www.gov.cn/zhuanti/2017-10/27/content_5234876.htm

and technological level, it is necessary to systematically promote green technological innovation and apply the latest achievements of green technology to various links such as green production, green consumption, ecological governance, and ecological monitoring, in order to build a government-led, enterprise-dominated, and market-determined green technological innovation system. At the institutional level, China must promote the improvement and implementation of the green development system in areas such as the laws and regulations of green development and the governance performance appraisal system for green development.

(V) The Open System: Properly Handling the Relationship between the Comprehensive Reciprocal Opening up of China, Economic Security, and People's Wellbeing

To achieve China's opening up, China needs to promote high-quality development by building a modernised economy. Centring on the construction of a diversified, balanced, secure, and efficient comprehensive opening-up system, it is necessary to focus on handling the relationship between a comprehensive reciprocal opening up of China, economic security, and people's welfare. *The Chinese will improve the structure of China's economy, expand its scope, and increase its returns if they can develop an open economy with higher standards.*

In the contemporary development of the world economy, the relationship between economic security, popular welfare and China's comprehensive, reciprocal opening up is a dialectical relationship that is both opposite and unified. China's comprehensive reciprocal opening up refers to the one that features equal status between an economy and other economies in terms of extent and scope. The dialectical unity between economic security, the people's welfare, and China's comprehensive, reciprocal opening up is reflected in the fact that when an economy's comprehensive reciprocal opening up meets the objective requirements of its own economic security and the improvement of the people's welfare, the two issues manifest themselves as a co-directional interaction. On the one hand, China's comprehensive, reciprocal opening up, in line with the actual economic development of the economy, can improve the innovation and competitiveness of its own economic system, thereby enhancing its ability to ensure economic security and improving people's welfare. On the other hand, the economic security assurance and the improvement of people's welfare can improve the quality and sustainability of the comprehensive, reciprocal opening up of China.

The contradiction between economic security, the people's welfare, and China's comprehensive, reciprocal opening up lies in the fact that when the opening of an economy fails to meet the objective requirements of the country's own economic security and the improvement of its people's welfare, the two issues manifest themselves as a reverse interaction. If an economy's economic openness to other economies reflects its equal status in terms of the extent and scope of the opening, but fails to meet the objective requirements of its own economic security and of the improvement of its own people's welfare, the economic risks to that economy are higher, and the capability of innovation and competitiveness of its own economic system is weaker with a greater extent and wider scope. Accordingly, the reduction in the welfare of the people will be larger.

In order to properly handle the relationship between comprehensive reciprocal opening up, economic security, and the welfare of the people as the opening-up system is constructed, China needs to eliminate the mindless act of *opening for the sake of opening*. Instead, it should seek to improve the security coefficient of its own opening up, and to proactively increase the welfare of the people while expanding the opening up of China. To open the real economy effectively, it is necessary to comprehensively implement an innovation-driven development strategy centred on independent innovation with Chinese characteristics, in a bid to enhance the country's own independent innovation capability for opening up China and for cooperation with other nations.

In the area of financial opening up, efforts should be made to improve control over the financial system and to enhance its international competitiveness while ensuring financial security. China should learn from the administrative systems and actual operating experience of the USA and other developed countries; for example, they should place reasonable limits and conditions on the percentage of shares owned by foreign financial capital in commercial financial institutions in China, limit the conditions for establishing business affiliates and the scope of their operations, take reasonable steps to determine the degree to which capital items are opened up, and the speed of this opening, and impose other measures to ensure financial security. Conversely, they should adopt the orientation of service that features strengthening the country through trade and innovating new forms of foreign trade, optimise foreign loan structures, scientifically determine the appropriate scale of diversified foreign exchange reserves, and progressively explore ways to create a scientific, rational, and safe foreign exchange formation mechanism.

Where international economic governance is concerned, they should adhere to the principles of mutual negotiation, construction, and sharing. It is necessary to take part proactively in revising and making international economic rules that are fair, unbiased, inclusive, and orderly.

(VI) The Economic Regulation System: Proper Handling of the Relationship between Market Determination and Government Guidance

In the area of economic regulation, China will promote high-quality development by creating a modernised economy. Focusing on the construction of an economic regulation system that utilises the functions of the market and employs government functions more effectively, it is necessary to properly handle the relationship between market determination based on the law of value and government guidance based on national regulation.

In our economic regulation system, the relationship between market determination and government guidance is dialectical, and thus both opposite and unified. The functions of the market and government are unified in that they are forms of the realisation of the law of proportion in the socialist market economy. According to the law of proportion, total social labour represented as persons, properties, and materials is distributed proportionally to all links of social production and areas of the national economy according to the structure and quantity of social demand. The results of social production maintain a comprehensive dynamic balance with social demand in the use value structure. In terms of the overall national economy, multiple industrial and economic structures should maintain an overall balance. In our socialist market economy, market regulation and government regulation can be organically integrated through the positive complementarity of function and effective synergy; the joint effect of market and government regulation is to realise the proportional and high-quality development of the national economy.

The contradiction between market determination and government guidance lies in the incongruity of their function mechanisms of economic regulation. Based on the law of value, the market spontaneously regulates the distribution of resources in every link of social production and every area of the national economy, with the aim of realising the short term and local interests of market entities. In the local, short term configuration of common resources, therefore, market regulation can effectively perform the function of resource distribution. But considering the disadvantages of market regulation, e.g., errors in the regulation targets (difficulty in realising full employment, stable goods' prices, a continuously stable economy, balanced international payments, and other economic development targets), and also its relatively slow speed, high cost, limited range of regulation, etc., market determination often fails in the long term configuration and global configuration of some important and special resources. In contrast, the government can realise long term and overall benefits in such areas through extensive democratic negotiations and decision mechanisms, active planning, and configuration of important economic resources, so as to promptly eliminate the negative impact caused by market failures before, during, and after the process.

In constructing a modern economic regulation system, China must correctly handle the relationship between market determination and government guidance; that is, they must organically combine market determination in the allocation of common economic resources with government guidance in the allocation of important economic resources, establishing an economic regulation system with sound functional complements, synergy in its effects, and incongruity in its mechanisms. As Xi Jinping has noted, 'The market plays the decisive role in resource allocation, but not for all of the functions'.[51] It is necessary to establish overall guidelines for regulating functions that are *not fully determined by the market*, while fully utilising the decisive regulation of the market in the short term and harnessing local market regulation of common resources. The government should activate the vitality of various market entities through streamlined administration and institutional decentralisation. In case of market failures due to regulation, it will be necessary to utilise every advantage of the guiding role of the government, participating in the allocation of public products, geological resources, and other special inputs. It will be necessary to actively plan and guide the long-term allocation of various common resources, such as education, health care, cultural amenities, and urban housing, as well as a range of uncommon physical resources. Proper planning and guidance of wealth and income redistribution will also be necessary.

---

51   Xi Jinping. Note on the Decision of the CPC Central Committee on Several Major Issues of Comprehensively Deepening Reform [N]. *People's Daily*, 2013-11-16.

http://cpc.people.com.cn/xuexi/n/2015/0720/c397563-27331312.html

(VII) The Property Rights System: Dealing Properly with the Relationship between the Dominant Public Economy and the Auxiliary Non-public Economy

In the area of property rights, it is necessary to promote high-quality development by constructing a modernised economy and maintaining and improving the property rights system in which the public economy is dominant. The state-owned economy must take the lead, and economic entities of diverse ownership should develop together. The relationship between the dominant public economy and the auxiliary non-public economy must be properly managed. These steps will lay the foundation of a solid basic economic system, improving the comprehensive competitiveness of our economic system.

In China's socialist market economy, the relationship between the dominant public economy and the auxiliary non-public economy presents itself as a dialectical relationship, which is opposite and unified. The unity in this case is reflected in the mutual development and win-win cooperation of both elements during the primary stage of socialism in China. In China's economic system, with its socialist character, the public and non-public economies form a development community with both sectors complementing each other. As President Xi Jinping has noted, 'The public and non-public economies are complementary and mutually beneficial, instead of mutually repelling or cancelling each other'.[52] The public and non-public economies both represent ownership forms appropriate to the productivity level of the primary stage of socialism in China. This condition allows for fair competition between them, except for those outside the scientifically developed negative list for market access. It also permits a focus on the development of varied forms of mixed ownership, with public capital as the controlling shareholder.

The contradiction between the dominant public economy and the auxiliary non-public economy is reflected in their significantly different status in the national economy and is stipulated in the *Constitution*. As Xi Jinping has stated' 'The public economy has made outstanding contributions to national construction, defence security, and the improvement of people's lives, so it is a precious treasure of all the people'.[47] In important fields that concern national development and people's livelihoods, the public economy plays the decisive role. The majority of the Chinese enterprises listed in the Fortune Global 500 are state-owned enterprises. In special fields such as national security that are on the negative list for market access,

---

52. Ibid

the public economy has also made strategic contributions to national security. The public economy also establishes a solid foundation for the common prosperity of the people by providing materials and developing the economic system, that is by eliminating the systemic basis of exploitation through implementing distribution according to work; ensuring a reasonable ratio between accumulation and consumption, and increasing the proportion represented by labour remuneration in primary distribution. As it is controlled by the law of private surplus value, the distribution according to capital that applies in the non-public economy embodies the tendency to income disparity, which undermines the common prosperity of the people and the stable operation of the national economy. In addition, the dominant role of public ownership provides a larger systemic space and creates a stronger interrelated power for coordinating the relationship between the government and the market, thus allowing the government to play a more effective role. Accordingly, the *Constitution* of China identifies the public economy as the mainstay of the primary stage of socialism in China. The state-owned economy, i.e., the socialist economy under the ownership of all the people, plays the leading role in the national economy, while the non-public economy plays an auxiliary role.

In constructing a modern property rights system, China must correctly handle the relationship between the public economy as the dominant player and the non-public economy as the auxiliary player; that is China must establish and improve a property rights system in which public ownership is dominant, state ownership takes the lead, and diverse forms of ownership develop together, realising the organic unity of the public and non-public economies. In the area of rural collective ownership, China needs to adjust and intensify the reform of the rural collective ownership system, and continuously improve the rural collective economy and the rural collabourative economy. China must improve the innovative capability and competitiveness of enterprises, and establish an innovative community in which large state-owned, private, small, and medium-sized enterprises support and cooperate with each other. It is very important to strengthen the competitive advantage represented by intellectual property rights, orientated toward controlling core technologies and famous brands. The goal is to develop these firms as world-leading competitive enterprises, and to prioritise the mixed ownership economy controlled by public capital. This will be accomplished through win-win cooperation aimed at constructing a community of development and innovation for domestic enterprises, featuring encouragement, support and guidance for private enterprises. This will apply especially to development and innovation by small and medium-sized enterprises, so as to promote benefit-sharing mechanisms for shareholding employees of private firms. It will establish a reward and penalty mechanism of integrity management to standardise and motivate the orderly vitality and creativity of the non-public sectors of the economy.

(VIII) The Distribution System: Dealing Correctly with the Relationship between Major Distribution According to Work and Auxiliary Distribution According to Capital

Within the distribution system, it is necessary to promote high-quality development by utilising a modernised economy. Focusing on the creation of a distribution system that reflects efficiency and promotes fairness, China must correctly manage the relationship between the major distribution according to work and the auxiliary distribution according to capital. This should be aimed at better promoting the rational distribution of wealth and income, at safeguarding social equality and justice, and at laying a solid foundation for a distribution system that provides for the common prosperity of the people.

In China's socialist market economy, the relationship between the major distribution system according to work and the auxiliary distribution system according to capital is a dialectical relationship, both opposite and unified. The unification lies in the fact that both are forms for realising distribution efficiency. Utilising distribution according to work, China can achieve both short-term and long-term efficiency of distribution. As the basic form of distribution in the public economy, the principle of distribution according to work takes the workload of employees in production or business as the basic criterion of distribution. It is able to reflect adequately the differing exertions of workers in the process of production or business, and to realise short-term efficiencies by promoting the motivation of workers through distribution. Alternatively, it helps labour remuneration maintain its predominant share in primary distribution, and as it seeks to achieve long-term distribution efficiency, fundamentally relieving the conflict between the unlimited expansion of production and decreasing effective demand. In a narrow sense, distribution by factors and property rights can be defined as distribution according to capital (not including the labour factor); that is cash, real property, technology, information, knowledge, and other elements are converted and quantified into certain amounts of capital or shares, and the share of capital contributed by a capital owner in a production or business entity is taken as the basic criterion for distribution of surplus value and of the profits or earnings derived from it. In a broad sense, distribution according to factors and property rights include labour as the most important main factor, and the worker's input to production or business is taken as the basic criterion for distributing compensation. This can reflect more accurately the difference made by labour in production or business.

The contradiction between major distribution according to work and auxiliary distribution according to capital appears in the fundamental difference seen in the realisation of fair distribution. By maintaining a larger share of labour remuneration in primary distribution, market distribution according to work for the public sector of the economy can better reflect the material contributions of workers in production and other operations, and thereby achieve equity of distribution in a better way. The law of private surplus value means distribution according to capital, so that private surplus value maintains the predominant share in primary distribution, where these conditions apply. In such a case of distribution according to capital, the predominant share of labour remuneration present in the public sector, cannot be realised. From the point of view of a dynamic state, distribution according to capital tends to widen the income distribution gap between capital owner and worker, so that equity of distribution cannot be achieved.

In constructing a modern distribution system that correctly handles the relationship between major distribution according to work and auxiliary distribution according to capital, China must perfect a basic system in which distribution according to work is the major form that coexists with other forms. This strategy will help them to achieve a harmonious and uniform fairness and efficiency in distribution. First, publicly owned production organisations (including public holding production organisations) need to insist on and improve the principles underlying distribution according to work. They should determine, on an appropriate basis, the general accumulation-consumption ratio required to maintain a predominant share of labour remuneration in primary distribution. Organisations should also consider, scientifically and in full measure, the different labour contributions made by workers, especially contributions that take the form of scientific research, management, and highly skilled production work. Second, the organisations should insist on, and steadily improve, a system of distribution according to factors and property rights. The rational property rights and interests of domestic and foreign enterprise investors should be protected under the law. Meanwhile, organisations should provide legal protection for the right of workers in domestic and foreign-owned private enterprises (including private holding enterprises) to enjoy reasonable remuneration and labour welfare. Finally, organisations need to insist on, and steadily perfect, a state system for the redistribution and adjustment of wealth and income. The government should continuously expand fair social security provisions that guarantee the bottom line of human development. Simultaneously, the government should improve taxation and other systems to adjust excessively high-income flow and wealth, while making adjustments to the social security and transfer payment systems so as to increase the incomes of low-income groups. It should also make adjustments to the legal system to ban unlawful incomes.

(Originally published in *Academic Research*, Issue 12, 2018. Lead Author: Gao Jiankun)

Chapter 2

China's Economy under the New Normal

China's economy has entered a 'new normal'. This is a necessary process if the economy is to evolve into a more advanced form, with a more optimised division of labour and a more balanced structure. To maintain rapid economic growth within this new normal, China must rely on reform.

* * *

Section I Value Orientation in China's New Economic Normal

1. The Connotations and Basic Characteristics of the New Normal of China's Economy

In China's economy, the term 'new normal' is used to describe the steady development trend that has emerged in recent years. The Central Economic Working Conference held in December 2014[53] pointed out that this developmental trend has the following four substantive characteristics:

First, the Chinese economy is shifting gears from high-speed to medium-to-high speed growth. Between 2002 and 2011, China's GDP maintained a growth rate above 9%. In six of those years, GDP growth was above 10%, with 2007 witnessing the highest growth at 14.2%. Since 2012, however, GDP growth has remained below 8%; the GDP growth rates for the first three quarters of 2014 were 7.4%, 7.5%, and 7.3%, respectively.

Second, China has shifted its economic growth from an extensive model that emphasised scale and speed to a more intensive one

---

53. https://news.12371.cn/2014/12/11/ARTI1418295777211338.shtml

emphasing quality and efficiency. In the first three quarters of 2014, energy consumption per unit of GDP decreased by 4.6% year-to-year (hereafter y-t-y).

Third, the economic structure has shifted from quantitative increase and capacity expansion to an in-depth adjustment that involves both stock adjustments and optimised increments. Importantly, the industrial structure is creating new breakthroughs. In 2013, the proportion in GDP of value added by tertiary industries surpassed that of secondary industries for the first time. In the first three quarters of 2014, the proportion in GDP of value added by tertiary industries was 46.7%. This represented an increase of 1.2 percentage points over the same period in 2013, some 2.5 percentage points higher than the corresponding figure for secondary industries. In addition, the demand structure has presented positive new changes. In the first three quarters of 2014, final consumption expenditure contributed 48.5% of GDP growth; this was 2.7 percentage points higher than in the same period of 2013, and about 7 percentage points higher than the growth rate of total capital formation. Moreover, the income distribution structure has improved. In the first three quarters of 2014, the per capita cash income of rural residents actually increased at a greater rate than the per capita disposable income of urban residents by 2.8 percentage points. Compared to rural residents, the difference-in-differences (or *DID*) per capita income of urban residents in the first three quarters of 2014 was 2.59 times lower, and 0.05 points lower, than in the same period of 2013. Finally, the regional structure has improved. Also in the first three quarters of 2014, the year-on-year growth rates of investment in the eastern, central, and western regions were 14.9%, 17.8%, and 17.9%, respectively. In the same regions, the year-on-year growth rates of industrial added value (for enterprises above the designated size) were 8.0%, 8.5%, and 10.6%.

Fourth, the driving force of China's economic growth has been shifting from input and investment to innovation. Overall, the economy showed a trend towards mid-to-high end industries, while emerging industries, new formats, and new products have maintained rapid growth rates. In the first three quarters of 2014, high-tech industries and the equipment manufacturing industry have shown growth rates of 12.3% and 11.1%, significantly higher than the industrial average.

In order to adapt to the new normal economy, China's economic development needs to be guided by a correct value orientation. The new normal economy has not only found new opportunities, with considerable economic growth, continuous optimising and upgrading of the economic structure, diversification of economic drivers, and an outpouring of market vitality, but it also faces potential risks and challenges, such as slowing economic growth, a larger gap between rich and poor, greater eco-environmental stress, increasing foreign control over investment, and a scaling-up in the proportion represented by the non-public economy. Only with the guidance of a correct value orientation can China seize new opportunities and overcome these risks and challenges. A correct value orientation makes it possible to adapt economic development to the conditions of the new normal. It includes a scientific development orientation that adheres to the laws of the economy, a sustainable development orientation that abides by the rules of nature, and an inclusiveness development orientation that follows the laws of society.

2. The Scientific Development Orientation That Follows Economic Laws

(I) Major Economic Laws to Be Followed in a Socialist Market Economy

The objective law of development to be followed by the socialist market economy is a system of economic laws. These include the laws of proportional development, value, surplus value, and state regulations.

1. The Law of Proportional Development

The law of proportional development (distribution of social labour in proportion) refers to the law of paradoxical movements between production and demand. What this law signifies is that in the course of the paradoxical movements between production and demand, various outputs and requirements need to maintain a dynamic and comprehensive balance within the value-in-use structure, so as to achieve maximum production results with minimum labour consumption under given conditions. Marx pointed out that 'To obtain the quantity of products that meets various needs, it is necessary to input various [types of] and a certain amount of total social labour'.[54]

The law of proportional development is a universal law that has applied to the allocation of resources in the production of human materials throughout all historical stages. Marx pointed out that 'No matter whether commodity exchange is used as a medium, the

---

54. Marx, Engels. *The Complete Works of Marx and Engels* [M]. Beijing: People's Publishing House, 1972: 541.

division of labour within a society is common to all socio-economic forms'.[55] In China's socialist market economy, the law of proportional development manifests itself in the combining of division of labour within an organised production unit with a planned and managed social division of labour.

The law of proportional development operates through organic integration with the law of market regulation (or the law of value) and the law of state regulation (or the law of planning).

2. The Law of Value

The law of value signifies that the value of a commodity is determined by the socially necessary labour time required for producing the commodity, and the exchange of commodities is carried out according to the principle of equal value. In a commodity economy, the law of value is actualised by the law of proportionality through the spontaneous fluctuations of exchange value (value form) caused by competition.

The law of value equates to the realisation of the law of proportional development at the stage of the commodity economy. In other words, it is the general law that governs resource allocation in a commodity economy. At the simple commodity economy stage, since the exchange value is only expressed as the remainder of the use value created by the producer for the purpose of survival, the law of value does not yet dominate the allocation of resources. At the stage of a more socialised commodity economy, the law of value plays a decisive role in the allocation of resources, because the exchange value gains a dominant position.

The functional strength of the law of market regulation (or the law of value) is mainly reflected in the following areas: short-term micro-allocation of general resources, auxiliary allocation of non-material resources such as education and culture, and spontaneous regulation of wealth and income distribution. The functional strengths include short-term resource allocation, micro-equilibrium, and signal transmission, etc. In the areas mentioned above, the market realises the short-term and local interests of market players through the spontaneous functioning of the *law of value*. In these areas, there is an equally competitive relationship between market players, including commodity suppliers and consumers. They act, based on the value of commodities, and follow the principle

---

55. Marx, Engels. *The Complete Works of Marx and Engels* [M]. Beijing: People's Publishing House, 397-398.

of equivalent exchange. Through market mechanisms, such as competition mechanisms, price mechanisms, and supply-demand mechanisms, allocations of resources among market players are achieved.

In the allocating of resources, the law of market regulation (or the law of value) also has its weaknesses. First, the market regulates the interests of commodity producers through its local interest-driven functions in a competitive system. Its weakness, however, is that it deviates from the overall interests of society. In one sense, regulation through the market leads to a growing income disparity among producers; commodity producers that have continuous competitive advantages are able to continuously expand their scale of production due to their high profits; while commodity producers that have continuous competitive disadvantages have to decrease their output or even withdraw from production due to their low profits, lack of profits, or losses. In another sense, market regulation channels commodity producers into aiming merely to maximise their own local interests while ignoring the overall interests of society. The issues at stake here include problems with environmental protection, cultural protection, and public health. The commodity producers are especially reluctant to invest in non-profit or low-profit sectors such as education, health, and basic research. This situation creates a downward spiral of negative externalities. At the same time, the market's technology innovation function, through the mechanisms of competition, stimulates commodity producers to improve their technology and management. This function also has a weakness: it may hinder technological progress. Producers of commodities that have gained a monopoly on technology are likely to impede the proper dissemination and use of technologies in society. Obviously, this is done in order for them to maintain their own technological advantages.

3. The Law of Surplus Value

The law of surplus value can be thought of as expressing the direct goal of investors in the production of commodities within the market economy to extract as much surplus value as possible through expanding the appropriation of surplus labour. The law of surplus value is the universal law of motion in capitalism and in a more controlled way in the market operations of socialist commodity economies in the primary stage of socialism.

In a capitalist private ownership economy, the law of surplus value manifests itself as the law of private surplus value. Capitalist ownership of the means of production means that the surplus value created by the workers employed by private capital will be appropriated by private capitalists. In order to extract as much surplus value as possible, private capital owners continue to convert surplus value into capital, increasing the scale of capital accumulation and production. The accumulation of private capital exacerbates the functional weaknesses of market regulation, which has the law of value at its core. Meanwhile, the relative labour surplus created by the accumulation of private capital through a continuous increase in the organic composition of capital has made high unemployment a normal feature of capitalism. Accumulated private capital has thus led to a deepening polarisation of society: at one pole is the accumulation of wealth in the hands of a few private capital owners, and at the other pole is the accumulation of poverty, toil, slavery, ignorance, barbarism and moral depravity among the proletariat engaged in the production of surplus value. In a market economy based on capitalist private ownership, the combined effects of market regulation laws, such as the law of value and the law of private surplus value, have led to periodic outbreaks of economic crises, which result in a huge waste of social resources.

In a socialist economy with public ownership, the law of surplus value is embedded in the law of public surplus value. Socialist public ownership of the means of production determines that the surplus value created by workers in public enterprises belongs either to the state or to the collective. Part of this surplus value is turned over to the state as profits and taxes, and the rest is converted into capital advances, which constitutes the source of overall and long-term benefits for workers. As for the allocation method of the publicly owned economy (that is, one owned by the entire people) total income can be divided into three components: state property income, accumulation, and labour compensation (consumption). Total income in a collective economy under sole proprietorship can be divided into accumulation and consumption (including labour compensation and labour share returns). Distribution in such an economy is in the form of mutual shareholding and cross-shareholding among different types of ownership held by public capital; the aggregate product can be divided into three parts in terms of distribution: share income (including public share income and private share income), accumulation, and labour remuneration. The accumulation of capital in a socialist economy with public ownership thus lays the foundation for eliminating exploitation and polarisation, thus achieving common prosperity for all workers.

4. The Law of State Regulation

The implications of the law of state regulation are that the state employs economic, legal, administrative, persuasive, and other mechanisms of state power, follows objective laws concerning the development of large-scale social production, and formulates in advance a general plan for social production in line with the specific operating conditions and development trends of the society concerned. The state also regulates the distribution of total social labour in the various production sectors in a proper scientific way.

The law of state regulation is a way of realising proportionality in the production of socialised commodities regulated by the state. Marx pointed out that in a society based on co-production, 'Society must rationally allocate its time to achieve production that meets all the needs of society. Therefore, savings on time and labour time planning among different production departments remain the primary economic law on the basis of co-production.'.[56] Under state monopoly capitalism and at the initial stage of socialism, due to the continued existence of the state, it is the responsibility of the government to complete the overall planning and comprehensive regulation of social production.

The functional strengths of the law of state regulation are mainly reflected in the following areas: macro-control and micro-regulation of the short-term allocation of general resources, direct allocation of special resources such as geological resources, long-term allocation of many general resources, dominant allocation of non-material resources such as education and culture, and planning and regulation of wealth and income distribution. The functional strengths of the law of state regulation mainly include macro checks and balances, structure coordination, competition protection, benefit optimisation, and income redistribution. In these areas, the state achieves long-term and overall benefits through active planning and the allocation of resources by professionally functional organisations.

In practice, these functions show weaknesses such as subjective preferences in regulation, sluggish transition between regulations, internal friction over regulation policies, and a lack of regulation impetus. A subjective preference in regulation means that adjustment behavior deviates from the objective laws of economic development, and a sluggish transition between regulations means

---

56. Marx, Engels. *The Complete Works of Marx and Engels: Volume 46* [M]. Beijing: People's Publishing House, 1972: 120.

that the regulatory agency fails to respond to a new situation by adjusting the direction and intensity of regulation in a timely manner, due to factors such as a lack of reliable information, complex decision-making procedures, long decision-making time, and excessive decision-making costs. Internal friction over regulation policies means that the functions of each policy counteract each other, due to a lack of coordination between the various policies within the adjusted policy system and a lack of regulation impetus. That is, state employees performing regulatory functions may be reluctant to implement conscious and effective regulation in response to changes in the economic situation, based on the narrow interests of individuals, their own region, their own sector, or their own class.

(II) Scientific Developmental Orientation under the New Economic Normal

In the situation of the new economic normal, scientific development orientation means that economic development must follow the objective developmental laws of the socialist market economy. This orientation requires that China's economic development under the new normal must, on the premise of adhering to the socialist basic economic system with Chinese characteristics, act effectively to combine the decisive role of the market in the general allocation of resources with the government's guiding (or leading) role in the allocation of key resources.

1. Adhere to the Basic Economic System of Socialism with Chinese Characteristics

The core of the socialist basic economic system with Chinese characteristics is that public ownership is the mainstay while economic entities of diverse ownership develop together. This system serves as the cornerstone for achieving development in a scientific way within the context of the new normal.

(1) Adhere to Public Ownership as the Mainstay

At the current stage of China's economy, the broadly defined publicly owned sector includes the forms of sole proprietorship, owned by all the people, and collective ownership, as well as the form of mutual shareholding and cross-shareholding between different forms of ownership held by public capital.

Under the new normal, the cornerstone of the public sector economy is the fundamental guarantee of scientific development of the economy.

First, within primary distribution, public-owned enterprises ensure that the economy runs smoothly by taking measures to narrow the gap between rich and poor. Publicly owned enterprises ensure that labour remuneration is at a reasonable proportion in the initial distribution by determining an appropriate ratio between profit, accumulation, and labour remuneration, and by promoting increases in labour remuneration in line with rises in labour productivity. At the same time, publicly owned enterprises need to improve specific income distribution mechanisms so as to reduce the irrationality of the pay gap between workers and to promote a more relative equality (common prosperity) in primary distribution. The dominant position of the public sector in the overall national economy has fundamentally eased the contradiction between the unlimited expansion of production and a shrinking level of effective demand. It thus prevents the periodic outbreak of economic crises and ensures the healthy and stable development of the economy.

Second, public enterprises provide the necessary guarantees and financial supports for the state to correct functional weaknesses that may exist in the law of value and law of market regulation. Unlike private enterprises or private monopolies that implement non-state regulation, publicly owned enterprises are willing to obey and cooperate with the state's overall economic regulations and control of the economy. Further, the publicly owned sector is one of the most important sources of capital that the state requires if it is to regulate the economy by smoothing out economic fluctuations. Since the reform, the profits and taxes paid by China's state-owned sector have always made up a considerable portion of national fiscal revenue. In the first three quarters of 2014, the total taxes paid by central enterprises totaled 1.5 trillion yuan, representing a year-on-year increase of 5.6%. The total profits of these enterprises reached 1.1 trillion yuan, up year-on-year by 6.6%.

Third, the publicly owned sector fills various gaps in the investment fields of other ownership systems, helping to solve problems that emerge in the laws of value and the laws of market regulation and promoting the balanced development of the economy in a universal way. Generally, the law of value (or the law of market regulation) plays an effective role in areas of the economy that are characterised by a short capital recovery period, low risks, and high profit margins (generally higher than the average profit margin in the short term). In these areas, fair competition can be ensured between the publicly owned sector and other economic sectors. The following areas, however, are under exclusive public ownership: (1) areas that are essential to the national economy and people's livelihoods and (2) areas that are not suited to other forms of ownership because of their long cycles of capital recovery, high risks, or low profit margins (even lower than average profit margins), or because of national security considerations. Publicly owned enterprises run these industries, not for the maximisation of profits but for the maximisation of social benefits.

(2) Adhere to the Common Development of Multiple Ownership Economies under the Premise of Public Ownership as the Mainstay

The common development of multiple ownership sectors under the premise of public ownership as the mainstay is an important aspect of the basic economic system of socialism with Chinese characteristics and is also an important embodiment of the scientific development of the economy under the conditions of the new normal.

To begin with, the common development of multiple ownership sectors under the premise of public ownership as the mainstay can stimulate market vitality in the current new normal situation. The economic fields in which multiple ownership sectors compete on an equal footing are mainly those in which the law of value (or the law of market regulation) can function effectively, that is, fields in which the cycles of capital recovery are shorter, risks are lower, and profit rates are higher (generally higher than the average profit in the short term). In these areas, publicly owned production units engage in fair commercial competition with production units of other types of ownership, thereby stimulating market vitality.

Next, an economy in which public ownership is the mainstay, and multiple ownership sectors develop together can effectively alleviate sharp fluctuations in economic development, since it can reduce the negative effects of the law of private surplus value. In a sector dominated by self-employed individuals there is generally no serious polarisation between rich and poor workers, despite differences in the quantity and quality of labour that the workers contribute to production. But in a Chinese-funded or foreign-owned area of the private sector that features a capital-based employment relationship, the law of private surplus value occupies a dominant position in the initial distribution, since for an owner of capital the fundamental goal of production is to appropriate as much surplus value as possible; meanwhile, the role played by the law of private surplus value creates the risk of severe economic fluctuations. During the process of capital accumulation, the law of private surplus value has in one sense widened the gap between capital owners and workers, thus exacerbating the contradiction between the unlimited expansion of production and a shrinking level of effective demand. Conversely, tax evasion is a serious problem within the non-public sector, weakening the financial base available to the country for improving people's livelihoods, correcting the law of value, and repairing other functional weaknesses in market regulation laws. Nevertheless, competition and cooperation between the public and non-public sectors can effectively curb the negative effects of the law of private surplus value. One view is that the principle of distribution according to work, as applying to initial distribution within a public ownership economy, serves as a model for distribution in the context of non-public ownership. Still another view is that in a mixed-ownership economy under the control of public capital, the effective participation of public shareholders in business operations can prevent tax evasion by their private counterparts.

In the current process of developing mixed ownership, adhering to and consolidating a basic economic system where public ownership serves as the main body and multiple ownership sectors develop together thus represents a fundamental institutional guarantee for the scientific development of the economy. In the modern service industry and in the strategic emerging industries that have gradually arisen during the transformation of China's economic developmental model, in the development of a circular economy, and in the coordinated interaction of urban and rural development, China must adhere to the mixed ownership of a public capital holding system as the mainstay. This by no means amounts to a one-way holding of non-public capital, or to the privatisation of public capital.

2. Adhere to the Organic Combination of Market Role and Government Role

The combining of the decisive role of the market in general resource allocation with the guiding (or leading) role of the government in allocating key resources is a basic way to satisfy the law of proportional development under the economic new normal.

One point to make is that an interactive combination of the market and government forms an organic integrity that is functionally complementary, synergistic in its effects, and anti-mechanical in nature, thus realising the law of proportional development. The market brings short-term and partial benefits to commodity producers through the spontaneous adjustment of resource allocation in line with the laws of market regulation, such as the law of value, while the government takes the initiative to use the laws of state regulation to plan and allocate resources to achieve the long-term and overall interests of society as a whole through professional institutions.

Another point is that the government's economic regulation should follow the objective economic law system, including the law of value and other market regulation laws. First, the government's economic adjustments should be based on timely, accurate, and adequate research that takes into account the state of economic development. Second, a timely and effective decision-making and coordination mechanism must be established within the government's structures of economic regulation, so as to avoid functional conflicts between various policies. Third, the process of state regulation must be subject to the supervision and management of specialised agencies. Before making adjustments, these specialised national agencies should hold hearings on important decisions with relevant stakeholders. During implementation, the agencies should check to see that decisions are being set in place; and after implementation, performance evaluations should be carried out.

Scientific development under the economic new normal thus requires an advantageous combination of the decisive role of the market in general resource allocation with the guiding (or leading) role of the government in allocating key resources. At the micro level, China must stimulate the functioning of various market players, strengthen innovation-driven forces, build a modern industrial system, and foster open economic development by streamlining administration, delegating power to the lower level, and giving full support to the decisive role of the market in resource allocation. At the macro level, it is necessary to receive the full benefit of the government's overall long-term planning and allocation of resources in areas such as scientific and technological progress, labour quality improvement, management innovation, resource conservation, the circular economy, and urban and rural development.

3. A Sustainable Development Orientation That Follows the Laws of Nature

(I) Natural Laws to Be Followed for Economic Development

The natural law that needs to be followed for economic development is mainly the objective law of harmonious development between humanity and nature. The core connotation of this law is that human beings originated from nature, have always been subordinate to nature, and depend on it.

The first aspect to consider is that human beings evolved as part of the natural world and are among its long-term developmental products. They have always been part of nature and have achieved their survival and development in the practice of interaction and integration with it.

The second aspect to consider is that human beings depend on nature. Since the beginning of human history, natural resources have been the basic link between population systems and natural systems. Human beings can only survive and develop by relying on resources obtained from the natural world. Humans obtain their means of livelihood directly from nature, and as they produce their means of existence, natural resources continue to enter the field of material production as labour objects and tools. Natural resources thus become the *inorganic body* of the human being.

The last aspect to consider is that human activities are constrained by nature. Under certain conditions of productivity, the capacity of nature to support human activities is limited. One point of view holds that humans have very limited natural resources, since the ecological environment that human beings depend on for survival has only a tightly restricted load capacity for human activities. Since the industrial revolution, human economic activities have not only increased the demand on natural systems for resources but have also increased the load represented by environmental pollution. When human activities do not damage the resilience and stability of the natural environment, humanity and nature can coexist in harmony. When the depth and breadth of human economic activity exceeds the load capacity of natural systems, nature will *retaliate* against humans. For more than half a century, the relationship between humans and natural systems has become increasingly tense. This conflict has led to a series of severe problems, including depletion of natural resources, energy shortages, and environmental pollution that threaten human survival and development. China's new economic normal is also constrained by resources and the environment. Under the new economic normal, the carrying capacity of China's energy resources and ecological environment is reaching or approaching its upper limit.

(II) Orientation to Sustainable Development under the New Economic Normal

To achieve sustainable development under the new economic normal, economic development must follow the objective developmental law of the paradoxical movement between humanity and nature. To develop China's economy in the new normal, China needs to firmly establish an orientation toward the concept of ecological civilisation, in which humanity develops in harmony with nature. China needs to chart a new development pathway that involves a green, low-carbon cycle relying on the system of ecological civilisation and promote a transition of economic development from extensive growth based on scale and speed to intensive growth focused on quality and efficiency. In this way, China can achieve the development goal of a sound ecological environment.

1. Firmly Establish the Concept of Ecological Civilisation in the Harmonious Development of Humanity and Nature

The core concept of ecological civilisation is the harmonious development of humanity and nature. Ecological civilisation is the sum of the results that have accrued to our material and spiritual civilisations through human beings following the laws of harmony and coordination between individuals, between humanity and nature, and between individual humans and society. The concept of ecological civilisation emphasises that in the process of economic, political, cultural, and social construction, human beings must respect, comply with, and protect nature at all times.

China's economic development under the new normal must firmly establish the concept of ecological civilisation, in which humans and nature develop harmoniously. First, China must continuously deepen our understanding of the laws of nature. This is an important premise of following the laws of nature. As Marx emphasised, 'Day by day we learn to understand the laws of nature more accurately and learn to understand the closer or farther effects caused by interference with the laws of nature'.[57] Second, China must establish the concept of treating nature well and of conforming to it. As Engels noted, 'We must always keep in mind that we dominate nature, not as conquerors dominating different peoples, nor as people standing outside nature'.[58] Third, China must establish the concept of protecting nature. Xi Jinping once stated, 'Protecting the environment equates to protecting productivity; and improving the environment

---

57. Engels. *Dialectics of Nature* [M]. Beijing: People's Publishing House, 1971: 521.

58. Marx, Engels. *The Complete Works of Marx and Engels: Volume 20* [M]. Beijing: People's Publishing House, 1972: 519.

also equates to developing productivity. We would never seek temporary economic growth at the cost of polluting the environment'.[59]

2. Rely on the Ecological Civilisation System to Promote Sustainable Development

To achieve sustainable development that follows the laws of nature, China must rely on the systems for promoting ecological progress. As Engels explained, to solve problems of the natural environment 'It is not enough to rely merely on knowledge. It also requires a complete change in the existing mode of production and even the entire social system connected to this mode of production today'.[60] Only by building mandatory and binding systems and laws based on an awareness of ecological civilisation can China transform people's activities, and finally achieve a reconciliation between humanity and nature.

The legislature should establish and develop a system of ecological civilisation, with a legal system of property rights over natural resources at its core. The initial need is to establish and steadily improve a legal system for property rights of natural resources, whose basis should be the ownership of natural resource assets by the whole people. The professional departments associated with the system should faithfully carry out the tasks of administering these resources on behalf of the entire people, who are the owners. The secondary need is to improve the legal system for territorial space development and protection, ecological compensation, environmental management, ecological restoration, and reporting and supervision.

Governments at all levels must establish and improve systems for evaluating administrative performance, including in the area of environmental assessment. The traditional view of economic development regarded it as consisting simply of economic growth. Guided by this view, GDP was considered the only indicator for evaluating performance. This attitude, however, led to excessive consumption of resources and to environmental destruction. To accelerate economic development under the new normal, the evaluation system should set sustainable development as the goal, and no longer see GDP as

---

59. Xi Jinping. Adhering to the basic state policy of resource conservation and environmental protection and striving for a new era of socialist ecological civilisation [N]. *People's Daily*, 2013-05-25. http://politics.people.com.cn/n/2013/0525/c1024-21610299.html

60. Marx, Engels. *The Complete Works of Marx and Engels*: Volume 20 [M]. Beijing: People's Publishing House, 1972: 521.

the standard of evaluation. Instead, it should consider resource consumption, environmental damage, and ecological benefits.

4. Inclusive Development Orientation That Follows Social Laws

(I) Social Laws to Be Followed in Economic Development

The social laws to be followed for economic development are a system of social laws. Social laws in the broad sense include the law according to which the relations of production reflect the level of productivity within a society, and the law which holds that the superstructure corresponds to the economic foundation. In a narrow sense, social rules exist in social organisations, social management, social coordination, social security, and so forth, all of which have rules to follow. The law of harmonious social development is among these precepts.

The core element in the law of harmonious social development is a harmonious relationship between the members of a society. This involves a society on an appreciable scale, within which the people figure both as the major player in development and as its purpose. Social development is a process in which purpose and regularity are unified, and social laws need to be manifested through the purposeful and creative activities of the people. In the development of human society, the people act as the creators of history and of social activities. Not only are the people the creators of material and spiritual wealth, but they are also the determining force for social change. In a society, however, where private ownership is the mainstay, the benefits of social development are mainly captured by the exploiting classes, who own the means of production. The working people and intellectuals, who make up the majority of the people, are not the primary beneficiaries of the fruits of social development. In a socialist society, where public ownership predominates, the fruits of social development should be shared mainly among the people. China's current reform and development aim to improve and strengthen this state of affairs, which is of great significance in practice and is closely linked to China's inclusive developmental orientation.

(II) Inclusive Development Orientation under the New Economic Normal

1. The Meaning of Inclusive Development

The concept of inclusive growth develops from the concept of inclusive increase. The concept of inclusive growth is a generalisation of the state of economic growth that is inclusive. The Asian

Development Bank and the World Bank have promoted the formulation and development of the concept of inclusive growth from the perspective of poverty reduction. According to the Asian Development Bank, seeking inclusive growth means advocating for equal opportunity growth; that is, the poor should enjoy equal social, economic and political rights, should be able to participate in and contribute to economic growth, and should share in the fruits of growth without facing denial of their rights or encountering institutional barriers or social discrimination. The World Bank's *2006 World Development Report: Equity and Development* argues that the best poverty reduction policies require inclusive institutions that provide a wide range of opportunities, instead of separating growth policies from equity policies.[9]

The concept of inclusive development represents an extension and deepening of the concept of inclusive growth. *The Growth Report: Strategies for Sustainable Growth and Inclusive Growth*, published by the World Bank's Growth and Development Committee in 2008, stated that the goal was to achieve sustainable and inclusive development. China had accepted the concept of inclusive growth earlier and had extended it from the economic field to the overall society through the concept of inclusive development. China proposes that the character of development must be scientific, follow economic laws, be sustainable, follow natural laws and be inclusive, and follow social laws. This concept closely integrates economic development, natural sustainability, and social progress.[61]

In the field of society as a whole, inclusive development refers in its essence to the notion that the entire population, including members of vulnerable groups, should be able to participate in the overall process of social construction. This should include economic construction, and should take place under equal conditions, with all sharing fairly in the benefits of social development.

2. The Orientation of Inclusive Development

An inclusive development orientation that follows social laws essentially requires a harmonious combination of fairness and efficiency, which make up a unity of opposites in the development of an economy. For a continuous strengthening of long-term economic development, and for a society to advance in a sustainable and healthy fashion, all members of the society must be able to participate under equal conditions and to share in the fruits of social

---

61. Wang Xinjian, Tang Lingkui. 'A Review of Research on "Inclusive Growth" [J].' *Journal of Management*, 2011 (1).

development fairly. However, there is an opposite side to fairness and efficiency in economic development: The principle of efficiency focuses on the short-term and local interests of individual economic actors, while the principle of fairness focuses on long-term benefits and on the overall benefits to society. Thus, equity and efficiency in economic development have some sense of antagonistic and conflicting aspects, and thus are not necessarily inclusive.

Inclusive development under the new economic normal, or the realisation of the law of social harmony, needs the support of systems and mechanisms as a guarantee. The following two systems and mechanisms are the most critical.

The first of these involves ensuring the dominant role of distribution according to work. A public ownership economy achieves inclusive development based on the principle of distribution according to work. Under this principle, publicly owned production units, after making necessary deductions from the total products created by workers, allocate the remaining products among the workers as personal consumption according to the amount and quality of labour provided by each worker during production. This is done so as to make sure that the workers are paid equally for equal inputs of work within the production units. A public ownership economy has ruled out the possibility that anyone can acquire social goods by virtue of their possession of the means of production instead of labour, thus laying the foundation for distribution according to work. Meanwhile, equality in the areas of labour and payment provides a fundamental manifestation of inclusiveness in society as a whole.

The second is a basic public service system where the inclusive development provides bottom-line protection. Basic public services are provided by the government and are compatible with the level and stage of economic and social development. They are designed to protect the fundamental needs of all citizens, and in a broad sense, include not only such livelihood needs as education, employment, social security, medical care, family planning, housing security, culture, and sports, but also fields that are closely related to the people's living environment, such as transportation, communication, public facilities, environmental protection, and many others. They also include areas that ensure security, such as public security, consumption safety, and national defence. In the inclusive development of China's new economic normal, the master plan for basic public services stipulates the equalisation of basic public services as its main goal and equal opportunities as its core.

In short, if China is to quickly adapt to the new economic situation, it needs to place a correct value on economic development.

Under this new economic normal, the country will only be able to take advantage of new opportunities, as well as to overcome potential risks and challenges, if it adheres to a scientific developmental orientation that follows the laws of economy, to a sustainable development orientation that follows the laws of nature, and to an inclusive development orientation that follows the laws of society.

(Originally published in *Exploration, Issue 1, 2015*, First author: Gao Jiankun)

* * *

Section II China's New Normal Economy Focuses on Improving Quality and Efficiency

In recent years, China's economy has entered a new normal. The essence of this lies in a more advanced form, a more complicated division of labour, and a more rational structure. From this point forward, China must adhere to and accurately grasp the logic of *understanding the new normal, adapting to the new normal, and leading the new normal*. China must do this to cope with complex environmental issues at home and abroad, so as to achieve the ambitious goal of building a moderately prosperous society in all aspects at the earliest date possible.

One of the basic characteristics of China's new normal economy is a medium to high-speed economic growth rate. Between 2002 and 2014, GDP increased at an average annual rate above 7%; however, there is an overall decreasing trend year by year. This indicates that the economic shift to a new normal is a gradual process. Although the growth of China's macroeconomy has slowed, growth remains near or above previous levels, and China still ranks second in the world in terms of its economic aggregate. At the same time, the new normal includes changes in quality and efficiency that the GDP indicators do not directly reflect. For example, China has shifted the focus of its economic development model from extensive growth, emphasising scale and speed, to intensive growth, emphasising quality and efficiency. From concentrating on the expansion of incremental capacity, economic policy has shifted to seeking in-depth adjustment of existing stocks while maintaining an optimised increment. Domestic demand is now considered the decisive factor underpinning economic growth, and from being driven by inputs and investment, the expansion of China's economy now rests increasingly on innovation.

Under the new normal, scientific and technological innovation has become the primary driver for economic development. In particular, the strategy of creating independent intellectual property has become the core of economic development driven by scientific and technological innovation. Only through independent innovation in key areas of core technologies can China truly ensure its prosperity and security. As China's President Xi Jinping has pointed out, implementing the innovation-driven development strategy is of fundamental importance if independent innovation is to be fostered. Within the new normal economy, China has thus set out to accelerate the pace of innovation, with a focus on promoting independent intellectual property rights. On the one hand, through the transformation of innovative achievements, new economic growth points will be continuously cultivated and developed. On the other hand, it is also important to give full play to the active role of the government, enterprises, research institutes, and workers in the improvement of the quality of human capital and scientific and technological progress; as China progresses, it will actively create an enabling and appropriate policy environment for improving industry's independent innovation capabilities.

Dissolving excess capacity through conversion, mergers, and acquisitions is an inherent requirement for the economy to improve quality and efficiency under the new normal. In order to promote the rationalisation and advanced industrial structure, it is important to focus on solving overcapacity while promoting coordinated development among industries. Large-scale investment in the past has caused severe production overcapacity in many industries, and has led to declining corporate profits, losses, and even bankruptcies. To promote the rationalisation and upgrading of the industrial structure, China needs to focus on promoting coordinated development between industries while reducing and eventually ending excess production capacity. The past stress on extensive production technologies has also resulted in severe environmental pollution. To optimise the industrial structure, an industrial division of labour must also be established, with various industries closely linked and supporting each other. For industrial development under the new normal, China must therefore avoid unilateral development that focuses on a few industries. Rather, it should promote a coordination and balance between primary, secondary, and tertiary industries and their internal branches. There is a particular need to upgrade technology in the agricultural sector, where support and protection for farm enterprises must be strengthened, agricultural technology service levels raised, and efficiency and sustainability improved. Through innovation, the industrial sector should transform its existing production capabilities, and promote a shift from an extensive to an intensive production mode. The service sector should continue to improve its capabilities and the quality of the services it provides. Doing so will not only help improve people's lives but will also boost labour productivity.

An integral component of economic development under the new normal is protecting the environment and using natural resources efficiently. Due to China's previous concentration on extensive growth, with the emphasis on scale and speed, the carrying capacities of energy, resources, and the natural environment have reached or are approaching their upper limits. Under the new normal, economic development will achieve a harmony between economic progress and environmental protection. We need to improve and implement relevant laws and regulations on environmental protection. The newly revised *Environmental Protection Law*, published in 2014, has clearly defined the responsibilities, powers, (rights), and obligations of governments, enterprises, and the public. China must also establish and steadily improve administrative performance evaluation systems for governments at all levels. This must include the evaluation of the ecological environment. This new administrative performance evaluation system must be guided by sustainable development, rather than being based on GDP, and it must track resource consumption, environmental damage, and ecological benefits as its main indicators for the evaluation of administrative performance.

The coordinated development of regional economies is another inherent requirement for achieving an overall improvement in the quality of economic development under the new normal. Coordinated regional economic development has an overall strategic significance for the development goals of upgrading industrial structures, protecting the environment, ensuring productive factor flows, and improving public living standards. China must coordinate the regional development strategies of various economic zones. At present, China has launched a number of key regional development strategies such as the Belt and Road Initiative, the coordinated development of the Beijing-Tianjin-Hebei region, the Yangtze River Economic Belt, the large-scale development of the western provinces, and the revitalisation of the old industrial bases in Northeast China. Economic development under the new normal should promote the organic integration of these strategies from a global perspective, promoting complementarity and positive interaction among the economic zones. This development must coordinate, classify, and guide the development of territorial space in various regions in line with the planning of China's main functional areas. Economic development under the new normal should be based on the positioning of the main functional areas of each economic region and should promote the organic combination of local economic development with population regulation and land and space development. In this way, it will be able to achieve the sustainable development of regional economies.

From the strategic perspective of improving people's livelihood equals development, planning for the development of wealth and income distribution, employment, medical care, housing, education, social security, and other fields is at the core of the fundamental value orientation of economic development under the new normal. This accords inherently with the fundamental purpose of socialist economic development. To plan for development in six areas under the new economic normal, China needs to improve the corresponding systems and mechanisms. The most critical of these is the distribution system, where distribution according to work is the main underlying principle. For example, China should adhere to and successively improve the system of distribution according to work in the public ownership economy, so as to ensure a reasonable proportion of labour remuneration in the initial distribution and to promote the simultaneous increase of labour remuneration and labour productivity. Moreover, it is necessary to support and further develop the government's system for regulating wealth and incomes. The government must improve the relevant laws and regulations in the area of initial distribution, while regulating the distribution of income and wealth in a more scientific way. Where redistribution is concerned, the government should adjust excessively high incomes by improving the tax system, enhance the incomes of low-income groups by improving the system of transfer payments, and end the receipt of illegal incomes by improving the legal system. The next broad goal must be to equalise services and to provide basic public service systems in the areas of employment, medical care, housing, education, social security, and other fields, so as to truly equalise opportunities for all.

A fundamental way to ensure that state-owned enterprises become larger and stronger under the new normal is to focus on developing the mixed ownership of public capital holdings. Under the premise that public ownership will remain dominant, this feature can create a community of interests in which the public and non-public shares are supervised, stimulated, and organically integrated. Simultaneously, it can effectively alleviate drastic fluctuations in economic development. The primary goal is to prevent the loss of state-owned assets. At present, some state-owned enterprises are expropriating state-owned assets, selling cheap but buying expensive, and taking whatever they want in the name of reform while establishing a modern enterprise system and other phenomena. To prohibit these wrongful activities, the government must pass legislation to strengthen comprehensive coverage, create a clear division of labour, coordinate cooperation, and fortify constraints on the system of supervision over state-owned assets. This legislation must provide for internal supervision of enterprises, supervision and auditing of investors, supervision of disciplinary inspections, and public supervision. The next step is to develop mixed ownership through two-way equity participation or holding structures. This can be achieved either through the participation of non-public capital, or through the holding of non-public capital by public capital such as state-owned capital. Further measures would involve a close integration with the developmental trends of science and technology. Whether this is for traditional industries in desperate need of optimisation and upgrading, or for emerging innovative industries and new service industries, China must adhere to the development of a mixed ownership system in which the public capital holding system is the mainstay and implement the *three conducive criteria* proposed by Chairman Xi Jinping[62] on the reform of state-owned enterprises. Reforms must be conducive to preserving and increasing the value of state-owned capital, conducive to improving the competitiveness of the state-owned economy, and conducive to enlarging the function of state-owned capital.

Making finance serve the real economy is a prerequisite for stable economic functioning under the new normal. The key is to adapt the speed and level of financial development to the real economy. If financial development lags behind, it will hinder the progress of the real economy. If, on the other hand, the development of finance accelerates too quickly, the result will be high financial risks. If supervision is lacking this will be especially true, and financial and economic crises will eventually follow. To safeguard China's economic autonomy and national security, foreign capital must not be permitted to create a financial monopoly in China. Preventing

---

62. https://news.12371.cn/2015/08/05/ARTI1438738513705105.shtml

such a monopoly from arising under the conditions of the new normal requires strictly limiting the shareholding ratio and conditions available to foreign capital when mixed ownership forms are developed in commercial financial institutions. Further, China must be cautious, insisting on full transparency, when it permits the opening of capital accounts. Control over capital accounts is an effective means of preventing national capital from adversely affecting domestic economic development. The degree and speed of capital account opening must be compatible with the ability of the domestic capital market to contain risks, and compatible with the regulatory capabilities of the financial supervision system. On top of this, the development of supervision over the entire range of processes of the financial markets must be accelerated, with supervision of the securities markets singled out for special strengthening. The measures needed include improvements to the legal system as it pertains to financial market supervision and adapting the legal system to the development and practice of the financial markets. Financial supervision departments must also continuously improve their capabilities in terms of the quality of their supervisors, technologies, and mechanisms.

Taking full advantage of the regulatory roles of the market and the government is the basis for efficient operation of the economy under the new normal. During the allocation of resources, cooperation between the government and the market aims to achieve a healthy complementary function, synergistic effect, and echo mechanism. Economic development under the new normal must adhere to the organic combination of the decisive role of the market in general resource allocation and the guiding role of the government in the allocation of key resources. In areas where the market can play an effective role, the government must fully stimulate the vitality of various market players, strengthen the driving force for innovation, build a modern industrial system, and foster new advantages for the development of an open economy through administrative streamlining and decentralisation. In areas related to the national economy and people's livelihoods, as well as in areas where the market fails, the government must take full advantage of the role of long-term and overall resource allocation in order to resolve various economic risks under the new normal and promote the healthy development of the national economy.

Since 2015, China's economy has shown the characteristics of quality improvement and efficiency during the new normal. Only by accurately grasping the logic of economic development and working hard in the above areas can our economy continue to maintain medium to high-speed growth and continuously improve the overall quality and efficiency of economic development.

(Originally published in *China Social Science News*, September 17, 2015, Second author: Gao Jiankun)

* * *

Section III The Dialectical Relationship between Supply and Demand in China's Economic Drive in the New Normal

1. Questions Raised

After more than thirty years of rapid development, China's economic achievements have been remarkable, but in recent years, economic growth has gradually slowed from 14.2% in 2007 to 6.9% in 2015. Since 2015, the value of newly approved infrastructure projects has exceeded two trillion yuan, and interest rates and the reserve ratio have been cut five times; however, the economic downturn has continued. The main reason for this is a mismatch between supply and demand in China's macro economy. This mismatch has become increasingly prominent, and the existing supply structure has become inflexible; it is now difficult to adapt to rapid changes in demand structure. China's development is in the midst of a new period of important strategic opportunities, but three profound changes have taken place. First, the world economy is slowing down, even while the size of China's economy is growing. Second, technological revolution and industrial transformation are accelerating; developed countries are promoting re-industrialisation, and developing countries are speeding up their industrialisation. Third, on the demand side, the sum of China's total supply, domestic demand, and international demand supported by debt in the past was generally in balance, while developed countries were *de-borrowing* and their markets were shrinking. It is quite clear that the principal aspect of China's economic contradiction is shifting from the demand side to the supply side, and what China is facing is for the most part not short-term cyclical and external shocks, but medium to long-term structural and internal pressures.

In the course of a collective study by the Political Bureau of the Central Committee of the CPC on 30 January 2016, General Secretary Xi Jinping therefore emphasised: 'While expanding the total demand moderately, we must work hard to promote structural reforms on the supply side, with emphasis on de-capacity, de-stocking, deleveraging, reducing costs, and making up for weak links, so as to enhance the adaptability and flexibility of the supply structure to changes in demand, and to promote an overall leap in China's social productivity'.[63] This indicates that China's macroeconomic policy has shifted from emphasising demand-side management to emphasising supply-side structural reforms. Work has shifted from focusing on short-term economic growth to focusing on sustainable development. Jin Hainian has put forward a theory of the economic growth of new supply. He believes that the decisive factor for long-term growth lies in *institutional supply on the supply side*. The study of supply and demand equilibrium from the supply side is the key to promoting economic growth.[64] By driving transformation and structural optimisation, the structural mismatch of supply and demand and the distorted elements of allocation will be corrected, and the economy will evolve to a higher level with a more complex division of labour and a more rational structure. This is an inevitable requirement for adapting to and leading the new normal of China's economic development and represents a major innovation. Nevertheless, people's understanding of the macroeconomic policy pattern under the new normal is still not clear enough. Based on the lack of perspectives of the micro- and macroscopic points of traditional economic theory, Jia Kang and Su Jingchun have put forward the perspective of specialisation and economic organisation[65] as a new framework for economic theory and for the characteristics of the new supply economics. It is worth noting that current academic research has placed more emphasis on study of the supply side, and there are even such misunderstandings as *China abandons Keynesianism* and *China embraces supply-side theory*. There is thus an urgent need to clarify why and how the demand and supply sides have been combined.

---

63. Xi Jinping stressed during the 30th collective study of the Political Bureau of the CPC Central Committee: accurately grasp and grasp the strategic focus of China's development and solidly turn the "13th Five-Year Plan" development blueprint into reality [N]. *People's Daily*, 2016-01-31

https://news.12371.cn/2016/01/30/ARTI1454141920834363.shtml

64. Jin Hainian. 'New supply economic growth theory: interpretation and prospects of China's economic performance of reform and opening up [J].' *Fiscal Research*, 2014 (11).

65. Jia Kang, Su Jingchun. 'The "new framework" and "new supply" of economics: the important linkage and the pursuit of the realm of "integration" in innovation [J].' *Fiscal Studies*, 2015 (1).

The supply-side school ignores both demand and economic structural adjustments. It also ignores the impact of China's social transformation on consumer demands and expectations. Changes in consumer expectations can lead to inflation, or falling prices, and even deflation. This is an issue that liberal economic scholars have largely ignored. Moreover, tax cuts as strongly advocated by the supply-side school may stimulate savings and investment. It is, however, also possible that they will stimulate leisure and consumption, the actual impact of which is difficult to determine. In practice, the supply-side school emphasises cutting tax rates, especially marginal tax rates, to weaken the progressive nature of taxation, which may simply have the result of a favorable tax-reduction policy for the wealthy. If tax cuts are purely designed to stimulate investment, they will lead to a rapid growth of aggregate demand or to a surge in inflation.

In summary, neither state interventionism arguing that demand pulls supply, nor economic liberalism maintaining that supply creates demand, can provide effective and comprehensive solutions to the problems of insufficient effective demand and excess production capacity in China's current economic operations. In the face of a complex situation and difficult tasks, the country must re-examine the dialectical relationship between supply and demand as a market-economy interaction variable in the drive for economic sustainable development. China must reconstruct the dialectical relationship between the supply side and the demand side and adhere to the unity of the Two-Point Theory and the Focal-Point Theory. It must emphasise a focus on the supply side, and the overall coordination of supply and demand relations.

2. 'Supply Creates Demand': The Supply-Side School

(I) The Supply Determinism of Say's Law

The history of economics deals with the conception, formation, disputation, coordination, and symbiosis of two economic ideas: economic liberalism (the 'invisible hand') and state interventionism (the 'visible hand'). Which hand is dominant depends on the supply and demand relationship during various periods. Throughout the history of economics, a lack of supply persisted until the early 20th century. All of the economic ideas and theories that emerged during this period in the history of human society argued that developing production should be the focus of theories and policies, and all the theories that were elaborated were dominated by supply determinism.

Classical economics represented by Smith, vulgar economics represented by Say, and neoclassical economics represented by Marshall insisted that supply is the central element, and that demand is a function of supply. The consensus was that supply is the main force that promotes the development of capitalist commodity production. These theories are mainly about how to improve labour productivity and how to accumulate capital so as to increase wealth. In the 19th century, the famous French economist Jean-Baptiste Say proposed what is now known as Say's Law: *There will be consumption when there is production, and the total supply and demand must be equal*. This idea has long dominated later Western economics. Although Say's Law is a primary form of economic liberalism, it is a concentrated expression of the neoclassical idea of 'automatic market clearing'. Say's Law is fatally flawed because it ignores the limitations on people's demand for specific material wealth, the contradiction between this limitation and the need for personal monetary wealth, the characteristics of needs and demands, and the influence on demand of income level and income distribution. In other words, its obvious mistake is that it absolutises the role of supply in creating demand and denies the possibility of effective demand being insufficient. The popular Product Life Cycle theory also shows that demand for specific products is limited, and the frequent crises of overproduction in capitalist economies cast grave doubt on Say's Law.

(II) The Revival of Say's Law by Supply-Side Economics

Supply-side economics are regarded by many as a resurrection of Say's Law, indicating that there are certain similarities between the two. The premises in each case are indeed similar. The premise of Say's Law is that industrial products are in short supply, while the premise of supply-side economics is that new high-tech products are in short supply, even though traditional products may be in severe surplus. A further similarity is a related approach. Both address the question of how to promote socio-economic development from a supply-side perspective.

In the area of economic drivers, the supply-side school stands for typical economic liberalism. It adheres to Say's Law: *Supply automatically creates demand*, emphasising both the role of market mechanisms and the effect of government policies on the supply of capital and labour. The views of supply-side economists include: First, the only source of economic growth is 'supply'. Second, the way to increase supply is through economic stimulus. Third, the main method available for stimulating the economy is tax reduction. Fourth, the external condition for economic stimulus is effective, limited government intervention; supply-side economics oppose excessive and over-detailed government intervention and excessive social welfare expenditures, emphasising the core role of enterprises and the market, and at the same time opposing currency issuance by the state. The supply-side school advocates a relatively tight monetary policy intended to make money supply growth adapt to long-term economic growth potential.

The most extreme element in the teachings of the supply-side school is the analysis it makes of the relationship between economic stimulus and growth. The school regards everyone as a rational 'economic person' who can respond sensitively to economic interest stimuli. Therefore, the market should have the freedom to regulate economic activities and promote economic growth by changing interest stimuli. The basic link and most effective means the supply-side school proposes for achieving this end, the essence of its economic theories and the core of its policy positions, is to increase total factor productivity through tax cuts.

Although Say's Law and supply-side economics share many similarities, there are also distinct differences between them. First, Say believes that supply equals demand and that there can be no over-production. By contrast, adherents of supply-side economics accept that supply often deviates from demand. Second, Say believes that the capitalist market economy has an inherent stability, and that supply and demand can adjust the balance spontaneously without the need for external intervention. Proponents of supply-side economics believe that appropriate state intervention is necessary, and that supply can be stimulated through tax cuts.

(III) The Policy Practice of Supply-Side Economics

The basic ideas of the supply-side school took hold in the mid-1970s. Due to the failure of Keynesian policies, in the stagflation era, there were many adherents of this idea, and it was finally named supply-side economics. As the name suggests, this idea is in direct opposition to Keynesian 'demand-side economics.' Representatives of the supply-side school include Robert Mundell, Arthur Laffer, etc. Supply-side economics in practice became the official economic thinking of the early 1980s and provided the main theoretical basis for Reaganomics. In early 1981, after assuming the presidency of the United States, Reagan announced that the government's primary task was to overcome stagflation. He proposed an economic recovery plan, which included reducing personal taxes and corporate taxes to stimulate work, savings, and investment, cutting social welfare spending to reduce the budget deficit, canceling or loosening the regulations governing enterprises to encourage them to actively expand their operations and investments, tightening monetary policy to curb inflation, and opposing any call to tackle inflation by raising interest rates.

The policies of the supply-side school fully reflect economic liberalism and have the following three aspects. First, its core objective is improving labour productivity. Through institutional innovation, technological innovation, management innovation, etc., the effective ability of supply to meet market needs is improved. The goal is thus to increase competitiveness and economic benefits, and to raise investment and consumer demand. Second, the role of the market mechanism is the means for boosting returns. Third, the responsibility of the government is to create an environment conducive to productivity improvement and industrial clusters.

In 2008, the financialisation crisis, of which subprime mortgages were the most vulnerable element of the process, broke out in the United States. This triggered a global financial crisis, directly leading to the questioning of the new supply-side economics in the economics community. At the same time, it led to a questioning of Keynesian demand management ideas. As the United States considered its policy options for escaping from the financial crisis, the 'Washington Consensus' was abandoned, and the U.S. administration implemented a policy of quantitative easing that was aimed at bailing out financial institutions and corporations.

(IV) The Rise of the New Supply-Side Economics and the Concept of 'Supply-Side' Regulation

The development of supply-side economics has gone through two stages: 'classical' and 'neoclassical'. The supply-side school was criticised by the first generation of Keynesians represented by Keynes himself and by Paul Samuelson. Later, with the rise of the new supply-side economics, supply-side theories underwent a first restoration. This was followed by the second generation of Keynesianism, which represented a second negation of liberal 'supply-side' regulation.

Two upward spirals of 'negation of the negation' in the development of economic thought demonstrated that the supply-side school no longer amounted simply to an attempt to resurrect Say's Law but represented the intellectual rationalisation for an out-and-out laissez-faire economy. Initially explained on the basis of Say's Law, the supply-side doctrines were subsequently raised to the status of a scholarly current and acquired a certain macro-theoretical weight. That is to say, the proponents of supply-side ideas maintained that economic policy had the function of driving economic development in the short term, while in the long term, the policy was invalid. The school developed to the point where its members addressed questions of supply management, applying their concepts in the field of institutional economics, and a trend developed for macro-supply management methods to be used in performing government functions. Supply-side research has evolved to include the study of more comprehensive and advanced institutional arrangements, and of the relationship between transition and economic growth, something that is no longer a mere study of policy instruments. The new Keynesianism that has emerged as part of this wave has come to incorporate important elements of supply-side thinking, providing the foundation for economists in the post-crisis era to reflect on 'supply management' in the United States and many other countries. Additionally, it has provided the basis for the rational return of the new supply economics, combining 'breaking' and 'establishing'.

The new supply-side economics does not abandon demand management but emphasises the combining of supply management with demand management, while incorporating a constructive and inclusive range of achievements from institutional economics and elsewhere. The basic framework of economics requires the strengthening of supply-side research and analysis, which despite originating from the classical liberalism of Say, has been supplemented with new ideas to remedy the defects of one-sided demand management in the context of the new era, the new economy, and emerging markets. Economic drive requires that the market and government should combine to work their magic. It advocates that a positive interaction be sought between the main body of the tertiary sector, the market, and the government, so as to form an effective supply response and to guide demand.

In short, the supply-side school puts forward the policy claims of supply management only on the basis of criticising and negating Keynes's effective demand theory and demand management policies. The school denies Keynes's Law, reaffirms Say's Law, re-emphasises the fundamental role of market regulation, and allows the market mechanism to regulate the economy on its own. The school also believes that the solution to stagflation caused by Keynes's policies is not 'demand creates supply', but 'supply creates demand'; it contends that 'supply comes first, demand comes later, production comes first, and consumption comes later.' From a static point of view, if the supply-side school incorporates the idea that demand also results in a dynamic reaction, then many of its views are justified.

The shortcomings of supply-side economics are that it obliterates the contradiction between production and consumption, denies the system as the determinant of economic supply potential, and denies the basic contradictions of capitalist society. Because the supply-siders overemphasise tax cuts and neglect the systematic study of other economic theories, their claims relating to tax reduction lack a scientific theoretical basis. The supply-side school is still immature, and lacks a rigorous, clear, and complete system of economic analysis. In many ways, it is chaotic and even contradictory.

3. 'Demand Pulls Supply': State Interventionism

State interventionism is represented by Keynesianism. Keynes inherited and developed Malthus's theory of effective demand and Mandeville's *Paradox of Thrift*, thereby establishing the basic theoretical system of effective demand. Through a clear division of demand and supply, Malthus shifted the focus of economics from the supply side to the demand side. He divided demand into demand degree and demand intensity, and on this basis took the lead in proposing the concept of 'effective demand' and ideas of demand management. On this basis, Keynes initiated his revolution in economics. Keynes also absorbed Wicksell's argument that the central bank should regulate interest rates. Wicksell suggested that overall price increases or decreases are due to bank interest rates being lower or higher than natural interest rates. Therefore, banks should increase their interest rates when prices rise, and when prices fall, should cut their interest rates.[66] This 'investment lure' theory became an important part of Keynes's theory of effective demand. In the face of an economic crisis caused by severe overproduction, Keynes totally altered the way in which the relationship of production and consumption was formulated from 'production comes before consumption', as asserted by the supply-side school, to 'demand comes before supply'.

---

66. Zhou Zhitai. *History of foreign economic doctrine* [M]. Hefei: University of Science and Technology of China Press, 2012: 247-250.

(I) Basic Theories of State Interventionism

Beginning with an analysis of the aggregate of the entire economic system, Keynes proposed his theory of effective demand. Effective demand refers to the level of aggregate demand at which the total supply price of commodities and the total demand price of commodities reach equilibrium. Capitalist economies generally lack sufficient effective demand, and unemployment is the norm. Keynes used three major psychological laws to demonstrate that aggregate market demand was insufficient and led to unemployment, a proposition that directly negates the supposed perfection of the market mechanism and Say's Law. Keynes's basic ideas are as follows: first, the psychological law of a decreasing propensity to consume leads to insufficient consumption demand. Second, the psychological law of diminishing marginal efficiency leads to insufficient investment demand. Third, the psychological law of currency preference also leads to insufficient investment demand. Keynes's theory of effective demand revolutionised the theoretical basis of traditional economics – Say's Law – and expressed it as a proposition that is the complete opposite: demand creates its own supply, namely, Keynes's Law.

In Keynes's theory of effective demand, investment demand plays a decisive role. That is, investment fluctuation is the main cause of insufficient effective demand and economic fluctuation. Keynes pointed out that the propensity to consume is relatively stable in the short term. To expand employment, investment must be increased, which can have a multiplier effect. He believed that a single investment could lead to multiple investments, thereby increasing employment levels, which naturally leads to increased demand. He also believed that effective demand has a multiplier effect on production, which is an inherent requirement of the self-generating capacity of an economy.

Keynes believed that there were two factors that determine the size of the investment multiplier: one is the degree of industrial relevance of the investment project, and the other is the marginal propensity to consume. The greater the marginal propensity to consume, the greater the multiplier, otherwise, the smaller. As the rich have a higher propensity to save than the poor, the consumption function will depend on the gap in income distribution. In view of the larger marginal propensity to consume of low-income earners, Keynes advocated redistributing income and increasing this propensity so as to magnify the multiplier effect. Since the propensity to consume is stable, its effect on national income is realised through the influence of the marginal propensity to consume on the investment multiplier.

Through increasing the disposable income of consumers and enterprises and raising the level of consumption demand and investment demand of the whole society, higher income and investment multipliers serve to raise the national income and to increase economic growth and employment. Keynes therefore believed that a country's total employment was determined by effective demand, and that the only way to expand employment was to increase demand. To this end, the government must intervene in the economy. Keynes advocated supplementing weak private investment with government investment and thoroughly transforming the purchasing power accumulated by savings into investment, so as to expand social demand. 'I hope the country will take more responsibilities for direct investment,'[67] he wrote.

(II) Demand Management: Policies of National Interventionism

In the context of the two major Western trends of interventionism and neoliberalism, one of Keynesianism's greatest contributions has been to point out the limitations of the self-regulating market regulation and to analyse the necessity and importance of state macroeconomic intervention and regulation. Keynes proposed that the state adopt an interventionist policy whose main feature would be demand management, which can have a certain positive effect on the stability of a capitalist economy. Keynes's call for increasing social consumption and investment to increase aggregate demand and address the unemployment problem was also reasonable. Insufficient effective demand means that the logical relationship between the variables of consumption demand and investment demand, which are effective demands and are supposed to have mutually causal impacts, is disordered and results in disequilibrium ending with total demand being less than total supply. External factors such as government policies thus need to be brought into play, so as to actively expand domestic demand and thereby change the shortage of effective demand to varying degrees. Only successful government investment can inspire people's confidence and their expectations of future development. Keynes's theory shifted the focus from the resource allocation issues of traditional Western economics, instead concentrating on issues of national income and employment.

Keynes not only emphasised the effect of investment demand on effective demand, but also made every endeavor to encourage

---

67. Keynes, John Maynard, *The General Theory of Employment, Interest and Money*, Commercial Press, 1999, p. 67

high levels of consumption. His thinking has had a great impact on American living patterns and government policies. The American government also frequently adopts deficit fiscal policies and inflationary monetary policies to expand government spending, increase effective demand, boost production, and promote employment.

Keynesian theory clearly defines the central position of demand management in macroeconomic management. The theory holds that when demand shrinks, the government should cut taxes, increase fiscal expenditure, increase the money supply, reduce interest rates, and seek to increase the marginal efficiency of investment so as to encourage investment. When demand is too strong, the government should moderate it by increasing taxes, by cutting fiscal spending or reducing the money supply, and by raising interest rates. Even if the economy is on the rise, Keynesian theory states that the fiscal deficit should be expanded in order to stimulate greater demand and promote faster economic growth.

Keynesianism swept across the western world for more than thirty years after World War II and became the principal theoretical basis on which governments formulated economic policies. It can be said that the United States is one of the countries that has implemented Keynesianism most consistently. Demand management policies, however, do not and cannot fundamentally resolve the contradictions inherent in capitalism. Throughout the 1960s, the United States ran deficits almost every year, yet the problems kept growing.

Demand management policies can thus magnify financial risks. In response to the limitations of Keynesianism, the supply-side school advocates promoting economic growth by increasing productivity rather than stimulating social demand. It was in the midst of the opposition to Keynesianism that the supply-side school emerged. The supply-side school had succeeded in riding the wave of opposition to Keynesianism.

4. Comparison between Supply Theory and Demand Theory

(I) The Difference between Supply Management and Demand Management and Their Respective Positions

Although both supply management and demand management are important means of macroeconomic management, there are many differences. In terms of timeliness, demand management is suited to short-term management, while supply management can often be slow in taking effect. In terms of specificity, demand management focuses more on regulating the total amount while supply management is more suited to structural management. In terms of policy instruments, demand management mainly uses fiscal expenditure and monetary policy, while supply management employs taxation, legal management, and administrative measures. Although Keynesian theory was also the rationale for tax cuts as demonstrated during the Kennedy administration and onward.

Of course, some policies have characteristics of both demand management and supply management. Such policies include tax cuts, which can reduce the burden on enterprises and are thus related to supply management, and which are also related to demand management through their ability to free-up savings for investment and provide more disposal income to stimulate demand. The theoretical boundary, however, between the two types of management is still apparent; their emphasis is different, even though some policies have attributes of both. By comparison, monetary policy attaches more importance to aggregate management, and carries a strong sense of demand management. Meanwhile, fiscal expenditure policy has obvious characteristics of demand management when stimulating economic growth, but in a period of relatively stable economic development, it is necessary to adjust the relationship of interests between various regions, industries, and social classes through a range of transfer payments, thereby affecting the development of production. These fiscal policies are important tools of supply management.

(II) Differences between Keynesianism and the Supply-Side School

Keynes's theory of insufficient effective demand is based on three basic psychological factors, emphasising economic expectations or psychological factors. Although the economic impact is objective, Keynes's analysis also has idealistic characteristics. The analysis carried out by his successors has been more profound and includes studies of the flaws in the role played by the market, based on examining internal market mechanisms and processes. The work of the Keynesian school has featured analyses of derived theories such as fine-tuning, watching for opportunities, and conducting studies of frictional and structural unemployment. Keynesian theory and supply-side economics have their applicable conditions, that is, both Western effective supply theory and effective demand theory are based on the conditions of a complete market economy. That first the market mechanism is sound, second, the market players are independent, and third, the supply of goods is effective. These three conditions are not yet fully in place in China.

Both Keynes and the supply-side school advocated tax cuts. Keynes, and his followers, however, proposed the alternate use of tax increases and reductions according to different economic trends as a temporary countermeasure, whereas the supply-side school has favored larger and longer-lasting tax cuts. Of course, this may be due to the different economic challenges the two trends have characteristically confronted. Keynes was faced with economic recession and unemployment. Accordingly, the Keynesians have advocated tax reduction to increase the disposable income of individuals and businesses, with a view to expanding demand, promoting economic growth, and increasing employment. The supply-side school, as opponents of Keynesianism, have dealt primarily with controlling inflation, which they did principally through a policy of tax cuts. The two schools have different economic backgrounds, so their policies and objectives are different.

5. The Unity of the Supply Side and the Demand Side

(I) The Unity of Keynesianism and Supply-Side Economics

Supply-side economics are the theoretical basis of the policies of neoliberalism, while Keynes's theory of insufficient effective demand provides the theoretical basis for state interventionism.

Keynesianism was created under conditions of excessive supply and insufficient demand. The new supply-side economics emerged ostensibly to correct the Keynesian 'overemphasis' on demand and its effect on the normal development of supply. However, supply-side economics were not developed solely as a question of functional economic policy. These neoliberal policies did not solve the effective demand problem and, in fact, were the justification for a new era of financialisation and globalisation, as the only short-term means to alleviate stagflation. Today's economic development is the result of a constant creative interaction between supply and demand. The respective policies of the supply side and the demand side are like the two blades of a pair of scissors. To meet the requirements of economic development at different stages, they must be used with each other instead of replacing each other. Once an economy has developed to a certain extent, it requires comprehensive management of supply and demand, which results in the integration of supply-side economics and Keynesianism. Keynes's demand theory and supply-side economics may seem to be complete opposites, but both in essence are supply and demand theories. Keynes's ideas and methods of 'expanding effective demand' were essential to increasing investment and revitalising supply in order to seek full employment and expand demand, so they still belong to the supply-side economics system

Since the development of the economic growth factor analysis method by the American economists Solow and Denison, most researchers have analysed economic growth in quantitative terms while proceeding from the supply side. Whether adherents of classical economics or of the prevailing mainstream economic growth theory, where supply-side research dominates the mainstream, these researchers all believe that capital increase and technological progress are the decisive factors for economic growth. Endogenous growth theory regards the differences in total factor productivity (TFP) among countries as the main determinants of economic growth. Most of the literature attributes the differences in TFP to differences in supply efficiency. These factors however, cannot fully explain the differences in growth among countries, and the impact of demand factors on economic growth must also be considered. It is worth pointing out that Lewis, who has had a major influence, believes that the greater the capital accumulation, the greater the benefits to employment. This view not only ignores the restrictive role of demand and income, but also the interaction of market supply and demand. It ignores the rate of the level and structure of income distribution and the degree of averaging in constraining supply and demand. In fact, 'supply adjustment' and 'demand adjustment' have significant impacts within each adaptive period. They are two in one, and together they affect economic growth.

In theory, there is no conflict or contradiction involved in whether supply or demand is dominant, simply because they each predominate at different stages of economic development. During a less developed stage of the economy, there is no demand problem, or the demand problem is not especially prominent; at this point, supply is naturally the overriding issue. At present, the emphasis on supply regulation stems from China's unbalanced development, caused by insufficiently effective supply mechanisms.

With continuous development of the economy, a series of changes have occurred in aggregate demand and demand structure. Economists have gradually come to realise that demand is also an important factor for economic growth. The improvement of income levels increased aggregate demand, and regular changes of demand structure all play critical roles in long-term economic growth. In the long run, economic growth is inseparable from the support of supply factors, but it is also affected by changes in demand factors. Analysing the economic development practices of different countries, Ji Ming has concluded that in economic growth, the logic underlying the evolution of demand structure reflects the logic of the evolution of demand dynamics.[68] The rationalisation of demand structure, together with its further development, can effectively suppress economic fluctuations. Ji Ming also believes that the government should fully consider the similarities and differences between the rationalisation of demand structure and the attainment of an advanced demand structure, since these affect economic growth and economic fluctuations. While efforts should be made to use demand structure to create an advanced economic environment, more consideration should be given to rationalising the demand structure itself.[69]

Keynes insisted on the assumption of a rational economic person and created the aggregate analysis method. He was, however, obsessed with studying the equality of quantities in relation only to quantity, ignoring a profound analysis of the inner structure of capitalist economies. He placed emphasis on aggregate analysis but made light of structure analysis, stressed demand analysis, but neglected supply analysis, and attached importance to short-term analysis but paid less attention to long-term analysis. As a result of Keynes emphasising only short-term interests and not paying sufficient attention to long-term interests, economic growth, or environmental protection, no mature theoretical system took shape on the basis of his ideas. Marxist theory overcomes these deficiencies in Keynesian national income theory. Marx's theory of the reproduction of social capital emphasises both aggregate and structural analysis and includes both aggregate and structural issues. It emphasises the analysis of both demand and supply, stressing the need to analyse both short-term and long-term phenomena. Marx explained that while supply and demand might appear on the surface to amount to no more than the transfer of goods in the market, they are in fact relationships between buyers and sellers and producers and consumers. Socialised mass production requires a proportional distribution of social labour, and there is an internal

---

68. Ji Ming. 'The logic of demand structure evolution and sustained balanced growth of Chinese economy [J].' *Social Science*, 2013(2):44-45.

69. Ji M, Liu Zhibiao. 'The impact of the evolution of China's demand structure on economic growth and economic volatility [J].' *Economic Science*, 2014(1):10-22.

proportional relationship between supply and demand. These are the ideological manifestations of Marx's value production and value balance. When the requisite labour hours in these two areas are equal, value production and value realisation will reach a balance, which is an essential requirement for the balance between supply and demand.

In short, both Keynesianism and supply-side economics have great limitations. They can only be used as a reference and cannot be used to guide China's current reform and development. As the above analysis indicates, it is necessary to learn from the theories and methods they use to analyse demand and supply, but it is even more necessary to employ up-to-date theories and methods derived from Marxist political economy. Further, it is necessary to conduct a comprehensive analysis from the standpoint of requirement of the relationship of production, promoting productivity, and the interrelationship of supply and demand.

(II) The Unity of Supply and Demand in Marxist Economics

Marx put forward the second meaning of socially necessary labour time in Chapter 10 of Volume 3 of *Capital*. Only when the amount of social labour consumed in the total amount of a certain commodity matches the social demand for this kind of commodity can supply and demand be balanced and can this commodity be bought and sold in accordance with its market value. When the market supply exceeds market demand, there will be excess product and the market price will fall below the market value. The current overcapacity is in violation of the socially necessary labour time requirements of this second meaning. The cause of the imbalance between supply and demand may be as follows: when the demand is constant, and the supply becomes too large or too small, there will be an excess or shortage. Or, if the supply is constant, but the demand is too large or too small, the current demand for high-quality goods will increase, while demand for inferior goods decreases. In other words, the imbalance between supply and demand may be caused by changes in supply, or it may be caused by changes in demand. The relationship between supply and demand not only regulates the distribution of resources among enterprises with different production conditions, but also regulates the allocation of resources among departments. Therefore, supply-side reform must adhere to market orientation, that is, the orientation of final demand.

Marx made clear that 'The real difficulty in defining the concepts of demand and supply is that they seem to be just synonymous repetitions (tautologies).'[70] Supply and demand arise in the course of production and are simply two sides of a single phenomenon. On opposite sides, they are hard to tell apart; from different angles, supply is demand and demand is supply. Production activities that increase supply also increase demand for factors of production. An increase in the demand for labour also leads to increases in the demand for consumer goods. Therefore, demand in the field of production can also be called supply. The essence of supply and demand is an issue of production and consumption as well as of the realisation of social reproduction. In the final analysis, it reflects the law of the proportional distribution of social labour.

Marx pointed out the identity of production and consumption from the general standpoint of production. First, production is directly consumption, and consumption is directly production. Second, production mediates consumption. Without production, consumption has no object. Without consumption, production has no purpose, and a product can only be a product of possibility, not a product of reality. Third, each party can create the other because of its own implementation. Production creates objects of consumption, the means of consumption, and motivation for consumption.[71] 'Production is the actual starting point', and therefore, production is also the dominant factor.[72] At the same time, 'no consumption, no production, this is because without consumption, production has no purpose.'.[73]

Marx also elaborated the relationship between production, consumption, distribution, and exchange. As he stated, 'They constitute all aspects of a whole, the differences within a unity...therefore, certain production determines certain consumption, distribution, exchange, and certain relationships between these different elements...There are interactions between different elements. This is true of every organic whole'.[74]

---

70. Marx, Engels. *The Complete Works of Marx and Engels: Volume 30* [M]. 2nd edition. Beijing: People's Publishing House, 1995: 33-34.

71. Marx. *Selected Works of Marx and Engels: Volume 2* [M]. 2nd edition. Beijing: People's Publishing House, 1995: 10.

72. Marx. *Selected Works of Marx and Engels: Volume 2* [M]. 2nd edition. Beijing: People's Publishing House, 1995: 97.

73. Marx. *Selected Works of Marx and Engels: Volume 2* [M]. 2nd edition. Beijing: People's Publishing House, 1995: 681.

74. Bureau of Compilation of the Works of Marx, Engels, Lenin and Stalin of the Central Committee of the Communist Party of China. *Collected Works of Marx and Engels: Volume 8* [M]. Beijing: People's Publishing House, 2009: 23.

In economic development, there is an interactive relationship between production and consumption, but their interactive relationship is asymmetrical. In Marx's view, effective supply determines and creates demand. Production determines consumption; this is because production creates materials for consumption, and production determines the mode of consumption, since production creates demand on the part of the consumer for what it initially produces as an object. [75] The improvement of the productivity level determines the increase of the consumption level, and the productivity level is positively related to the consumption level. Consumption, however, also has an adverse effect on production. In short, production and consumption are in a dialectical relationship that has been mutually determined, and that is both antagonistic and unified. The growth of supply ultimately requires the growth of consumer demand, and it cannot be a real and lasting driving force of the economy. Supply does not exist independent of demand, nor does demand function independent of supply. The effect of demand in promoting supply is mainly reflected in the following: when the demand for a certain consumer product increases, it will lead directly to an increase in the supply furnished by the production sector that produces this consumer product, which will lead to an increase of investment in this department of production and eventually to an increase in total investment. When investment increases, part of the investment is transferred to the compensation of labour. To put this differently, the disposable income of workers is raised, thus bringing about growth of personal consumption demand and promoting an expansion of consumption. The infinite nature of demand and the finite nature of supply make an excess of demand over supply an eternal social phenomenon, which provides an infinitely broad space for the development of supply-side theory. Market demand signifies demand for products that are affordable with the real money that is available, so infinite demand will turn to finite demand. The normal state of economic operations is the underemployment equilibrium. When the absolute finiteness of supply changes to relative infiniteness, the total market supply is greater than the total market demand, and the market economic system is in a normal state of insufficient demand.

Production and consumption, however, can each be converted to the other. First, 'production determines consumption'. Production provides consumption objects for consumption activities.

---

75. Marx. *Selected Works of Marx and Engels: Volume 2* [M]. 2nd edition. Beijing: People's Publishing House, 1995: 10.

Production determines consumption methods and creates new production methods. In social reproduction, production is the *actual starting point* of the entire process, and therefore the *dominant factor*. Under the new economic normal, the creative effect of production on consumer goods, consumption methods, and consumers requires that supply innovation should drive demand and create demand. It requires that efforts be made to strengthen supply-side structural reforms, to promote economic structural reforms, and to improve the quality and efficiency of the supply system, so as to realise economic structural transformation and upgrades.

Second, *consumption produces production*. On the one hand, a good that is produced can only realise its use value in the course of consumption; on the other hand, consumption also creates *the motivation for production*. The huge response of consumption to production requires that while strengthening supply-side reforms, China must also find objectives, directions, and driving forces for supply-side structural reforms from the perspective of the demand-side response to the supply-side. This is done so as to expand effective demand, thus propelling reforms to the structure of supply, and establishing the ranges of effective investment and effective supply through a new demand structure. Impetus from both the supply side and the demand side will finally realise structural transformation and upgrades.

In the contradiction between supply and demand, the main aspect of the contradiction is supply, and the level and method of supply determine the level and method of demand. Supply creates demand, and also suppresses it. Effective supply and effective demand are two sides of the same thing. Effective supply is supply that adapts to and guides demand and has multiple characteristics. One is that the value of the product must be determined by the amount of socially necessary labour, while the market price is determined by the amount of value or the production price formed by competition. A second characteristic postulates that the total amount of products provided by each department must meet the scale of social needs. A third is that effective supply signifies the supply that corresponds to a certain demand, with effective demand meaning primarily the ability to pay. In short, only when there is demand can there be supply, and vice versa. A balance should be achieved between supply and demand. Supply and demand are regulated at both sides, and the two sides work together to complement each other.

Marx believed that the contradiction between the supply and demand of commodities is the unity of imbalance and relative balance. The balance of supply and demand is relative and accidental, while the imbalance of supply and demand is absolute and normal. The equilibrium of supply and demand must be achieved through competition, proceeding from their imbalance. The state, in accordance with the needs of the society for all kinds of commodities, should guide the distribution of total social labour in a forward-looking manner and promote the balance between supply and demand.

The supply side determines the demand side, which in turn determines the speed and direction of economic growth. The supply side influences the evolution of the demand side in the following ways: the change in the structure of the production factors will affect the income structure, which may change the elasticity of income demand, resulting in changes in demand and its structure.

Demand-side evolution affects supply-side evolution in the following ways. First, the evolution of preferences has an impact on technological progress. Preference affects consumer demand, constitutes a market selection environment for technology, and determines the benefits of various technologies, which in turn directly affects technology selection and diffusion. Second, changes in the structure of demand will cause changes in the supply side and will also bring about changes in the factor structure. These changes affect the evolution of the entire supply structure. Evolution of the supply side includes evolution of the supply structure (factor and output structure) and technological progress, while evolution of the demand side includes evolution of the demand structure and of preferences. In the process of economic evolution, the supply and demand sides are affected by each other, and jointly affect the speed and quality of economic growth. The institutional system affects the evolution of both the supply and demand sides and has a profound impact on their joint evolution. The dynamic mechanism that underlies sustained economic growth is the coordinated evolution of the supply side, the demand side, and the system, together manifested in the dynamic and effective matching and coordinated upgrade of the supply structure and the demand structure. Institutional reform is a dynamic mechanism, operating at a deep level, that promotes the coordinated upgrade of the supply and demand structures.

Achieving a balance between supply and demand requires a reasonable increase in demand, expansion of domestic demand, and optimisation of the demand structure. At the same time, it involves reducing excess capacity, increasing effective supply, and optimising the supply structure Supply and demand, however, still have a different status. Supply is more about long-term, structural, and quality matters, while demand is more about short-term, aggregate, and economic stability issues. One cannot say, however, that supply is more important than demand. Although supply can create new demands under certain circumstances, whether this concerns the general relationship between production and demand or the requirements of socialist production, demand is the purpose, while supply is only a means, and a means that serves the purpose. That is to say, supply serves demand.

(III) China's Response to Surplus Economy: The Unity of Supply and Demand

China's overproduction problem is caused by both demand and supply. Whether in theory or in practice, to put undue emphasis on the demand side or the supply side is to display bias. In theory, the macro policies of expansion and austerity have both advantages and disadvantages. Both supply-side and demand-side policies have their pros and cons, and both should be weighed carefully. In practice, although supply-side reforms are promising in the long run, some reforms may curb demand in the short term. Priority should be given to reforms that can increase demand in the short term, while reforms that may suppress short-term demand should be postponed. To be specific, projects should be selected on a basis that includes effective investment aimed at making up for shortcomings and solving infrastructure bottlenecks, so as to create demand in the short term. In the long run, projects need to be selected taking into account improvements to labour productivity and competitiveness, added value, reduced transaction costs, and increased taxes. Such investment will not cut consumption but increase household income and consumption.

The 'three engines' of China's economy are consumption, exports, and investment. They represent the demand-side approach, and their opposite is the supply-side approach. The supply side signifies the supply and effective utilisation of production factors. Prof. Cheng Enfu has proposed the 'new three engines' on the supply side, with technological innovation, structural optimisation and improvement of factor quality acting as the three drivers. In essence, the goal here is to improve the quality of the various elements and the efficiency of their use through advances in science, technology, and education, and through optimisation of the industrial structure. This requires more than simply reforming science and technology education, improving the quality of education and technology, improving the quality of factors, realising unified social security, medical care, and unemployment relief services across the country, and promoting the free movement of labour across regions and industries. It also requires the government to build a market economy system and to promote the decisive role of the market in allocating resources, so as to optimise the industrial structure. As the development stage shifts, the demand for enhanced quality rises rapidly, and the demand structure will accordingly undergo fundamental changes. Changes to demand management will necessarily affect the nerve center of supply, and it is impossible for any measures to promote or restrict supply without touching the pulse of demand. Demand determines supply, and first, any change in demand structure will affect the direction in which the adjustment of industrial structure proceeds and second, similar demand preferences influence the process of industrial structure adjustment. Supply-side reform is, in fact, creating new demands, and these new demands are more sustainable. Meanwhile, supply determines demand, which refers to the improvement of product quality and product grade brought about by technological progress, to the increase of effective supply, and to the transformation and upgrading of industrial structures.

Countries are at different stages of development. The developed countries of the West have long been at the advanced stage in relation to overproduction/overcapacity, and they are faced with chronic problems of effective demand. China has remained, for a long time, at the stage of material shortages and backward production capacity, but as a developing country, it is primarily confronted with constraints on the side of supply. Therefore, when an understanding of aggregate demand gained from the practices of developed Western economies is combined with an understanding of aggregate supply derived from the practices of developing countries, and when their specificities are abstracted, a unified aggregate supply and demand model and a complete set of universal macroeconomic theories can be formed. Theoretical work of this kind can provide a direction for the further development of macroeconomics. Through combining the experience of demand management from Western countries and supply management from China, a new macro-control system that includes both demand management and supply management can be formed, and macro-control will shift from the one-dimensional space of demand management to a two-dimensional space in which demand management and supply management can be unified. Therefore, the introduction of supply management does not mean giving up demand management, which is still an important means of macroeconomic regulation. The combination of the two can solve most of the problems in the real world and achieve multi-objective management simultaneously.

(IV) China's Response to Economic Surpluses: Mutual Transformation of Supply and Demand

Issues relating to agriculture, rural areas, and farmers are a prominent concern, and the main response has been to adopt a supply-side approach, which involves promoting the transformation of agricultural management structures from those of a small-scale farming economy to large-scale operations. According to theory of new labour migration, the transfer of surplus rural labour to non-agricultural industries is part of a reallocation of human resources that can significantly improve marginal labour productivity in agriculture and effectively address the sector's weaknesses, thus promoting the growth of the national economy. The outflow of agricultural labour and the rise of marginal agricultural productivity is affecting marginal income per worker, with the prospect that it will eventually equal the current wage level, and that the dual economy will become monistic. Studies have shown that changes in China's labour force allocation contributed 20% to the country's economic growth between 1982 and 1997. Since China's reform began, the existence of wage differences and the lack of mandatory regulations for paying social security levies have meant that migrant workers have effectively contributed a development fund of 11.6 trillion yuan to the industrial and urban economy.[76] Remittances of migrant worker incomes to rural areas have improved the consumption power of rural families and aided investment in entrepreneurship. The shift to large-scale agriculture will not only free up labour for industrialisation but will also increase the productivity of agricultural land and labour, improve the quality of agricultural products, increase fiscal revenues, reduce real interest rates, and help achieve price stability and economic growth. Further, the shift will increase investment, improve employment, raise household incomes and expand

---

76. Zhou Zhitai. 'Research on farmers' income increase in a multidimensional perspective [J].' *Scientific Socialism*, 2013 (1): 108-111.

consumer demand. Market expansion will in turn promote industrial development, spurring technological innovation and improving the quality of economic growth. This is the case for carrying through the transformation from the supply side to the demand side, and for making use of their synergies to promote economic development.

Overcapacity in the coal, electricity, and steel industries is becoming serious, and the most effective way to deal with the problem is to start with demand. China should comply with the laws of the market economy and reduce electricity tariffs. Electricity is a commodity with a very high elasticity of demand. If electricity charges are decreased, consumption will rise, and the demand for household appliances will also increase. This will lead to an increase in the demand for steel, and associated industries will become profitable. More broadly, reduced electricity prices can be expected to have the following results. First, employment will expand, bringing an increase in consumer demand; this will achieve one of the goals of socialist production and will create a virtuous cycle that promotes economic development. Second, more funds will go into R&D and staff training to develop related industries, and the effect will be to promote national economic development. Of course, this development will help expand employment, and consumption will also rise. This again proves the case for making the transformation from the demand side to the supply side, and for taking advantage of their synergies in order to foster economic growth.

(Originally published in *Contemporary Economic Research*, Issue 3, 2016, First author: Zhou Zhitai)

Chapter 3

China's Five New Developmental Concepts

China's five developmental concepts are a sublimation of the perceptual knowledge it has acquired in promoting economic development. They are also a theoretical summary of our practice in promoting economic development. China must be resolute in leading and promoting economic development through the use of innovative developmental concepts and creating new prospects for economic development.

*　*　*

Section I Pioneering the Economic New Normal with Five New Developmental Concepts

For the first time, the Fifth Plenary Session of the 18th CPC Central Committee put forward the developmental concepts of innovation, coordination, greenness, openness, and sharing. In addition, the session even initiated a far-reaching change related to China's overall development. Although the above five concepts have been reflected in past work, under the new normal economic policy important connotations of these ideas have evolved in significant ways. Since the 18th National Congress of the Communist Party of China, the Party Central Committee, under the direction of Comrade Xi Jinping and basing its innovative developmental stage on China's reform and opening up, has put forward a new governing policy. This policy characterises the new normal as a transition from high-speed growth to medium-to-high speed growth. It includes continuous optimisation and upgrading of the economic structure and a shift from factor-driven and investment-driven development to innovation-driven development. The Central Economic Work Conference, in December 2015, reiterated the need to redefine the new normal, to be flexible and to adapt to the new normal, and to promote and lead the new normal developmental model. It will therefore be beneficial for theorists to focus on the key nodes and corresponding implications of the five developmental concepts under the new economic normal.

1. Innovative Development

Innovation can be understood in broad and narrow senses. At the Fifth Plenary Session of the 18th CPC Central Committee, it was pointed out that in order to pursue innovative development China must put innovation at the core of the country's overall development, while constantly promoting innovation in theory, systems, science, technology, culture, and other relevant aspects. China must ensure that innovation runs through every work project of the party and country, and that it becomes a trend in our entire society. The innovation involved here is mainly innovation in the broad sense.

Scientific and technological innovations, meanwhile, are discussed by the present text in a relatively narrow sense. Innovation is very important in both its broad and narrow senses, but due to limited space, the focus here is on independent innovation in the field of science and technology.

At present, special emphasis must be placed on using scientific and technological innovation as a driving force to break through the *bottleneck* hindering economic development. More specifically, the *bottleneck* that currently restricts China's economic development is insufficient motivation. Only through innovation can this obstacle be cleared away. To foster the necessary new developmental drivers through innovation, in line with the requirements set down by the Third Plenary Session of the 18th CPC Central Committee, the nation must utilise all its advantages, embracing the lead role of scientific and technological innovation, fortifying overall innovation, strengthening basic research, revitalising original and integrated innovation, and strengthening its capabilities in the areas of imports, absorption, assimilation, and re-innovation. China's past development was driven fundamentally by factor inputs and low-cost labour, which created a pattern that typically featured quantitative and extensive development. The stress on extensive development has resulted in severe overcapacity, constraints on resources and the environment, insufficiently effective innovation, and a large economy that is not as strong as it could have been. Today, continuing to rely on factor inputs has become less tenable; the era when China could compete on the basis of low labour costs has passed.

Where the demand side is concerned, it is obviously no longer enough to rely solely on the traditional *three carriages*. China must now focus on reforming and developing the *three new carriages* (factor quality, structural optimisation, and technological innovation) on the supply side. It has become clear that the need for innovation in economic development is stronger and more urgent than at any time in the past. Only purposeful innovation can fundamentally break through the *bottleneck* restriction of insufficient developmental power. When identifying innovation-driven development as a major strategy orientation for our country's future, China must focus on promoting the close integration of technological innovation, economic growth, and social development, so that enterprises can truly become key players in technological innovation. Moreover, the government should play an active role in areas related to the national economy, people's livelihoods, and industrial lifelines. The government must be active in strengthening support and coordination, in determining overall technical directions and pathways, and in making good use of major national science initiatives, technology projects, and other major undertakings. The government must also concentrate the nation's efforts on areas of strategic importance. The key to implementing an innovation-driven development strategy lies in enhancing our capacities for independent innovation and in striving to master key core technologies.[77]

Among the widespread but mistaken views and policies that have appeared since the reform and opening up, a notable example places emphasis on the *market for technology* strategy, which has argued that it is better to buy than to manufacture and better to rent than to buy. Practice has confirmed that this strategy is unsuccessful. For example, the opening up of the auto industry in China has been an obvious failure, and the large aircraft industry an even bigger one. In the early 1980s, China's research and development in the area of large aircraft was quite well developed, and aircraft manufacturing plants flourished. Soon after these factories had opened, the leadership defied opposition and discontinued the Y-10 large aircraft project. Large aircraft Research and Development (R&D) and production eventually resumed after an interval of thirty years, when the Commercial Aircraft Corporation of China was launched with a base in Shanghai. The reason for these frustrating changes of direction was a misreading of openness as a substitute for indigenous innovation, along with a mistaken belief that core technologies could be acquired

---

77. Cheng Enfu. 'Xi Jinping's Ten Strategic Economic Ideas [J].' *Contemporary Perspectives on Social Sciences*, 2014 (1).

through joint ventures. One instance in which this faulty view was successfully resisted was in the R&D and production of high-speed rail systems. The Ministry of Railways seized the initiative and broke the technological monopoly of several big western companies. High speed rail was ultimately to become one of the *international business cards* of *Made in China*.

Flawed policies often stem from flawed theoretical orientations. The economist Wu Jinglian argued at one point that systems are more important than technology, which represents a departure from commonsense views in economics and philosophy.[78] It is clear that the most important element in productivity is technology utilised by people, and that each system is closely related to production relations and superstructure. To state in general terms that systems are more important than technology is to say that production relations and superstructure are always more important than productivity. This is an obvious falsehood.

China's economic opening can be divided into several stages. The first stage emphasised the exclusive strategy of *bringing in* foreign capital and technology. The second stage emphasised *bringing in* and *going global*. While continuing to pursue *bringing in*, it also implemented *going global* measures by calling on more Chinese enterprises to make overseas investments. In 1998, Jiang Zemin maintained that in the future, equal importance should be attached to both *bringing in* and *going global*.[79] Since then, the central government implemented a strategy that placed equal emphasis on both *bringing in* and *going global*, and the nation entered the second stage of opening up. The third stage emphasised the new strategy of *independent innovation* and implemented measures to make China an innovative country with independent intellectual property rights. After the 16th National Congress, multinational companies were often reported as implementing *decapitation campaigns*. The Party Central Committee stressed independent innovation, and the State Council followed this by launching a revitalisation plan for the machinery industry.

Nevertheless, there are still differing opinions on these matters in the academic and political communities. The economist Lin Yifu has urged that China take the necessary steps to avoid falling into

---

78. Wu Jinglian. *System over technology: Developing China's high-tech industry* [M]. Beijing: China Development Press, 2002.

79. Cheng Enfu, Hou Weimin. 'The "New Open Policy Theory" for Transforming Foreign Economic Development [J].' *Contemporary Economic Research*, 2011(4)

the *independent innovation trap*.[80] He believes that the costs and benefits of independent innovation are sometimes uneconomical, and that it may be better to introduce new technology. In response to the increasing number of multinational companies setting up R&D institutions in China, the *Guangming Daily* at one point published an article stating that this provided a good opportunity to promote the technological progress of Chinese enterprises, and that the prospects for technological innovation in China were promising. People may ask, 'Are Western multinational companies here to help our country master core technologies?' In fact, their strategy is to utilise our relatively cheap and abundant human resources to develop technologies and products suitable for China. They then turn around and sell them to us at high prices. These practices ultimately restrict our own core technological development. In the 1930s, a Japanese professor wrote an article stating that Japan should develop *colonial technology*, and he emphasised that if colonial technology was not developed at all, then the sovereign state would also be adversely affected. He cautioned, however, that a technology gap of about fifteen years should be maintained during this developmental period. Although developed countries do not mention it publicly, they actually use this strategy off the record. Therefore, promoting independent innovation after the 16th National Congress, proposing to build an innovation-oriented country at the 17th National Congress, and creating an innovation-driven strategy after the 18th National Congress have all represented thoroughly logical propositions.

After 2000, I proposed the theory of the advantages of independent intellectual property rights (IPRs) and have pointed out that in addition to employing dynamic comparative advantages and comprehensive competitive advantages, China must focus on cultivating and exerting IPRs as a third advantage.[81] The first two theories of advantage have their flaws. The theory of comparative advantage implies that the resource endowment characteristics of various economies remain unchanged. In practice, this tends to lead to the *comparative advantage trap*. That is, the economy that has a comparative advantage only at the lower end of the international industrial chain will typically remain stuck there. For countries with this industrial structure, moving towards the mid-to-high end can be

---

80. http://finance.sina.com.cn/roll/20051101/1110378949.shtml

81. Cheng Enfu, Ding Xiaoqin. 'Constructing the theory and strategy of intellectual property advantage - Also on the theory of comparative advantage and competitive advantage [J].' *Contemporary Economic Research*, 2003 (9).

extraordinarily difficult. The concept of competitive advantage pro-posed by Michael Porter in the United States, because of its emphasis on a number of factors, failed to grasp the crux of this problem. I, therefore, propose a third theory and strategy in this area: the the-ory and strategy of independent intellectual property advantages. Obviously, the primary way to realise this theory and strategy is through independent innovation. Therefore, the Fifth Plenary Ses-sion of the 18th CPC Central Committee put innovation at the top of its five developmental concepts, continued to foster national innova-tion, and enhanced the level of endogenous economic growth. This was further evidence indicating that the theory and strategy of the advantages of independent IPRs are fully consistent with the think-ing of the Party Central Committee.

2. Coordinated Development

Among the five new developmental concepts mentioned in the communique of the Fifth Plenary Session of the 18th CPC Central Committee, coordinated development was of high theoretical and policy significance. From a problem-oriented perspective, it is nec-essary to establish ten new ideas and measures for coordinated development, along with consideration of the current difficulties of China's economic and social development and the countermeasures required.

First, China must coordinate economic and social development. The development of the entire national economy should be stable, progressive, effective, and efficient; but it is very important to be mindful that the starting point and ultimate goal of economic devel-opment is the improvement of people's livelihoods. Consequently, the value orientation that *improving people's livelihoods is development* is intrinsically unified with the fundamental purpose of socialist eco-nomic development. At present, social development in the six major areas, that is, wealth and income distribution, employment, med-ical care, housing, education, and social security must be planned from the strategic standpoint of improving people's livelihoods and development. This tenet amounts to the main content of coordinat-ing economic and social development under the new normal.

Second, China must coordinate developmental speed and effi-ciency. Looking at global economic growth, 1% ~ 3% is *low speed*, 4% ~ 6% is *medium speed*, 7% ~ 9% is *high speed*, and more than 10% is *super-high speed*. Therefore, one of the signs that China has entered the new normal state is its transition, representing the combined effect of objective laws and policy control, from high speed to medium-to-high speed growth. To coordinate the relationship between speed and efficiency, China needs to pay attention to the economic development mode, adapting it from extensive large-scale growth to intensive growth focused on quality and efficiency, to shift the economic structure from incremental capacity expansion to in-depth adjustment together with stock adjustments and growth optimisation, to transform the economic development impetus from the traditional factor-driven and investment-driven growth points to their new, innovation-driven successors, and to promote the continuous rationalisation and improvement of the industrial structure.

Third, China must coordinate development between regions. The key points are as follows: First, it is necessary to coordinate the regional development strategies being applied in different economic zones. At present, while continuing to develop the Yangtze River Delta, the Pearl River Delta, and the Central Economic Zone, China has implemented a number of key regional development strategies such as the *Belt and Road Initiative*, the coordinated development of Beijing, Tianjin, and Hebei, the development along the Yangtze River Economic Belt, the large-scale development of the country's western regions, and the revitalisation of the old northeastern industrial bases. Next, in line with the planning of the main functional areas within China, China should coordinate and guide the development of territorial space in different regions according to their characteristics, enhance the organic integration of these strategies from a global perspective and promote the complementary advantages and positive interaction between economic zones and main functional areas.

Fourth, there must be coordinated development of urban and rural areas. Currently, the gap between the economic and social development of China's urban and rural areas is relatively large. Therefore, the construction of public facilities in rural areas, the development of compulsory education in primary and secondary schools, the creation of township and village enterprises, and the integration of urban and rural areas and urbanisation are the keys to coordinating urban and rural development. Innovative urbanisation should be designed to provide benefits and efficiencies to both urban and rural areas, rather than simply to realise the migration of rural dwellers into the cities.

Fifth, China must coordinate the synergistic development of people and nature. The relationship between economic development, population growth, the use of natural resources, and environmental protection must be handled properly. With a new policy, each family may now have two children. It is estimated that there will be about 100 million more people than there were during the one-child policy era. This will exacerbate the already severe deterioration of the natural environment and scarcity of resources. Therefore, it is necessary to strengthen the protection and restoration of the ecological environment and enhance the efficient use of natural resources, including by implementing restrictions.

Sixth, coordinated development of the public and private sectors is necessary. In strict compliance with the *Constitution* and a series of documents of the Party Central Committee, which maintains and consolidates the general framework of public ownership as its mainstay while also developing diverse forms of ownership, China must implement the principle of unswervingly developing both public and non-public economies, and resolutely implement the *three conducive criteria* proposed by General Secretary Xi Jinping and the Party Central Committee. These three conducive criteria are intended to reform the strength and vitality of state-owned enterprises, return enterprises to new levels of competitiveness, increase the functionality of state-owned capital, and implement a general policy of strengthening and expanding state-owned enterprises. Their joint focus is on the development of a mixed-ownership economy with public capital holdings as the pillar, rather than on simply developing and expanding the domestic and foreign private economies, or on making the private economy the cornerstone.

Seventh, thought must be given to coordinating the development of *getting rich first* and *common prosperity*. At its core of this coordination are improvements to the distribution system, where distribution according to work is the main form and diversified modes of distribution coexist. There must be an adherence to and improvement of the distribution system according to work within the public ownership economy. Subsequently, China must adhere to and improve the government's regulation of wealth and income. In the area of primary distribution, the government must scientifically regulate the distribution of income and wealth by improving and enforcing relevant laws and regulations on income distribution. Where redistribution is concerned, the government is obliged to adjust the excessive incomes of high-income groups by improving the tax system, to raise the income of low-income groups by improving the transfer payment system, and to end illegal incomes through improvements to the legal system.

Eighth, deliberation must be given to coordinating material and spiritual development. Building a moderately prosperous society in a universal way includes continuously improving the level of material production and consumption, as well as the level of cultural production and consumption. The latter involves the cultivation and enhancement of the core socialist value system. That is, the spirit of quality, the spirit of making progress, the spirit of maintaining health, and other mainstream issues under the socialist market economy are all significant considerations. It is critical to also be conscious of issues concerning the enhancement of ideological and cultural soft power and international competition with Marxism-Leninism and its Sinicised Theory as its soul. It is rather obvious that this coordination is of great significance.

Ninth, a coordinated effort must be made in the fields of technical and institutional development. Technology belongs to the sphere of productivity, while institutions belong to that of production relations and superstructures. It is not appropriate to carry on believing that *systems are more important than technologies*, just as it cannot be maintained that production relations and superstructures are more important than productivity. Attention must be paid to General Secretary Xi Jinping's assertion that 'Innovation is the primary driving force for development'[82], and to coordinating the interactive development of the science and technology-led productivity system with reform of production relations and the superstructure.

Tenth, internal and external development must be coordinated. Establishing the idea that the purpose of opening up to the outside world is for the betterment of domestic development must be propagated. China must avoid taking opening-up measures merely for the sake of openness, and steer clear of initiatives that do more harm than good. For the present, China's public and private enterprises should set about strengthening their cooperative efforts and gradually regaining control of many industrial sectors – including popular websites – from their foreign counterparts. It is necessary to affirm the concept of serving the real economy and enriching the country through financial development, prevent foreign capital from forming financial monopolies in China, handle the issue of capital account openings cautiously and proceed only after full discussion, and accelerate pre-supervision, procedural supervision, and post-supervision of the financial market. If China is to strengthen the legal system and the efficacy of stock market oversight so as to effectively

---

82. Central Documentary Research Office of the Communist Party of China, *Excerpts from Xi Jinping's Discourse on Science and Technology Innovation*, Central Literature Publishing House, 2016

avoid, navigate, or manage any potential or inadvertent crisis, this is especially pertinent.

3. Green Development

There is a view that it is wrong for Marxists at home and abroad to attribute the deterioration of the natural environment mainly to the capitalist system. Is China's environmental degradation actually caused by capitalism? In my opinion and from a global perspective, the deterioration of the environment has been caused by the capitalist system, and Chinese and foreign left-wing scholars in China and abroad have analysed the situation correctly. In the case of China, the main problem has been that ideas, institutional arrangements, policies, and the corresponding technologies have not kept up with the pace of economic development. Among these, the construction of a socialist ecological system with Chinese characteristics is the key and should be a top priority.

First, the integrated planning and management system of the government is the core of the ecological governance. The government must take the lead in protecting the ecological system. A good ecological system first requires long-term planning and sound scientific management on the government's part. It is urgent that China improve and implement a governmental planning management system that includes a planning and environmental impact assessment, an evaluation of political achievements, resource accounting, and ecological management. For example, China must establish a strict environmental protection management system, construct an evaluation system for economic and social development that will assess progress in building ecological civilisation, and make improvements to the accountability system for the natural environment. Along with these tasks, it is necessary to implement a system for placing top leaders in roles where they have overall responsibility, establishing the necessary one-vote veto system for ecological protection, and maintaining a life-long accountability system. Those who violate the requirements of scientific development and cause severe damage to resources and the environment should be identified and made subject to lifelong accountability. They should not be promoted or transferred to important positions, and those who have already been transferred should also be held accountable. Officials who do a poor job in promoting ecological progress should be admonished. Those who blindly make decisions with no regard for the constraints of the natural environment and cause serious damage must unfailingly be held accountable. In cases of ineffective performance of duties, lack of supervision, or dereliction of duty, the administrative superior responsible for the personnel concerned must be investigated in accordance with disciplinary code and the law.[83]

Second, a clearly defined system of property rights ownership provides an incentive for ecological protection. Such a system plays a substantial role in determining the prices fetched by assets in market transactions. Making use of the role of the market in general resource allocation may allow prices to reflect the scarcity of natural resources, as well as helping to adjust the relationship between the supply and demand of resources, savings resources, and reducing environmental pollution. However, the ecological market mechanism, including the system of asset property rights, is not always effective and can be harmful in ecological terms in real life. The ecological market mechanism, including the system of asset property rights, is not always effective in real life. Because the ecological environment and natural resources are public goods, and the market mechanism suffers from the limitations imposed by individual interests, spatial and temporal location, decentralisation of power, and information asymmetry, the following situations can easily arise. Property rights over assets are not always clearly defined; for example, it is difficult to specifically distribute the air and to determine who owns it. When there are too many parties involved in negotiations and the transaction costs are excessively high, property rights over assets are not always transferable even if these have been clearly defined. In cases where there is informational asymmetry, clear property rights over assets and the free transfer of assets do not translate into an optimisation of resource allocation. Since the system of asset property rights plays a role in regulating natural resources and in improving the ecological environment only under certain conditions and within a certain range, it is necessary to exercise the leading role of government regulation to the fullest, and not simply to believe blindly in marketisation. Making full use of the dual authority of the government and of the market in ecological protection, and utilising their respective advantages, can effectively avoid the devastating effects on the natural environment caused by the capitalist system with its basis in private ownership. Capitalism is a system in which the market economy is the mainstay, and the government plays the role only of a *night watchman*. China represents a concentrated reflection of the superiority of the socialist system with Chinese characteristics.

---

83. Opinions of the CPC Central Committee and State Council on accelerating the construction of ecological civilization [N]. *People's Daily*, 2015-05-06.

In view of this, and while continuing to promote the construction of a market in natural resource property rights, the country must also improve the natural resource asset management system and its use control system.

Third, the compensated (paid) system of natural resource use represents only a restricted means of ecological development. Due to a lack of awareness of the need for ecological protection, ecological management has lagged behind for a significant period. Ecological values have been ignored, urban resources have been used free of charge, and low sewage charge levies have not been adequate to effectively constrain enterprises in their discharge of pollutants. These harmful activities have caused tremendous damage to the ecological environment, without providing compensation. To remedy this situation, China's need to develop and implement a green tax and fee system, an ecological compensation system, and a damage compensation system. China needs to implement the just principle according to which *those who develop should protect, those who destroy should restore, those who benefit should compensate*, so that the people and enterprises that engage in dynamic economic development and that fail to repair the environmental damage they cause are obliged to compensate the state. Furthermore, China should actively promote the reform of environmental protection taxes and resource use fees and should establish an ecological compensation system that takes account of market supply and demand relations, while also reflecting the scarcity of resources, the cost of damage to the ecological environment, and the benefits of restoration. It is critical to establish an ecological damage compensation system with clear responsibilities, unobstructed channels, standardised technology, strong guarantees, adequate compensation, and effective provisions for restoration. In particular, it is important to create a consultation mechanism to cover compensation for ecological damage, to improve the relevant litigation rules, to strengthen the implementation of compensation and restoration, to improve supervision, and to standardise appraisal and assessment. In this way, it is possible to effectively compensate the nation for the damage caused to ecological functions by environmental pollution and the destruction of ecological systems.[84]

Finally, a strict governance system that combines prevention and control is needed as a fundamental guarantee of ecological balance.

---

84. Wang Erde. 'Nationwide reform of ecological environmental damage compensation system to be implemented in 2018 [N].' *21st Century Business Herald*, 2015-09-18.

Faced with achieving economic transformation and technological upgrades but subject to resource constraints, China must stop the abuse of ecological resources that has resulted from rapid economic development, improve resource utilisation by enterprises and residents, reduce energy consumption, promote resource recycling, and manage publicly used resources within a reasonable range. The country should employ a strict governance system combining prevention and control as its fundamental guarantee that pollution will be contained. Specifically, in order to prevent environmental pollution, it is necessary to strengthen market access standards in all the diverse ways they affect energy, land, water conservation, the environment, technology, and safety. Minimum ecological impact standards must be set for air, water, soil, and the protection of species, and to ensure that these apply to all members of society and all levels of commercial activity. Market prices need to reflect the true costs of economic activities, and these costs include resource depletion and damage to nature.

Only by incorporating such costs into the national economic accounting system will it be possible to determine appropriate marginal social costs, and to stimulate enterprises to increase the efficiency of their resource use. In the field of environmental governance, governments at all levels should assume major ecological responsibilities, perform ecological functions, maintain ecological security, change the mode of economic development, and coordinate the relationship between economic development and ecological protection. To this end, it will be necessary to increase financial investments and coordinate related funds so as to support resource conservation and recycling, new and renewable energy development and utilisation, environmental infrastructure construction, and ecological restoration and construction, along with expediting the demonstration of advanced and applicable technologies. Enterprises should play the primary role in green development, through technological and management innovations. They should save energy, reduce emissions, improve production efficiency, and meanwhile realise economic, social, and ecological benefits. A corporate environmental behavior rating system should be devised and differentiated credit support policies should be applied to guide enterprises in implementing green production and operational models. Organisations should play active, independent roles in the environmental education of the public, in environmental damage assessment, and in responding to environmental emergencies. Individual citizens should change their consumption concepts and lifestyles and participate systematically in environmental protection and supervision.

They should promote the creation of a clean, beautiful, and harmonious ecological environment and the formation of a scientific lifestyle that is green, low-carbon, and recyclable.

4. Open Development

The Fifth Plenary Session of the 18th CPC Central Committee proposed that to properly enact open development, China must follow the trends of deeper integration of the economy into the world economy, pursue a mutually beneficial open market strategy, develop an open economy with higher standards, actively participate in global economic governance and public product supply, improve China's influence over international regimes in global economic governance, and build a broad community of shared interests. To enter a new stage of opening up to the outside world, China must enrich the meaning of opening up, improve the quality of opening up, and more effectively coordinate the promotion of strategic mutual trust, economic and trade cooperation, and cultural exchanges. The Session determined that China must strive to form a deeply integrated and mutually beneficial cooperation pattern. In December 2015, the Central Economic Work Conference pointed out that it is necessary to continue to optimise the regional layout of opening-up, promote foreign trade both internally and externally, actively utilise foreign capital, strengthen international cooperation in the areas of production capacity and equipment manufacturing, accelerate negotiations on free trade zones and investment agreements, and actively participate in global economic governance. China will ensure the implementation of the *Belt and Road Initiative* and implement every beneficial aspect of the financially supportive role of the Asian Infrastructure Investment Bank and the Silk Road Fund in order to ensure the implementation of major landmark projects.

At present, the key to implementing the Central Committee's policy of *developing an open economy of higher standards* is to establish a *lean* opening-up mode featuring *low loss, high efficiency, two-way interaction, and independent innovation*. Additional aspects will involve the coordination of the relationship between domestic economic development and opening up in order to promote the sustained and healthy development of the national economy.[85] For example,

---

85. Cheng Enfu, Yin Luanyu. 'Accelerating the transformation of foreign economic development must achieve "five controls and enhancements" [J].' *Economic Dynamics*, 2009 (4).

to promote high-level and two-way opening up, China should first focus on the implementation of an independent intellectual property strategy, accelerate the construction of an innovative country, and participate in the international division of labour from the lower end to the mid-to-high end while actively improving the quality of economic opening up to the outside world. In addition to implementing *Made in China 2025*, China must also plan industry in advance with reference to the spirit of *Industry 4.0* in Germany. It is not possible for every industry to develop late-mover advantages. In the area of high-speed rail, China possesses a very successful first-mover advantage. Independent innovation requires long-term continuous investment and long-term accumulation. In the past, China did not do enough in this regard, and our investment in scientific and technological research and development was too low. In 2014, scientific and technological research and development expenditure accounted for only 2.1% of GDP. This statistic lagged far behind that of developed countries; it was even lower than that of India.

Second, it is important to learn from Japan's experience and specifically determine the degree and speed of opening up of each industry according to its independent innovation capabilities. By doing so, China will be able to create a more relaxed environment for industry to improve its independent innovation capabilities. Japan opened its industries one after another, and this method was learned from Germany. Under the influence of the historical school of the 19th-century economist Friedrich List, Germany's economy accelerated quickly. The measures taken were designed to protect Germany's national industries before opening up to the UK. Actions were taken to develop technologies through domestic competition, while waiting for the industries concerned to become competitive in relation to the UK; only then did Germany open up to the UK, to the mutual benefit of both nations. Much the same is true of South Korea. Economic nationalism in Japan and South Korea is now stronger than in China. Instead of learning more from the United States, China should seek lessons from Japan and South Korea, and from what they were able to accomplish after World War II.

Finally, regarding the development and opening-up of our financial sector, it is necessary to establish an ideology of using the financial sector to serve the real economy and prosperity of the country. This is essential for the stable operation of the economy under the new normal. The basic function of finance is to serve the real economy, and for this function to work properly, the speed and level of financial development must be compatible with the real economy.

If the level of opening up and developing the financial industry lags behind the real economy, the development of the latter will be hindered. If the opening up and development of the financial industry outstrip the real economy, financial risks will continue to accumulate, and in the absence of financial supervision, will lead eventually to financial and economic crises.

Under the new normal, financial development needs to serve the real economy, the wealth of the people, and the country's prosperity. To achieve this goal, focus is necessary on the following areas. First, foreign capital must be prohibited from forming financial monopolies in China. Such monopolies will capture large quantities of financial profits, will cause China to lose its economic autonomy, and will cause it to lower its guard in the area of national security. To prevent foreign capital from creating financial monopolies under the new normal, China should adopt legislation strictly limiting the percentage of shares held by foreign capital in commercial financial institutions, while restricting the conditions under which foreign capital can be placed in these institutions and developing a system of mixed ownership.

Second, the question of opening capital accounts must be cautiously and fully investigated and verified. Capital account controls are an effective means to prevent the entry of foreign capital into an economy from having a severe impact on domestic development. The degree to which capital accounts are opened, and the speed with which this is done, must be compatible with the ability of the domestic capital market to guard against risks, and with the capabilities of financial regulatory departments.

Third, China should speed up the entire process of developing general supervision of the financial market before, during, and after the opening of capital accounts. In order to effectively manage any potential stock market crashes, it is especially necessary to strengthen the legal system and ensure enhanced oversight of the stock market. An important consideration is that the National People's Congress must improve the areas of the legal system that relate to the supervision of the financial market and ensure compatibility between the relevant legal structures and the supervision of financial market development. Meanwhile, the departments charged with overseeing the financial sector must continuously improve the quality of their supervisors, along with the technology and other mechanisms these supervisors employ.

Fourth, and even though the RMB was included in the basket of special drawing rights (SDR), financial reform should still be based on the principles of national security in order to strengthen a high-level autonomous opening up. The inclusion of the RMB in the SDR basket is not meant to signal an immediate opening of capital accounts. Based on the Impossible Trinity, there is a *pendulum effect* between the free flow of capital, the stability of the exchange rate, and monetary policy. That is, while one of these three objectives of macroeconomic policy may be attained, the other two can only achieve a limited degree of swing. The four Nobel Laureates Mundell, Krugman, Stiglitz, and Tinor, the international financial experts Lin Yifu, Yu Yongding, Lang Xianping, who have now returned to China, and the well-known professor Fang Xingqi are all unanimously opposed to the scientific theory and policy analysis of the immediate opening of our capital accounts. The policy options that China should now adopt are to ensure the effectiveness of monetary policy and to seek to combine the flexibility of the exchange rate system with a degree of capital flow. Specifically, while ensuring the effectiveness of monetary policy, a managed floating exchange rate system should be implemented in conjunction with regulated capital flows.

5. Shared Development

The Communique of the Fifth Plenary Session of the 18th CPC Central Committee proposed that insisting on shared development means insisting on development in the interests of the people, relying on their support, and seeking to directly benefit them. China must make more effective system arrangements, give the entire population an increased sense of shared gain in the process of co-construction and co-sharing, strengthen development dynamics, and unite the people further in moving toward the shared goal of common prosperity. It is critical to narrow the income gap while pursuing the simultaneous growth of the economy and of residents' incomes, at the same time as synchronising increases in labour remuneration with labour productivity, improving the scientific mechanisms for wage determination, normal growth, and payment guarantees, and improving minimum wage growth and the way contributions are distributed. Insisting on shared development involves the issues of people's livelihoods and common prosperity, and here the issue of distribution is especially prominent. Disparity in the distribution of property and income in China is now large, with China's Gini coefficient exceeding that of the United States; the richest 1% of families receive one-third of China's household income, which is the same as in the United States. It should be noted that the key indicator of polarisation between rich and poor is not income. Income is merely the flow of wealth, while the key is the stock of wealth or household net worth, which is the primary indicator of wealth polarisation. According to a report in *Reference News* from 17 October 2015, *Hurun Wealth Report* stated that China had more billionaires than the United States. The wealth tracking report said that although China's economic growth had slowed, the number of billionaires increased in 2015 from 354 to 596, an increase of 242. By comparison, the number of billionaires in the United States was 537. The number cited for Chinese billionaires did not include those living in Hong Kong, Macao, or Taiwan. During the past decade or so, the Party Central Committee has always emphasised *narrowing the income gap*, but this issue has attracted a fair amount of controversy in academia and politics. There have even been articles written, which state that *the rich are the economic engine and the social role model*.

A common misconception is that the current gap between rich and poor is not the primary issue, and that it is unaffected by the large-scale development of the non-public economy; according to this view, it is the *middle-income trap* that China needs to be concerned with. This is a prominent issue that needs to be carefully scrutinised. The term *middle-income trap* was coined in a World Bank one-page report from 2007, entitled *An East Asian Renaissance: Ideas for Economic Growth*[86]. No clear definition of the term was given; the report only described several aspects of the supposed trap, including a lack of economies of scale, large economic fluctuations or economic stagnation, and difficulties in economic growth. These scant details provide room for ambiguity, even if unintentional. It is worth noting that there are some Westerners with rigorous academic styles who, through independent research, have come to disagree with the concept of a *middle-income trap*.

In the first place, the real reason for Latin America's fall into the so-called *middle-income trap* is the result of rampant neoliberalism. Neoliberalism is an extreme development of classical liberalism. It advocates complete marketisation and deregulation and gained momentum after the failure of Keynesianism. Next, all of the thirty-one low-income countries analysed, except for North Korea, have adopted capitalism, and most of them are African countries. The so-called *systemic superiority of capitalist countries* has not been demonstrated in these countries. On the contrary, low-income capitalist countries have serious problems. Taking African countries as

---

86. https://openknowledge.worldbank.org/handle/10986/6798

an example, they are more or less tied to the capitalist system, and they suffer from issues such as an overall ideological backwardness, political instability, constant conflicts at home and abroad, food shortages, inadequate public health, serious shortages of educational resources, and staggering unemployment problems. Have high-income countries fallen into this trap? The United States-led Western, high-income countries have now experienced financial crises, economic crises, and fiscal crises for nearly eight years. A few years ago, the Occupy Wall Street movement theorised a 1% *and* 99% polarisation between rich and poor. Frequent outbreaks of economic, political, and military hegemonic expansion have shown that the United States, the European Union, and Japan have fallen into a *high-income trap*.

Today, one of the keys to truly implementing the new concept of achievement-sharing and common prosperity emphasised by the Fifth Plenary Session of the 18th CPC Central Committee is to strengthen and improve public ownership, with distribution according to work as its pivot. China must unswervingly consolidate and develop a public ownership economy. This necessitates the inclusion of the state-owned economy and various forms of collective and cooperative economies. The public economy is the economic foundation that excludes exploitation, eliminates polarisation, and is an actualisation of shared prosperity. It is the market pillar that develops modern socialised productivity, and it represents an important way to restrict non-public economic exploitation while improving labour wealth and income. Over the years, the dominant position of public ownership and distribution according to work has gradually weakened, and the proportion of labour income has declined. In the final analysis, this is because the dominant position of the public economy is being sidelined. It is of the greatest importance to develop mixed ownership, with public ownership in the dominant role and public capital as the controlling shareholder. A second key to shared prosperity involves building a state-led labour rights protection mechanism. Currently, most of our workers are employed in non-public enterprises, and owners have the final say on whether to increase wages or not. Therefore, there has been little room for government intervention. Western governments, reflecting the standpoint of the employer class, rely on post-regulation to coordinate labour relations. A socialist government that is a people's government rather than a *neutral government* should learn from the lessons of the West. It should take a stand for the employee class and adopt proactive measures to coordinate labour relations in advance. In the past, under the employee ratio system and income co-determination mechanism of the board of directors in enterprises of the Federal Republic of Germany, labour unions negotiated reasonable increases in the incomes of employees in line with rises in labour productivity within the enterprises. In Japan, increases in employee incomes were based on seniority, that is, the number of years spent working for a particular employer. These guidelines may provide useful references for the Chinese government. If the government carries out strict checks and implements statutory labour hours and the *Labour Contract Law*, the interests of workers will be fully protected. This would be a proactive measure to coordinate labour relations and maintain social stability. If governments at various levels coordinate their activity only after labour conflicts occur, they will find themselves in a passive position and will hardly be able to reflect the working-class nature of the people's government. This would be entirely inconsistent with the positive spirit of strictly and comprehensively governing the country according to law.

(Originally published in the *Journal of Nanjing University of Finance and Economics*, Issue 1, 2016)

*   *   *

Section II Promote Economic and Social Development with Innovation as the Primary Driving Force

The *Proposals of the Central Committee of the Communist Party of China on Formulating the 13th Five-Year Plan for National Economic and Social Development* stated, 'To achieve the development goals of the 13th Five-Year Plan period, solve developmental problems, and consolidate the advantages of development, we must firmly establish the developmental concept of innovation, coordination, greenness, openness, and sharing.'[87] To implement the spirit of the Fifth Plenary Session of the 18th CPC Central Committee, the most important thing is to grasp and adhere to the five developmental concepts put forward by the plenum. China should use the new developmental concepts to guide development, solve developmental problems, enhance the driving forces for development, and expand the scope of development. *Innovation* ranks first among the five new

---

87. http://www.gov.cn/xinwen/2015-11/03/content_2959432.htm

developmental concepts. This section will explore what innovation is, why and how to innovate, and more.

1. Deepen Understanding of the Importance and Scientific Implications of Innovation

The concept of innovative development put forward by the Fifth Plenary Session of the 18th CPC Central Committee differs from innovation at the general technical level and is more than just innovation in the field of science and technology. It is an important guiding element in the ideology of the Communist Party of China as the Party sets out to lead economic and social development, and it represents the core concept guiding our overall development. It covers theoretical innovation, institutional innovation, scientific and technological innovation, cultural innovation, and other relevant aspects. It is related to the comprehensive establishment of a moderately prosperous society and the realisation of the great rejuvenation of the Chinese nation. In order to fully understand the innovative developmental concept, put forward by the Fifth Plenary Session of the 18th CPCCC, China must thoroughly grasp the scientific implications and special importance of this concept of innovation.

(I) Deepen Understanding of the Scientific Meaning of the Concept of Innovation

To uphold and implement the concept of innovation, China must first correctly grasp the scientific meaning of this idea. The Communist Party of China views the concept of innovation as the guiding ideology of the development effort that the Party leads and assigns it the core position in national development overall. China can thus see that this concept is different from innovation in the general sense, both in its connotations and extended meaning. From the perspective of its connotations, the concept features three elements: first, technological and economic innovation, led by technological innovation; second, institutional innovation, based on innovation in the areas of systems and mechanisms; and third, innovation in thinking, based on innovation in ideas, concepts, and modes of reasoning. In its extended significance, the concept includes innovations in productivity and production relations, as well as in economic foundations, superstructures, and ideology. It also includes innovation in production modes, consumption patterns, modes of thinking, and social governance.

(II) Deepen the Understanding on the Importance of the Concept of Innovation

Xi Jinping has repeatedly emphasised the particular importance of the concept of innovation, stating at one point: 'Innovation is the primary driving force for development. China's economic and social development must break through bottleneck constraints and resolve deep-rooted contradictions and problems.[88] Innovation is the fundamental way for our country to be at the forefront of the world. Innovation means development, and innovation means the future. Without innovation, we will lag behind, and if we are slow to innovate, we will lag behind as well'.[89] The Fifth Plenary Session of the 18th CPC Central Committee explicitly stated: 'To pursue innovative development, we must place innovation at the core of the country's overall development, constantly promote innovation in theory, system, science and technology, culture, and other aspects, and ensure that innovation runs through all of the party's and country's work. We must ensure that innovation becomes a continuous trend in our entire society'[13].

First, the concept of innovation is an important guiding ideology that allows the party to lead the way in development. Leading economic and social development in the new era requires new developmental concepts. If a concept is outdated and cannot match the developmental requirements of the times, it will inevitably hinder overall development and reduce its effectiveness. Even with the most vigorous of efforts, such a concept will achieve only a limited amount. Xi Jinping emphasised: 'Developmental concepts are the trailblazers of developmental action. They determine the management of the overall situation, the fundamentals, the direction, and the long-term vision. They are the concentrated embodiment of developmental thinking and developmental direction and are the focus of development. If we have the right developmental concepts, we will set our goals, tasks, policies, and measures accordingly'[90]. The new developmental concepts put forward by the Fifth Plenary

---

88. Xi Jinping. 'Achieving real growth - on promoting sustainable and healthy economic development [N].' *People's Daily*, 2014-07-07.

http://cpc.people.com.cn/n/2014/0707/c64387-25245316.html

89. http://www.xinhuanet.com//politics/2015-07/19/c_1115970819.htm

90. Xi Jinping. 'Note on the Proposal of the Central Committee of the Communist Party of China on Formulating the Thirteenth Five-Year Plan for National Economic and Social Development [N].' *People's Daily*, 2015-11-04.

http://www.gov.cn/xinwen/2015-11/03/content_5004118.htm

Session of the 18th CPC Central Committee are an important guiding ideology and action plan for the Party to lead economic and social development in the new period. *Innovation* is among the top five major developmental concepts. Party committees and governments at all levels must grasp the particular importance of innovative ideas that derive from the party's guiding ideology. They must view these ideas as guiding principles for the actions of the region, department, and unit; they must hold to these ideas as a common thread that runs through the whole process of development and must promote and lead development through innovative thinking.

Second, innovation is the core concept that leads the country's overall development. The Fifth Plenary Session of the 18th CPC Central Committee stated clearly, 'Innovation must be placed at the core of the overall development of the country'[91]. Xi Jinping has emphasised: 'These five developmental concepts are the crystallisation of China's developmental thinking, developmental direction, and developmental focus during the 13th Five-Year Plan period and beyond. They are also the concentrated reflection of China's developmental experience of more than thirty years of reform and opening up. They reflect the new understanding of China's developmental pattern. Innovative development is not a general policy but a concept that occupies the core position in the overall development of the country. It is directly related to the success or failure of the country's modernisation. Innovation is the soul of a nation's progress, the inexhaustible motivation for a country's prosperity, and the most distinctive national endowment of the Chinese nation'[92]. Innovation is of immediate importance to the entire country's modernisation strategy and affects the overall long-term situation. At present, innovation is easing downward pressure on the economy and boosting economic development. In the near future, innovation will still be important for achieving the goal of building a moderately prosperous society by 2020. In the long run, innovation will basically determine whether China achieves modernisation by the second centennial. Innovation-driven development requires strategic vision and global thinking. China should not only stress the evolution of technology, but also pay attention to the interaction between various technologies and industries. In fact, innovation-driven development requires not only coordinated innovation in the development of high, medium, and low-tech industries, but also a balance between innovation-driven development, foreign

91. Ibid
92. Ibid

direct investment (FDI), and the size of an enterprise. Therefore, China needs long-term planning, comprehensive strategising, and a range of supporting policies.[93]

Finally, innovation is the primary driving force for economic and social development. The innovative concept put forward by the Fifth Plenary Session of the 18th CPC Central Committee was essentially designed to solve the issue of developmental momentum. Economic and social development must first have a strong impetus. As the saying goes, *the train runs fast because of the locomotive*. The impetus is the *locomotive* that leads economic and social development. At present, China's economic and social development *bottleneck* is a lack of old and new impetuses. There is an urgent need to solve the problems of a shortage of impetus and of a lack of innovation in the areas of economic and social development in China. This can be resolved through pursuing innovation. Solving these problems will inject a powerful impetus into sustainable economic and social development. At present, China's economic development not only faces the arduous task of solving the *three-phase superposition* of our domestic economy and structural transformation, but it also faces the tremendous pressure of fierce competition on the world stage of science and technology. In response to this grim situation at home and abroad, the fundamental way out is through innovation. Only by vigorously pursuing innovation as the primary impetus for development can China allay the *three-phase superposition* risk, solve the problem of overcapacity, realise sustained and beneficial transformations, upgrade the economic structure, and maintain the pace of the world's scientific and technological revolution. Only by utilising innovation as the top priority for promoting development, transforming old impetus with innovation, cultivating new impetus with innovation, rejuvenating old impetus with new vitality, and developing new and continuous ways for impetus to emerge, will China be able to enhance the impetus to lead economic and social development.

2. Lead the New Normal Economic Development with Technological Innovation as the Impetus

The fundamental way out of the current dilemmas of economic development is through innovation, and the fundamental driving

---

93. Wang WG, Ma S, Jiang B. 'Research on the influencing factors of innovation-driven growth of low-tech industries in high-tech industries [J].' *China Industrial Economy*, 2015 (3).

force for achieving sustainable economic development is also innovation. As Xi Jinping has said, 'Under the new normal, China's economic development shows three characteristics: change of speed, structural optimisation, and impetus transformation. The growth rate should be shifted from high-speed to medium-to-high speed. The developmental model should be changed from one of speed and scale to one of quality and efficiency. The economic structure should be shifted from incremental expansion to stock adjustment and increment optimisation. And lastly, the developmental impetus should shift from relying mainly on resources, low-cost labour, and other factors, to relying on innovative drive'[94]. The new normal needs new impetus. To realise the dream of economic recovery under the new economic normal, the main avenue must be to improve quality and increase efficiency. Only by adapting to the new normal, grasping the new normal, and leading the way in developing the new normal can China actively transform its impetus and cultivate new impetus. The principal problems of China's current economic development are weak and insufficient impetus and lack of new impetus, and these have become bottlenecks that restrict economic development.

(I) Breaking Through the Bottleneck of Economic Development with Technological Innovation as the Impetus

Insufficient impetus is the bottleneck that currently restricts China's economic development, and the only way to break through the bottleneck is through innovation. The cultivation of new impetus through innovation is required to *enhance the leading role of scientific and technological innovation in comprehensive innovation, to strengthen basic research and original innovation, to fortify integrated innovation, and to conduct introduction, absorption, and re-innovation.* This ideology is in accordance with the requirements of the Third Plenary Session of the 18th CPC Central Committee. Science and technology are the primary productive forces and the primary driving forces for economic and social development. Scientific, technological, and economic innovation intrinsically foster the momentum for new development, expand the space for new development, create new industrial systems, and vigorously promote agricultural

---

94. Xi Jinping. 'Note on the Proposal of the Central Committee of the Communist Party of China on Formulating the Thirteenth Five-Year Plan for National Economic and Social Development [N].' *People's Daily*, 2015-11-04. http://www.gov.cn/xinwen/2015-11/03/content_5004118.htm

modernisation. In the past, China's development essentially relied on factor inputs and low-cost labour, which amounted to a typical pattern of extensive development based on expansions of scale. Extensive development has resulted in serious overcapacity, in resource and environmental constraints, in a lack of innovation capacity, and in a large but not a vibrant economy. Continuing to rely on factor inputs has now become untenable; the era of competition based on low-cost labour has passed. The demand for innovation in our current economic development is stronger and more urgent than at any time in the past. The fundamental way to achieve economic development is through innovation. The future is all about innovation, and the key is innovation. Only innovation can fundamentally break through the bottleneck constraints of insufficient developmental momentum. When China looks to innovation-driven development as the major strategy for China's future, the need to focus on promoting a close integration of technological innovation and socioeconomic development is clear. This path will allow the market to truly become a force for the allocation of innovation resources, and companies will indeed become the core players of scientific and technological innovation. Moreover, the government should take action in areas related to the national economy, to people's livelihoods, and to the lifeline of industry. The government needs to strengthen support and coordination, determine the nation's overall technical direction and route, make good use of such drivers as major national science and technology projects, and concentrate on achieving the full extent of our economic potential. The key to implementing an innovation-driven development strategy is to enhance independent innovation capabilities and to strive to harness core technologies.[95]

(II) Leading the New Round of World Scientific and Technological Revolution and Industrial Transformation with Technological Innovation as the Impetus

It has now been more than sixty years since the founding of the People's Republic of China; and thirty years since reform and opening up triggered a new phase in China's rapid economic development. China's previous scientific and technological backwardness has been decisively ended, and the global influence and status of Chinese

---

95. Cheng Enfu. 'Xi Jinping's Ten Strategic Economic Ideas [J].' *Contemporary Perspectives on Social Sciences*, 2014 (1).

scientific and technological innovation has risen to a new level. In the past, figuratively speaking, the Chinese were followers, but now they are not simply following. China has caught up and is now running side-by-side with other competitors, even leading the race in some areas. Catching up depends mainly on learning and imitation but running side-by-side and taking the lead requires innovation, originality, and initiative. Without innovation, there is no possibility of matching others or leading the field; there is even the danger of missing the developmental opportunities brought about by the world's new scientific and technological revolutions and of witnessing the widening gap with the most advanced countries in technological and economic development. From the perspective of the international development environment, a new round of scientific and technological revolution and industrial transformation is set to begin. If China wants to forge ahead in the world's scientific and technological competition, providing both leadership and cooperation, it must vigorously promote scientific and technological innovation, record more pioneering achievements in this field, and use technological innovation as the driving force to enhance its ability to lead and cooperate in the world's scientific and technological development.

3. Promoting the Modernisation of the National Governance System with Institutional Innovation as the Impetus

Modernisation and innovation of the national governance system is an important symbol and driving force for the progress of social civilisation. *The national governance system is an institutional complex that manages the country under the leadership of the party, and that includes the systems, mechanisms, and legal and regulatory arrangements that govern the economy, politics, culture, society, ecology, and party-building. The national governance system is also a set of national systems closely linked to and coordinated with each other.*[96] To advance the modernisation of our national governance system, China must attach great importance to institutional innovation. The national governance system is not only tasked with the mission and responsibility of promoting scientific, technological, economic, and ideological innovation, but is also entrusted with the requirements and tasks of advancing with the times and innovating internally. It is necessary to give full play to

---

96. Fan Fengchun. 'Innovative social governance to achieve "five changes" [N].' *Guangming Daily*, 2014-07-20.

the important role of the national governance system in promoting innovation in science, technology, the economy, and ideology, and to pay attention to the modernisation and innovation of the national governance system itself.

(I) Promoting Scientific, Technological, Economic, and Ideological Innovation through Innovation within the National Governance System

Scientific, technological, economic, and ideological innovations require a rational and scientific governance system. Although the current governance system has played an important role, there is still a sizeable gap as regards the requirements for comprehensively promoting innovation in science, technology, the economy, and ideology. Due to system imperfections and shortcomings within the mechanisms of the national governance system, China has, at times, witnessed the hindering, delaying, and even stifling of innovation in science, technology, the economy, and ideology. For example, some innovations have remained stuck at the *first kilometer* because of failures to improve systems and mechanisms. Other innovations have been stuck at the *last kilometer* due to poor systems and mechanisms. Still other innovations have been stillborn because the systems and mechanisms have suffered from more serious defects. To allow innovation to prevail throughout the whole of society, China should first promote innovation and modernisation in the national governance system, with institutional innovation as the driving force. It should utilise institutional innovation to clear obstacles, open up new pathways, and provide guarantees that social innovation will be promoted. At the level of the national governance system, China needs to stimulate the vitality of social innovation, foster the impetus for social innovation, broaden the opportunities for social innovation, set the stage for social innovation, and unclutter the channels through which social innovation proceeds.

(II) The National Governance System Must Keep Pace with the Times and Undergo Innovation

The national governance system should play a key role in promoting science, technology, the economy, and ideological innovation. The most significant aspect here is that the national governance system has an obligation to improve the nation's level of modernisation through innovations to its own structures.

To promote innovation and modernisation within the national governance system, China must first streamline institutions and decentralise power. The main drawbacks of China's national governance system are organisations that have grown too large; they wield power that is inefficient and too centralised. To modernise the national governance system, China must resolve to streamline institutions and implement a *super-ministry system*. For longer than anyone can remember, government agencies have had overlapping functions, too many detailed divisions, redundant establishments, huge organisations, and mutual constraints. These drawbacks have adversely affected efficiency and have not been conducive to stimulating the vitality of social innovation. The key to modernising the national governance system is to slim down the government and transform its functions. The focus must be on building a lean, efficient, strong, and authoritative government; China must transform our focus on functions so as to strengthen the government's service functions, its regulatory functions, and the authority of decision-making and guidance. China must establish a service-oriented government. Regarding matters of governance, governments should manage their duties in a strict and precise manner. Matters that do not fall within the bounds of true governance should be eliminated. In areas of power that require centralisation, governments must ensure that their authority is strong and highly concentrated, so that power is exercised fully and effectively in the proper places. The power that is subject to decentralisation should be decentralised firmly, and returned to society, enterprises, and the people. By appropriately structuring governmental institutions and functions, China will improve the modernisation of the national governance system, optimise the allocation of social and political resources, and stimulate social innovation. It should be pointed out that while the market economy enjoys an inherent functional strength in promoting innovation-driven development, itmay also give rise to opportunism, thus leading to insufficient innovation impetus. That is, this opportunism may eventually lead to an innovation-driven *market failure.*[97]

Next, to advance the modernisation of the national governance system China must adhere to socialism. To modernise national

---

97. Chen Bo. 'On the connotation characteristics and realization conditions of innovation-driven---The realization of "Chinese dream" as a perspective [J].' *Journal of Fudan University: Philosophy and Social Science Edition*, 2014 (4).

governance, China must base itself on the national conditions, adhere to a socialist direction, and not simply copy Western models. Western developed countries have accumulated a wealth of experience in building their national governance systems. They have created relatively well-developed systems that have included numerous achievements in human civilisation, which reflect well on the common law of social governance. In promoting modernisation and innovation in the Chinese national governance system, China should consider thoughtfully the more advanced and useful experiences and practices of Western social governance, so as to improve the quality of the civilisation. However, China must not copy the practices concerned indiscriminately, let alone worship the Western systems of which they are part, or fully Westernise the Chinese systems. China must base itself on the specific national conditions and keep to the socialist course. Even in the case of the most advanced and beneficial experiences and practices of the West, China must be selective, transformative, and able to digest the core of these experiences, rather than simply transplanting and grafting them onto China's culture. Attention must be paid to the *Westernisation trap and* prevent people from touting detrimental concepts such as *separation of the three powers*, *multi-party system*, *parliamentary system*, and *nationalisation of the army* under the guise of promoting innovation and modernisation in the national governance system. Further, China should resolutely counter any opposition to the party's leadership over the country and the army. It should guard against opposition to the people's congressional system, threats to the country's fundamental political system, and changes to its socialist nature.

4. Promoting Emancipation of the Mind through Innovative Ideas and Modes of Thinking

Emancipation of the mind is the prerequisite for promoting innovation, and effective innovation in turn requires emancipation of the mind. Only by emancipating the mind can China dare to think, to act, to break through, to take risks, and to attempt innovation. Without emancipation of the mind, innovation cannot even begin, and people's enthusiasm and potential for innovation are likely to be suppressed or even stifled. To uphold and practice the concept of innovation put forward by the Fifth Plenary Session of the 18th CPC Central Committee, it is necessary to further promote the emancipation of the mind, with innovation in ideas and modes of thinking.

(I) Promoting Emancipation of the Mind through Innovative Ideas and Modes of Thinking

Innovative ideas and modes of thinking are complementary to the emancipation of the mind and serve to condition it. Innovation in ideas and modes of thinking is not only a sign of emancipation of the mind, but also the essential meaning of that emancipation, and at the same time the force that drives it. Without emancipation of the mind, it is difficult, if not impossible, to achieve innovation in ideas and modes of thinking. If China is to promote economic, social, and ideological innovation, it is necessary to break from stereotypes and traditional ideas, to overcome customary thinking and subjective prejudices, to break the shackles of habitual restraints, and to bring innovation to the ideas and patterns of thought. In a social environment where ideology is confined, rigid, and conservative, achieving innovation is arduous, and producing new ideas and new concepts becomes problematic.

To uphold and implement the innovative ideas put forward by the Fifth Plenary Session of the 18th CPC Central Committee, China must take the emancipation of its ideology further and use it as a guide to promote innovative development. Over the past thirty years of reform and opening up, China has made tremendous advances in emancipating its mind, but there is no consensus on whether this mental emancipation now needs to continue. There are people who consider that after more than thirty years of reform, the minds of the Chinese people have been emancipated almost completely, and that the main task now is to unify and stabilise their thinking. Others make the observation that emancipation cannot continue forever. Still others believe that emancipation of the mind has gone too far and should now stop. Influenced by these debates, many people have, to varying degrees, experienced a waning of their passions. Their fighting spirits are now flagging, and mental fatigue has become the dominant threat to the emancipation of their minds.[98] This situation is extremely detrimental to innovation in ideas and modes of thinking.

To adhere to and implement innovative ideas, China needs to be intensely aware that there are no limits to the emancipation of the mind. The ideological activity of human beings has always been combined closely with practice. Meanwhile, it is the endless development of social practice that determines the endless, innovative

---

98. Tan Jinsong. 'Thought emancipation without industry, emancipation with principles [J].' *Observation and reflection*, 2015 (4).

liberation of the human mind. Human thinking is always marked by a process, in which old ideas are constantly being replaced by new ones, and advanced ideas continually conquer and eliminate backward ones. The activities of the human mind will never cease. Simultaneously, people's ideological stances have a certain independence of social practice. Once a new thought or concept has been formed, it will not alter rapidly in line with changes to social practice, nor will it immediately quit the historical stage after the social practices associated with it have disappeared. Once people have formed a certain view, understanding, concept, thought, or theory, they will consciously or unconsciously stick to it, maintain it, and stabilise it. This is what is often termed their mindset. Mindsets tend to lead to conservative thinking, rigid cognition, thought imprisonment, conformism, and scholasticism. The existence of mindsets result in a dullness and tardiness in the way people reflect on social practices. Mindsets are the biggest obstacle to people liberating their thought and embracing innovation. If it is true that there is no end to social development and innovation, then China may reason that there is no end to the emancipation of the mind. This is the eternal theme of the sustained development of human society.[99]

(II) Guiding and Driving Social Innovation through Innovative Ideas and Modes of Thinking

Innovations in ideas and modes of thinking are the precursors to all innovations. Whether innovations are in the fields of science, of technology, in the economy, or in the national governance system, which includes innovation within systems and mechanisms, innovations in all areas take their origins from innovations in ideas and modes of thinking. This requires the Chinese to emancipate their minds and dare themselves to break with the stereotypes of their thinking. Innovations in ideas and modes of thinking need to start from the following aspects.

First of all, China must cultivate a mental mode of self-transcendence. Self-transcendence means never being satisfied and always pursuing excellence. People who are content with what they have, and who do not want or dare to develop further, have no urge to innovate; so, it is impossible for them to innovate no matter in what work they are engaged. Only by means of innovation can the Chinese people surpass themselves. Adhering to new, innovative

---

99. Ibid

ideas, and realising them in practice, requires the cultivation of self-transcendent thinking.

Next, it is necessary to cultivate a mode of thinking that includes self-transformation. Innovation stems from self-change. China can only achieve innovation through self-change. Yet self-change also requires innovation; the two complement each other. It is easy for people to behave according to their routines and to think according to their habits; they fear change and get into a rut. This is the major obstacle that hinders innovation. To adhere to innovative ideas and turn them into reality, China needs to incorporate self-transformation into its mental practice.

Finally, the Chinese people must develop a mode of thinking that encourages them to take the lead on a global scale. Innovation comes largely from the spiritual drive to dare to be the first in the world. How can China be the *first in the world*? Only through innovation, and only by embracing the idea of always doing better than others can China seize opportunities, take the lead in the race, capture the high ground, and control development. Without innovation, China will be unable to take the lead; instead, it will lag behind and be eliminated. To allow China to be satisfied with a mediocre status in life, never dare to forge ahead or seek greater challenges and live a life of easy contentment and complacency will rob China of the ability to be innovative.

5. Creating an Innovative Atmosphere and Conditions for the Entire Society

To uphold and practice the innovative ideas put forward by the Fifth Plenary Session of the 18th CPC Central Committee, it is necessary to create an innovative atmosphere, clear the terrain for innovation and build an innovative country and society. In line with the requirements of the Fifth Plenary Session of the 18th CPC Central Committee, China needs to *make innovation the basis of development, form an institutional framework for promoting innovation, and shape more innovation-driven, first-mover oriented development.*[100] It is clear that innovation is not only a requirement for science and technology workers, but also an urgent task for the entire Party and the whole society. Innovation is not only the first driving force for the development of productivity, but also the driving force behind the progress of the entire society. China must promote mass entrepreneurship

---

100. https://news.12371.cn/2015/10/29/ARTI1446118588896178.shtml

along with universal innovation, wide-ranging innovation, and a complete involvement in innovation, so that innovation becomes the source of technological progress, social development, and the vitality of the times.

(I) Cultivating Innovative Talents and Workers with Innovative Consciousness

Talent is the foundation of innovation. To make innovation the primary driving force for social development, the most important thing is to cultivate innovative talent and workers with innovative consciousness. The fundamental reason why China lacks innovation power is a glaring shortage of innovative talents, especially the leading talents required for major innovations. Workers often lack consciousness of innovation and an enthusiasm for it. To uphold and practice the innovative ideas put forward by the Fifth Plenary Session of the 18th CPC Central Committee, China must start by cultivating workers' innovation awareness and innovative talents.

Initially, China should attach importance to the cultivation and introduction of high-level innovative talent. To promote social innovation, especially scientific and technological innovation, China needs high-level innovative talent. China should attach great importance to the cultivation and improvement of the existing high-level talent and give full play to their roles in leading and consolidating innovation. At the same time, it is necessary to pay attention to the introduction of high-level talents, especially those who have been identified as leading talents. At present, the world is full of high-end innovative talents, and competition in the international talent market is fierce.

China should seek to attract first-rate talents from abroad, especially from among overseas Chinese and students, through preferential policies. China must handle the relationship between cultivation and introduction properly, and place strong emphasis on both. Whether high-level innovative talents are cultivated or introduced, they should be treated equally, taken seriously, respected; China should build working platforms for them, and help them with the difficulties that they encounter in their work, study, and life. China should assist them in their lives and studies, offer them preferential policies, promise them good job opportunities, promote their welfare, and treat them with sincerity. They must be provided with a stage so that they will have an opportunity to exercise their talents, and China must try to allay their worries and fears so that their enthusiasm for innovation can be fully expressed and their intelligence and wisdom can be fully utilised.

Furthermore, it is necessary to cultivate and stimulate workers' innovative thinking and enthusiasm. Workers are the main force of mass entrepreneurship and innovation. Sticking to and implementing the concept of innovation is based on the cultivation and improvement of workers' awareness of innovation and the enhancement of their qualities and ability to innovate. First, it is necessary to stimulate the enthusiasm of on-the-job workers for innovation. Party committees and governments at all levels should support and protect the enthusiasm of workers for entrepreneurial innovation, while stimulating the vitality of entrepreneurial innovation, tapping the potential of entrepreneurial innovation through policy support, and providing public opinion guidance and material encouragement in accordance with the requirements of the central government to encourage *mass entrepreneurship and innovation*. Those who venture to start their own businesses and who become prosperous first will gain the respect of the country and society. Moreover, China must pay attention to vocational and technical education, to innovation awareness in higher education, and to the cultivation of innovative talent. Tens of millions of young students in the country enter middle and high schools every year, and they represent a large reserve army of labour. In accordance with the central government's strategic requirements of *mass entrepreneurship and innovation*, middle and high schools should pay attention to and strengthen the cultivation of young students' awareness of entrepreneurship and innovation, developing their readiness to embrace entrepreneurship and innovation. These endeavors will enable them to carry the banner of entrepreneurship and innovation and to become fresh troops for entrepreneurship and innovation in the future. The government and the Party shall encourage them to become explorers of future breakthroughs in innovation, practitioners of entrepreneurship and innovation, and promoters of the world's innovation trends. Additionally, innovation education should start from childhood; it should cultivate students' problem-solving abilities and awareness of innovation and infuse the innovative genes they possess with fresh and promising ideas. China must fundamentally change exam-oriented into innovation-based education, so that the students' awareness of innovation and their spirit of exploration through innovative educational and teaching methods is embraced. In this way, China will be able to make education truly serve national entrepreneurship and innovation.

(II) Strengthening Incentives for Social Innovation

Innovation needs incentives, and incentives are the driving force for innovation. The Chinese people must adhere to and practice the innovative ideology put forward at the Fifth Plenary Session of the 18th CPC Central Committee. China must work hard to improve the incentive mechanisms for social innovation, unleash the innovation potential of society, mobilise initiatives for innovation, and take full advantage of the wisdom of innovation, so that innovation will become common practice throughout society. The Fifth Plenary Session of the 18th CPC Central Committee called for *accelerating the formation of a market environment, a property rights system, an investment and financing system, a distribution system, and a mechanism for the introduction of talent cultivation and its use in ways conducive to innovative development.* The session also called on the Party to *inspire entrepreneurship and protect entrepreneurial property rights and the benefits flowing from innovation in accordance with the law.*[101] Practice has shown that original innovation is the decisive factor in the current economic development of all countries in the world, and that it is accurately reflected in a country's comprehensive strength. To uphold the sustained power of original innovation, it is necessary for China to not only stimulate the interest, curiosity, spirit of academic competition, and other innate potential of researchers but also to attach more importance to external factors such as demand pull, national policy promotion, and incentives, so as to jointly promote the continuous development of original innovation.[102] It is recommended that the government and enterprises improve the incentives for innovation in such areas as salaries, bonuses, taxation, and achievement transfers. China should give high priority to innovation and reward it well. China's innovative talents should receive generous recompense for their achievements. People who dare to innovate, and who prove good at it, should have more income and better lives and should become rich ahead of others. People with pioneer spirits should be respected and praised by society, and innovative talents should become role models for various industries. They should be awarded with corresponding honorary titles and should be promoted according to their innovative contributions. Let the public's enthusiasm for innovation burst forth; let the innovative

---

101. Ibid

102. Yu Suisheng. 'A study on the sustainable dynamics of original innovation [J].' *Journal of Management*, 2015 (5).

wisdom of diverse talents spring forth; and let the whole society be full of innovative vitality.

(III) Creating an Atmosphere of Public Opinion and a Social Environment That Promotes Social Innovation

Innovation needs a proper social environment, a sound atmosphere for public opinion, and cultivation of *the soil that nurtures* it. To uphold and practice the innovative ideas put forward by the Fifth Plenary Session of the 18th CPC Central Committee, through publicity, cultural influence, and policy guidance, China should *cultivate this fertile soil* for innovation and create a climate of innovation throughout our entire society. China should also develop a social consensus that innovators are honorable people who deserve to prosper and be well respected, so as to encourage others to actively pursue innovation.

To achieve these goals, China needs, first of all, to create a social environment that promotes entrepreneurial innovation. The more attention paid to innovation, and the greater the support it receives, the greater its effectiveness will be. If this point is not fully understood and importance attached to it, it will prove difficult to achieve good results from innovation. Party committees and governments at all levels should not only appreciate the importance of innovation from the perspective of science, technology, and the economy, but should also attach great weight to it in line with the principle that *the party guides the ideology of development*, and accordingly, should support innovation by increasing its investment. These same committees and governments must promote innovation based on a national developmental strategy, so that it can realise significant benefits. China should not only increase financial investments and material support for innovation, but also support and guarantee innovation through the institutional arrangements embodied in policies, regulations, systems, and mechanisms. It is also necessary to attach importance to innovation from the perspectives of ideology and leadership, and to ensure that innovation and development are on the agendas of party committees and governments, running through the entire process of their work. A new situation should be created in which entrepreneurial and innovative talents can stand out, so that everyone has the opportunity to excel in entrepreneurship and innovation and has a platform to show his or her talents in these fields.

Second, China should create an atmosphere of public opinion that promotes entrepreneurship and innovation. To uphold and practice

the innovative development concept put forward by the Fifth Plenary Session of the 18th CPC Central Committee, China must work
hard at changing public opinion, using publicity and education to
make entrepreneurship and innovation a culture, an ideology, a
consensus, and a social trend. China must create a strong base in
public opinion for a social trend that advocates, praises, respects,
and supports entrepreneurship and innovation, inspiring active participation throughout society.

**(IV) Improving the System and Mechanisms for Promoting and Ensuring
Innovation**

Innovation in science, technology, ideas, and the economy requires
the promotion and protection of a scientific, civilised, and democratic
modern system. Only by establishing such a system can society create a political situation that combines freedom with discipline, unity,
tension, and seriousness. Only within such a social system can the
members of society feel comfortable, speak out freely, think and act
boldly, emancipate their minds, seek new innovations, keep forging
ahead, and keep pace with the times. In a social system that is seriously lacking in democracy, everyone is cautious, frightened, and
fearful of punishment if they speak their minds. These hazards result
in an atmosphere in which only one person has a say, in other words,
a patriarchal system marked by ideological imprisonment and a
lack of vitality. History has shown that society can only emancipate
people's thinking if it is built on a scientific, civilised, and democratic system, and only this emancipation of the mind can trigger
innovation in the field of concepts and ideas along with innovation
in science, technology, and the economy. If China fears to break the
shackles on its thinking, then how can it emancipate its minds, not to
mention seeking innovative ideas?

In summary, to adhere to and implement the innovative ideas put
forward by the Fifth Plenary Session of the 18th CPC Central Committee, China must firmly grasp the concept that innovation is the
key driving force for development and the primary factor in stimulating social vitality. China must place innovation at the core of its
overall development as the main line running through the work of
the party and the country. It should create the social environment
and social trend that advocate, encourage, support, and practice
innovation within society. Only through such measures is it possible
to set the winds of innovation blowing across the country. China can
shine the light of innovation upon its land, kindle the spark of mass

innovation into a great conflagration for the benefit of the country, and turn a healthy dose of developmental momentum into a great rejuvenation for the Chinese nation.

(Originally published in *Marxism & Reality*, Issue I, 2016, Second Author: Tan Jinsong)

* * *

Section III Shared Development Is the New Discourse of Our Socialist Political Economy with Chinese Characteristics

At a symposium on philosophical and social science work on 17 May 2016, General Secretary Xi Jinping pointed out: 'For foreign theories, concepts, discourses, and methods, there must be analyses and identification. If they are applicable, use them; if not, then don't copy them. If China's philosophical and social sciences are to play their role, we must pay attention to strengthening the construction of our discourse system. We should have the best say in interpreting Chinese practices and in constructing Chinese theory'.[103] These words give voice to a completely correct and extremely important theoretical innovation. The new concept of shared development proposed by General Secretary Xi Jinping emphasises that the fundamental purpose of development is for the people, the strength of development is its reliance on the people, and the fruits of development are shared by the people. These words of General Secretary Xi Jinping thus present a new discourse and a new idea of socialist political economy with Chinese characteristics. There is an urgent need for in-depth interpretation and active dissemination in comparison with the relevant Western discourse.

1. The Formation of a New Idea of Shared Development

The new idea of shared development was included in a series of important speeches by General Secretary Xi Jinping. In March 2013, he stated: 'The Chinese people living in our great motherland and living in these great times all enjoy equal opportunities to achieve

---

103. Xi Jinping. 'Xi Jinping's speech at the symposium on the work of philosophy and social sciences [N].' *People's Daily*, 2016-05-19. http://cpc. people.com.cn/n1/2016/0519/c64094-28361550.html

their potential, to realise their dreams, and enjoy equal opportunities to participate in the development of the country'[104]. The Fifth Plenary Session of the 18ᵗʰ CPC Central Committee incorporated *sharing* into the four developmental concepts of *innovation, coordination, greenness, and openness,* providing the first comprehensive and systematic description of shared development. The Session also put forward an idea that may be summed up as follows: *to attain shared development, China must uphold the principle of development for the people and by the people, with the achievements of development shared among the people, and China must construct governance systems that can more effectively give the entire population an increased sense of shared gain. This will enhance development momentum and unite the people further in pursuing a shared goal of common prosperity.* These ideas may be considered the core of the concept of shared development. The Plenary clarified our country's people-centered developmental value orientation, spelt out the starting point and goal of our economic and social development, and provided a valuable summation of the economic development ideas underlying Xi Jinping's thoughts on governing the country.

China has now entered the new normal of rapid economic growth and is taking on the task of comprehensively deepening reform and economic governance. The shared development concept highlights the fact that the fundamental purpose of development is for the people; the strength of development depends on the people; and the fruits of development are shared by the people. It thus indicates the correct direction for economic and social development.

2. The Difference between a Sharing Economy and a Shared Economy

In Western economics there exists the concept of a *sharing economy*, but this needs to be distinguished from the concept of a *shared economy*, which has been widely discussed online in recent years. The latter concept refers to a business model that uses idle resources to provide consumers with low-priced goods or services through a highly efficient information publishing platform. Sharing of this kind is aimed essentially at profits rather than public welfare, and the situation with other market transactions is essentially the same. The *sharing economy* in Western economics refers to the theory, put forward by American economists in the 1980s, that the problem of domestic stagflation can be solved through linking wages to corporate profits. This

---

104. http://www.chinanews.com/gn/2013/03-17/4650319.shtml

theory holds that fixed wages can only cope with a normal economic environment. Under a fixed-wage model, an unexpected shock to the economy means that employees have to be laid off, which in turn results in insufficient demand. The use of aggressive monetary policy to spur job creation then leads to inflation. But linking wages to profits, the theory maintains, can automatically reduce wage costs during a recession and avoid layoffs and stagflation. During a boom, by contrast, workers are motivated to work more efficiently and increase overall returns. Influenced by the *sharing economy* theory, many companies in the United States have implemented profit-sharing plans based on employee shareholding. As of 2012, some 11 million workers had participated in such plans, with shared profits of 870 billion U.S. dollars. This situation has a definite progressive significance.

It seems that under such schemes, all working people participate in the distribution of new values. The *shared economy* proposed by General Secretary Xi Jinping, however, has important differences from the *sharing economy* found in Western economic theory. First, the two are based on different property rights and distribution subjects. The *shared economy* is connected to the basic property rights system with public ownership as the main element. Within this system multiple forms of ownership are developed, and multiple forms of distribution coexist. In the basic distribution system, however, distribution according to work serves as the central component. The shared part is principally achieved through the publicly owned enterprises that occupy a dominant position in the economy; in these enterprises, each worker shares and uses the means of production; labour remuneration is distributed according to work; and the income gap within the enterprise is kept moderate. Conversely, the non-public enterprises that play an auxiliary role use the national income of labour and capital for initial distribution and redistribution, and sharing can also be achieved to a certain extent. The *sharing economy* is connected to a basic system of property rights and income distribution whose mainstay consists of private ownership and distribution according to capital. The *sharing* is achieved predominantly by private enterprise; that is, the means of production are privately owned, and the workers use them subject to control by the capitalist. Profits are distributed in the form of shares, resulting in a pattern of sharing in which a large number of workers with relatively few shares receive less profits.

Second, the *shared* and *sharing* economies have different purposes. A *shared economy* is developed to serve people-centered developmental ends. It promotes the common enjoyment of development achievements by the whole people, increases the benefits of ownership inclusively, and jointly realises the common ultimate goal of raising the level of prosperity. A *sharing economy* is motivated by a wish to delay economic crises and represents a means of achieving this. It sets aside a small number of shares for distribution to workers in order to maximise the long-term profits of capitalists.

3. The Sharing Economy and Capital Restoration

The *sharing economy* is essentially an external manifestation of capitalist society's quest for capital reproduction. The reproduction of capital restoration refers to the reproduction by capitalists of their profits/accumulation through various means. While capital brings incremental value, its profit-seeking nature means that it also gives rise to a broad range of economic, social, and ecological problems. These problems will accumulate to a certain extent and will *break out* in the form of financial and economic crises. They will likely result in economic recession, unemployment, polarisation between rich and poor, environmental degradation, and other consequences that endanger the existence of the system. If these contradictions are to be alleviated, and if the operations of the capitalist economic and social system are to be maintained, capital must be restored.

There are many ways to reproduce capital, and a *sharing economy* is one of them. Of the surplus value that workers create, capitalists share a part with them in the form of equity dividends, so that employees have a sense of belonging to the company and feel responsibility for it. This in turn improves work efficiency, promotes productive use of resources, and ultimately brings more profits to the capitalists than if sharing is not practiced. It also provides certain gains for employees in the form of higher incomes and greater benefits.

In addition, raising the incomes of workers helps increase their ability to purchase goods, thereby stimulating effective demand, realising physical compensation and value compensation for capital, alleviating structural imbalances in the economy caused by insufficient effective demand, delaying the onset of economic crises, and prolonging the economic cycle. Moreover, by sharing a portion of enterprise profits with workers, capitalists can narrow the income gap between owners and employees. It can help the workers' leaders gain more income, thus weakening the resistance and bargaining power of labour unions and easing class contradictions.

In the long run, however, economic crises stem from the fundamental nature of capitalism, reflecting the basic contradiction between the socialisation of production and the private capitalist ownership of production materials. A *sharing economy* may alleviate class contradictions, but imbalances will still be exacerbated as a result of continuing accumulation, and class contradictions will gradually become more acute as the wealth gap widens. The *Occupy Wall Street* movement, which has spread to more than 80 capitalist countries in the past few years, has demonstrated this by pointing to the rich-poor divide between *the 1%* and *the 99%*.

4. Shared Economy: Dual Restoration of Labour and Capital

The reproduction of labour in the course of economic operations is more important than the reproduction of capital. The reproduction of labour refers to the reproduction of the labour force and to the improvement of workers' skills; it includes the primary matter of ensuring workers' survival and propagation, the intermediate question of workers' education and training, and the advanced issue of workers' comprehensive development. The factors involved in the reproduction of labour include workers' income levels, living conditions, educational levels, personal development, social welfare, and political rights. Under the capitalist system, private capital consumes labour through the production process that creates commodities and private surplus value. Workers are regarded only as tools of production. Their subjectivity cannot be truly established, and labour cannot be fully restored.

Even under the premise of the reproduction of capital by a *sharing economy*, the purpose of capitalist production determines the limits of labour reproduction. Although a *sharing economy* raises workers' incomes, it does not change the nature of capitalist production; that is, capitalist production pursues the maximisation of private profit. The means of production and social reproduction are all in the hands of private capital. First of all, the sharing of profits in this era of economic prosperity means that the primary reproduction and part of the intermediate reproduction of labour can be carried out smoothly. During an economic crisis, however, large numbers of workers are unemployed, and their living standards decline. Primary reproduction cannot be guaranteed in this situation. Second, with the advance of technology and the extensive use of large machines and computers, the organic composition of capital continues to increase, and more workers will be absorbed into the capitalist production system.

In contrast to the *sharing economy*, the *shared economy* not only has all the capital reproduction functions of the *sharing economy*, but also embodies the main purpose and functions of labour reproduction. The *shared economy* differs from the *sharing economy* in that the capital restoration of the *sharing economy* is only reflected in the field of distribution. Meanwhile, the reproduction of labour in a *shared economy* is comprehensively reflected in the whole range of economic activities including production, distribution, exchange, and consumption.

In the productive operations of public enterprises, mutually beneficial sharing of production materials, technologies, and information means that enterprises can make use of the easy communicability of knowledge, increased returns to scale, and decreased marginal costs in order to break the man-made barriers to knowledge dissemination that are created by private capitalist ownership and monopolism. The goal of this strategy is to achieve a maximum release of the growth dividends created by innovation, to make the economic aggregate larger, and to lay a material foundation for the common prosperity of every citizen.

Next, and in line with the concept summed up as *development depends on the people*, working people play a managerial role and occupy a dominant position in production. This aids them in realising their personal value and overall development and helps them achieve complete high-level labour restoration. Workers are able to accumulate work experience and production knowledge through their practice, and to realise intermediate labour restoration through the *learning by doing* effect.

Additionally, the development achievements are shared by the people, and the profits are shared by the workers and investors. This emerges clearly in the fact that the workers concerned participate in distribution according to their labour contributions, and it is also evident in the gradual promotion of labour and capital by non-public enterprises during the initial distribution and redistribution of national income. This is quite different from the way a capitalist, under a *sharing economy,* will obtain a large proportion of his or her income from capital ownership. A fair and reasonable distribution structure can bring about a rational and harmonious production structure, thus achieving the goal of fairly dividing up the *cake* while at the same time making it bigger.

Moreover, the transaction costs involved in exchanges between different entities are greatly reduced in a *shared economy* due to the mutually beneficial sharing of product information. This has the obvious advantages of reducing production costs, increasing economic profits, and increasing the benefits distributed to working people.

Further, the country manages economic profits in a rational manner, centralises portions of the profits in the form of taxes, and spends those funds on public goods with positive externalities, such as parks, hospitals, and schools. This not only allows for a more beneficial consumption structure, but also ensures that high-expenditure services such as education, medical care, and environmental protection are fully consumed. The labour restoration process of workers is then complete.

In short, under the concept of a *shared economy*, public capital reproduction and labour reproduction become two engines that promote complementarity and drive economic development. The contradiction between the two types of reproduction that exists under the *sharing economy* is eliminated. On the basis of recovering public capital to obtain more economic profits, China will expand the total amount of social and economic profits and then share the economic profits with the whole people by way of a fair and rational distribution system, thereby promoting the completion of labour restoration at all levels. At the same time, efficient and sound reproduction of labour will strengthen the subjective consciousness and sense of responsibility of all working people, increase their sense of progress and happiness, improve the quality and efficiency of their labour, and thus promote accelerated economic development while striving for more economic profits to complete the reproduction of capital.

(Originally published in *Guangming Daily*, July 6, 2016, First Author: Ding Xiaoqin)

* * *

Section IV Coordinated Development is the Key to the 13th Five-Year Plan

General Secretary Xi Jinping has pointed out that the new normal is an objective state that is certain to emerge at this stage of China's economic development. Since the 18th National Congress of the Communist Party of China, it has been necessary to put forward and implement the new concept of coordinated development, in order to adapt to and guide the new normal of the economy, to solve the long-standing uncoordinated problems in economic and social development, and to adhere to the people-centered development approach.

1. The Concept of Coordinated Development Includes the Dialectical Idea That Things Have a Universal Connection

The internal components of economic entities are interrelated, and the national economy and society make up a unified and interconnected whole. It is necessary to understand the real ties between them, to improve their qualities on the basis of their inherent connections, and to establish new and optimal interrelationships. Coordinated development means to firmly grasp the overall layout of socialism with Chinese characteristics, to correctly handle major developmental issues, and to promote the overall sound development of our society. China's Yangtze River Delta, Pearl River Delta, Beijing-Tianjin-Hebei area, central and western regions, Yangtze River Belt, northeast region and other regions along the Belt and Road routes have a wide range of interactive and symbiotic connections and require coordinated development. The focus of domestic regional coordination is on shaping a new pattern of coordinated regional development with orderly and free flowing factors, effective restraint of main functions, equal basic public services, sustainable resources, and a healthy environment.

At present, China is still confronted with uncoordinated regional development. Especially in the western region, old revolutionary areas inhabited by ethnic groups, border areas, and poverty-afflicted areas are still weak links in development. It is essential that these deficiencies should be fixed as soon as possible. A coordinated policy should initially focus on and support the weakest regions and areas. Meanwhile, support for regions with good ethnic unity and stability should not be less than that provided to unstable regions. Such areas should get prosperous first and set themselves up as a model to demonstrate their efficiency and good governance. It is necessary to use statistical data and objective facts to publicise the breakthroughs that are occurring. Since the founding of the People's Republic of China, and especially since its reform and opening up, the country's overall support for various ethnic regions (in terms of the income of ethnic regions) has greatly exceeded the value of the natural resource support contributed by the ethnic regions to the country as a whole (calculated on the basis of the expenditures or costs of ethnic regions). The policies involved here were followed because national unity and stability are beneficial to the economy and provide improved living standards for all.

2. Coordinated Development Includes the Dialectical Concept That Everything Has Two Aspects

General Secretary Xi Jinping has stressed that China should adhere to the reform direction of the socialist market economy, embracing the dialectical method and the doctrine that everything has two aspects. In other words, China should look at problems in two ways. China has always stressed that material and spiritual civilisations should be developed concurrently, but the development of these two types of civilisation have not proceeded in a bilateral fashion. This is why the 13th Five-Year Plan specifically calls for the coordinated development of two civilisations. When China sets out to build a moderately prosperous society in all respects, including those related to both material and spiritual civilisation, it is comparatively easy to achieve *hard civilisation* indicators, such as those of material, economic, and cultural development, as well as to bring material and cultural improvement to the lives of urban and rural residents. Nevertheless, spiritual civilisation, linked to the abstract human values such as integrity, ethics, and beliefs that together are known as *soft civilisation,* needs to be strengthened as well. These two civilisations are closely related. For example, the creation of social media hot topics and the sale of shoddy or counterfeit commodities both involve material civilisation. In the end, however, there are issues here that touch on moral character and spiritual civilisation.

The Party's determination and strictness in combating corruption should be used as a model for firmly managing the integrity of the business community, the atmosphere in the political sector, the writing style of the media, the scholarship in academia, the civil style of the community, and the military style of the army from the two aspects of ideology and sectoral regulation. It is necessary to establish *soft civilisation* rules and regulations throughout all walks of life, and when necessary, to strictly implement rewards and punishments. In this new era, China should vigorously publicise the spirit of Lei Feng and the pacesetters of spiritual civilisation in all walks of life. It must be ensured that this spirit permeates the national education system and the system of party schools. China should acquire skills in organically combining Marxism, in its Chinese-style outlook on life and values, with the essence of our traditional culture. China should promote the unity of knowledge and practice of social ethics, professional ethics, and family ethics by individuals and groups. Party and government departments at all levels should make full use of and improve the existing system that provides an index for the measurement of spiritual civilisation. They should use this index as a binding guide in assessing officials and the units and regions under their leadership. Only in this way can China ensure that this work does not become a mere formality and goes on to achieve significant and tangible results in giving the broad masses a true sense of gain.

3. Coordinated Development Includes the Dialectical Concept of the Relationship between Quantitative and Qualitative Change

Change and development in the economy, along with all other national advances, starts with quantitative changes. When looking at issues, China should keep in mind the idea that quantitative change leads to qualitative change. It is necessary to adhere to the principle of moderation, pay attention to the accumulation of quantity, and learn to optimise structure. At present, the key to promoting the coordinated development of urban and rural areas is to gradually improve the integrated system of urban and rural development, to improve the long-term mechanism of rural infrastructure investment, to promote the extension of urban public services to rural areas, and to improve the level of new rural construction in the socialist system. Especially in terms of the quantity, quality, and structure of the new people-centered urbanisation, there are several issues that urgently need attention and solutions. First, the quality of urbanisation needs to be improved. The urbanisation rate of China's permanent residents has exceeded 50%, while the urbanisation rate of the actual registered population is less than 40%. The second issue is the urgent need to guarantee urban services to rural people who have moved to cities. Approximately 240 million migrant workers and their dependents who are counted in the urban population have failed to enjoy the basic public services to which urban residents are entitled in the areas of education, employment, medical care, old-age care, and affordable housing. Third, the spatial distribution and structure of large, medium, and small towns needs urgently to be improved. The distribution of cities in the eastern, central, and western regions does not match the carrying capacity of resources or the environment. In small and medium-sized cities, there are insufficient industries and inadequate populations. Large cities have a *big city disease* issue. Fourth, it is urgent to strengthen the characteristics of urban and rural development. Some cities show a craving for things big and foreign, which leads to the *homogenisation* of architecture, etc., while some rural areas simply borrow urban elements, which lead to a loss of local characteristics and culture.

The key to solving these problems involves thinking in dialectical terms about the relationship between quantitative and qualitative changes, strengthening institutional arrangements and guidance based on classification, and promoting new urbanisation with unique characteristics based on local conditions. The people must be placed at the core of urbanisation, ensure that the permanent residents of urban areas are covered by basic public services as soon as possible, and strengthen vocational education and training for new citizens. It is necessary to synchronise urbanisation with informatisation, industrialisation, green development, agricultural modernisation, convenient transport, and a high quality of life. The promotion of the equal exchange of urban and rural factors and the balanced allocation of public resources is important. There is a definite need to coordinate new industrial-agricultural relations and urban-rural relations, optimise spatial layouts, intensively and efficiently promote urbanisation, and improve the efficiency of land and space utilisation.

In short, China must scientifically grasp and apply the materialist dialectics included in the concept of coordinated development, enhance the coordination and integrity of development, broaden the development space in coordinated development, enhance the momentum of development through strengthening weak areas, and promote the development of the five major areas of economic, political, cultural, social, and ecological civilisation. China must implement the content of the Four-Pronged Comprehensive Strategy, so as to continuously open up new prospects for the governance of the country.

(Originally published in *Theory Guide*, Issue 5, 2017)

Chapter 4

Reform of China's Distribution System

The interests of the people are paramount. Only by adhering to the principle of distribution according to work, improving the system and mechanism of distribution according to factors of production, and promoting a more rational and orderly distribution of income, can China deliver more of the fruits of reform and development to each individual in a more equitable way, and ultimately achieve prosperity for the entire people.

* * *

Section I Analysis of Labour Income Distribution

Since the financial crisis, the policies introduced by the Chinese government to stimulate economic growth have mainly been investment-oriented. Sluggish domestic demand is the bottleneck that restricts China's future long-term economic growth. Compared with developed countries, the proportion of consumption expenditure in China is obviously low. The reason for this has to do with the still relatively low average income of citizens, and especially and with the decline in the labour share of income, which is the most important factor restricting the growth of consumption.

1. The Current Distribution Status of China's Labour Income

Since the 1990s, labour income as a share of the total in China has been declining. Research by Li Daokui et al. (2009)[105] shows that the labour share in China's initial distribution rose slightly from 1992 to 1996 and declined gradually thereafter. In 1999, the labour share of income in China was about 54%, but by 2006 it had dropped below

---

105. Li Daokui, Liu Linlin, Wang Hongling. 'U-shaped Law of Labour Share Evolution in GDP [J].' *Economic Research*, 2009 (1)

50%. Research by Bai Chongen and Qian Zhenjie (2009)[106] shows that China's labour income share was about 50% in 1978, and that it increased slightly over the next decade. Since 1990, however, it has again declined, with the downward trend particularly obvious since 2004. The same research showed a drop to 47.31% in 2006. These detailed data indicate clearly that China's labour income share has fallen to its lowest level in history.

Research by other scholars has added to these findings and echoes the obvious conclusion that labour's share of income in China has indeed fallen to its lowest historical level. Zhao Junkang's (2006) research shows that between 1996 and 2003, China's urban and rural employment increased by 54.82 million people, while the share of income represented by labour compensation fell from 54.3% to 49.62%. With exceptions such as Inner Mongolia, Liaoning, Zhejiang, and Shandong, the labour remuneration share in twenty-seven provinces and cities declined to varying degrees. Studies by Xu Xianxiang and Wang Haigang (2008)[107] show that the income distribution in China's initial distribution continued to shift to the right from 1978 to 2002. The share of capital income generally increased, while that of labour income continued to decline. Research by Luo Changyuan and Zhang Jun (2009)[108] found that between 1995 and 2004 labour compensation in China fell from 51.4% of the total to 41.6%. Research by Zhuo Yongliang (2007)[109] shows that China's labour income share rose steadily in the early days of reform and opening up, from 42.1% in 1978 to 56.5% in 1983. But from 1984, this share began to decline, and by 2005 had fallen to 38.2%.

Although scholars differ greatly in their measurements of the absolute share of labour remuneration in China's GDP, it is an indisputable fact that in recent years this share has declined to a record low. Optimistic estimates of the share of income going to workers between 2002 and 2006 are in the region of 50%, while the pessimistic appraisal is around 40%.

---

106. Bai Chongen, Qian Zhenjie. 'Who is Crowding Out the Income of Citizens—Analysis of the Distribution Pattern of Chinese National Income [J].' *Chinese Social Sciences*, 2009 (5).

107. Xu Xianxiang, Wang Haigang. 'The polarization in China's primary distribution and its causes[J].' *Economic Research*, 2008(02):106-118.

108. Luo Changyuan, Zhang Jun. 'The Proportion of Labour Income in Economic Development: An Empirical Study Based on China's Industrial Data [J].' *Chinese Social Sciences*, 2009 (4).

109. Zhuo Yongliang. Plate drift, ready? [J]. *Decision*, 2007 (5).

Against this backdrop, another phenomenon accompanying the reduction in the labour income share has been a year-by-year widening of the labour income distribution gap. Research by Li Shi (2005)[110] shows that between 1995 and 2002, whether on the basis of data relating to urban citizens, rural citizens, or citizens in general, the Lorenz curve for China has shifted outward in a significant way. Li's research indicates clearly that China's income gap has constantly widened. Using income distribution data from the *China Statistical Yearbook* (1995-2005), Wang Zuxiang (2009)[111] concluded that in both the urban and rural sectors the current Gini coefficients are not large, neither of them exceeding 0.34. But since 2003, China's aggregate Gini coefficient has exceeded 0.44, far beyond the warning level of 0.4. It is generally believed that in market economy countries, a Gini coefficient between 0.3 and 0.4 signals a relatively reasonable income gap. Since 2000, China's Gini coefficient has been above 0.41, indicating that the gap between rich and poor is still widening.

Labour income share and the income gap are closely related. The rapid growth of capital income and the slow growth of labour income are the main reasons for the current national income gap. Under normal circumstances, the income gap is influenced by differences in labour productivity, and higher labour productivity means higher labour compensation. This can also be illustrated from the perspective of labour productivity, the opposite of capital productivity: if capital productivity grows more rapidly than labour productivity, then in the process of income distribution wealth will lean toward the party that owns capital, thereby reducing the share of labour income and increasing the inequality of income distribution. Wage income is the most important source of citizens' income, and the decline in its proportion is related to the slow growth of wages. There are about 100 million to 150 million working people in China who are either unemployed or underemployed. This prevents wage income from increasing along with labour productivity, which in turn has brought the continuous decline in the national share of wage income.

The decline in the share of labour income has thus led to an increase in the proportion of capital income and government income, which to a certain extent further widens the income gap between citizens who earn wages and those who receive capital returns.

---

110. Li Shi, Wei Zhong, Ding Sai. 'Empirical Analysis of the Unequal Distribution of Chinese Citizens' Property and Its Causes [J].' *Economic Research*, 2005 (6).

111. Wang Zuxiang, Zhang Kui, Meng Yong. 'A study on the estimation of Gini coefficient in China [J].' *Economic Review*, 2009(03): p. 14-21.

In other words, the decline in labour's income share is the reason for the widening income gap.

2. Reasons for the Widening Labour Income Gap

The main reason for the widening income gap is the combination of an increase in the share of capital income with a decline in the share of labour income. Therefore, if the cause of the decline in the share of labour income is discovered, a clearer understanding of why the income gap is widening will be gained.

Since the 1990s, the decline in labour's income share in China has primarily been due to the evolution of the country's ownership structure. The share of income going to labour reflects the economic and social status of workers in relation to income distribution. The lower the share, the lower the economic and social status of labour. Statistics show that within China's different types of ownership economy, the share of labour income in the non-public economy is generally low, and the average wage of workers is also low. Meanwhile, and in comparable settings, the share of labour income in the public economy is higher, and the average wage of workers is also higher. In the private economy, where employers seek the maximum profit, they are diligent about keeping wage levels low so as to obtain the benefits of improved labour productivity mainly in the form of usable capital. As labour productivity increases, the proportion of enterprise income going to labour remuneration is bound over time to fall lower and lower. At present, China, in its economic restructuring, emphasizes the development of the private economy and foreign investment, and a large number of existing state-owned and collective enterprises have been privatized through the sale of shares. This will inevitably lead to a decline in the proportion of labour remuneration.

According to the currently disclosed data and the economic laws of income and ownership, the decline in the proportion of labour remuneration is an objective result of the decline in the proportion of public ownership in China's economy, and of the failure of the government and labour unions to play a fuller role in the market economy. With other conditions unchanged, the greater the non-public sector of the economy, including domestic and foreign capital, the lower the proportion of labour remuneration tends to be. In a public economy, workers can protect their rights through workers' congresses, labour unions, and other institutions. The wage decisions of the public economy are directly managed by the government, and workers' social security and welfare benefits are relatively sound. In a private economy, wage decisions are entirely determined by employers. Workers' voices are rarely heard, and social security and welfare benefits have been greatly reduced; the private economic sector has no reasonable wage growth mechanism. These are the main reasons for the decline of China's labour income share.

In addition, the decline in the share of labour income during China's reform and opening up has had two other causes. One is the slow growth in the incomes of migrant workers, and the other is that urban enterprise workers' income growth lags behind managers' wage increases.

Since the reform and opening up, the number of migrant workers in China has continued to grow, and the proportion of the incomes of rural households made up by wages has increased year by year. Between 1984 and 1996, the proportion of the net income of rural households represented by the wage incomes of migrant workers increased from 17.17% to 23.59%. By 2008, this proportion had grown further to 37.42%. The highest proportion, up to 70%, has been recorded in Shanghai, and throughout the eastern coastal areas the figure has generally been over 40%.[112] Although the proportion of the net incomes of agricultural households provided by the incomes of migrant workers is increasing, the wage growth of migrant workers has been painfully slow due to the lack of policies ensuring the minimum level for their wages. Employers have even implemented discriminatory policies against migrant workers. The rate of wage increases for migrant workers has often been lower than the average rate of wage increases for urban workers. Since migrant workers are an important part of the new workforce in China's non-public economy, the slow growth of migrant workers' wage incomes has become one of the main reasons for the declining share of wages in national income.

Within enterprises, the labour incomes of ordinary employees have continued to decline compared to the incomes of managers, and the wage gap within enterprises has thus continued to widen. According to a survey conducted from 2002 to 2004 by the All-China Federation of Trade Unions, the wages of 81.8% of China's enterprise employees were lower than the average local social wage. Some 34.2% of employees received wages that were less than half the average social wage, and in 12.7% of cases, wages were below the local minimum. Compared with 1998-2001, the number of employees whose wages were less than half of the local social average wage

---

112. Wan Guanghua, 'Economic Development and Income Inequality: Methods and Evidence,' *Shanghai People's Publishing House*, 2006

increased by 14.6 percentage points. This was an obvious sign that the proportion of low-income workers in China had expanded.[113]

3. The Significance of Expanding the Labour Income Share and Narrowing the Income Distribution Gap

Labour's income share in China has been declining for more than a decade, and there is great uncertainty as to when it may begin to rise. But there is no doubt that expanding the share of labour income and narrowing the income distribution gap is of major economic significance.

(I) The Need to Stimulate Domestic Consumption and Economic Growth

To improve China's economic efficiency, it is necessary to change the nation's mode of economic growth. China's economic growth has always been driven by high accumulation and high investment. During the planned economy era, the state was the dominant player in high accumulation and high investment, and in the transition to the socialist market economy, the role of the dominant player in high accumulation and high investment was played by state-owned, collective, and non-public enterprises. In a market economy, high accumulation and high investment are reflected in a higher share of capital income and a lower share of labour income in the distribution of newly increased value. The effects will inevitably include reducing the share of labour income, depressing domestic consumption, and influencing the contribution of domestic household consumption to the economy. Because China has long implemented a high-accumulation and high-investment development strategy, the share of labour income within the national income has grown slowly and, on occasion, even declined. Household consumption has had a limited role in driving economic growth. Under China's growth model of high accumulation and high investment, the rate of return on investment has traditionally been very low, and economic growth has had a limited effect on improving the living standards of the people.

If China can gradually increase the labour income share and narrow the income distribution gap, China will be able to promote economic growth and rely on an expanding level of domestic demand, thus breaking the vicious cycle of the past where China has relied on investment and exports to promote economic growth.

---

113. http://www.moa.gov.cn/ztzl/lhnyjj_1/2006/200603/t20060313_569174.htm

Growth patterns of high investment and low returns will change to a certain extent, but the future long-term growth of China's economy will have a very solid base in domestic consumption.

(II) The Need to Upgrade Industrial Structure and Foreign Trade Structure

China's low share of labour income is closely related to the country's export-oriented foreign trade strategy. In the process of reform and opening up, business development and investment attraction in coastal areas have been weighted too heavily towards foreign processing industries. Drawn by China's large rural labour surplus, foreign companies have relocated processing industries with low added value to China. These industries also have low requirements for labour skills. Chinese companies, too, make use of the country's cheap labour to process materials for foreign customers. The risks involved in starting a business are low, and profits are easy to obtain; therefore, export-oriented processing enterprises have developed rapidly. In the early days of reform and opening up, there was nothing wrong with developing low-tech and low-wage processing industries, but many companies had no long-term vision for their further development. Obsessed with the profits brought by low technology and low costs, they did not attach importance to technology updates, talent training, or brand innovation. Under this developmental model, Chinese processing companies obtained only a very low share of the value added in international industrial chains. This was a major reason why China's industrial structure lagged far behind its economic development.

If the share of labour income can be increased, production costs in some manufacturing industries will inevitably rise. To make up for the cost increases caused by wage growth, many companies will be forced by the mechanisms of competition to increase their industrial added value through introducing advanced technical equipment and talent, and through pursuing internal technological innovation. Enterprises improve their efficiency with the deft use of capital and turn gradually towards higher value-added products and industrial sectors, so as to achieve a mutually beneficial and virtuous cycle of increased labour income share and upgraded industrial structure. This is an essential condition if China's industrial development is to make the shift from extensive to intensive development. Two benefits come from carrying out this transformation of industrial development. One of these is that the driving effect of domestic demand on economic growth will increase. The other is that China's dependence on foreign trade will be greatly reduced. It is quite evident that this process will require the government to promote education and improve the quality of the labour force so as to provide the appropriate conditions for upgrading the industrial structure.

4. The Role of the Government in Narrowing the Labour Income Gap

In view of the problems caused by the gradual decline of China's labour income share in recent years; it has become necessary to increase this share in a timely fashion. The government must not shirk the task of narrowing the labour income gap, because increasing the labour income share and narrowing the labour income gap are profoundly necessary for implementing a scientific outlook on development and for adequately sharing its benefits. These safeguards are also needed to stimulate domestic consumption and economic growth. Further, they are needed to promote upgrades to the industrial and foreign trade structures. None of these three goals can be accomplished without the government's macro-control.

(I) Strengthening and Improving the Ownership Base with Distribution According to Work as the Mainstay

This is a primary condition for increasing the share of labour income. The ownership relationship determines the distribution relationship. To maintain and actively increase the proportion of labour income for the entire society, China must insist on distribution according to work as the mainstay, and resolutely consolidate and develop the public economy. These efforts must include development of the state economy and of various forms of collective and cooperative economies. The public economy is the economic foundation for eliminating exploitation and polarisation while achieving common prosperity. It is the main market playing field for developing modern socialized productivity, an important means and economic basis for restricting exploitation in the non-public economy, and an effective mechanism for increasing labour income. Studies over the years have shown that the dominant position of public ownership and distribution according to work has gradually weakened, and the proportion of labour income has declined. In the final analysis, this is because the dominant position of the public economy has been sidelined; public assets have been sold or subjected to mergers. China should summarise these relevant lessons, clarify the ideological trend of privatisation that devalues and weakens public ownership, and endeavor to develop and improve the public economy. This is a pivotal point for deepening the reform of the income distribution system, and it is of great significance for rapidly increasing the labour income share.

(II) Establishing a State-Led Labour Rights Protection Mechanism

Establishing a state-led labour rights protection mechanism is essential for increasing the share of labour income. At present, more than 70% of China's workers are employed in non-public enterprises, and it is up to their bosses whether or not to increase wages. This situation leaves little room for government intervention. Western governments are in the position of the employer class, and mainly rely on post-regulation to coordinate labour-capital relations. A socialist government, as a people's government rather than a neutral government, should learn from the lessons of the West, take the position of the employee class, and coordinate labour relations or labour-capital relations through active and proactive measures. In Federal Germany, under the system that included income co-determination mechanisms and required a certain ratio of employee representatives on boards of directors, labour unions, in the past, negotiated reasonable increases in employee incomes based on rises in corporate labour productivity. In Japan, enterprises typically raise employee incomes according to length of service. These mechanisms can provide useful references for our government. If the government implements statutory labour hours and the *Labour Contract Law*, and backs these measures up with close inspection, then the interests of workers can be fully protected.

(III) Relevant Government Departments Must Strictly Implement the Minimum Wage System

A minimum wage system is the basis for increasing the share of labour income. The crux of the labour-capital conflict is the conflict of interest distribution. To effectively alleviate the labour-capital conflict under the market economy, a tripartite coordination mechanism must be established among labour, capital, and government. For about twenty-five years following the second world war, the Western countries established relatively effective labour, capital, and governmental coordination mechanisms. However, their ability to do so rested upon their increased exploitation and oppression of the developing countries, using globalisation and financialisation, and these mechanisms have been inoperable now for nearly half a century.

1. The Minimum Wage System Is Conducive to the Mandatory Transformation of the Enterprise Development Model

Since the reform and opening up, Chinese companies, especially non-public companies, have followed a low-wage and low-tech development model. The consequences of this model are that employers benefit, while workers and the rest of society suffer. Under the low-tech and low-cost model of development, workers are unable to share the benefits of social development, and society has to bear the costs, such as environmental pollution. This low-cost development model is destructive to normal market competition. Some enterprises that rely on low technology and low costs to survive will take measures to extend working hours, to increase labour intensity, and to reduce workplace health and safety standards. In contrast, companies that operate in compliance with the law pay relatively high wages to their workers and incur higher work safety costs. This prevents enterprises of both types from being able to compete fairly. Due to the inconsistency of competitive regulations, the development of Chinese enterprises is still in a very undeveloped state. While efficient enterprises may prevail over competitors, inferior enterprises are also able to survive.

By enforcing a minimum wage system, the government can eliminate inferior enterprises and promote fair competition. A government-enforced minimum wage system is conducive to the formation of a reasonable labour cost mechanism within society. The market is incapable of spontaneously forming a reasonable mechanism for determining labour costs. If left to the discretion of the labour market, labour costs will tend to fall towards subsistence wages. A reasonable labour cost mechanism is part of a reasonable product pricing mechanism. Socially unified enterprise accounting standards, minimum product quality standards, and minimum labour standards are the necessary components of a reasonable pricing mechanism. A reasonable product pricing mechanism and a reasonable labour cost mechanism are essential to protect the interests of the public and its workers. To establish a reasonable labour cost mechanism, it is necessary to implement a unified weekly work time standard and minimum workplace health and safety standards. Right now, in China's non-public enterprises, it is common for employees to work overtime without pay. If the weekly working hours of employees are not managed well, a minimum wage standard will be virtually useless. The law of value requires companies to reduce costs, but competition between companies to reduce costs is only beneficial to society if the companies do not reduce product quality, do not cause environmental pollution, and do not harm workers' health. Cost competition must be based on reasonable costs; otherwise, the pressure to reduce costs will cause enterprises to try to reduce their outlays on labour and environmental pollution management. The end result will be the destruction of any reasonable pricing mechanism. Occupational diseases and environmental pollution incidents, which are constantly being exposed, are the results of destroying a reasonable pricing system.

2. The Minimum Wage System is Conducive to the Implementation of Third-Party Labour Supervision and the Raising of Labour Income Share
Third-party labour supervision involves an independent organisation evaluating the labour situation in an enterprise, with reference to prevailing labour. At present, the comprehensive competitiveness of third-party labour supervision is based on the International Labour Standards, which refer to the various principles, norms, and guidelines adopted by the International Labour Organisation (ILO) to deal with labour affairs on a global scale. They form the international labour system with the International Labour Conventions (Conventions, 185) and International Labour Recommendations (Recommendations, 195) as the core.

SA8000, one of the most widely recognised international labour standards, is based on the *Charter of the International Labour Organisation*, the *United Nations Convention on the Rights of the Child*, and the *Universal Declaration of Human Rights*. On 12 December 2001, Social Accountability International (SAI) published the first corporate social responsibility standard: SA8000: 2001. This was the first international standard of social responsibility that could be used for third-party certification. The main contents include nine aspects: child labour, forced labour, safety and health, freedom of association and collective bargaining rights, discrimination, punitive measures, working hours, wages and remuneration, and management systems. Currently, more consumers around the world have begun to pay attention to whether the products they buy meet the standard of SA8000. They have started to refrain from purchasing cheap, substandard products, and this has become a significant consumption trend in developed countries.

As a member state of the ILO, China has ratified twenty-four international labour conventions and faces the problems of how to implement ILO conventions and how to coordinate international labour standards with domestic ones. Despite the best intentions of SA8000, which posits a continuous reduction of general non-tariff barriers, it is easy for protectionists to exploit SA8000 as a powerful tool to restrict the export of labour-intensive products from developing countries. China's current trade frictions with Europe and the United States are largely due to labour standards. Not only is there a misunderstanding of our country by the international community, but there are also problems of our own making. One accurate view is that some Chinese companies have become sweatshops by trampling on labour standards and not complying with any minimum wage standard. However, this is not a widespread issue in the Chinese business community. Conversely, the Chinese government has failed to use reasonable channels to communicate with the international community, and this has led to a one-sided foreign perception of the labour situation in our country. The end results have generated misunderstandings and even distrust. Foreign nongovernmental organisations have taken advantage of public suspicions about China to initiate anti-dumping investigations and to boycott Chinese products, which have hurt the Chinese companies that actually comply with international labour standards. Due to the Chinese government's insufficient understanding of SA8000, foreign certification agencies are not legally able to operate in China. Additionally, Chinese export companies, suppliers of large international enterprises, find that they must undergo international labour standard assessments and pay high assessment fees in order to conduct international business. Even when they have passed these assessments, it is not considered appropriate to publicise these facts in China, thus resulting in a great deal of waste. In view of this, it is recommended that the Chinese government adopt an open mind and act deliberately to introduce international labour assessments. Not only can third-party assessments and certifications greatly reduce the assessment costs borne by the assessed enterprises in China, but they can also promote the development of a third-party certification industry. In order to maintain the fairness and transparency of assessments and certifications, the whole process should be established by an internal Chinese assessment company. The third-party assessment of labour standards should be combined with minimum wage standards promulgated by local governments across the country. Since third-party assessments would be contracted by enterprises on a voluntary basis, taking this step would make outstanding enterprises known to the public and make compliance with labour laws and regulations the brand of enterprises that are capable of strengthening the implementation in China of the minimum wage system and of the relevant labour laws and regulations. Moreover, in the face of overcapacity in many Chinese industries, the minimum wage standard should be gradually increased and strengthened in its implementation so as to eliminate weak enterprises and create a more equitable economy.

References

[1] Cheng Enfu. 'Interpretation of Current Labour Income Distribution Issues—Interview with Famous Economist Professor Cheng Enfu and Professor Yu Bin', *Chinese Academy of Social Sciences* [J]. *Journal of Management*, 2010 (5).

[2] Zhou Zhaoguang. 'How to Promote the Harmonious Development of Fairness and Efficiency in China's Distribution System [J].' *Shanghai School of Economics Quarterly*, 2008 (1).

[3] Bai Chongen, Qian Zhenjie. 'Who is Crowding Out the Income of Citizens—Analysis of the Distribution Pattern of Chinese National Income [J].' *Chinese Social Sciences*, 2009 (5).

[4] Chang Kai. 'Report on Labour Relations in China—Characteristics and Trends of Contemporary Labour Relations in China [M].' *Beijing: China Labour and Social Security Press*, 2009: 265.

[5] Zhu Miaokuan, Zhu Haiping. 'Starting from Perfecting the Distribution System to Improve the Basic Economic System [J].' *Shanghai School of Economics*, 2008 (23).

[6] Gong Gang, Yang Guang. 'Looking at the Inequality of Income Distribution in China from the Perspective of Functional Income [J].' *Chinese Social Sciences*, 2010 (2).

[7] Luo Changyuan, Zhang Jun. 'The Proportion of Labour Income in Economic Development: An Empirical Study Based on China's Industrial Data [J].' *Chinese Social Sciences*, 2009 (4).

[8] Li Daokui, Liu Linlin, Wang Hongling. 'U-shaped Law of Labour Share Evolution in GDP [J].' *Economic Research*, 2009 (1).

[9] Li Shi, Wei Zhong, Ding Sai. 'Empirical Analysis of the Unequal Distribution of Chinese Citizens' Property and Its Causes [J].' *Economic Research*, 2005 (6).

[10] Yang Junqing, Wei Bin, et al. 'Investigation and Research on Labour-Management Relations of Non-State-owned Enterprises in Shanxi [J].' *Labour Economic Review*, 2008 (12).

[11] Zhao Junkang. 'Analysis of the Proportion of Labour and Capital Distribution in China [J].' *Statistical Research*, 2006 (12).

[12] Zhao Xiaoshi. 'A Study on the Adjustment Mechanism of China's Labour Relations during the Transition Period [M].' Beijing: *Economic Science Press*, 2009.

(Originally published in *Comprehensive Competitiveness*, 2010, Issue 6)

* * *

Section II The Role of Government in Functional Income Distribution and Size Income Distribution

1. Basic Concepts of Functional Income Distribution and Size Income Distribution

(I) The Difference between Functional Income Distribution and Size Income Distribution

Functional income distribution and size income distribution are two basic methods used to study national income distribution. Functional income distribution, also known as factor income distribution, explores the relationship between various factors of production and income. It allows for the study of income distribution from the perspective of income sources and focuses on the relative contributions to income of capital and labour. Size income distribution, also known as individual income distribution or household income distribution, discusses the total income of different individuals and families. It focuses on the relative income share of the population or families of different classes. Functional income distribution focuses mainly on the initial distribution of national income, while size income distribution focuses mainly on the final distribution of national income.

The first economist in history to study functional income distribution was Adam Smith, who divided income into wages, profits, and land rents. The nature of wage income is labour income, and the nature of profit and rental income is capital income. Following Smith, economists such as Ricardo and Marx insisted on studying income distribution from the perspective of functional income. The indicators commonly used to measure the distribution of functional income are labour income share and capital income share. The economy includes many compound incomes, such as the incomes of farmers and of small business owners in cities and towns. The methods used to decompose compound incomes into labour incomes and capital incomes will significantly affect the calculation of labour income share and capital income share. Since the dividing up of the nature of income carried out in functional income distribution involves normative analysis, contemporary western economics, which emphasise empirical analysis, have shifted its focus from functional income distribution to size income distribution.

Vilfredo Pareto was the first economist to study size income distribution. Size income distribution does not distinguish either the source or the nature of income. It takes individuals or households as the unit of analysis, and in order to analyze the proportion of income received by different households, ranks them from *low* to *high* based on total household income. This method of analysis can be utilised to explore the relationship between the proportion of the population or of families who belong to a given class and the share of income that class receives, and analyze what factors determine the income distribution structure of an individual or family. Indicators commonly used to measure size income distribution are the 80/20 rule, the quintile method, the Gini coefficient, and the Taylor coefficient. In the past, economists used the Gini coefficient to measure size income distribution, but now the Taylor coefficient is becoming more popular.

In the Gini coefficient method, the formula for calculating the Gini coefficient of discrete row data is $g = \sum_{i=1}^{n} \frac{2i-n-1}{n^2} \frac{xi}{u}$. The Gini coefficient can be viewed simply as the weighted sum of the relative income $\frac{x_i}{u}$ of all individuals and the weight in the i-th position, which is $\frac{2i-n-1}{n^2}$. The Taylor coefficient method examines the deviation of real income distribution from perfect equality by calculating the ratio of people's income share to population share. The calculation formula is $T = \sum_{i=1}^{N} \frac{y_i}{Y} \log\left(\frac{y_i}{Y/N}\right)$, where Y_i is the income of the i-th individual, Y is the total income, and N is the total population.

(II) The Relationship between Functional Income Distribution and Size Income Distribution

There is a close relationship between functional income distribution and size income distribution. Generally speaking, the greater the difference in functional income distribution, the greater the difference in size income distribution, and vice versa. Any measures to strengthen the functional income distribution gap will affect the pattern of size income distribution. The functional distribution of income determines the size distribution of income. Functional income distribution studies income distribution from the perspective of income source, and its analysis is based on the principle of economic efficiency, while size income distribution studies the relationship between population or household size and income scale. The results can be used to explain the mobility of social classes or trends in the formation and change of income distribution among different socio-economic groups. The functional income distribution determines and influences the size distribution, because the share of income gained by the population of an economic group depends largely on the amount of production factors they possess.

An economic system affects the relationship between functional income distribution and size income distribution. According to the marginal productivity theory of neoclassical economics, in a perfectly competitive market environment functional income distribution will lead to the equalisation of owners' income of each factor. But this is not realistic. In reality, due, for example, to collective bargaining between employers and labour unions and the manipulation of capital, land, and product prices by monopolists and wealthy land-owners for their own personal benefit, the effects of the theory of functional income distribution are greatly reduced.

Both functional income distribution and size income distribution are very significant causes of income inequality. There are generally two reasons for this; one is the inequality of property income, and the other is the inequality of wages. Lower wages will cause property income to rise, while rising property income will increase income inequality. Alternatively, rising wage inequality will also cause income inequality. In developing countries, people's income gaps are often caused by property income inequality, but in developed countries, wage inequality is the main reason for the rise of income inequality. In China, for example, labour income accounts for only 40% of the national income, and income inequality is mainly derived from capital income inequality. In the United States, labour income accounts for two-thirds of the national income, and the contribution rate of labour income inequality to U.S. income inequality is much higher than in China. Friedman believes that all in all, the rise of inequality in labour incomes, which account for two-thirds of total income in the US, is the main reason driving the expansion of American income inequality. In the United States, the main reason for the rise in wage inequality is that workers with higher education and advanced skills have seen their wages grow faster. But this argument ignores the fact that in the United States, the people with the highest labour incomes also receive income from property. This suggests that labour income inequality and capital income inequality promote each other. The combination of wage inequality and property inequality has widened the national income gap in the United States.

(III) The Relationship between Functional Income Distribution, Size Income Distribution, and the Final Use of National Output

Functional income distribution and scale income distribution are the two basic methods used to study national income distribution. In recent years, an ever-increasing number of scholars have realized that the distribution of national income should be studied from a third perspective, that is, the final use of national output.

The final use of national output = investment demand + consumption demand (1)

Where investment demand = government investment + enterprise investment = ① + ③ + ⑤   (2)

Consumption demand = government consumption + household consumption = ② + ④ + ⑥   (3)

In Formula (2), the source of corporate investment is residential households. Among these, high-income families account for the bulk of corporate investment, because the ownership of enterprises is often in the hands of a few high-income families. Low-income families also have investment needs, but the sums involved are very limited.

In the relationship shown in Figure 4-1, government is excluded from functional income distribution and size income distribution. From the perspective of functional income distribution, government is a third party, outside of labour and capital in production; functional income distribution only considers the manner in which the benefits of production are divided between labour and the owners of capital. The government is not an investor in production factors, so it is excluded. The household is the unit of analysis for size income distribution, and a considerable portion of governmental income is broken down to the level of each household in the form of income transfer. Therefore, size income distribution also excludes

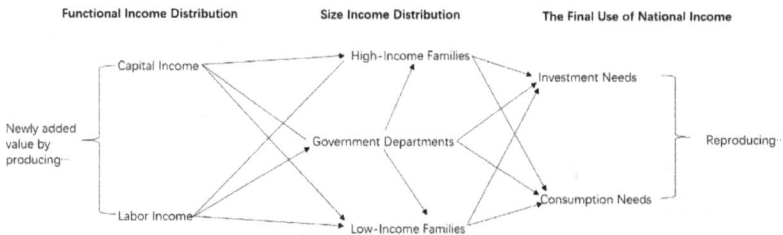

Figure 4-1 The role of government in functional income distribution and size income distribution

the government. The advantage of studying national income distribution from the perspective of final use is that this method can show the relationship of government to functional income distribution and size income distribution.

As shown in Figure 4-1, the final use of national output involves three major economic entities: the government, enterprises, and households. Fang Fuqian used the Basic Input-Output Flow Table published in the *China Statistical Yearbook*[114] to estimate the proportion of the three major economic entities in the final use of China's national output. In the real economy, ranking of households by income from high to low provides a continuous series. In Figure 4-1, however, we simplify households into high-income families and low-income families, assuming that high-income families are the main owners of enterprises. By introducing the government into functional income distribution and size income distribution, we ensure that these two income distributions will be effectively linked through the role of the government.

2. The Influence of the Government on Functional Income Distribution and Size Income Distribution

(I) The Influence of the Government on Functional Income Distribution

According to Marx's basic theory, the value of a single commodity is:

$$z = c + (v+m) \qquad (4)$$

For the national economy, the sum of the values of all commodities can be written as:

$$\Sigma z_i + \Sigma c_i + (\Sigma v_i + \Sigma m_i) \quad (5)$$

But if Formula (5) is to be valid, there must be stringent conditions set in place; namely, all products are final products, so as to avoid the double counting of intermediate products.

There are two parts in Formula (5), Σc_i is constant capital, which is stock; $\Sigma v_i + \Sigma m_i$ is the newly added value, which is the flow. In the current national economic statistics, GDP is a concept of flow, and only includes the second part of the total value of commodities, namely $\Sigma v_i + \Sigma m_i$. We thus obtain:

---

114. Fang Fuzian. 'Progress of research on the relationship between government consumption and private consumption [J].' *Economic Dynamics*, 2009 (12).

$$\text{GDP}= \sum v_i + \sum m_i, \qquad (6)$$

According to Formula (6), GDP can be divided into two parts: labour income $\sum v_i$ and capital income $\sum m_i$.

In reality, the division of national income is far more complicated than the above theoretical division implies. The above division of national income assumes that the government does not exist. But in contemporary capitalist countries, government-controlled income will account for approximately 20%-40% of GDP. Therefore, government revenues must be broken down. The government's influence on functional income distribution is realised through two channels. First, the government can regulate the bargaining power of both employers and employees through labour legislation, and then regulate the division of added value between capital income and labour income. Second, the government can regulate capital income and labour income through the allocation of tax derived from them. The taxation of capital income is mainly realised through corporate income tax, and that of labour income through income tax on wages and salaries.

Assuming that all government revenue comes from taxation, that is, that the government has no capital income, governmental taxation can be divided into two types according to different standards. On the basis of the objects of taxation, it can be divided into taxation of labour income and taxation of capital income. Utilising taxation methods, it can be divided into direct tax and indirect tax. Under different taxation methods, the division of national income is also different. In the real economy, the government's tax revenue sources are mainly divided into direct tax and indirect tax. Whether these are beneficial to capital income or to labour income depends on the specific situation. In reality, the income of each family is compound income, which includes labour income and capital income. Generally speaking, the income of high-income families is mainly capital income, while the income of low-income families is mainly labour income. Under the conditions of direct tax, if the threshold of personal income tax is high and the marginal tax rate of progressive income tax is high, the result is unfavourable to high-income families. This is equivalent to increasing the tax burden on capital income. If the individual income tax threshold is low and the marginal tax rate of progressive income tax is low, this is bad for low-income families. These conditions are equivalent to increasing the tax burden on labour income. Under the conditions of indirect tax, it is more difficult to analyze whether indirect tax is beneficial to capital income or labour income. The consumption tax on luxury goods, an indirect tax, is typically not good for high-income families; its effect is equivalent to taxing capital income. Meanwhile, the taxation distribution of VAT is neutral. Due to the low tax distortion effect, VAT has become an increasingly important indirect tax. Under the conditions of VAT, the national revenue is divided into three parts. On the premise of not considering whether the government revenue comes from capital income or labour income, the formula of commodity value can be modified from the perspective of microscopic commodity value as follows:

$$z = c + (v+m) = c+ (v_t+m_t+t) \qquad (7)$$

Where v_t is after-tax labour compensation, m_t is after-tax residual value, and is governmental tax revenue.

In the national economy, the value of all commodities can be written as:

$$\Sigma z_i = \Sigma c_i + (\Sigma v_{ti} + \Sigma m_{ti} + \Sigma t_i) \qquad (8)$$

Gross domestic product (GDP) can be written as:

$$GDP = \Sigma v_{ti} + \Sigma m_{ti} + \Sigma t_i \qquad (9)$$

The three parts in Formula (9) correspond to: labour income, capital income, and government revenue. In some literature, labour income is termed household income, and capital income is referred to as corporate income.

(II) The Influence of the Government on Size Income Distribution

The influence of the government on the final income distribution is mainly evidenced through the adjustment of expenditures. Changes in the scale and structure of government expenditures affect final income distribution.

1. The Impact of the Scale of Government Expenditure on Size Income Distribution

To a certain extent, changes in the scale of governmental expenditure will have a *crowding-out effect* on household expenditure and corporate expenditure. The government's consumption demand will have a *crowding-out effect* on consumption by the household sector, while the government's investment demand will crowd out investment by the corporate sector. Whether the crowding-out effect is harmful depends on the efficiency of government spending. Where consumption expenditure is concerned, if government spending on the purchase of public goods can make up for the public sector's insufficient supply of public goods, then government consumption efficiency will be higher than that of the household sector. In the case of investment, if government investment can make up for the deficiencies of private enterprises in large-scale and long-term investment projects, then governmental investment efficiency will be higher than that of the corporate sector.

This also means that the relationship between the government, the household sector, and the corporate sector must be complementary rather than competitive. If the relationship is competitive, the efficiency of government expenditure will be low. Government expenditures may produce *compulsory consumption* and *excessive consumption*. For example, the government's administrative apportionment may cause compulsory consumption, while its spending on receptions, vehicles, and overseas trips may amount to excessive consumption. Compulsory consumption and excessive consumption will reduce the efficiency of government spending. Government investment, meanwhile, may exercise effective monopoly power, restricting the access of private capital so as to earn monopoly profits. The effect is likely to be that government investment displays low efficiency.

2. The Influence of Government Expenditure Structure on Size Income Distribution

Government spending can be divided into investment expenditure, nonproductive expenditure, and expenditure for social security. The government's investment in infrastructure, regional development, ecological protection, high-tech R&D, etc. for the purpose of economic construction is investment expenditure. The government's expenditure on national defence, public security, and management of administrative institutions in order to maintain their normal operation is nonproductive expenditure, which is also known as governmental spending on public goods and services. The government's transfer payments, agricultural expenditures, education expenditures, medical expenditures, and social security expenditures in backward areas are expenditures for social security. The higher the proportion of social security expenditure in governmental expenditures, the more transfer payments low-income earners receive, and the more equitable the distribution of social wealth. When government consumption expenditures grow too fast, this may have a *crowding-out effect* on household consumption (consumption from payroll funds).

3. The Role of the Government in Functional Income Distribution and Size Income Distribution in China's Fiscal Revenue and Expenditure

(I) Functional Income and Size Income in China's National Income Statistics

China's national income statistics have undergone a transition from the Material Product System (MPS) to the System of National Accounts (SNA). The former was implemented in 1985, and the latter was formally implemented in 1993, with a transitional stage in between. The MPS focuses on functional income distribution, and its calculation formula is:

$$\text{National income} = (\text{salary} + \text{employee welfare fund}) + (\text{profit} + \text{interest}) + \text{tax} + \text{others} \quad (10)$$

The SNA focuses more on the final use of national output, and its calculation formula is:

$$\begin{aligned}
\text{National income} &= \text{total consumption} + \text{total investment} + \text{net exports of goods and services} \\
&= (\text{household consumption} + \text{social consumption}) \\
&\quad + (\text{fixed asset formation} + \text{inventory increase}) \\
&\quad + (\text{export of goods and services} - \text{import of goods and services}) \quad (11)
\end{aligned}$$

Neither the MPS nor the SNA can directly obtain information on size income distribution. Size income distribution involves only households, not enterprises or governments. Further, it assumes that the income of both enterprises and governments will ultimately boil down to household income. The calculation of size income distribution is often measured by the Gini coefficient. In the sections that follow, the current situation with China's functional income distribution and size income distribution will be analyzed, together with the final use of national output.

1. China's Functional Income Distribution

Today, China's national income statistics adopt the income approach, which breaks down added value into workers' remuneration, net production tax, depreciation of fixed assets, and operating surplus. This statistical method cannot directly reveal the share of labour income and capital income. Zhou Minghai, Xiao Wen, and Yao Xianguo[115] believe that in this national statistical accounting, the net production tax represents neither labour income nor capital income, and that an increase in the tax share will lead to the share of labour income being understated. In calculating China's labour income share, there are still difficulties with decomposing the labour income share of the individual economy. In 2004, our statistics indicated that the income of individual workers was regarded as the remuneration of workers, and thereafter the labour remuneration and operating profits of individual economic owners were regarded as operating profits.

The above difficulties affect the absolute measurement of labour income share in China, but the effect of relative measurement on labour income share is not significant. The research results of Bai Chongen and Qian Zhenjie[116], as well as of Zhuo Yongliang, Zhou Minghai, Xiao Wen, Yao Xianguo, and others all show that the share of labour income in China rose from 1978 to 1984, while the share of capital income declined. From 1984 to 2007 the share of labour income declined, while the share of capital income rose. Figure 4.2 shows changes in China's Labour Income Share 1978-2007.

The decline of China's labour income share since 1984 can also be accounted for by the changes in corporate profitability. Zhang Jie et al. used the statistical database of industrial enterprises from 1999 to 2007 issued by the National Bureau of Statistics to establish a multiple regression model. The results of the Spearman correlation coefficient matrix show that there is a significant and stable negative correlation between corporate profitability and the per capita wage level. In essence, this indicates that the higher the profits made by enterprises in China, the lower the wages paid to employees. It is evident that corporate profits are being aggregated through *squeezing the wages* of employees; this seems to provide a test of the fact that 'profits crowd out wages' at the micro level of Chinese companies.[117]

---

115. Zhou M.H., Xiao W., Yao X.G. 'Uneven economic growth and imbalance of national income distribution in China [J].' *China Industrial Economy*, 2010(6).

116. Bai Chong'en, Qian Zhenjie. 'Factor distribution of national income: the story behind the statistics [J].' *Economic Research*, 2009 (3)

117. Zhang J, Huang Taiyan. 'Research on the trend of wage changes and determination mechanism of Chinese enterprises [J].' *China Industrial Economy*, 2010 (3).

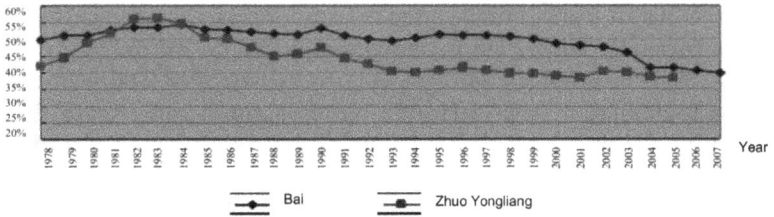

Figure 4-2 China's Labour Income Share 1978-2007

2. China's Size Income Distribution

According to an estimate by Wang Zuxiang (2009), based on income distribution data provided by the *China Statistical Yearbook* (1995-2005), the Gini coefficients for both urban and rural sectors indicated by those data were not large, neither exceeding 0.34. Since 2003, however, China's overall Gini coefficient has exceeded 0.44, far higher than the warning level of 0.4. Wang Zuxiang believes that the urban-rural income gap is the main reason for the widening inequality in China. The slow increase in the wages of migrant workers is certainly a reason for the widening urban-rural income gap, but the main reason for this gap is the rapid growth in the capital income (property income) of urban citizens. Since the reform and opening up, the number of migrant workers in China has become progressively larger, and the wage component in the income of rural households has increased year after year. From 1984 to 1996, the proportion of rural migrant worker wage income in the net income of rural households increased from 17.17% to 23.59%. By 2008, this proportion had further increased to 37.42%. Shanghai claims the highest proportion, up to 70%, with the figures for eastern coastal areas generally above 40%.[118]

Figure 4-3 shows the trend of changes in the ratio of urban and rural household consumption in China. It can be seen that the gap widened sharply from 1984 to 1995. Since the mid-1990s, the multiple of urban household consumption to rural has remained above 3.5 times. The widening urban-rural income gap is due to the fact that the income of urban citizens is higher than that of rural citizens, and that the property income of urban citizens is also higher than that of rural citizens.

---

118. Wang Zuxiang, Zhang Kui, Meng Yong. 'A study on the estimation of Gini coefficient in China [J].' *Economic Review*, 2009 (03):14-21.

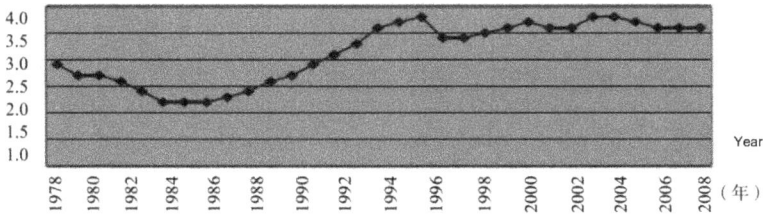

Figure 4-3 China's Urban/Rural Consumption 1978-2008

3. The Final Use of China's National Output

According to China's current national income statistics, national income can be divided (using the gross income approach) into labour compensation, net production taxes, fixed asset depreciation, and operating surplus. Using the expenditure approach, gross domestic product can be divided into final consumption expenditure, total capital formation, and net exports of goods and services. A link is thus established between functional income distribution and the final use of output. Using this method of division, the capital formation rate (investment rate) and the final consumption rate can be calculated. The final consumption expenditure can then be divided into household consumption expenditure (rural, urban) and government consumption expenditure. Figure 4-4 shows the difference between the statistical items of the income approach and expenditure approach in the current national income statistics of China.

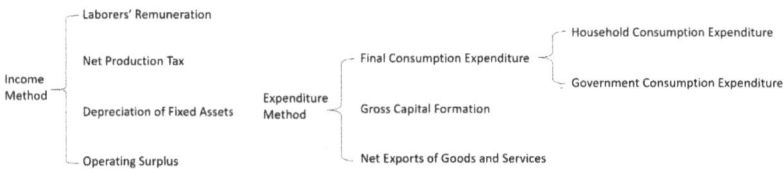

Figure 4-4 Composition of GDP by Income Approach and Expenditure Approach in China's Statistical Yearbook[119]

Table 4-1[120] shows the composition of China's GDP measured by the expenditure approach. The advantage of this approach is that it is easy to measure where the final demand goes. Final consumption, investment, and net exports are the three *final flows* of national income.

---

119. Ibid
120. Ibid

Table 4-1 China's GDP Composition from 1978 to 2008 (Expenditure Method)

Year	Final Consumption Expenditure (%)	Gross Capital Formation (%)	Net Exports of Goods and Services (%)	Year	Final Consumption Expenditure (%)	Gross Capital Formation (%)	Net Exports of Goods and Services (%)
1978	62.1	38.2	-0.3	1994	58.2	40.5	1.3
1979	64.4	36.1	-0.5	1995	58.1	40.3	1.6
1980	65.5	34.8	-0.3	1996	59.2	38.8	2.0
1981	67.1	32.5	0.3	1997	59.0	36.7	4.3
1982	66.5	31.9	1.6	1998	59.6	36.2	4.2
1983	66.4	32.8	0.8	1999	61.1	36.2	2.8
1984	65.8	34.2	0.0	2000	62.3	35.3	2.4
1985	66.0	38.1	-4.0	2001	61.4	36.5	2.1
1986	64.9	37.5	-2.4	2002	59.6	37.9	2.6
1987	63.6	36.3	0.1	2003	56.8	41.0	2.2
1988	63.9	37.0	-1.0	2004	54.3	43.2	2.5
1989	64.5	36.6	-1.1	2005	51.8	42.7	5.4
1990	62.5	34.9	2.6	2006	49.9	42.6	7.5
1991	62.4	34.8	2.7	2007	49.0	42.2	8.9
1992	62.4	36.6	1.0	2008	48.6	43.5	7.9
1993	59.3	42.6	-1.8				

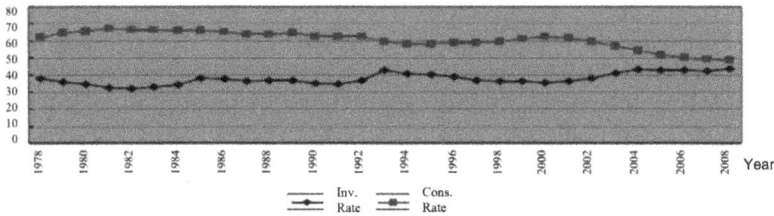

Figure 4-5 China's Investment and Consumption Rates

In the final flow of national income, investment and consumption are the two most important items. As can be seen from Figure 4-5[121], China's investment rate continued to rise from 1978 to 2008, while its final consumption rate continued to decline.

The above analysis shows that functional income distribution and size income distribution are closely related to the final use of national output, and that government revenue and expenditure activities are an important link connecting the three (as shown in Figure 4-1). The following section will further analyze the role played by the government in this instance.

(II) Issues and Policy Recommendations Concerning the Government's Fiscal Revenue and Expenditure in Functional Income Distribution, Size Income Distribution, and Final Use of National Output

1. Problems and Countermeasures in China's Functional Income Distribution

As previously discussed, the main obstacle facing China's functional income distribution is that the labour income share is too low. In the United States, the share of labour income in GDP has been maintained at 65% to 68% since the 1970s. For the healthy and stable development of the economy, the Chinese government must, in the near future, increase the share of labour income within functional income distribution. This increase in labour income share will affect economic growth in the following beneficial ways. First, the increase in labour income share will increase social consumption demand and avoid an economic crisis. Second, the increase in labour income share will raise the incomes of low-income families and narrow the income gap of final distribution. This is due to the fact that the major income source for low-income families is labour income. Third, the increase in labour income share also helps improve investment efficiency. According to traditional theory, high-income families are the

---

121. Ibid

major participants in capital investment. However, under the modern financial system, as the developed credit system facilitates direct and indirect investments, investment behavior has been socialised, and no longer corresponds to the behaviour of individual capital owners. Labour income will also be converted into capital, with low-income families receiving capital income, as a rising share of labour income allows many families of wage workers to become investors. These developments are conducive to the formation of a stable middle class within society.

In the field of labour legislation in China, the government needs to move deliberately to increase the bargaining power of workers, so as to raise the share of labour income. Furthermore, the tax burden on labour income should be reduced. In another article, Cheng Enfu has noted that the wage levels of employees of Chinese enterprises are sufficient only for simple labour reproduction, or are even below this point, and that the members of China's labour force lack opportunities to develop further skills so as to improve their position. Labour is thus caught in the so-called *comparative advantage trap,* where the low value of labour yields a comparative advantage. It is an untenable position for China that it maintains the competitiveness of the previous labour-intensive industries by reducing and lowering the protection of employees' rights and interests. The low-end, labour-intensive industrial market is characterised by intense competition. Only by improving the level of technology, by creating core intellectual property that can guarantee competitiveness, and by upgrading our industrial level can China achieve sustainable economic development. China is a socialist country that represents the fundamental interests of the working people. China should consciously embrace the position of working people, take the initiative in protecting and enhancing the rights and interests of employees, formulate and effectively implement laws and regulations aimed at protecting employees' rights, and strictly enforce those rights. At the same time, China should rely on the active participation of trade unions and employees. It should require enterprise executives, relevant industry and commerce associations, and employers' associations to work together to protect and improve the rights and interests of employees. Meanwhile, China should create an effective socialist labour relationship and labour-capital relationship, so as to lay a solid economic and social foundation for building a harmonious socialist society.

2. Issues and Countermeasures in China's Size Income Distribution

The main conundrum in China's size income distribution is that the income gap between citizens is too large, reflecting a weakening of the function of government redistribution. The government plays a very important role in the redistribution of income, where the mechanisms available to it include fiscal revenue and fiscal expenditure.

In the case of fiscal revenue, it is generally true that the smaller the proportion of indirect taxes in government revenue and the greater the proportion of direct taxes, the more obvious the role of public finance is in regulating the final income distribution. Yang Wenfang and Fang Qiyun[122] have conducted a comparative study on the fiscal revenue structure and expenditure structure of the United States and China. What they discovered was that the fiscal revenue of the United States has been dominated by direct tax. In fact, income tax has always accounted for nearly 60% of the U.S. government's fiscal revenue, followed by the social security tax, which has accounted for about 35%. China's fiscal revenue has always drawn on indirect taxes to account for more than 70% of its total sum. The U.S. government's fiscal expenditures are mainly transfer payments and security expenditures, which have remained stable at about 62%; China's fiscal expenditures are mainly consumer expenditures, which have always accounted for more than 65%. These are followed by investment expenditures, stable at 23% ~ 30%, while the proportion of security expenditures is the smallest, always below 10%. These statistics show that the fiscal expenditure of the United States focuses on the revenue distribution function of fiscal policy, while China's fiscal expenditure structure reflects the function of fiscal policy in exerting macro-control over the economy. In the future, China's fiscal expenditure needs to focus more on the function of fiscal income redistribution.

The direction and structure of fiscal expenditure will directly affect the final income distribution. Research by Wang Yiming and others shows that in China, the government's administrative expenses have significantly widened the urban-rural income gap at the national level. The impact of capital construction expenditures and of cultural, educational, and health and welfare spending on the urban-rural income gap, differ from region to region. In the eastern region, the above expenditures narrow the urban-rural income gap, while in the western region they widen it. The main reason for this is that in the western region, rural financial inputs are seriously deficient, while the above expenditures are skewed heavily towards the urban areas, thus further widening the urban-rural income gap. In subsequent articles, Cheng Enfu stated that the key to promoting

122. Yang W.F., Fang Q.Y. 'Fiscal revenue, fiscal expenditure, and consumption rate [J].' *Contemporary Finance and Economics*, 2010 (2).

consumption is to remove the bottleneck that restricts personal consumption. That is, the solution is to improve the entire medical and social security system, to increase public investment in basic education and health, to effectively improve people's consumption expectations, and to motivate them to consume. The above research shows that in the future, China must focus on reducing government administrative expenses and on increasing its spending on culture, education, science, health, and social security in rural areas.

3. Complications and Countermeasures in the Final Use of China's National Output

The three central complications in China's use of its national output are that the proportion of investment is large, the proportion of consumption is small, and the total social demand is insufficient. The principal reason for the shortfall in social demand is to be found in the long-term downturn of the household consumption rate. It is an indisputable fact that China's household consumption has been sluggish for many years, but a variety of plausible explanations have been advanced to account for this situation.

The first view is that the low household consumption rate stems from the widening income gap. For example, Yang Wenfang and Fang Qiyun[123] believe that China's low household consumption rate has its origins in the following factors. First, since the reform and opening up, the income gap of citizens under numerous forms of distribution has gradually widened, and this has resulted in a reduction of the overall propensity to consume. Second, the development of China's social security system has lagged behind, and citizens have been faced with increasing uncertainty as to their income and expenses. These worries have increased the motivation for precautionary saving and have strengthened the tendency for social consumption to fall. Research by Wu Dong et al.[124] reveals that the change rate in social security spending in China has a significant positive effect on the consumption rates of both urban and rural citizens. Social security expenditures, by nature, are able to transfer payment and improve the structure of income distribution, creating a proclivity for increases in social consumption. Similarly, rises in

---

123. Yang W.F., Fang Q.Y. 'Fiscal revenue, fiscal expenditure, and consumption rate [J].' *Contemporary Finance and Economics*, 2010 (2).

124. Wu D., Zhou P. 'Research on the impact of fiscal spending on residents' consumption rate under the urban-rural dual structure [J].' *Contemporary Economic Research*, 2010 (6).

education and health spending have a positive impact on the growth rate of social consumption, and this is possibly due to the fact that fiscal investment in human capital is more likely to impel economic growth than is investment in physical capital.

A second view holds that the *crowding-out effect* of governmental consumption on household consumption is the real reason for China's low household consumption rate. For example, Fang Fuqian[125] thinks that the widening income gap between citizens is also a cause of the insufficient consumption demand on the part of the population, but it is not the primary cause. China's income distribution has been tilted towards the government since 1996 and towards enterprises since 2004. As the *economic pie* has continued to expand, the shares going to the government and enterprises have increased, while the share going to ordinary citizens has been shrinking. Since the second half of 1997, China's macro economy has shifted from insufficient supply to insufficient demand. Any lack of total demand in developed countries is due to insufficient investment demand, while the shortfall of total demand in China is due to insufficient consumer demand; this is evident from the country's low final consumption rate (the proportion of final consumption expenditure in the GDP by the expenditure approach), which has been decreasing gradually since 2000. Between 1998 and 2006, China's consumption rate was less than 62%, while the world's average consumption rate was approximately 75% during the same period, and that of developed countries was around 80%. In China's final consumption structure, household consumption and governmental consumption show a reciprocal relationship. Since 2000, the growth of China's household consumption rate has lagged behind both fixed asset growth and GDP growth. This is mostly due to the rapid growth of China's economy, an economy supported by the rapid growth of fixed asset investment.

These two views may seem contradictory, but they are not. The reason for the low consumption propensity of China's citizens is that the government's social security expenditure is too low, and the excessive growth of government consumption has led to a decline in household consumption. If the government could cut down administrative expenses, increase social security spending, and increase the efficiency of fiscal expenditure, then both of these problems could be overcome.

---

125. Fang Fuqian. 'A study on the causes of insufficient consumer demand in China - based on data from urban and rural China by province [J].' *China Social Science*, 2009(2).

4. Complications and Countermeasures Involving China's Government Expenditure

The scale and structure of government expenditure will affect the consumption propensity of urban and rural citizens, which in turn will affect total social demand. There are many problems with China's functional income distribution, size income distribution, and final use of output, and they all require controlling the growth rate of fiscal expenditure and optimising its structure.

First, measures should be taken to control the growth rate of fiscal expenditure so that its level is compatible with economic growth. According to World Bank statistics, the proportion of fiscal revenue in countries with per capita GDP of less than 3,000 U.S. dollars generally amounts to 20%-30% of GDP. For countries with per capita GDP of 3,000-10,000 U.S. dollars, the proportion is generally 30%-40%. For countries with per capita GDP greater than 20,000 U.S. dollars, the corresponding figure is generally 40%-60%. China's fiscal revenue, this suggests, should account for 20%-30% of its GDP.

According to the research by Guo Yanqing[126] and others, between 1978 and 1992 the proportion of China's fiscal revenue to GDP was 30%-50%, with an average value of 37%. Between 1993 and 1999 this proportion dropped to less than 20%, with an average value of 17%. Since the year 2000, the proportion has been stable at over 20%, with an average value of 23%. Judging from these data, the proportion of China's fiscal revenue to GDP might seem to have remained within a reasonable range. Some scholars, however, believe there are leakages in China's fiscal revenue statistics, and that the actual ratio is higher. The uncounted fiscal revenues are said to include extra-budgetary revenue, extra-system revenue (not included in extra-budgetary management), and various forms of revenue collected by local governments and public institutions at their own discretion. These forms may include various types of fee income, extra-price markups, funds, fund-raising, apportionment, etc. In view of this, some economists, basing themselves on the neoliberal economic proposition, believe that China should limit the scale of its government expenditure.

Neoliberal economists advocate restricting and reducing government intervention in the market, which is an overly idealistic approach. In fact, the size of government is constantly expanding even in Western capitalist countries such as the United States, and the proportion of government expenditure to GDP has remained

---

126. Guo Yanqing, Li Lanying. 'Analysis of the Current Situation and Optimal Value of Fiscal Revenue Size in China [J].' *Journal of Central University of Finance and Economics*, 2009 (12).

high. According to the famous law formulated in 1882 by the German economist Adolph Wagner, the size of government expenditure will continue to increase. Wagner's law holds that there is a positive functional relationship between the expansion of a country's government functions and national income. As the economy develops, the functions of the state will continue to expand. To ensure the exercise of state functions, the proportion of public expenditure will also increase. This rule is also known as the *Law of Increasing Public Expenditure* or the *Law of Expanding State Activity*. After human society entered the era of industrialisation and urbanisation, the scope of human-to-human interaction expanded, the public realm of social life increased, and the proportion of public expenditure indeed expanded, which seems to verify Wagner's law.

If Wagner's law is correct, the size of China's fiscal revenue will not decrease in the future but will continue to rise. Therefore, policy recommendations to reduce fiscal expenditure in the long run may not be in line with the reality of social development. In the short term, however, properly restricting the excessive growth of this spending will help the government improve the efficiency of fiscal expenditure. In recent years, China's tax revenue has grown significantly. From 2000 to 2006, it increased by an average of 30% annually, much higher than the growth rate of GDP. Controlling the growth of fiscal expenditure within an appropriate range and adapting this expenditure to the tasks of enhancing economic growth, standardising fiscal revenues, and reducing extra-budgetary revenues are primary issues that China's government should solve.

China should also optimise the structure of government spending and enhance its transparency. The main problem with China's fiscal expenditures is not their size but their structure, which has many unreasonable characteristics. One aspect of this situation is that non-productive fiscal expenditures have grown too fast. Another is that transfer payments for public services and social security are seriously inadequate.

A study by Han Guiying[127] and others has revealed that among China's fiscal expenditures, administrative expenditures have been increasing year by year. From 1998 to 2002, the proportion of China's fiscal spending represented by administrative expenditures exceeded 14% annually. This was significantly higher than in other countries. Han Guiying views the rapid expansion of government agencies

---

127. Han Guiying, Mao Yan, Tang Liping. 'International Comparison of Fiscal Expenditure Structure and Its Reference and Implication for China [J].' *Journal of Southwest University for Nationalities*, 2004 (10).

and staffing as the linchpin for the sharp rise in the proportion of administrative expenditures. Xu Xiongqi and Zhu Qiubai[128] have observed that while the total amount of China's financial investment has increased, quality has declined. Fiscal expenditures lack macro-control, investment structures are dysfunctional, there are many redundant and unplanned construction projects, and the salaries and administrative expenses of government functionaries consume a large proportion of fiscal revenue. The inevitable result has been a quantifiable degradation in the efficiency of fiscal expenditure.

Currently, China's fiscal spending on education, science and technology, culture, health, radio and television, social security, and environmental protection still accounts for a small proportion of the total. These expenditures have strong social and external effects. Inadequate spending in these sectors leads to an insufficient supply of public goods and services, seriously affecting economic and social development. A major future challenge facing the Chinese government is how to realise the transformation of government functions and how to improve government efficiency, in essence, how to bring about the change to a service-oriented government. To achieve this transformation, China must improve the transparency of government revenues and expenditure and strengthen social supervision over them.

In conclusion, the government is an important economic entity in the field of national income distribution. Governmental activities play a major role in guiding the distribution of functional income and size income through fiscal revenue and fiscal expenditure, and through related laws and regulations. Studies in developmental economics have long shown that the government either plays an important role in promoting economic development or plays a poor role, which seriously hinders development. Neoliberalism seeks to excise the role of government from the economy, something that does not correspond to the requirements that must be met if a market economy is to develop. For a healthy market economy to emerge, regulation is required, and the government should take on the role of supplying it. Whether China's future income distribution is rational, and whether the market economy can develop in a healthy and stable fashion, depends on whether the government has the necessary mechanisms in place for regulating it.

---

128. 'An empirical study on the relationship between fiscal revenue and fiscal expenditure in China [J].' *Finance and Economics Research*, 2004 (3).

(Originally published in *Research on Marxism,* Issue 6, 2011, Second Author: Hu Jingchun; Third Author: Hou Hehong)

*   *   *

Section III China's Low Rate of Consumption and Insufficient Consumption

Insufficient consumption has been a critical issue for China's economic development in recent years. In the face of China's long-term low consumption rate and serious economic imbalances, it is urgent that China work on theories and countermeasures to expand domestic demand and boost consumption. Since the mid-1980s, I have paid close attention to the question of consumption and have studied the economic theories associated with it; I have written and published several books on the topic, including *Ancient and Modern Consumption Theories: A Consumer Handbook,* which expounds consumption behavior and consumer psychology. In recent years, the elementary, intermediate, and advanced textbooks of *Modern Political Economy* have also discussed consumption issues at great length, while at the same time introducing the theories of consumption ability and consumption relations emphasised by the famous scholar Professor Yin Shijie. It should be said that the issue of consumption is not only related to the realisation of production, the upgrading of the industrial structure, and the improvement of people's living standards, but also to the success of the internal and external transformation of China's entire economic development model. Consumption depends not only on the distribution of production conditions and the distribution of income, but also on the long-term, stable development of China's economy. At present, many contradictions in China's economic development are related to consumption or are directly reflected in the consumer sector. Here is a brief analysis of the rate of consumption and of the difficulties associated with inadequate consumption in China.

1. Analysis of the Low Rate of Consumption in China

It is widely known that in the past five years the central government has realised that economic growth cannot be driven predominantly by investment and foreign trade, and that it has therefore emphasised repeatedly that growth must be driven by consumption. But what has been the actual effect? In my view, things have not worked out very well. Let's look at the changing trend in the rate of consumption. In 1978, China's consumption rate was 62.1%, and by 2008 it had dropped to 48.4%. The annual rate of consumption fell to an historic low of 47.4%, and even continued to decline further. Although it rose from time to time, the general trend has been downward. The information from today's media is that the income of China's citizens is increasing, as are total retail sales. Such reports partly reflect the expansion of China's total consumption, but for the public they can also be misleading. First, an increase in the income of citizens does not equate to a growth in consumption; there is a distinction between the two. Second, the growth of total retail sales never quite equals the growth of consumption. In addition to household consumption, the data for total retail sales of social goods include not only sales of consumer goods manufactured by enterprises and institutions, but also sales of building materials used by urban and rural citizens for construction. These latter sales are not included in the category of household consumption. Consequently, a distinction also needs to be drawn between the two indicators, growth of retail sales and growth of consumption.

If an objective and scientific comparison is made, it can be said that China's rate of consumption is below the average world level, and that it continues to decline. Generally speaking, the consumption rate of most developed countries today is between 70% and 86%, and the trend has been highly stable, showing a slight increase. Compared with developed countries, China's consumption rate is more than 20 percentage points lower and is now at the dangerously low level of less than 50%. Compared with developing countries such as India, China's average rate of consumption is also much lower. Although the Indian consumption rate has declined in recent years, it has remained stable in most years at around 70%. Data published in the *World Development Report (2002-2009)* show that the final consumption rate of the world's low-income countries was 72% in 1980 and 83% in 2007. The same publication reports that the final consumption rate in middle-income countries was 76% in 1980 and 75% in 2007. Though there were small fluctuations in the middle years of this data-set, the figure basically remained stable. The South Korean government has also used a high-investment, low-consumption growth model since the end of World War II. South Korea has exhibited a similar level of development, and its final consumption rate gradually recovered after falling below 61.7% in 1988; it has now remained at 65%-70% for the past twenty years. China's consumption rate has changed as follows: 62.1% in 1978, 62.5% in 1990, 58.1% in 1995, 62.3% in 2000, 52.9% in 2005, 48.2% in 2009, and

47.4% in 2010. From this perspective, China's consumption rate is indeed relatively low.

It is worth observing that although the consumption rate for China's entire society has shown a downward trend, this decline is notably evident in the falling share of consumption by the country's citizens. It can be said that the low final consumption rate is primarily caused by the low household consumption rate, which essentially reflects the imbalance in the relationship between household consumption and government consumption. In the area of household consumption, it should be pointed out that in relative terms the consumption level of rural citizens has continued to decline. In recent years, China's rural economic and social development has lagged behind, and the problem of how to increase agricultural output amid relatively slow rises in agricultural income has become more and more challenging. At present, China's rural population, which accounts for nearly half of the total population, is responsible for only 1/3 of total national consumption. Statistics show that between 2001 and 2008 the per capita disposable income of China's urban citizens increased at an average annual rate of 9.9%, while the average annual growth rate of net income per capita for China's rural citizens during the same period was only 6.4%. Historically, the consumption level of urban citizens in China has not been high, and the deterioration in the relative income level of rural citizens has further inhibited the consumption capacity of most people in China.

2. The Negative Impact of Insufficient Consumption in China

Whether in theory or in reality, insufficient consumption is detrimental to the steady long-term growth of the economy. China's current low consumption rate has many negative consequences, reflected especially in the following phenomena.

The decline in the rate of consumption has led to a long-term imbalance in aggregate demand. It is widely understood that maintaining a reasonable ratio between investment, consumption, and exports is an inherent requirement for the coordinated development of the national economy. The declining consumption rate, added to already insufficient consumption, will inevitably disrupt the internal balance of the national economic development. This will cause the balance of total domestic demand to be broken. Within total domestic demand, the growth of final consumption lags dramatically behind the growth of capital formation; in essence, this will result in the contribution made by capital formation becoming greater than that of final consumption and will make fixed capital formation the primary factor in domestic demand. Accordingly, household consumption will become a secondary factor in demand. The relative decline of domestic consumption in recent years has also forced domestic production to turn outward, which has led directly to the growth of China's net exports of goods and services outstripping the growth of total domestic demand. This means that the relationship of total domestic supply and demand has shifted from a basic equilibrium in the past to an imbalance in the current period, making China more dependent on external demand. For proof of this point, one needs only observe the rising inventories of domestic goods. If net exports do not fill the gap between domestic supply and demand, then the rate at which inventories are increasing will accelerate. In particular, any downturn in the international economy will send external demand into a severe slump, which will further aggravate the imbalance in China's total domestic supply and demand.

Further, inadequate consumption can result in large excesses of domestic production capacity. The steel industry may be taken as an example. Statistics from the China Iron and Steel Association show that China's crude steel production capacity reached about 900 million tons at the end of 2011. But in 2010, China's crude steel output was only 683 million tons, and domestic steel production capacity is still expanding. This degree of overcapacity is alarming. In the current situation of high domestic savings and high investment, low consumption, over the long term, has caused excess capacity to appear in most domestic industries. Overcapacity typically involves the formation of a large volume of inefficient investment, with seriously redundant construction; the reduced overall investment efficiency has the effect of holding back economic growth. When economic growth cannot be sustained, the loss of dynamism will become one of the main factors hindering upgrades to the industrial structure and will also restrict the development of China's international division of labour. Under the investment-led growth model, overcapacity has also contributed to China's low level of industrial concentration, to intensified competition between homogeneous products, and to vicious competition among domestic companies. From an objective point of view, China, since the financial and economic crisis in the West, has adopted a proactive fiscal policy and has stabilised economic growth, but the existing overcapacity has been further aggravated. This has brought great harm to the long-term, sustainable development of China's economy at both the micro and macro levels. From a micro perspective, overcapacity has caused some domestic enterprises to overstock their inventories and reduce their production and sales ratios. Many enterprises have been operating at less than their production capacity, causing serious underutilisation and misuse of resources. As a consequence, the operating costs of enterprises have increased, and losses have been intensified. Many enterprises in the Yangtze River Delta and Pearl River Delta have already faced problems with maintaining ongoing operations. From a macro perspective, overcapacity directly affects the stability of overall price levels, and for bank portfolios results in an increase of non-performing assets. These detrimental effects may act as a trigger for deflation, for increased financial risks, and for greater macroeconomic uncertainty. In addition, overcapacity has lowered corporate investment expectations and household consumption expectations, adversely affecting domestic employment and social stability.

In short, China must objectively evaluate and deal with the negative effects of insufficient consumption.

3. The Core Explanation for Insufficient Consumption in China

An important prerequisite for fundamentally solving the problem of a low consumption rate is to discover the reasons behind this phenomenon, and especially the root causes. Doing so will allow us to address the issues and take effective measures to expand consumption. In my view, the current insufficient consumption in China can be explained on the following basis.

The first reason for the problem is China's high savings rate. High rates of saving and investment are common features of economic growth in Asian countries but are more obvious in China. We do not deny that savings rates in developing countries can be higher during economic development, but China's rate is currently too high. According to the relevant statistics, the average Chinese household, in recent years, has saved 25% of its disposable income. This is six times the savings rate for American households, and three times the rate in Japan. Even when expressed as a proportion of GDP, it is fifteen percentage points higher than the weighted average for Asian countries. One of the characteristics of China's existing socialist economy, with its mix of planning and market mechanisms, is that it is liable to produce a cycle of *high savings-high investment-economic growth*, unless the scientific outlook on development for people's livelihoods is truly implemented.

In addition, the shortcomings of China's investment and financing system, together with a lack of innovation, mean that the pace of industrial upgrades is slow. This has led to a large gap between deposits and loans in the banking system, and to the accumulation of large quantities of idle funds. It is worth noting that the current massive surplus of funds in China's banks first emerged in 1996 and has increased year by year. A *dual surplus* has actually created a situation in which foreign capitalists are making good use of Chinese capital. Within a policy environment that emphasises one-sided investment promotions, foreign capital entering China tends to produce a *crowding-out effect* rather than a *spill-over effect*. These effects continue to lower China's real labour costs, thereby reducing domestic investment efficiency and forcing China to strengthen its dependence on investment in order to maintain high growth. To a considerable extent, China has not been using Chinese capital for foreign investment, but instead, foreign capital has been using Chinese capital. It is, therefore, not surprising that domestic spending on consumption has been excessively restricted by a number of factors that have kept the savings ratio high.

The second reason relates to distribution. Wealth and income are the basis of consumption, and under-consumption directly translates into low wealth and income levels. The key problem here, however, is not that the pie to be distributed is insufficiently large, because China's economy has grown rapidly since the reform and opening up, and the expansion of total social wealth has been unprecedented. The real dilemma has been the slow growth of the incomes and wealth accumulation of workers. This has been especially true of the slow growth of wages in the initial distribution. Statistics show that since 2000, the total annual profits of industrial enterprises above a designated size in China have increased by an average of 35.3%, but employee wage growth has only increased by 14.1%. Here is another illustration that will make this clearer. In 2008, wage payments, which are the main source of workers' income, accounted for less than 10% of the operating costs of enterprises, a much lower level than in developed countries. The proportion in developed countries is generally 50%, and the gap is widening. Therefore, there is plenty of room for wage increases in China. If labour's share of the benefits of the *reform* cannot be greatly improved, it will be difficult to fundamentally reverse the tendency for the consumption rate to decline.

It must also be pointed out that the current imbalance of distribution in China is not simply a matter of income distribution, but also involves assets and wealth. Western scholars like to narrow the issue of economic equity down to income distribution, and simply and unilaterally measure it using the Gini coefficient and household income quintile, as if these two indicators effectively defined the income gap between rich and poor. In Chinese public opinion, there is now a widespread view that income distribution is unfair. This view focuses on the income gap between the managers and employees of state-owned monopoly enterprises, and largely fails to take into account the much wider gap between managers and wage earners in private enterprises. It also fails to acknowledge the fact that the assets of state-owned enterprises are shared by the state and the people. This latter point never seems to be brought up for rebuttal. Obviously, it is not enough to confine the discussion of distribution to the issue of income distribution. Otherwise, it is easy to fall for the illusions and fallacies of Western economics and sociology.

Therefore, my opinion is that the polarisation of household assets leads to the polarisation of family wealth and income, and further, to polarised consumption levels. Household assets are essentially property rights. The root of household asset polarisation lies in the excessive development of the non-public economy, reflected in the speed of its growth, and in the continuously increasing proportion it represents within the economy. As a result of this development, the most prosperous 10% of China's households currently receive 57% of total social income. It is also noteworthy that 20% of households hold 80% of bank savings. Some scholars have urged that fair distribution be promoted by substantially increasing the property incomes of citizens. Obviously, this argument ignores the social disparity of property ownership. Only a very small number of people are able to get rich quickly through the non-public economy, financial markets, and real estate markets. Most households cannot increase their property income to a greater extent or at a faster pace, and neither can workers in developed countries. Compared with private entrepreneurs, how many channels do ordinary workers have for increasing their property income? In addition, China's current channels for workers to share company profits from the capital market are not without problems. The latest information shows that 85% of the investments made in recent years have been loss-making, with the losses amounting to roughly 40% of the original sums. This is another significant issue that has severely curbed citizens' consumption.

In *Capital*, Marx pointed out that although under-consumption may appear to be the equivalent of low purchasing power, its root cause is the irrational ownership and arrangement of property rights. China's current situation indicates that under-consumption caused by low purchasing power is closely related to the lack of balance of the country's social income distribution, but at its root, under-consumption is still determined by the ownership structure of society.

Due to the unequal control of production conditions by workers and asset owners, labour and capital factors are naturally in an asymmetrical income distribution position. In recent years Liu Guoguang, Wei Xinghua and many other prominent Chinese Marxist economists have examined and clarified the relevant theoretical principle: *consumption depends on distribution, and distribution depends on property rights*. This is a basic theorem of economics, and those who fail to take it into account look only at the surface of the problem. China, in recent years, has stressed the need to achieve greater equity in initial distribution; for example, the wages of front-line workers have been raised nationwide since 2010, and some measures have been taken to improve minimum wage standards and subsidies for farmers. Nevertheless, it remains an obvious fact that the pendulum on the *scales of distribution* have not fundamentally been made to swing in favor of the majority of workers. In enterprises, the proportion of income distributed on the basis of capital is increasing, and the share of disposable income in the household sector continues to decline. This share is now even lower than that received by workers in Russia, which is generally regarded by us as a capitalist country.

The third reason is that the marginal propensity of citizens to consume has also decreased. Strictly speaking, this decrease is a result of the earlier-mentioned two reasons. The decline in the marginal propensity to consume is related to the high level of savings and is also rooted in income imbalances. There are profound institutional factors behind China's high savings. Since the reform and opening up, China's economic development has accelerated rapidly amid quickly evolving market-oriented reforms, but the social security system has not kept up. Its shortcomings mainly take the form of problems with housing, education, medical care, pensions, and employment. These areas were originally the responsibilities of the government, but market-oriented reforms have meant that the burdens involved are now borne mainly by the people themselves. Individuals are now required to pay more for the services concerned, which has prompted citizens to maintain a high level of savings. To make these passive savings, society's lower and middle classes are compelled to reduce their expenditures and consumption. Therefore, no policy based on stimulating consumption can achieve the desired results. Under such policies, large amounts of wealth are concentrated in the hands of a few rich people, which only intensifies their quest for wealth appreciation, making our high investment trend irreversible. Moreover, due to the polarisation in the distribution of wealth and income, China's household consumption structure has shown two extreme trends: the wealthy are overly enthusiastic about luxury goods and investment products, while large numbers of people on low incomes have limited purchasing power, resulting in slow sales of ordinary consumer goods. Today, China's consumption of luxury goods is among the greatest in the world. This was spelt out in a report, entitled *Heavy Crown of the No. 1 Luxury Country*[129], published in the international news section of *Guangming Daily* on 24 June 2011. In the area of investment products, the real estate bubble has become a persistent problem for economic development, and even some agricultural products have been targeted by investors. This has put tremendous pressure on the consumption levels of low and middle-income people and has further reduced the propensity of ordinary citizens to consume.

The fourth reason is that the proportion of government consumption is too high. In general, the final consumption rate is limited by the total economic volume and by the overall level of social consumption. Within the structure of social consumption, excessive consumption by the government means that household consumption will be suppressed. Unfortunately, not only has China's overall consumption rate decreased, but from a social consumption structure perspective, while household consumption has declined, governmental consumption has risen. A number of studies of China's domestic economy have pointed out that since the reform and opening up, the proportion of government consumption in the final consumption rate, after remaining stable at 21% – 23% during the 1980s, has since trended upward; between 2000 and 2010 it was in the region of 26% – 27%, and it has now exceeded 28%. The government's outlays on everyday administrative expenses, on construction of office buildings, and on official overseas trips, vehicles, and receptions are relatively large. This is especially true due to the frequency with which the government and its affiliates hold high-cost international forums, inviting foreign experts who are hired for large fees to expound meaningless, superficial, or unoriginal views. Despite the determination of the central government to take measures to strictly control governmental spending in the past two years, the results have not been very effective.

It can be seen that one of the typical manifestations of the imbalance of Chinese national income distribution is the relative decline in the share of household income during the current period of rapid economic growth. According to data from the National Bureau of Statistics, in 2010 the per capita disposable income of urban citizens in China increased by a nominal figure of 14.1% over the 2009

---

129. https://finance.qq.com/a/20110624/001914.htm

level. After deducting price factors, the actual growth rate was 8.4%, which was 0.8 percentage points lower than the GDP growth rate. On 14 September 2012, the *2011 China Salary Report*[130], released by the Labour and Wage Research Institute under the Ministry of Human Resources and Social Security, showed that China's public fiscal revenue increased that year by 24.8%, which was 1.76 times the nominal increase in per capita disposable income for urban citizens and 1.39 times the nominal increase in per capita net income for rural citizens. The growth rate of corporate income during the same period was about 20%, far higher than the income of citizens.

The reason why government consumption has grown so fast is that disposable fiscal revenue in China has risen too quickly. Using statistical data, one can see that the annual growth rate of China's fiscal revenue in the past ten years has generally been in the range of 11% to 15%, which is higher than the growth rate of GDP. It has been argued that since the proportion of China's fiscal revenue in GDP (30% in 2011) is lower than the average level for developed countries (generally around 40%), it is not possible for China's government consumption to be higher than the world average. Those who hold this view draw a simple equation between the government's disposable fiscal revenue and tax revenue, which is an untenable position. China's government revenue is objectively different from that of western countries. The government's disposable fiscal revenue stems not only from tax revenue, but also from other sources outside budget management, such as land transfer fees, confiscation revenue, and even profits created by state-owned enterprises. These sums have also provided the financial basis for the excessive growth of government consumption. Clearly, the current high proportion of government consumption in China has occurred at the expense of the relative shrinkage of labour consumption capacity. Since part of the growth of government consumption in China is due to the expansion of government agencies and personnel numbers, and to an increase in unwarranted expenditures, it has not been possible to achieve a long-term increase in the final consumption rate, and this has been a major cause for the continued insufficient consumption of goods by the country's citizens.

In short, high savings and investment, inequity in property ownership and income distribution caused by excessive development of the non-public economy, citizens' low marginal propensity to consume, and an excessive government consumption ratio are the four main reasons for China's current low consumption rate and

---

130. https://china.huanqiu.com/article/9CaKrnJx6XT

insufficient consumption. If these problems are left unsolved, it will be almost impossible to achieve China's goal of expanding consumption and domestic demand.

(Originally published in *Consumer Economy*, Issue 6, 2012)

* * *

Section IV Theoretical Interpretation and Practical Analysis of Common Prosperity under Socialism

As an important scientific conclusion regarding future social development, scientific socialism projects the gradual elimination, on the basis of the development of the productive forces, of the social inequality that accompanies private ownership. The goal of common prosperity is the fundamental position of Marxism where future standards of social value are concerned. In Deng Xiaoping Theory, common prosperity, as the essence of socialism, determines the direction of socialist reform and development in China. In the long run, achieving common prosperity requires a comprehensive implementation of the corresponding system of distribution, on the basis of consolidating the socialist economic system. In the short term and basing ourselves on China's national conditions at the primary stage, China needs to effectively curb the growing gap between urban and rural areas, between regions, and between rich and poor by consolidating and developing public ownership, adjusting primary distribution, and directing the redistribution of national income to promote economic fairness and improve labour efficiency.

1. The Essence and Practical Significance of Common Prosperity

(I) Common Prosperity as a Socialist Value Standard

Understanding the specific connotations and historical significance of common prosperity as the goal of socialist development involves both theoretical and practical elements.

From a theoretical perspective, common prosperity is a scientific conclusion drawn from the laws of historical development and represents the basic developmental goal of a socialist society as stipulated by the founders of scientific socialism. Looking back and reviewing Marx's thoughts on the future of society, we find that common prosperity first emerged as the opposite of *polarisation*. In his analysis of capitalist society, Marx regarded capital accumulation as both the motive force and the result of the capitalist mode of production, and he explained the historical nature of *polarisation* under the conditions of capitalism. Basing himself on his scientific method, he pointed out that 'the nature of the production relations in which the bourgeois movement is carried out is by no means uniform and simple, but two-fold; poverty also arises in those relations, which produce wealth; a power of oppression also develops in the relationships that develop the productive forces'[131]. The contradictions of the capitalist system, under which both wealth and poverty accumulate, will eventually lead to the collapse of the entire social reproduction process. Therefore, a future socialist society must fundamentally eliminate capitalism by rooting out the system of private property ownership on which social exploitation depends. That system is an historical phenomenon within which the minority owns the labour achievements of the majority. In his *Economic Manuscripts*[132] from 1857 to 1858, Marx proposed that in the new social system, 'The development of social productive forces will be so rapid, ... production will be aimed at the prosperity of all the people'. 'Production will be developed to a scale that can meet the needs of all the people; the situation of sacrificing the interests of some people to meet the needs of others will be ended.' It is clear from these words that the founders of Marxism inscribed the concept of the common prosperity of all members of society on their banner from the very beginning, and these tenets have become a guide to the social practice of socialism.

Common prosperity is the concrete path of socialist practice, and it is the inevitable choice for strengthening the national cohesion of socialist countries and consolidating the socialist system. Just as any new social system must, as it emerges, confront the remnants left by the old society, the socialist system also needs to choose a developmental path consistent with its institutional situation at the point when it begins to be established. China, in this regard, has traversed a long and difficult road forward. As a backward agricultural country, China as early as 16 December 1953 proposed the concept of *common prosperity* in the *Resolution of the CPC Central Committee on the Development of Agricultural Production Cooperatives*[133] (hereinafter referred to as the *Resolution*). The *Resolution* stated, 'In order to further improve agricultural productivity, the fundamental task of the

---

131. Marx. *Capital*: Vol. 1 [M]. Beijing: People's Publishing House, 1975: 708.

132. Marx, Engels. *The complete works of Marx and Engels*: Volume 46 [M]. Beijing: People's Publishing House, 1980: 222.

133. http://www.71.cn/2011/0930/632197.shtml

Party's work in the countryside is to educate the mass of peasants and gradually promote unity among them with principles and methods that are understandable and reasonable, and to organise and gradually implement the socialist transformation of agriculture, so that agriculture can carry through the change from the individual economy of backward, small-scale production to an advanced, cooperative economy of large-scale production. This is done so as to gradually overcome the incompatible contradictions in the development of the two economic sectors of industry and agriculture, and to enable farmers to gradually overcome poverty and achieve common prosperity'[134]. Through the socialist transformation of agriculture, the fundamental goal was to achieve common prosperity on the basis of developing the forces of production; the organic unity of socialist methods and aims was thus set forward in a scientific fashion. It follows that only by pursuing a common path of prosperous development will China be able to break the historical cycle of ups and downs of prosperity and chaos caused by the unevenness of the development process. Only in this way can China overcome the difficulties and crises that have arisen from the economic and social development of capitalist countries. Only through the search for common prosperity can China unite the whole of society to accelerate the growth of productivity and improve our quality of life. It may be said that common prosperity has become not just the value standard of socialism, but also a realistic path for China's socialist modernisation drive, and a concrete manifestation of the institutional advantages China has achieved through the establishment of our socialist system.

In examining the specific practice of China's socialist reform, the comprehensive elabouration of common prosperity should be attributed to Comrade Deng Xiaoping. In 1992, he stated: 'The essence of socialism is to liberate the productive forces, develop the productive forces, eliminate exploitation, eliminate polarisation, and ultimately achieve common prosperity'[135]. These five phrases on the essence of socialism make up a unified whole and placing common prosperity at the end of the list does not mean that its importance is less than that of developing the productive forces. On the contrary, in Deng Xiaoping's theory of the essence of socialism, it

---

134. Liao Gailong, Zhuang Puming, editors; with contributions by Lin Yunhui, et al. *Chronology of the People's Republic of China*. Zhengzhou: Henan People's Publishing House. ISBN 7-215-04679-6.

135. Deng Xiaoping. *Selected Writings of Deng Xiaoping*: Volume 3 [M]. Beijing: People's Publishing House, 1993: p. 373.

is precisely the liberation and development of the productive forces, the elimination of the exploitation inherent in private ownership, and the containment of polarisation that will enable the realisation of common prosperity. In September 1986, when answering a question from the American journalist Mike Wallace, Comrade Deng Xiaoping made his position clear: 'Socialist wealth belongs to the people, and the prosperity of socialism is the common prosperity of all the people. The first step is to develop production and the second is to get rich together. Our policy is not to cause polarisation in society'[136]. It can be seen that Comrade Deng Xiaoping adhered to the basic principles of Marxism here, and that he also explained *common prosperity* as the opposite of *polarisation*. This theoretical statement clarifies the standards by which China's socialist nature under the conditions of reform and opening up should be judged and sets out the developmental requirements for common prosperity. It thus amounts to a unified theory of the purpose and methods of socialist development.

(II) Common Prosperity as the Path to the Realisation of Socialism, and Related Disputes

Although common prosperity was established as the value standard and development goal of socialism at the beginning of the reform, there have been divergent understandings of how to realise the goal in practical terms. By 'common prosperity', Comrade Deng Xiaoping did not mean *simultaneous prosperity* or *equal prosperity*. Addressing the imbalances in the development of China's productive forces in a 1983 talk, Comrade Deng Xiaoping advanced the idea: 'Let some people and some regions get rich first. This is a new method that everyone supports, and it is better than the old one'[137]. At the same time, he stressed: 'Let some people and some regions get rich first, to lead and help the backward areas. It is an obligation for advanced areas to help the backward areas'[138]. The essence is to start from the actual situation, that is, from the characteristics and conditions of different regions of the country, and correctly deal with the developmental relationship between different groups and regions. This idea of 'allowing a group of people to get rich first and then let them help others get rich later', so as to achieve common prosperity has

---

136. Ibid, p. 172
137. Ibid, p. 23
138. Ibid, p. 155

undoubtedly played a role in emancipating the mind in the practice of reform and opening up. The position he took aroused enthusiasm at all levels, and greatly promoted the rapid development of the country's economy.

As is true of many scientific theories when they are applied in practice, Comrade Deng Xiaoping's idea of *getting rich first and getting rich later* is nevertheless at risk of being understood unilaterally. In particular, the question now arises: *Is the current debate about common prosperity in China not about whether to achieve common prosperity, but about how and when to achieve common prosperity?*

The core issue in this matter is ownership. A typical misunderstanding evoked by Deng Xiaoping's concept of *getting rich first and getting rich later* has been to separate common prosperity from the issue of ownership, to understand it purely in the sense of the ultimate goal, and to treat *getting rich first* and *getting rich later* in practice as two different developmental models that are spatially independent of each other. For example, the view is put forward that Deng Xiaoping's theory of the essence of socialism does not mention public ownership, and that consequently, public ownership is no longer important. But once separated from public ownership as its mainstay, distribution according to work as the main body will no longer exist, and the goal of common prosperity will be impossible to achieve. In the same way, the conditions of a socialist market economy mean that since various factors of production enter the market simultaneously, those who get rich first and those who do so later will all face the same market. They will inevitably be connected to each other and will find that their interests diverge. For example, coastal areas and inland areas are in different positions in terms of resource utilisation; thus, market behavior alone cannot simultaneously enrich the people who are supposed to get rich later. The reason why Deng Xiaoping proposed to let some people *get rich first* was mainly in order to liberate the productive forces at that specific time. That is, at a point when the economy was generally lagging behind, his idea was to let some eligible regions and individuals get rich first. The current situation, as pointed out by the renowned economist Liu Guoguang, is that the gap between rich and poor in China has expanded for more than thirty years, and that the formation of a trend to polarisation has resulted from a shift of ownership structure and property relationships from *public* to *private*. Moreover, the accumulation of wealth has quickly become concentrated in the hands of a few private individuals. These are the root causes.

Regarding the latter question, another typical misreading of Comrade Deng Xiaoping's ideas on *getting rich first and getting rich later* is to treat *getting rich first* and *getting rich later* as two different stages of development, separated by time. This amounts to blindly copying so-called modern economic theories current in the West, and to searching for ways to excuse the widening gaps of wealth and income. Various scholars heedlessly follow the so-called *inverted U curve theory*, believing that economic development, to a certain degree, will produce an inflection point conducive to fair distribution. In other words, they contend that unfair distribution is an inevitable phenomenon at the lower stage of economic development. Such people maintain dogmatically that in the areas of system design and economic policy, *making a bigger pie* is always more important than *properly dividing the pie*, and they fail to recognise that production and distribution need to interact closely. This attitude is obviously not conducive to implementing the scientific outlook on development, with its stress on sharing the benefits of reform and development, and in practice the above viewpoint has become one of the theoretical sources of the *GDP-only theory*. In reality, the *inverted U curve* is simply a hypothesis, and since the 1990s has been questioned in a large number of empirical analyses by Western scholars, to the point where it has become untenable. A large number of theoretical studies, together with historical experiences of economic development in various countries, have proved that making the pie bigger can certainly provide favorable factors for achieving a better division, but also that good things can sometimes turn bad. That is, if the pie keeps growing but the gap between rich and poor keeps widening as the pie is divided, then any favorable factors will be cancelled out. Only a fair and reasonable distribution of the pie can maximise everyone's enthusiasm, and as a result, help to make the pie bigger.

Objectively speaking, the word *prosperity* has its own historic meaning, and Comrade Deng Xiaoping in his theory used the term *common prosperity* in a deliberate, realistic fashion. Judging from the situation at that time, he clearly believed that *common prosperity* should be possible once China's economic development reached the level of per capita income of moderately developed countries. There is now a widespread view that reaching this level of per capita income will allow China to end the *getting rich first* stage and to enter the *common prosperity* stage. This view, however, clearly runs counter to Comrade Deng Xiaoping's original intentions. On the question of a timetable for common prosperity, he remarked as follows: 'It is conceivable that this issue will be highlighted and resolved when the *well-off level* is reached at the end of this century (the end of the 20th century)'[139]. Comrade Deng Xiaoping's concerns were not unreasonable. In the context of ever-increasing wealth and a continuing income gap, it is even more important to pay attention to the danger of polarisation. While remaining conscious that achieving common prosperity is an arduous long-term task, China must also be aware of its inevitability and urgency. Liu Guoguang[140], a member of the Presidium of the Chinese Academy of Social Sciences, summed up the situation accurately when he stated that it is not a matter of first transforming *national wealth* into *civil wealth*. Instead, a clear announcement is needed that the policy of *'letting some people get rich first'* has run its course. It is time for this policy to be transformed into one of *achieving common prosperity*. For completing the transition from *getting rich first* to *achieving common prosperity*, this is what is required.

2. Measuring the Degree of Common Prosperity or the Gap between Rich and Poor

When it comes to the goal of common socialist prosperity and its realisation, one cannot avoid the discussion surrounding its measurement criteria. Common prosperity is the development goal of socialism, which necessarily requires that it be viewed and measured by the standards of scientific socialism. In the view of the founders of Marxism, when they contemplated the future of society, common prosperity referred to *letting all the people enjoy the welfare created by the whole of society*. Since Marx's vision of the future of society was that the whole society would jointly own the means of production, and there would be no currency intermediary due to the dissolution of the commodity economy, the embodiment of common prosperity would be *welfare*. Obviously, the word *welfare* here should be understood as the sum of the material and spiritual wealth of a society.

Common prosperity always appears as the opposite of polarisation between rich and poor. Taken in a negative sense, this polarisation can be used as a reference standard to judge common prosperity, the more polarised a society, the lower the degree of common prosperity, and vice versa. At present, the staple measurement indicators of polarisation are *wealth distribution indicators* and *income distribution*

---

139. Deng Xiaoping. *Selected Writings of Deng Xiaoping: Volume 3* [M]. Beijing: People's Publishing House, 1993: p. 374.

140. Liu Guoguang. 'Should "the country's wealth be given priority" or "the people's wealth be given priority", or "some people get rich first" to "common wealth" [J].' *Exploration*. 2011(4).

indicators. The difference between the two is that wealth indicators are not only linked to income, but also to the extent to which people possess means of production. More unequal income distribution will exacerbate polarisation and is not conducive to the realisation of common prosperity. From an historical perspective, however, and in accordance with the realities of Western capitalist countries, polarisation reflects not so much the income distribution gap, as the gap in wealth possession. And notably, the gap in wealth is usually tied directly to the widening of the gap in income distribution.

When measured by indicators of wealth ownership, the degree of polarisation in capitalist countries is often staggering. In the ownership of various financial assets, for example, the richest 10% of American households possess from three to sixty times as much of each item as the remaining 90% of households. The richest 1% of households own 62.4% of total commercial assets, while the next 9% of households own 30.9%, and the remaining 90%, only 6.7%. This gap is much greater than in most capitalist countries and in socialist China. In 2011, the contemporary Keynesian economist Joseph Stiglitz, analyzing the current crisis that is sweeping the capitalist world, pointed out: 'The top one percent of Americans now control nearly a quarter of the nation's income every year. In terms of wealth rather than income, the top one percent control forty percent. Their lot in life has improved considerably. Twenty-five years ago, the corresponding figures were twelve percent and thirty-three percent'[141]. Stiglitz believes that if the property ownership system is not changed, the *trickle-down economy,* in which the people who get rich first help others get rich later, may be only a delusion!

The indicators of income distribution that are widely used in Western theoretical circles are the Gini coefficient of income and the household income quintile figures; the latter are generally used to compare the incomes of the richest 20% and poorest 20% of households. These indicators, however, partly obscure the real polarisation between rich and poor, and they are not completely scientific. In the household income quintile method, for example, the richest 1% of people at the top of the pyramid are grouped into the 20% group with higher incomes. In essence, this conceals the reality of polarisation under monopoly capitalism. If we recall the slogan of the Occupy Wall Street movement, *We are the 99%,* we can see that the income quintile method employed by bourgeois economists and sociologists is indeed limited by class.

---

141. https://www.vanityfair.com/news/2011/05/top-one-percent-201105

Where common prosperity and the wealth gap are concerned, the present status quo in China is as follows.

(I) The Wealth Gap Is Widening Faster

According to statistics, the degree of imbalance in wealth distribution in China recently has been far greater than the imbalance in income distribution. The concentration of wealth in the hands of high-income groups is growing at an average annual rate of 12.3%, which is twice the global average. In 2009, the number of individuals in China with assets greater than one million dollars reached 670,000, the third-highest figure in the world. The number of individuals with assets exceeding one billion dollars was second only to the United States. According to a report by the Boston Consulting Group, the number of millionaire families in China increased by 16% in 2010 to 1.43 million. During the same period, the United States saw a decrease of 129,000, with a total of 5.13 million. According to another World Bank report, 5% of the population in the United States controls 60% of the wealth, while 1% of Chinese households control 41.4% of the national wealth, which is an even greater degree of concentration than in the United States.[142]

(II) The Income Gap Has Been above the Warning Line

Although various calculations have been made of China's Gini coefficient, it is generally believed in academia that this value has reached 0.45–0.49, with the World Bank reporting a figure of 0.47. Both of these calculations are above the internationally recognised warning line of 0.4. According to the National Bureau of Statistics, which chose the income quintile method for measurement in 2010, the per capita net income ratio of high and low-income groups for rural citizens in China, though down from 8.0: 1 in 2009 to 7.5: 1, was still relatively high. The result for urban citizens was also found to have maintained a high level of 5.4: 1.

It should be pointed out that both of these measurements are from Western sources. In practice, they cannot provide a fully accurate reflection of the polarisation between rich and poor, but the situation is already grim. Another reflection of the gap between rich and poor is that the ratio of labour compensation to GDP in China has

142. Bloomberg News. 'Asia Pacific's wealthy grow "alone" [N].' *Reference News*. 2012-06-02.

continued to decline. According to data from the National Bureau of Statistics, between 1990 and 2009, this figure fell from 53.42% to 46.62%. During the same period, the gap between different industries also widened. This phenomenon of imbalance between personal efforts and social achievements, and value creation and social contributions has become a major challenge for China as it seeks to achieve common prosperity and build a harmonious society.

(III) The Urban-Rural Income Gap Is Too Large

Statistical analysis shows that the income gap between urban and rural citizens in China has widened from the mid-1980s to the present; from 1.88: 1 in 1985 (assuming 1 in rural areas), it increased to 2.21: 1 in 1990, to 3.48: 1 in 2005, and to 3.66: 1 in 2009. According to data released by the National Bureau of Statistics in 2010, the per capita net income of rural citizens in China was 5,919 yuan. The annual per capita disposable income of urban citizens was 19,109 yuan, and the urban-rural income ratio reached 3.23: 1. Although this was lower than the above-cited estimate, the widening income gap is still glaringly obvious. It should be pointed out that the above figures depict only the income gap between urban and rural citizens in each year, not the property gap analyzed from the perspective of stock ownership. If the difference between the property owned by urban and rural citizens is taken into consideration, the gap will be even greater. First, income can be converted into investment assets under market economic conditions, but low-income rural citizens need to spend most of their income on daily necessities, education for their children, and medical treatment, meaning that their ability to accumulate wealth is strictly limited. Second, the income of rural citizens as measured in current statistics often includes their income from working in cities, so comparisons based on these data cannot fully reflect the true gap between urban and rural economic development.

The current income gap between urban and rural areas should neither be exaggerated nor ignored. There is a one-sided view that regards the urban-rural gap as the main cause of the income gap. The evidence for this view is insufficient. It is obvious that the urban-rural gap emerged before the reform and opening up, and that it was also large at that time. The income gap, however, did not widen excessively, nor did it lead to serious polarisation between rich and poor. Another explanation for the gap between urban and rural areas is rapid industrialisation and urbanisation. But the statistical data at different times in China and abroad do not fully prove this conclusion. The gap requires a more deep-seated explanation, on the basis of the change of ownership structure and the leading factors of economic development. It can be said that the main reasons for the urban-rural income gap are the rapid development of privatisation at home and abroad, and the imbalance involved in *putting emphasis on cities while overlooking rural areas.*

(IV) Attention Needs to Be Paid to the Regional Income Gap

According to statistics, the ratios of per capita incomes in the eastern, central, and western regions of China expanded from 1.37: 1.18: 1 in 1978 to 2.42: 1.2: 1 in 2000. For urban citizens, the ratios of per capita annual incomes in 2008 in eastern, central, and western regions of China reached 1.51: 1.01: 1, while the annual net income ratios for rural citizens were 1.88: 1.27: 1. One scholar pointed out that in 2000, the per capita GDP of the eastern region was 1.98 times that of the central region, while the per capita GDP of the western region was 77% of that of the central region. By 2010, GDP per capita in the eastern region was 1.74 times that in the central region, while GDP per capita in the western region was 80% of that in the central region. Although the gap has been narrowed, it is still relatively large. There are historical reasons for regional disparities as well as reasons related to geographical factors, industrial policies, and resource conditions. The widening income gap between regions is a new problem that China has had to face as economic development has proceeded in recent years.

(V) The Industry Income Gap Is Too Large

In the 1980s, the wage gap between the highest and lowest-paid sectors of industry in China generally remained at the level of 1.6–1.8 to 1. By 2010, the industry with the highest average wage was the financial sector, and the average wage of its employees had reached 70,146 yuan. Meanwhile, employees in agriculture, forestry, animal husbandry, and fisheries had the lowest average wage, which was a mere 16,717 yuan. The ratio of the highest to the lowest was 4.2: 1. If calculated by industrial segments, the ratio of the highest to the lowest could be more than 10 times. According to other sources, average annual wages in the manufacturing and construction industries, which accounted for 40.5% of all employees of urban non-private entities in 2011, were only 36,494 yuan and 32,657 yuan. These figures were about one-third of the average annual wage of 91,364 yuan in the financial industry. An international comparison of industrial wage gaps released by the Wage Research Institute of the Ministry of Human Resources and Social Security in 2011 showed that the gap between the highest and lowest-income industries in China had expanded to fifteen times. The gap revealed by National Bureau of Statistics figures released the previous year was only eleven times.[143] Data from other market economy countries show that the wage gap between the highest and lowest-income industries in 2006–2007 was 1.6–2 times in Japan, the United Kingdom, and France. In Germany, Canada, the United States, and South Korea, it was 2.3–3 times. China's industrial income gap, by contrast, has jumped to the top rank in the world.

3. Two Important Pathways to Promoting Common Prosperity under Socialism

Another urgent task for us is to *take our lead from public opinion,* instead of merely *making a show.* We must earnestly implement Comrade Deng Xiaoping's idea of *putting forward and solving the problem* of *polarisation.* We need to focus on narrowing the excessive gap in wealth and income, and to move economic reform and development onto the scientific track of accelerating the realisation of common prosperity.

(I) Jointly Develop the State-Owned and Privately-Owned Economies, and Make the Public Sector Bigger, Stronger, and Better

The essence of socialism with Chinese characteristics lies in the establishment of a basic system in which public ownership plays a dominant role and diverse forms of ownership develop together. Only by consolidating and developing socialist public ownership, can we fundamentally guarantee the people's ownership of the means of production and eliminate the institutional obstacles to combining the means of production with labour. At the beginning of the reform, Comrade Deng Xiaoping pointed out: 'In the reform, we must always adhere to two fundamental principles: one is taking the socialist public economy as the mainstay, and the other is common prosperity'.[144] From a macro perspective, we

---

143. Song Xiaowu. 'China's industry income gap widens to 15 times, leaping to world's top [N].' *Economic Reference News.* 2011-02-10.

144. Deng Xiaoping. *Selected Writings of Deng Xiaoping: Volume 3* [M]. Beijing: People's Publishing House, 1993: p. 142.

should recognise that within a certain range the existence of the private economy is of positive significance for the development of the social productive forces. But we must also see that adherence to public ownership is not only a necessary condition for preventing the wealth gap from becoming too large, but also an important prerequisite for implementing the system of distribution according to work as the mainstay, and for curbing the tendency for the share of labour income in the national economy to fall. Compared to the private economy, the wages of employees in the public economy are relatively high, and provisions for the welfare of employees are also better. This not only serves to restrain the differentiation in wealth ownership, but also helps generally to raise the income level of ordinary workers and to narrow the income gap. Only in the publicly-owned economy can corporate profits be transformed into wealth owned in common by the whole of society or the collective. This makes accumulation a bridge to common prosperity. Research also shows that there is an inconsistency in the trade-off between the growth of labour income and the increase of capital gains in China, a situation that intensifies the contradiction between the bourgeoisie and the working class. In addition, competition between the public and private sectors of the economy is deepening day by day. The areas and forms in which this competition appears include economic resources, control of markets, the competition of professional and technical talent, the field of services to the public, and the exclusion of public capital from joint ventures. It can be seen that the contradiction between the public and the non-public economy has an objective existence, and it is impossible to ignore this contradiction as we strive to make public enterprises stronger and better. Using the *creation of an environment of fair competition* as an excuse for advocating the so-called principle under which *the state-owned economy retreats while the private economy advances* or advocating *share ownership for all people* and other such practices will only hamper and destroy state assets. Fundamentally, these slogans and practices run counter to the path of common prosperity.

From a micro perspective, scientific management in accordance with the inherent requirements of public-owned enterprises, and regulation of the development of private enterprises on the basis of protecting the rights and interests of workers, are important guarantees for achieving common prosperity. The manner in which enterprise theory and the practices of modern firms have developed also shows that advances in the productivity of labour in modern society need to be made on the basis of strengthening the status of employees, technicians, and management personnel, and that there is a need to promote the fundamental equality of stakeholders in enterprises. In the process of economic reform and development, we should not, therefore, simply emphasise the get *first-rich effect* in the private economy but should also pay more attention to a *common prosperity mechanism* in the public economy. We should not only consolidate and develop the state-owned economy, but also encourage, develop, and expand urban and rural collective and cooperative economies in particular. Practice has shown that when we engage in double-tier management on the basis of co-production contracting, special attention should be paid to collective-level management. The active development of the true rural collective economy is the key to enhancing rural cohesion and the appeal of the party organisation. This aids the rural economy in adapting to the path of larger-scale operations, intensification, and modernisation, and can enhance social stability and common prosperity. Therefore, we should place special importance on the role of the rural collective economy in promoting the coordinated development of urban and rural areas and in narrowing the gap between these two areas.

In the course of reform and opening up, excessive privatisation policies in some regions and departments have allowed the private economy to develop on a large scale. In the name of marketisation, large numbers of state-owned assets have undergone a restructuring that has seen them pass into private hands. Resources of land and minerals have also been taken over by the private economy, and in recent decades this has made China one of the countries with the fastest-widening gaps between rich and poor in the world. At the same time, as we continue to develop the non-public economy at home and abroad, we must therefore vigorously strengthen the guidance and management to which it is subject, and while fostering its positive aspects, suppress its negative effects.

(II) Establish a Development Model That Focuses on Improving People's Livelihoods, and Shifts Government Inputs and Policies Towards a Model of Inclusiveness

The improving of people's livelihoods is itself a direct manifestation of social prosperity. It can enable people to enjoy the benefits of the development of social productive forces. At the same time, enhancing the quality of people's livelihoods through expanding social welfare coverage and providing basic social security can effectively reduce the negative impact that the income gap is having on various social groups, regions, and sectors as economic development proceeds. Practice has shown that to achieve common prosperity during the primary stage of socialism, when productivity is still underdeveloped, we must take full advantage of the socialist state's political power to intervene, to regulate economic life, and to release the energy and creativity of the people who will get rich later. Therefore, we should not only pay attention to the root problems of primary distribution, but also take full advantage of the government's role in regulating national income redistribution.

In establishing our new development model, we should specifically and substantially increase our investment in constructing better livelihoods for the people. We should improve employment policies, increase transfer payments through measures such as social security, housing security, special consumption subsidies, holiday subsidies, and special fee reductions, and strengthen investment in education. We should improve our policies relating to the control of income levels in various industries, raise investment in environmental protection and the Expedite City Program, continue to meet the living and development needs of urban citizens, and promote the orderly flow of rural citizens into cities. The focus of the development model, with its orientation toward people's livelihoods, should be on expanding social security, increasing the income levels of low and middle-income earners, and narrowing the wealth and income gaps at such levels as groups, regions and industries.

(Originally published in *Marxism Research*, Issue 6, 2012. Second Author: Liu Wei)

Chapter 5

Reform of the Relationship between the Chinese Market and Government

China's reform has entered a crucial stage. To further strengthen reform, we need to respect the rules of the market, give full play to the role of the government, and seek more space for development by grasping the advantages of the policies of opening-up.

* * *

Section I Establish a New Regulation Mechanism Based on Market Regulation and Guided by State Regulation

So far, no single consensus has been reached on the roles of the market and state regulation or on the relationships between them, though within China's academic circles many useful studies have been conducted. In this section, I call for gradually establishing a new regulatory mechanism within the system of economic reform. This is an initial stage mechanism designed to be based on market regulation and to be guided by state regulation in order to better meet the objective need for the development of a socialist planned commodity economy.

1. The Meaning and Overall Characteristics of the New Mechanism Based on Market Regulation and Guided by State Regulation

(I) The Basic Meaning of *Based on Market Regulation*

Market regulation is the control of value through market governance based on economic operations and economic behaviours. It is manifested as the *coordination effect* or *adjustment effect* of the interaction between market mechanism elements such as price, supply, demand, and competition. The phrase *based on market regulation* refers to taking advantage of such functions of the market mechanism as short-term allocations, micro-equilibrium, signal transmissions, technological innovations, and interest motivations. These features directly regulate enterprises and individual workers. However, the functional strength of market regulation cannot conceal its inherent weaknesses. These weaknesses can be briefly summarised in four points.

1. The Deviation from the Target of Market Regulation

It is impossible for an enterprise solely guided by the market to gain insights into the developmental goals or the direction of the national economy. This is because the nation is in the process of striving towards the overall goals of the operation of the national economy, and under market regulation there is no macroeconomic decision-maker. As a result, it is easy to deviate from these goals during the pursuit of profit maximisation, causing the macro-plan to fail.

2. Limited Market Regulation

In sectors subject to external factors, particularly infrastructure such as transportation, utilities such as water supply and sanitation, services such as postal and telecommunications, as well as in the production of goods that require the use of scarce resources and other basic industries with low profitability and long investment cycles, market regulation is not deep enough to be effective. Even increasing the divergence between price and value and stimulating competition is not effective in the short term at producing rapid growth in these goods and services. In areas like non-profit education, health, basic research, national defence, and other sectors, the possibility of suitable market regulation is even smaller.

3. The Slow Pace of Market Regulation

Market regulation, by its nature, suffers from a time-lag or hysteresis in exerting its effects, and it is relatively slow at promoting the evolution and upgrading of the industrial structure. This arises from the imbalance that exists between market supply and demand and leads to price changes. Responding to these price signals, the enterprises adjust their business decisions, which may bring about a temporary balance between market supply and demand. This chain reaction is not instantaneous; in practice, it can take a prolonged period. Moreover, since the market information is never completely transparent, the known *white information*, unknown *black information*, and semi-known *gray information* coexist. In reality, the market system and its mechanisms are never perfect, and under the conditions of low market visibility, producers are only able to plan their immediate next steps on the basis of current prices and the latest status of supply and demand. It may be concluded that the business decisions taken by enterprises taken as a whole will inevitably turn out to be shortsighted, or even to have been made blindly. Additionally, enterprises always encounter difficulties in consistently implementing technological transformations, and this will be harmful to the optimisation of the social industrial structure.

4. The High Cost of Market Regulation

Features of market regulation such as goal deviation, time delays, and frictional losses do exist. These features give rise to the need to invest a large amount of labour in dealing with issues such as collecting market information, balancing economic fluctuations, and curing static and dynamic negative externalities. Further challenges flow from the need to prevent excessive monopolies, to alleviate high unemployment and inflation, to eliminate abnormalities in distribution, and deal with irrational consumption choices. All of these must be considered, because they directly or indirectly increase the cost of market regulation. Observed from an empirical perspective, a considerable portion of these adjustment costs is a pure waste of resources.

In short, the advantageous functions of market regulation mean that it has established a fundamental position in the socialist economic regulation system. But at the same time, the inherent functional deficiencies of market regulation lead inevitably to the emergence of state regulations.

(II) The Basic Meaning of *Guided by State Regulation*

State regulation refers to the use of economic, legal, administrative, and persuasive measures by the state to consciously allocate total social labour and manage general economic behaviour in accordance with the overall goal of economic development. The essence of state regulation is planned regulation. A complete state-planned regulatory mechanism is composed of plan indicators, economic policies, and economic levers. Only if these three interrelated factors are integrated into the functions of the system, can its latent potential be fully activated. The basic meaning of *guided by state regulation* refers to making fully effective use of the functions of the national mechanism including macro-balance, structural coordination, competition protection, benefit optimisation, and income redistribution. These factors primarily regulate the macroeconomy. Like market regulation, state regulation displays certain disadvantages throughout the macroeconomy and in certain microeconomic areas. The socialist practice of the past has demonstrated that state regulations are prone to the following four types of functional shortcomings.

1. State Regulation Is Subjective in Its Preferences

The governmental system (the Central Peoples' Government or State Council) and the National People's Congress (NPC) are the two major players of state regulation. All economic management organisations in China, including the People's Bank of China and the national statistical departments, are affiliated with the government. It must be noted, however, that governments and competent economic departments at all levels may exhibit irrational short-term behaviour, as they are excessively eager to record political achievements or even to perform miracles. In cases where the mechanism of mutual restraint that governs relations between the institutions of the government and NPC is not sound, that is, if the national preference deviates from the strong endogenous demands of the existing productive forces and the planned commodity economy, this unscientific state regulation will unavoidably fall into voluntarism and unilateralism. Functional disorders of some kind will then be the result.

2. State Regulation Is Slow to Change

Due to the development of potential factors such as the lack of reliable information for national macroeconomic regulatory decisions, the overly complex procedures for decision-making, the lengthy time of decision-making, and the high cost of decision-making, the state is often incapable of moving effectively, even if it is found that the state mediation involved was erroneous or there was an urgent need to change the form and content of the regulation according to the new situation. The government is too often incapable of legislating expeditiously and making flexible adjustments and conversions, resulting in a phenomenon of *state regulation failure* that corresponds to the *failure of market regulation*.

3. Internal Frictions Arising from State Regulation Policy

When fiscal, financial, price, income, tax, exchange rate, consumption, manpower, and other economic policies are used by the state to regulate the market system and corporate behaviour, and if the national policy system is internally uncoordinated or even counter-productive in its effects, *internal frictions* will occur. This means that various policy functions will offset one another. Of course, if the national decision-making mechanism is relatively sound, these internal frictions of the policy function will be decreased, but they will not disappear completely.

4. Lack of Motivation for State Regulation

State regulations should be legislated through the proactive formulation and organisation, by civil service experts, of various regulatory objectives, steps, and specific methods. Due to a narrow concern for the interests of individuals, local bureaus, departments, or classes, these civil servants are often unwilling to mediate, in a timely manner, the problems and contradictions that emerge in economic developments. Especially in the face of *countermeasures* taken by many enterprises and individuals, the *measures* of state regulation and control often appear feeble. The results are either rigid centralisation or disorder resulting from decentralisation.

The positive function of state regulation establishes its dominant position in the socialist economic regulatory system. But the functional weaknesses of state regulation cannot be completely avoided, and it is these weaknesses that determine the need for market regulation.

(III) The Suitability and Synergy of Market Regulation and State Regulation

There is a dialectical relationship of *the unity of opposites* between market regulation and state regulation. The nature of this combination can be understood on the basis of its following three aspects.

1. Functional Suitability

The complementarities in this case can be summarised as follows: Micro-macro complementarity at the level of equilibrium, short- and long-term complementarity in the allocation of resources, individual and overall complementarity in the adjustment of society's interests, internal and external complementarity in the change of benefits, and high and low complementarity in the distribution of income. The functions of market regulation and state regulation are complementary from the aspects of both focus and permeability. On the whole, market regulation clearly functions better than state regulation in terms of the activities of individual economic units, short-term allocation of common resources, daily adjustment of income and benefits, and general economic behaviour. Market regulation, however, also requires the injection of planning mechanism factors and the implementation of state guidance. In terms of industrial structure, national economic aggregate, social ownership structure, major projects, products of particular importance, long-term allocation of critical resources, and major adjustments in income and benefits, the functioning of state regulation is significantly stronger than that of market regulation. Nevertheless, state regulation also requires an injection of market mechanism factors that can provide market feedback and exercise constraints on state plans. It can clearly be seen how the functional combination and complementarity of market and state regulations demonstrate, at a profound level, that at this stage, the new mechanism of economic regulation has essentially been unified.

2. Synergy of Effects

Under certain external conditions, an open economic operational system inevitably produces a synergistic effect through nonlinear interaction between its internal market regulation system and the state regulation system. If the antinomy present in the mechanisms of the two major regulation systems is gradually expanded, the synergistic effect may be negative, causing disorder in the operation of the economic system. If the functional complementarity of the two major regulation systems is gradually exerted, the synergistic effect may be positive and beneficial in forming a high level, economically stable, and orderly organisation, which is commonly referred to as a *dissipative structure*. We will examine, in detail, the positive synergy between market regulation and state regulation as reflected in the following:

First, let's look at the scope of synergy. Both the market and the state plan should embrace society as a whole, and the market relationship, or the commodity-currency relationship, should become the general form of connection for every social and economic activity. Its basic criterion is equivalent exchange. Meanwhile, a state plan will define the goal orientation for all social and economic activities. This plan will regulate and, therefore, affect all economic behaviour. The non-segmented and organic integration of market and plan throughout society has laid the foundation for a positive synergy.

Second, let us review the objective of synergy. The most attractive goal is for the market and the state plan to achieve a two-way compatibility. That is to say, the planning mechanism should penetrate into the market, and the market mechanism should be absorbed into the plan. The plan guides the market; and with feedback from the markets, the market guides the plan. The integration of the two establishes an efficient and flexible *feedforward-feedback* control mechanism. At last, we can discern a synergistic trend. Market regulation leads from micro to macro, and it presents itself as the economic circulation process of an *enterprise-market-state*. State regulation leads from macro to micro and presents itself as the economic circulation process of a *state-market-enterprise*. This convective transmission between the market and the state plan communicates the connection between the micro and macro levels, each of which is improved synergistically. In short, the positive synergistic effects between market regulation and state regulation strongly show that by this stage the new mechanism of economic regulation has reached an essential unity.

3. Mechanism Antinomies

When a market regulation mechanism works according to the law of value, the law of supply and demand, and the law of competition, the value targets may exclude the use-value production that society desperately needs. In a worst-case scenario, counterfeit goods will hit the market, seconds will be sold at top-quality prices, and smaller quantities of products will be sold to customers, thus harming the interests of the state and the public. Market fluctuations will result in a degree of fictitious demand, and the spontaneous tendencies that result may lead to haphazardness in economic development. Putting particular interests first may have an impact on macroeconomic and other social benefits, allow the formation of various types of monopolies, and hinder the organic integration of short-term, long-term, local, and overall interests. These results all run contrary to the goals and mechanisms of state regulation. Similarly, when a state regulation mechanism functions according to basic economic laws and the laws of planned development, the use-value target may distort economic accounting and prevent exchange at equal values, leading to the creation of a range of *'political products'*, such as *'secure food, political vegetables'*, and the steel production seen during the Great Leap Forward. An orientation toward planning may result in improper adoption of mandatory planning and direct administrative controls, resulting in the concentration of power and a rigid structure. National interests may be overemphasised, damaging the interests of enterprises and individuals, and dampening the enthusiasm and creativity of workers. All of these effects are contrary to the objectives and mechanisms of market regulation. Therefore, the mechanism antinomy that exists between market regulation and state regulation is an objective phenomenon and cannot be completely avoided, which shows that at this stage, the new mechanism of economic regulation embodies essential contradictions.

In theory, the purpose of understanding the characteristics of the combination of market regulation and state regulation is to prevent the functional misalignment of the regulatory system and to strengthen the functional complementarity when the two are specifically combined. The combination of the two reduces the negative entropic value of the regulatory system and enhances the synergistic positive effect; it reduces the contradictoriness of the regulation system mechanism and expands the consistency with which this mechanism operates. On what basis, therefore, do we plan and organise the combination of market regulation and state regulation in practice? We present a brief outline of the four dimensions involved, intended to clarify the basic principles of this combination and to provide a general overview.

The first principle is the dimension of products (including labour services), which consists of three elements. The first is the type of product and its role. It is necessary to distinguish the products of basic facilities such as energy, transportation, postal services, and telecommunications, along with other important products related to the national economy and people's livelihoods, from scientific and technological evolution, foreign trade, less important goods, and general products. The second element is the type and level of the industry to which a particular product belongs, as well as its role. The type of product determines to which industry the product belongs, and it is necessary to distinguish between different industries as well as internal levels within each industry. Products in different industries have varying degrees of importance. The third element consists of the types and functions of the various fields and links to which the product belongs; on the basis of the previous two points, it is necessary to distinguish between the field in which the product is located and the links within the field. For example, it is necessary to distinguish the production field, distribution field, exchange field, consumption field, material economy field, cultural economy field, military economic field, and non-military economic field, as well as the primary product link, the reprocessed product link in the production field, and the wholesale and retail links in the circulation field, etc. The products in different fields and links have different meanings and significance. There is no doubt that market regulation and state regulation must first determine the

degree, manner, and scope of their combination around the product dimension. Generally speaking, for products that are part of the
output of leading industries, non-competitive industries, and of
industries that produce other important and special products, state
regulation is stronger, and the methods adopted are more direct.
Meanwhile, market regulation is weaker; even in cases where very
few products are created and exchanged, there is no proper market
regulation. For other less important products, by contrast, this situation is reversed.

The second principle is the dimension of property rights. This
consists of three elements, of which the first is represented by
enterprises with property ownership of various kinds. Nationally-
owned enterprises, collectively-owned enterprises, cooperative
enterprises, private enterprises, Sino-foreign joint ventures, wholly
foreign-owned enterprises, and various hybrid enterprises feature
different property ownership and have different relations with the
state. The type of property ownership determines the characteristics
of their acceptance of both market regulation and state regulation. The second element is involved with the degree of separation
between ownership and management rights of enterprises with the
same form of property ownership. For example, when state-owned
enterprises function on the basis of contracts, leases, shareholding
arrangements, and direct operations, the difference between the
respective ownership and management powers is very large, which
in turn inevitably determines the manner in which these enterprises
are subject to market regulation and state regulation. The third element relates to the size of the enterprise governed by the property
rights relationship. Overall, joint-stock enterprises are large, as are
many state-owned enterprises, while the size of private enterprises,
collective enterprises, cooperative enterprises, and leasehold enterprises is relatively small. Large, medium, and small enterprises of
different sizes have an objective need to adopt diverse and flexible
regulatory measures, which will inevitably determine the way in
which they are subject to market and state regulations. Undoubtedly, the relationship between ownership rights and the size of the
enterprises that are restricted by them is one of the cornerstones of
socialist economic regulation. Large-scale, state-owned, and some
medium-sized enterprises are mainly subject to relatively strict state
regulations. Conversely, non-public-owned enterprises, collective
enterprises, cooperative enterprises, and numerous state-owned
small and medium-sized enterprises are subject to relatively loose
state regulations, or even operate under an incomplete market
regime.

The third principle is related to the regional dimension and has two elements that apply to urban and rural areas. Industrial and commercial cities such as Shanghai, important central cities such as Chongqing and Wuhan, medium-sized developed cities such as Changzhou and Wuxi, and small emerging cities such as Jiangyin and Fuyang show considerable differences in their economic status and in the roles they play in various provinces, regions, and even the whole country. The economic development of vast rural areas in Wenzhou, Quanzhou, Southern Jiangsu, and Northern Jiangsu, etc. also has different characteristics and is extremely diverse. In urban and rural areas, where situations vary, methods and means of market and state regulation must be adapted to meet specific local conditions. The next element includes areas that are both open and non-open as regards the orientation of their economies. The depth and range of market regulation and state regulation inevitably differ greatly between Shenzhen, Hainan, and other fully open, outward-oriented regions and non-open, inward-oriented regions, and the situation in internal and external bidirectional regions is different again. To function optimally, the mechanisms of economic regulation must have different characteristics and utilise different functions in each of China's distinct regions, whether eastern, western, central, old, new, border, poor, or any other economically developed areas. It should be noted that their statuses can be partially covered by the two elements above. Needless to say, the regional dimension is of great significance to the socialist system of economic regulation. For the state to intervene and regulate activities in a particular economic location (production location, market location, etc.), a wide variety of considerations must be taken into account. These include economic factors such as resources, transportation, trade, scale, labour, and science and technology, the geographical characteristics of the location, and social factors such as political, cultural, and ethnic. Economic policies and indicators such as differential tax rates, differential interest rates, differential prices, differential incomes, and regional fiscal expenditures are used to implement regional regulation at the meso-economic level. Generally speaking, additional mechanisms of market regulation should be introduced in rural areas, in small and medium-sized cities, and in coastal open areas, while more state regulation mechanisms should be introduced in large cities and non-open areas.

The fourth principle that should be pointed out concerns the dimension of time and includes two primary elements; the first is related to economic expansion and contraction. In the short-term analysis, when the economy is in a period of expanding, relatively speaking, there is a shortage of supply, a booming market, and a loose monetary policy. This market environment facilitates a more market-regulated role. State regulation, however, cannot simply be abandoned. Comparatively speaking, when the economy is in a period of contraction, there is a relatively abundant supply, weak markets, and a tightened monetary policy. During such times, the role of state regulation in the market environment needs to be appropriately strengthened, but equally, market regulation must not be neglected. The second component involved here consists of the primary and intermediate stages. Employing a long-term analysis, the government, during the primary stage of socialism, implements a plan-led, commodity-based economic system. Market regulation gradually and inevitably comes to act as the basic form of regulation, while state regulation consequently, and progressively, takes a dominant position. During the intermediate stage of socialism, the government may implement an economic system based on planned production, while market regulation gradually becomes an auxiliary form of regulation, and state regulation progressively becomes dominant. From this point of view, when exploring the actual combination of market and state regulation, it is necessary to use *time* as a scale to describe and express the relationship between the two. Whether the context is an empirical analysis of China's economic history since the founding of the People's Republic, a countermeasure study of the current period of governance and rectification, or a selection of targets for the entire primary stage and later stages, the time dimension is extremely important. It can be asserted that only by incorporating the time dimension can we thoroughly explain and scientifically validate the different combinations of market and state regulation in various periods.

The above explanations show that the dimensions of product, property rights, and region amount to a *three-dimensional combination* of market regulation and state regulation. If the time coordinates are added, a *four-dimensional spatial combination* will be formed. If we establish the concept of space-time positioning and follow the objective requirements and basic content of these *four dimensions*, we can accurately and systematically grasp the depth, mode of fusion, wide or narrow range, and strengths and weaknesses of the combination of these two forms of regulation. We can then, in actual practice, continuously adjust the use made of instructional plan regulation, of guiding plan regulation, and of regulation by the spontaneous operations of the market, etc., so as to effectively implement various specific forms of dynamic allocation.

2. Grasping the New Regulation Mechanism by Comparing Socio-Economic Systems and Stages of Social Development

In order to further understand and better grasp the *basic and dominant functional combination* of market regulation and state regulation in practice, comparative research must be performed. It is necessary to explore the economic environment in which this combination appears, and the various types of economic systems that determine how the regulation mechanism varies during the evolution of the socio-economic system and the stage of social development. On this basis, a deeper insight may be gained into the essence of the current mechanism of economic regulation, and into the causes and effects of the changes it undergoes.

(I) Combinations of the Four Types of Economies

Leaving aside the ownership and distribution of the means of production, human social and economic formations can be summarised according to two sets of corresponding categories: (1) free economy and planned economy and (2) product economy and commodity economy. From the point of view of economic operations, the former set of categories indicates whether the process of social and economic development is driven by spontaneous activity outside of planned control, or whether it occurs in line with conscious activity and is subject to planning. The latter set of categories, reflecting the content of economic operations, indicates whether the nature of the social economy (or entity or organism) is composed directly of countless labour products or is transformed from countless labour products into commodities. The actual socio-economic formation is an organic combination of economic operational forms and economic operational content, both of which are indispensable. Sometimes the planned economy and the commodity economy can be analysed together, but this does not mean that the two belong on the same logical level.

Figure 5-1 describes the different combinations of these two categories. According to the differences between their degree and status, freedom and planning, product and commodity (connected with dotted lines) can be abstracted into the following four combinations (indicated by solid arrows).

Combination AI – Free product economy. The characteristics of this combination are that the products of labour do not take the form of value, and social and economic activities can be carried out freely. Throughout history, the self-sufficient mode of production dominated primitive, slave, and feudal societies.

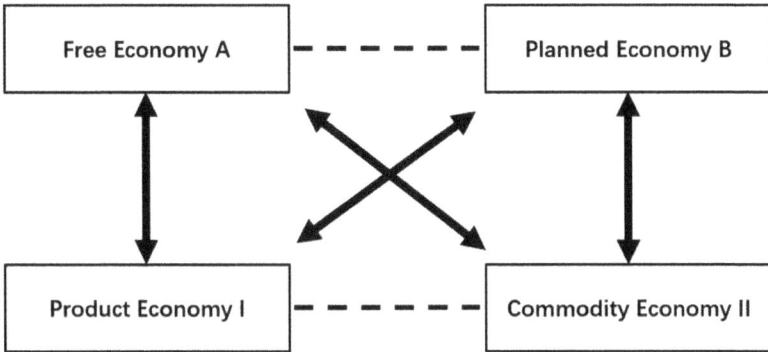

Figure 5-1 The Combinations of Four types of Economics

Combination AII - Free commodity economy. The characteristics of this combination are that the products of labour take the form of value, while socio-economic activities can still be carried out freely. Historically, its actual forms have been the simple commodity economy and the capitalist commodity economy.

Combination BII - Planned commodity economy. The characteristics of this combination are that the products of labour take the form of value, while socio-economic activities are regulated by conscious planning. The actual form it assumes is the socialist economy at the initial stage.

Combination BI - Planned product economy. The characteristics of this combination are that the products of labour do not take the form of value, while socioeconomic activities are still subject to conscious planning and regulation. Based on the history of social development, the actual forms the planned product economy assumes will be the advanced stage of socialism and the economy of communist society.

Three additional explanations are needed for the above four economic combinations. First, inspired by Marx's theory of the law of the negative dialectics of negation, the author believes that the first negation in the evolution of social and economic activity is the one found in the free product economy (referred to as the *natural economy*), linked to low productivity levels. The second negation is that of the commodity economy by the planned product economy (described as the *time economy*), linked to a high level of productivity development. On this basis, the following consensus should be reached: the current vigorous development of the socialist planned commodity economy not only represents a sublation of the capitalist commodity economy, but also a negation of the models of our country's natural economy and traditional rigid planned product economy (a distorted

and unrealistic model). This will be a prolonged, natural historical process. Second, transitional types may occur between various
economic combinations. Assuming that the transition from combination BII to combination BI occurs over a fairly long historical period,
during which some qualitative changes in economic operation will
transpire, it is very likely that a combination BIII will occur. In other
words, the planned economy is, at present, mainly combined with
the product economy, but is still largely related to the commodity
economy. This transitional combination may be referred to simply as
a *planned commodity-product economy*, and its actual form may appear
at the future intermediate stage of socialism. Third, Marx and Engels
primarily analysed combination AII, foresaw combination BI, and
made certain limited mentions of combination AI. On the basis of a
unique deepening of previous studies, Lenin and Stalin put forward
the *economic combination theory* relating to the transition period from
capitalism to socialism and the economic combination theory after
the establishment of socialism (the famous *commodity shell theory*).
The reform of China's economic system requires a large-scale discussion on combination BII. China's economic system reform calls
for a large-scale discussion on combination BII, which is a significant
exploration on and contribution to Marxist-Leninist theory and the
ongoing development of socialism.

(II) Six Economic Systems and Six Economic Regulation Mechanisms

Various economic combinations will definitely give rise to different
economic systems and economic regulation mechanisms.

The first of these involves a completely free product economic
system and a single natural division of labour mechanism that is
compatible with it. In the natural economic system of pre-capitalist
society, people implement a natural division of labour regulated by
gender and age. This division of labour is a purely physiological
division of labour and has nothing to do with either market regulation or social regulation.

The second type involves a completely free commodity economic
system and a single market mechanism compatible with it. During
the stage of free competition in the evolution of capitalism (the characteristics of a simple commodity economy are the same), economic
activities are laissez-faire ('allowed to do' free from government
intervention), social and economic development is unplanned, state
intervention is minimal, and the regulation of economic operations
is carried out by the *invisible hand*, amounting to regulation by the
market alone.

The third type involves a planned commodity economic system and market mechanism with a planning mechanism that goes with it. At the stage of state monopoly capitalism, some key questions such as the overall direction of the national economy, its basic pattern, and the proportional relations between its major sectors are ultimately determined by market regulation. State regulation is only used as a necessary supplement to market regulation, and as an auxiliary means for implementing its processes. In this type of system, market regulation therefore acts as the foundation, while state regulation takes an auxiliary position. It is true that there are differences between various developed or undeveloped capitalist countries, but none of these differences affects the fundamental manner in which a capitalist economy operates.

The fourth type features a commodity economic system with a plan-leading mechanism, combined with a market mechanism and a plan-leading mechanism compatible with it. During the primary stage of socialism, this type does not resemble state monopoly capitalism. A *national economic plan is not regarded as a strict, binding plan that must be followed by the government*, and the state's plans and interventions are limited to correcting shortcomings that appear in the regulation by market entities. Nor is this fourth type like the intermediate stage of socialism; during this stage, national planning regulation is already in a dominant position, mainly adopting the method of direct regulation, and the function of administrative coordination is more prominent. Instead, the fourth type implements economic regulation restrictions that are *based on market regulation and are dominated by state regulation*.

The fifth type consists of a product economic system with planning as its core, and a planning mechanism with a market mechanism compatible with it. By the intermediate stage of socialism, the main components of the economic body have changed from those of a commodity economy to those of a product economy, while at the same time there is a considerable degree of commerciality. Once the changes in question have occurred, the plan moves from a leading to a dominant position. The state now uses direct regulation and administrative coordination as its basic means for regulating the functioning of the entire macroeconomic and microeconomic complex, while using indirect regulation and market coordination as its secondary means.

The sixth type involves a completely planned product economic system and a single planning mechanism compatible with it. At the advanced stage of socialism and in communist society, the commodity economy and market regulation have basically ceased to exist.

Table 5-1 shows the comparisons in systems and stages of the economic regulation mechanisms.

Combinations of Economy	Economic Mechanisms	Economic Regulation	Stages of Economic System and Deviation
AI Free Product Economy	Completely free product economic mechanism	Single natural division of labour	Pre-capitalist natural economic system
AII Free Product Economy	Completely free commodity economic mechanism	Single market regulation	Free competition stage of capitalism
BAII Planned-Free Product Economy	Commodity economic mechanism with planned action	Market mechanism with planning mechanism; market regulation as its base, state regulation as its auxiliary	State monopoly stage of capitalism
BII Planned Commodity Economy	Commodity economic mechanism with planned action	Market mechanism with plan-guiding mechanism; market regulation as basic, state regulation as dominant	Primary stage of socialism
BII I Planned Commodity-Product Economy	Product economic mechanism with planned action	Planning mechanism with market mechanism; state regulation as its base, market regulation as its auxiliary	Intermediate stage of socialism
BI Planned Product Economy	Fully planned product economic mechanism	Single planning regulation	Advanced stage of socialism; communist society

Economic operation is now fully planned, and all economic activities are regulated by a relatively pure planning mechanism. At the advanced stage of socialism, only the center of social and economic organisation still exists as a *state*.

In short, only by introducing the methods of institutional analysis, and by observing the changing context of economic regulation against the historical background of the evolution of human society, can we eliminate various errors that arise if economic regulation at this stage is discussed in isolation. If we employ this approach, we can anticipate finding a more common language on the difficult issue of *what kind of economic system and regulation mechanism should be built in order to drive reform forward*.

(Originally published in *Financial Research*, Issue 12, 1990)

* * *

Section II The Characteristics and Internal Structure of the Socialist Market System

1. The Definition and Characteristics of the Socialist Market System

To understand the market system, we must first understand the meaning of the market. To explore the meaning of a market system and the characteristics of a socialist market system that conforms to the norms of a modern market economy, we must analyse the actual concept of the *market*.

(I) The Four Characteristics of the Market

The market arises out of the development of the social productive forces when these have reached a certain historical stage. In its formation and development, the market shows distinctive characteristics; because it arises from a material production mode and is connected to a certain level of material productivity, it has objective materiality. The market also has a social character, since it breaks through the constraints of the natural division of labour, connects with the social division of labour, and embodies the social and economic connections among the people. The market possesses an historical character since it has evolved gradually in the course of the historical development of civilisation and is associated with certain social forms and a certain history of social development. In addition, the market grows and develops within various cultural contexts, and is powered and restricted by certain ideas, morals, and spiritual values; therefore, it is civilised as well. So, what is the precise definition of the *market*? On the basis of economic reality and Marxist-Leninist theory, the category of *market* can be described by four characteristics, each with its own parameters.

First, the market is the institution and place within which commodities circulate. Where there is commodity production and exchange, there must be a market. With the development of commodity production and exchange, markets as instruments of commodity circulation will increase in number and scale.

Second, the market is the sum of all exchange relations between commodity producers and operators, rather than representing individual aspects of commodity exchange relations or exchange relations between individuals.

Third, the market is an exchange factor in a commodity economy and performs the function of a medium in the links of social reproduction, where it plays a central role. The market with commodity exchange as its content is the central link connecting production, distribution, and consumption, and it commands a special position that cannot be replaced.

Fourth, the market may be understood as a regulation mechanism, as resource allocation, or as a mode of operation. As far as the commodity economy is concerned, the basic regulation mechanism and mode of operation is the market itself, and that is the reason why the market and the market mechanism are sometimes interchangeable with each other.

(II) The Concept and Key Features of the Market System

A point of view exists whereby the socialist market system refers to a completely unified market with a multi-layered spatial structure that is compatible with the development of a socialist planned commodity economy. In fact, to define the socialist market system in this way is to equate the market system with a unified market, which often causes confusion between these two connected but different categories. The category of the *market system* emphasises the organic combination of various markets, and the market emphasised by the category of *unified market* cannot be artificially divided. It can also be said that the unity of the market is an important part of the content of the market system, but not the whole. In my opinion, although the socialist market system can be viewed from multiple perspectives, the general meaning of the term should refer to the whole, or to the system of the organic combination of various socialist markets that are mutually interrelated and restricted. A sound socialist market system must have the following characteristics.

First, it must be well structured and rationally organised. The socialist market system should include not only markets for consumer goods and markets for means of production, but also markets for capital, labour, real estate, technology, and economic information.

Second, it must be open domestically and globally with complete mechanisms in place. In principle, all markets are open to the inside; no administrative monopoly markets exist; all unnecessary *sectoral divisions* and *local divisions* have been eliminated; and increasingly close ties have been maintained with international markets. The opening of the domestic market to the outside world should be selective, progressive, and limited. On the whole, this pattern should be dominated by coastal areas and combined with the opening up of border areas, regions along certain rivers and roads, and provincial capitals.

Within a socialist market system, the mechanisms governing competition, supply and demand, price, risk, currency circulation, etc. are relatively sound. Market players show a high degree of initiative and display a good sensitivity and responsiveness to changes in market signals. As market variables, market signals such as prices, interest rates, exchange rates, and wages function to a considerable extent automatically, so that the positive role of the law of value is fully exercised. Not only should we seek to prevent all kinds of undesirable *excessive competition* phenomena in the markets of capitalist countries, but we should also be conscious of *insufficient competition* in our country, at the same time as engaging vigorously in legal market competition. To make a specific distinction between economic monopolies, it is necessary to completely oppose monopolised markets. While we should resist the type of market in which there is only one seller of a certain commodity, we also need to consider the case of oligopolistic markets, in which a few enterprises that produce most of a certain product control the sales volume and price of that product. Here, different countermeasures should be taken according to the actual situation, and such oligopolies should not be opposed outright. This is because what we want from socialism is not a classical market economy, nor a market system with completely free competition, but a modern market economy and market system that conforms to the trend of socialisation and internationalisation of production. A moderate monopoly mechanism and a competition mechanism can still complement each other.

Third, we need to consider the penetration of the plan and the need for the market to be favorable to buyers. The socialist market system takes publicly-owned enterprises as its mainstay and is constrained by various regulatory mechanisms, with planning as the main content; it thus becomes a *plan-driven market system*. Under the traditional market system, sovereignty within the market has always been biased towards sellers; total demand is always greater than total supply; and serious imbalances have even repeatedly occurred. Practice has decisively demonstrated that the chaotic price increases of production materials and consumer goods, rampant inflation, the poor quality of business services, and low levels of economic efficiency and technological innovation of enterprises are related to the relative expansion of market demand and the relative shortage of supply. This situation has caused tension and confusion in reform, development, and people's lives. It is, therefore, necessary to correct the tendency of demand outstripping supply, to recreate the situation in which supply slightly exceeds demand, and to build a modern market system in which market sovereignty favors buyers.

2. The Internal Structure of the Socialist Market System

There are different perspectives for examining the internal structure of the market system, and different classifications that can be employed, but the basic elements are still evident. There are objects to be exchanged, that is, market objects. There are owners of exchange objects and parties to exchange activities, that is to say, *market space*. There is a development process for the beginning and end of exchange; that is, *market time*. The broad market system is mainly composed of these three elements, each of which is a subsystem within an open market system.

(I) The Objective Structure of the Market

In the broadest sense, everything that is exchanged in the market can be called a commodity, and this concept can be subdivided further.

First, if we take into account the function of market objects in social reproduction; there are *general commodity markets* and *factor markets*. The general commodity market refers to the market for consumer goods and the market for means of production. The factor market encompasses the capital market, the market for means of production, the labour market, the technology market, and the land market. There is an intersection between these two types of markets. For example, the market for means of production belongs to both the general commodity market and the factor market.

Second, according to the correlation between market objects there are strong alternative markets and weak alternative markets. The consumer goods market, the market for means of production, the labour market, and the technology market are strong alternative markets. Various factors within each market can be flexibly substituted. In contrast, the land market, capital market, etc. are weak alternative markets in which there is little room for choice between various factors, especially when, as in China, the markets are not fully developed.

Third, market objects exist in three forms: there are ordinary tangible commodity markets, intangible commodity markets, and special commodity markets. The ordinary tangible goods market mainly refers to the consumer goods market and to the market for the means of production that exist in a physical form. The intangible commodity market refers mainly to the tourism market, transportation market, technology market, information market, labour market, and so forth. The special commodity market refers to the labour market, the financial market, and the markets for land and other natural resources. Some markets are more complicated. For example, the cultural market falls within the category of the general consumer market when people buy TV sets and audio tapes to enjoy at home. However, it becomes a part of the intangible commodity market if people go to public places to watch TV and listen to audio recordings.

(II) The Main Structure of the Market

The market subject is the owner of all market objects, with this category also including parties to market exchanges. Under the conditions of a commodity economy, the place where people's economic activities are conducted is the market. Market subjects dominate market objects through playing various economic roles, becoming the most active and revolutionary factor in market exchange, and promoting the evolution of the market system. The structure of a market subject can be examined from multiple perspectives.

First, according to the scope and scale of economic activities, market players can be divided into three groups: (1) individuals and their families, (2) enterprises, and (3) states or governments.

In market exchange activities, the parties representing the smallest units are individuals and their families. They provide labour to the society as the owners of labour power, obtaining a corresponding income and consumer goods; or they engage in private operations and securities transactions as independent production operators and investors, in order to obtain operating income. Enterprises such as industry, commerce, finance, services, and information are the major exchange forces in the market and play a pivotal role. The state is not only a party to market activities, but also conducts equal exchanges with other players in line with the law of value. At the same time, market activity coordinators and managers are responsible for establishing and maintaining market order and for adjusting internal and mutual interest relations within and among various market players, including themselves.

Second, in accordance with their different roles in social reproduction, market players are divided into producers, consumers, exchange intermediaries, and market investigators. Producers provide various products and services as part of market supply. Consumers represent market demand and exist as buyers. They consist of consumers engaged in production activities, and simple consumers. Exchange intermediaries are intermediate contacts between buyers and sellers, and they function as merchants, brokers, and agents. Market regulators appear in the form of national and governmental mechanisms at all levels; they perform the functions of organisational coordination, management, and supervision, and promote the rational operation of the market.

Third, according to the nature of ownership and the degree of separation of the two rights, market players are divided into state-owned economic units, collective economic units, cooperative economic units, self-employed workers, private owners, foreign investors, joint-stock enterprises, leasing enterprises, and contracting enterprises. These various types of enterprises and individuals have distinctive features in purpose, behaviour, and conduct in market activities. As market players, they exhibit numerous differences.

Fourth, in accordance with the transitional relationship of economic rights, market players are divided into the ownership market, the market of possession, and the rights of use market. The ownership market means that the parties to an exchange can fully transfer the possession, use, profit, and right of disposal of the exchange objects. The possession market means that the parties to the exchange retain the ownership of the exchange objects and transfer their possession rights or rights of use.

(III) Spatial Structure of the Market

The space of the market consists of the active areas and scope for market players and market objects. The spatial structure of the socialist market is a vertical and horizontal network based on a single market with multi-level regional markets as its *circulatory system*, the national market as its *skeletal structure*, and the international market as its overall situation. The socialist market is a unified market or integrated market in a broad sense.

First, a monomeric market can be thought of as an individual *cell* within the structure of the market space, and it belongs to the most basic level. If a monolithic market formed by micro-transactions between individuals, families, and enterprises on both the supply and demand sides is not fully developed, other high-level markets will face barriers to growth. Currently, because the reform of China's economic system has not fundamentally changed the state of soft restraint with regard to enterprises, and because of a weak situation with respect to individual economic rights, the positions of enterprises and individuals as market players are unstable, and the concept of independence is fragile. Except where the markets for consumer goods and means of production are relatively well developed, the markets for land, real estate, labour, information, technology, capital, and some other categories still need improvement. Therefore, we must reverse these inadequacies as soon as possible and strenuously expand and invigorate the monomeric market.

Second, a regional market is a market in which the exchange of goods and services takes place. The regional market, which is situated at the middle level of the market spatial structure, takes on at least two forms. One is the *administrative regional market*, and the other is the *economic regional market*. Administrative regional markets are prone to producing *regional blockades,* as they artificially prevent the free circulation of goods and services. In order to surmount regional market barriers and dovetail the regional market into the spirit of the unified market of socialist China, it is necessary to take robust measures to carry out reforms, gradually dilute the administrative regional market, and strengthen the economic regional market. It is true that local governments at all levels cannot completely abandon market management in the areas under their jurisdiction. They should, however, comply with the objective need of the market economy to establish a new order within the market economy and maintain a unified market throughout the country. They should not poke their noses into businesses in which they are not expected to interfere, and instead, should fulfil their responsibilities to the businesses that fall within the scope of their official duties.

Third, a national market is a market in which the exchange of objects takes place nationwide, and it involves an organic combination of individual markets and regional markets within society. A national market implies national political unification, but the primary reason why a certain commodity or service needs to be circulated nationwide is that there is an exchange of comparative interests, which gives it an intrinsic motivation to spread across the country. From the perspective of consumer goods, means of production, and information, it is necessary to establish a national market, but in the case of particular commodities and services, a specific analysis is needed.

Fourth, an international market is a market formed by the exchange of objects worldwide. The law of international value or of international production prices is a law that applies throughout the international market, and its scale is constrained by an international division of labour and international collabouration. In most cases, it is impossible for a country's commodities to circulate into every country in the world; the likelihood is that they will reach only a restricted number of countries. This holds true for developing countries like China, whose commodities can only gain a limited market share, even if they succeed in making their way into the international market. The main way in which this situation can be changed is through the vigorous development of export-oriented enterprises. Export-oriented enterprises can expand their sales to the international market once the domestic monomeric market, the regional markets, and national markets have been formed. Or they may skip the domestic market and directly target and explore the international market.

(IV) Time Structure of the Market

Market time is the continuity and sequence of the process in which market players exchange market objects. In markets of varying types, or even of the same type, the buyer-seller or debtor-creditor relationships between the supply and demand sides always have variable and irregular lengths, thus revealing variations in exchange times and methods.

In the case of the general commodity exchange, the time structure of the market is composed of spot trading, futures trading, and credit trading. In the land market, for example, if land ownership is completely transferred the exchange times and methods will be quite similar to ordinary commodities. If the land is leased, the process surrounding an exchange will depend on the duration of the lease, which may be fifty or sixty years. In the technology market, the procedures for exchanging technology patents are quite diverse. If the amount of a technology transfer fee is based on the actual economic benefits after the application, its transfer will take longer than the general transaction. Another example is the capital market, where financial markets may be either short-term or long-term. Those of the short-term variety include deposit markets, loan markets, discount markets, foreign exchange markets, and loan fund markets, with loan periods of six months to one year. The long-term variety, offering a loan period of more than one year, comprises long-term loan markets and the bond market. In addition, the differences between multiple exchange methods in the labour market are also manifested as differences in market time.

(Originally published in *Exploration and Contention*, Issue 2, 1993)

*   *   *

Section III Protecting Private Property and Public Interests

Modern western economics are concerned solely with protecting individual property rights and private interests. The presumption is that an individual's free actions, aimed at maximising his or her own interests, will inadvertently but effectively promote the interests of society as a whole. This is obviously a one-sided viewpoint. In fact, private property and interests often conflict with public property and interests. Therefore, the phenomenon of encroaching on private rights and private property in the name of *public interests* must be eliminated. It is also necessary to correct the tendency of embezzling public property and violating the public interests in the restructuring of state-owned enterprises. In an era of economic globalisation and the mixed economy, it is necessary to jointly establish the concepts of national property, national rights and interests, and of international competition to safeguard private and public property, rights, and interests.

In the process of building a harmonious socialist society, the protection of private property and the maintenance of public interests have now become the *focus* of people from all walks of life; a focus that is embodied in a series of issues such as land expropriation, enterprise restructuring, anti-corruption measures, and the prevention of tax evasion by foreign enterprises. All of these are worthy of analysis. The protection of private property refers to the protection of every kind of property obtained by citizens through lawful means, ensuring that no one else can violate the law and infringe on the private property rights involved. The protection of public interests refers to the legal protection of the common interests of society, ensuring that no one can violate the law or infringe upon public interests. There are three main types of public interests: those that maintain national security and legal order, such as national defence, those that promote economic development and social progress, such as infrastructure and public undertakings, and those that maintain the survival and development of the weak, such as philanthropic work or public welfare.

Practice has shown that the relationship between private property and the public interest may take four forms: the common gain of private property and the public interest, the common loss of private property and the public interest, a gain for private property leading to a loss for the public interest, and a gain for the public interest leading to a loss for private property. It can be seen that the two are able to share in positive effects, but that a contradiction may also be present, advantaging one while disadvantaging the other.

In order to deal with the relationship between the protection of private property and the maintenance of public interests, we must pay attention to the following issues.

First, we must eliminate the frequent encroachments on private rights and private property that occur in the name of *public interests*. For example, private owners are often forced to make donations for the building of roads, bridges, and schools, and for other public works and utilities. Taking the expropriation of land without economic compensation as an example, we see that some local governments first acquire farmland at low prices in the name of the national and public interests, then transfer this land to Chinese or foreign private enterprises at low prices. Additionally, governments may transfer land to enterprises at open market prices as a way of gaining profits. Unfortunately, such moves have the effect of jeopardising the private interests of individual farmers. Some of the differential income that results from the rise in land prices caused by government investment ends up as fiscal revenues through land expropriation prices or land transaction taxes. Nevertheless, attempting to expand fiscal revenue and gain political credit through compensating for price differences in land acquisition represents an incorrect view of political performance that has done serious damage to private property, private rights, and private interests. These issues must be addressed and corrected.

Second, we must reverse the tendency of state-owned enterprises embezzling public property and encroaching on the public interests of our citizens. The state-owned asset management system and the state-owned enterprise management mechanism must undergo substantial market-based reforms that embody the spirit of the 16th National Congress, that is, *developing and strengthening the state-owned economy*, and fundamentally safeguarding and enhancing the public interests of all citizens. Certain state-owned enterprises that are relatively small in scale, that cannot turn around their losses, and that have no future in the market may be transformed into collective or private enterprises. The problem is that during restructuring in some places state-owned assets are sold to enterprise managers at low prices without any public bidding. Some enterprises have even been forced to suffer losses, which has resulted in the large-scale loss of state assets and a further erosion of public interests. One lesson we should learn from developed countries is that the sale of shares in certain state-owned enterprises needs to be subject to discussions by legislative bodies at the corresponding levels or at public administrative hearings. Just as in the case of the SARS epidemic (and more recently in the context of COVID-19), we must strengthen the supervisory and administrative bodies of state-owned assets and the system responsible for protecting the personnel. We must implement an accountability system and a system under which those at fault take the blame and resign; and we must stop the serious loss of national assets and violation of public interests at the outset, especially at key linkages of the principal-agent relationship of property rights.

Third, we must safeguard private and public property rights and interests. It is essential to jointly establish the concepts of national property, rights, interests, and international competition. In this era of economic globalisation and a mixed economy, a country's private and public property and private and public interests are often integrated and are presented to the world as the country's common national property and interests. Whether a particular case involves an individual citizen or a legal organisation, and whether the latter is a private enterprise, state-owned enterprise or institution or government department, whenever they engage in economic activities such as international trade, international finance, international investment, or economic diplomacy, the protection of private property and rights is generally beneficial to public societal interests. The defence of the rights involved here is also a component of the maintenance of national property and rights. Conversely, the protection of social property and rights is usually beneficial to private property and rights since it is also a component of the maintenance of national property and rights. For example, Chinese private and state-owned enterprises have responded to lawsuits against foreign enterprises, and the Chinese government supports private and state-owned enterprises in combating foreign dumping. Another example is that at roughly the same starting point of development globally, China's land public property system has facilitated the development of the Internet and greatly contributed to the rise of public and private property for the entire Chinese nation, compared to countries with private land property systems such as India.

Fourth, it is necessary to emphasise the ethical regulation of the coordination between private and public property and interests, and to implement the *three simultaneous promotions* of ethical regulation, state regulation, and market regulation. Modern western economics only touch on the protection of individual property rights and interests. The belief is that an individual's free action in pursuit of his or her own interests will inadvertently but effectively promote the interests of society as a whole, which is obviously a one-sided viewpoint. In reality, private property and interests often conflict with public property and interests. In coordinating the relationship between private and social interests under the conditions of a socialist market economy, we should use market regulation means, such as the price mechanism, the competition mechanism, and the supply and demand mechanism, to carry out as much self-regulation as possible. Meanwhile, the state should conscientiously employ laws, economic factors, any necessary administrative measures, and other assets and means to carry out regulation. But there is another aspect that should not be overlooked: that is, we should never neglect to emphasise ethical and moral considerations, to encourage people to consciously observe self-discipline as well as the law, and to encourage them to pursue their private interests and exercise their rights on the basis of maintaining collective norms and social morality, and of not violating the integrity of others. No matter how perfect the institutional constraints and market mechanisms are, there are always gaps or deficiencies. Once people lose the requisite moral self-restraint, they will readily violate the interests of others and of society.

Fifth, we must protect legal private property according to the law, but it is impossible to sanctify and absolutise it. Some people believe that the new constitution stipulates that *each citizen's lawful private property is inviolable,* and that *socialist public property is sacred and inviolable.* This view does not treat private property and public property equally, nor does it emphasise that legitimate private property is also inviolable; it, thus, lacks a profound understanding of the spirit and substance of constitutional evolution in countries around the world. Out of the need for an anti-feudal dictatorship, the *Declaration of Human Rights* drawn up during the French Bourgeois Revolution stated that *property is a sacred and inviolable right.* The Republicans later realised, however, that private property was subject to a higher social goal, and when necessary, should be sacrificed in favor of the public interest. How can a socialist country sanctify and absolutise private property and its rights? This has nothing to do with China's current private investment or legal accumulation of private property, etc. It is even more unreasonable to use such arguments as *private property is sacred and inviolable* to justify various instances of illegal private property-holding.

(Originally published in *Wen Hui Bao,* April 11, 2005)

*   *   *

Section IV Improving the Dual Regulation System: The Decisive Role of the Market and the Role of the Government

The economic regulation system is the core of the economic operation mechanism, and it plays a key role in the optimal allocation of resources. In his speech to the National People's Congress and the Chinese Political Consultative Conference in 2013, General Secretary Xi Jinping emphasised that 'We should more closely follow the rules of the market and exercise the role of the government to a higher degree'[145]. At the 3rd Plenary Session of the 18th Central Committee, he went on to state that the market should play a decisive role in the allocation of resources as should the government exercise its role more effectively. At the same time, he pointed out: 'China is implementing a socialist market economic system, and we still have to insist on fully developing the superiority of China's socialist

145. Xi Jinping. 'Note on the Decision of the CPC Central Committee on Several Major Issues of Comprehensively Deepening Reform [N].' *People's Daily,* 2013-11-16. http://cpc.people.com.cn/xuexi/n/2015/0720/c397563-27331312.html

system and the active role of the party and government. The market plays a decisive role in the allocation of resources, but not in all of the roles'[146].

Fully developing the roles of the market and the government is not only directly related to shaping the new economic normal, such as promoting reforms, stabilising growth, changing modes, adjusting structures, increasing efficiency, and preventing risks, but also bears directly on whether a fully competitive market mechanism can truly solve the real, urgent problems of society, such as high housing prices, high medicine prices, rapid price increases, limited welfare provisions, polarisation between rich and poor, unemployment, food and drug safety, serious bribery, frequent labour-management conflicts, and the low quality of urbanisation. The relationship between the market and the government is not only among the basic theoretical concerns of political economy but is also the key to deepening the reform of the economic system and the sound and rapid development of the national economy. Therefore, it is of great practical significance to study this issue thoroughly.

1. Gradually Deepening the Understanding of the Roles of the Market and the Government

Practice is the sole criterion for testing truth, and Marxist scientific theory has constantly evolved through practice. The same is true of the theory surrounding the socialist market economy, and China's exploration of economic adjustment methods has gradually deepened as well. Beginning with utopian socialism, commodities, money, and markets have been regarded as a source of evil and sin. As Winstanley, for example, said, 'After humans begin to buy and sell, they will lose their innocence and purity' and 'oppress and fool each other'[147]. The founders of scientific socialism believed that there could be a certain degree of commodity-currency relations and cooperative economy during the transition period to a communist society, but that the development of the capitalist market economy had exposed maladies such as fraud, wealth polarisation, and cyclical economic crises. Speculating on developments after humanity had entered the communist society of the future, they predicted that *once the society occupies the means of production, the production of commodities will be eliminated, and the rule of products over the producers will*

---

146. Ibid.

147. Gerrard Winstanley. *Selected writings of Winstanley* [M]. Ren Guodong, Translation. Beijing: The Commercial Press, 1965: 100.

also be eliminated. The anarchy within social production will be replaced by the conscious organisation of the plan.

After Russia's October Revolution and in the face of economic difficulties arising from the *policy of 'war communism'*, Lenin raised the issue of using *markets and commerce* as a socio-economic basis, and even proclaimed, 'We have to admit our entire view of socialism has fundamentally changed'[148]. The practice of Lenin's New Economic Policy initially showed that relatively backward productivity and complicated social and economic conditions determined that economic construction could not go beyond the stage of commodity production and commodity exchange. After Lenin's early death, the Soviet Union, under Stalin, established a strict planned economy.

At the founding of the New China, our country learned from the Soviet experience and established another planned economic system. Although the Chinese Communists, represented by Mao Zedong, were later to carry out investigations into many sectors, the system they generally implemented was founded on a planned economy. Since the capitalist market economy and the planned economy at the primary stage of socialism both possessed insurmountable defects, the objective goal of reform has been to combine a basic socialist economic system with a market economy.

After the reform and opening up in 1978, Deng Xiaoping led the whole party in making bold experiments, and repeatedly discussed issues related to the market economy. In 1992, he addressed this topic ten times before his *Southern Talks*, and a further two times afterwards (twelve times in total; see *Deng Xiaoping Chronicle*)[149]. In 1992, the 14th National Congress of the Communist Party of China finally proposed that the goal of China's economic reform was to establish a system based on a socialist market economy. Practice has shown fully that the market is an effective means of resource allocation and economic regulation, and that it can be used by both capitalism and socialism. The superiority of the socialist market economy, however, is demonstrated by the fact that through the basic socialist economic system with public ownership as its foundation, and through a more effective role of the government, ailments such as the wealth polarisation between rich and poor and the cyclical economic crises produced by the capitalist market economy can be cured. Since 1992, China's average annual economic growth rate has exceeded 9%, and

148. *Lenin's complete works: Volume 42* [M]. Beijing: People's Publishing House, 1987: p. 367.

149. Leng Rong, *Deng Xiaoping Chronicle: 1975-1997*, Central Literature Publishing House, 2004. ISBN: 9787507316773

China has quickly become a major economic power with important international influence.

After more than twenty years of practical experience, China's socialist market economic system has been established and improved to some degree, but there are still many drawbacks that have restricted the vitality of market players and hindered the effective progress of the market and the law of value. These core issues are as follows. The market order is irregular, and the phenomenon of seeking economic benefits through improper means is widespread. Next, the development of the market in production factors has lagged behind; a significant number of factories are idle; there is excessive consumption of resources; and large amounts of effective demand have not been met. Additionally, market rules are not uniform, and sectoral and regional protectionism exists on an extensive scale. Lastly, insufficient market competition has hindered the *survival of the fittest* and structural adjustment. At the same time, inadequacies in market regulation itself (spontaneity, blindness, and slowness in responding to stimuli) have been clearly exposed. Specific detrimental phenomena include illegal businesses, speculative trading, ecological crises, the division between rich and poor, regional gaps, high housing prices, high drug prices, etc. All of these maladies show that there are numerous gaps, redundant interventions, and misalignments in our governmental regulations. As General Secretary Xi Jinping has pointed out, 'If these problems are not effectively solved, it will be difficult to form a sound socialist market economic system, change the development mode, and adjust the economic structure'[150]. In this context, the questions of whether it is necessary for the market to play the decisive role in resource allocation and of how the role of the government can be made more effective have become unprecedentedly salient. These issues have become a general hub for seeking solutions to various contradictions in economic and social development.

2. Market Regulation and its Strengths and Weaknesses

The law of *value* is the intrinsic and essential relationship between commodity *production* and commodity *exchange*. The market economy is an economic system and mode of economic operation that

---

150. Xi Jinping. 'Correctly play the role of the market and the role of the government to promote sustainable and healthy economic and social development [N].' *People's Daily*, 2014-05-28.

http://www.gov.cn/xinwen/2014-05/27/content_2688228.htm

is regulated by the law of value itself. Market regulations will be continuously enhanced through increases in both the degrees of socialisation of the national economy and of export orientation of the economy. Objectively, it requires a greater scope and greater emphasis on the role of the law of value and its manifestation, i.e., market regulation.

Market regulations adjust the supply and demand of commodities and resources through the combined effect of mechanisms such as price, competition, and supply and demand. They guide the flow of economic resources in all areas of society and distribute economic interests among different stakeholders to promote growth and the healthy development of the national economy. Specifically, the strength or positive effect of the market regulation function is reflected in five aspects. The first is the microeconomic equilibrium function. Through this function the market directs independent decision-making, individual production, and operational behaviours to closely follow the changes in real demand, so that they can regulate the relationship of supply and demand at the micro-level, as well as its balance. Another aspect is the short-term resource allocation function. This function enables the market to quickly guide the flow of economic resources to areas with high efficiency in the short term. The benefit of this function is that it directly affects the short-term resource allocation of economic entities. The next aspect is the market signal transmission function. This allows the market to more accurately reflect market supply and demand, competition, etc. through the price signal; it guides production operators in making quick and independent decisions. Subsequently, we have the scientific and technological innovation function. This function empowers the market to guide production operators to improve production materials, improve production technology, enhance product quality, and increase social productivity. Lastly, the local interest-driving function empowers the market to drive producers to strengthen business management and internal and external cooperation based on local interest considerations, thereby promoting economic development.

Market regulation, however, also has its own functional weaknesses that are difficult to overcome. First, it is easy to deviate from macroeconomic goals. Amid the spontaneity, time-lags, and disorder in the functioning of market regulation, market players, due to conflict with their own interests, have often failed to pursue their macroeconomic goals and the long-term interests of society. Second, areas of regulation are easily restricted; in reality, not all areas are suitable for market regulation. Unlike the field of general commodity production and exchange, in some areas where natural monopolies are caused by economies of scale, such as transportation, water supply, and power supply, the effect of completely adopting market regulation is not ideal. In welfare and non-profit sectors, such as education, health, environmental protection, cultural protection, basic research, national defence, etc., assigning a leading role to market regulation will also intensify adverse consequences. Third, market regulation can easily widen the gap between rich and poor. If the distribution of wealth and income is left completely to the control of the market, then it is bound to result in the *Matthew effect*, or the tendency for the rich to get richer and the poor to get poorer. In actuality, it has been left to the control of capital, especially private capital. Fourth, the coordination of industry becomes problematic. Market regulation often prompts producers to pay closer attention to short-term resource allocation and short-term profitability. Basic industries with long recovery periods and long-term strategic significance are often overlooked, and production capacity leans towards overcapacity. Fifth, the actual transaction cost is relatively high. In an increasingly large, modern market economy, factors such as supply and demand and transaction prices affect each other and change frequently. These factors inevitably cause market entities to invest in research and development costs, decision costs, adaptation costs, and even error correction costs, which result in higher costs to micro-individuals and society.

It should be pointed out that the understanding of market regulation, among Western economic theoreticians, changes constantly. Basing himself on the commodity economy of bartering, Jean-Baptiste Say claimed that 'supply creates its own demand,' and called for the universalising of market regulation. Faced with the reality of free-competition capitalism, Adam Smith advocated that the market act as an *invisible hand* to allocate resources. Smith's laissez-faire thinking was premised on the internal consistency of individual and social interests but was limited to consolidating the vision of capitalist interests and was unable to provide an effective approach to realising the overall interests of society. In response to the disordered and out-of-control social production that occurs under monopoly capital, both the old and new schools of Keynesianism have advocated government intervention and compensation in the event of market failure. This confirms the existence of various defects in market functions. To meet the need of international monopoly capital to continue expanding in the context of economic globalisation, neoliberalism abandons government intervention and advocates *market omnipotence, market activism,* and *market-only reform* (critical terms coined by Joseph Stiglitz and Paul Krugman, representatives of contemporary Keynesianism).

In general, with regard to the functional defects of the market allocation of resources, Western scholars have put forward the market structure theory, public product theory, spillover or external effects, informational asymmetry, market incompleteness, and unfair distribution. In practice, from the stage of free capitalism to the stage of private or state monopoly capitalism, and even under the capitalist globalisation system, the scope and degree of the market allocation of resources have not been the same, and the results have been quite different. In real life, the role of the market in allocating resources is not without constraints, and neither is it fully nor spontaneously realised. Since the beginning of the 19th century, numerous large and small economic crises, financial crises, and fiscal crises, and the wealth gap between rich and poor in Western capitalist market economies, have all served to prove the objectivity of the above-mentioned theoretical analysis, and have confirmed that the advantages of market functions need to be supported while the disadvantages need to be rejected.

3. The Issue of Government Regulation and Its Strengths and Weaknesses

Government behaviour is an important part of modern economic activity. What is government regulation? In the broad sense, it encompasses the regulation exercised by a country's legislative and administrative institutions and is equivalent to regulation by the state. After the Great Depression of the 1930s, government intervention and regulation became a normal feature of economic life in various countries. Government regulation involves the ruling power using economic, legal, administrative, persuasive, and other means to regulate the economic behaviour of various economic entities in order to achieve its overall, long-term goals of economic and social development. Government regulation is not arbitrary or chaotic, but there are no inherent laws that it follows. It seeks to realise such objectives as proportional development and planned development. The sustained and healthy development of modern economic society essentially requires that, while the market plays a decisive role in resource allocation, society consciously enacts macro-, meso-, and micro-level regulation in accordance with the overall goal of economic development. For the government to assume this function is an objective necessity. So, what are the strengths and weaknesses of government regulation?

At the macro level, the advantage of the government's scientific adjustment function lies in the formulation and realisation of overall economic and social development goals. The primary goal of government regulation is macroeconomic stability. *Scientific macro-control is an inherent requirement for promoting the full development of the advantages of the socialist market economy, which is exactly the same as the function of the government. An ability to solve problems in this field is not among the advantages of the market.* Employment is related to social stability, but general market players do not care about the overall employment situation. The stability of prices determines the accuracy of market price signals and individual market operators, seeking profit, often use transparent or opaque signals. The balance of total supply and demand and the balance of international payments are determined by the overall behaviour of thousands of producers and operators, while general operators have no ability or motivation to maintain the equilibrium between the two. The imbalance of international payments has already had a huge impact on the economies of some countries, especially developing countries, and has caused serious problems. The negative impact of the non-public economy is a concern for realising microeconomic benefits, and it is extremely difficult to solve the problem of disparity between rich and poor within an enterprise or even a society through market regulation.

The *concerns of a single market subject* are related to microeconomic benefits, and acting on the basis of such concerns, it is hard to deliberately improve the overall economic, social, and ecological benefits to society. Various scholars have pointed out that *another level of governmental functions and of macro-control is the role of the entire economy, society, culture, ecological civilisation, and other aspects.* The questions at issue here *go far beyond the scope of resource allocation and cannot be determined by the market.* Practice has demonstrated that in order to achieve macroeconomic and social development goals, the government is entitled to override economic decisions made by individual enterprises on the basis of short-term and local interests. Acting from an overall global perspective, the government is better able to adjust resource allocation and economic operation, thus maintaining macroeconomic stability and ensuring the achievement of full employment, price stability, balance of total supply and demand, balance of payments, common prosperity, and the sustainable development of the population, resources, and environment.

At the meso-level, the advantage of the government's scientific regulation function lies in its ability to resolve the imbalance in economic development between the industrial structure and the regional economy. Because government regulation has a certain forward-looking, comprehensive, and strategic nature, it can focus on coordinated development and seek an overall balance in industrial and regional development. Unlike market regulation, which centers on the short-term allocation of resources, government regulation concentrates on making up for the *weak linkages* of economic and social development. It invests in new industries that have strategic significance, but in which returns materialise slowly; it promotes basic industries, and regional development strategies related to the national economy and the livelihoods of individuals. For example, the government has the ability to use tools such as fiscal and taxation policies to promote the large-scale application of new technologies, accelerate the elimination of backward production capacity, and thus accelerate the transformation of industry and upgrades to the productive structure. China's Pearl River Delta, Yangtze River Delta, Beijing-Tianjin-Hebei area, Midwest and Northeastern regions, and other *regional and Belt Road economies* (the Yangtze River Belt, and the onshore and offshore Silk Roads) have already experienced rapid development, which has necessarily depended on active regulation and control by central and local governments.

At the micro-level, the functional advantage of scientific government regulation lies in the effectiveness of the essential supervision and control that it exercises. The organisation and efficiency of a modern market economy cannot simply be based on the awareness and self-discipline of market players. Government regulation is ideally fair and authoritative. It is possible for it to effectively regulate the operations of economic subjects, thus ensuring that these operations are legal and honest. It can also maintain the normal order of the market through economic and administrative management methods such as market access, punishment, and blacklist systems. Among these methods, supervision before, during, and after the process, depending on specific circumstances, has its own indispensable role to play. For example, in the areas of the minimum wage system, worker rights and interests, and environmental protection assessments, the government is able to constructively help protect the interests of workers and safeguard the interests of the public by standardising policies and regulations. There is no mechanism through which these can be properly regulated by the market.

Government regulation in China has also suffered failures. The disadvantages and deficiencies of the government's regulatory functions are largely related to the subjectivity of the government's preferences, the conversion system used for undertaking adjustments, and the coordination between departments. Specifically, the first disadvantage is that governmental regulatory preferences are inappropriate, and it will make governmental regulatory goals prone to deviate from the requirements of society. For example, the preference often summed up as *GDP first* can lead to ill-considered investments, excessive investment attraction, the neglect of citizens' livelihoods, and a lack of concern for ecological protection. The second potential disadvantage of government regulation is that the procedures may be handled improperly, making it easy for the decision-making process to deviate from the path of democratisation, for measures to be delayed, and for costs to escalate; moreover, changes in the market are unlikely, under these circumstances, to spur a timely and flexible response. The third disadvantage is the possibility that regulation will be weakly coordinated between different areas of government. This can make it easy for a regulatory target to be controlled by the interests of specific executive departments as well as by local interests, thus causing policy-based internal friction. The fourth disadvantage may reflect a lack of motivation in government officials charged with implementing regulations; this can weaken the impact of the measures involved. Typically, such a situation leads to delays in resolving problems and contradictions after these have been exposed. The results are felt as bureaucratism in government agencies, and as a reduction in the effectiveness of government regulation. Practice has shown that the current problems of overstaffing, procrastination in granting approvals, poor information flows between departments, and the tendency to local protectionism fostered by the government's *'non-big-ministry' system* can, to some extent, lead to the phenomena summed up as *improper ordering* and *difficult implementation*. This greatly reduces the scientific nature and effectiveness of government regulation.

4. Different Characteristics of Market Regulation and Government Regulation

The Third Plenary Session of the 18th Central Committee of the Communist Party of China proposed *the decisive role of the market in the allocation of resources and* called for the government to play a more developed and effective role[151]. Unfortunately, some people have understood this unilaterally, and have even formed certain neoliberal interpretations. For example, several articles have argued that the decisive role of the market represents the breakthrough and roadmap for reform, and that reform of the basic economic system, the market system, government functions, and macro-control should all be based on it. This view expresses the idea that the decisive role of the market also furnishes the principle and yardstick for the approach to reform known as *crossing a river by feeling for the stones*. We, therefore, need to understand accurately the connotations of the *theory of the decisive role of the market* under socialism with Chinese characteristics as proposed by the Third Plenary Session of the 18th Central Committee and General Secretary Xi Jinping. Overall, this theory emphasises dual regulation by the market and the government. However, the roles and functions of these two are different, and a dialectical relationship exists between them. So, what are the different characteristics of the dual regulatory roles played by the market and the government?

At different macro and micro-levels, the *theory of the decisive role of the market* under socialism with Chinese characteristics emphasises the need to adopt national macro-control and micro-regulation to jointly correct certain *decisive market roles*. General Secretary Xi Jinping explained that in China's socialist market economy the market plays a decisive role in the allocation of resources, but not in every case. It is necessary to *improve the macro-control system that is guided by national development strategies and plans, with fiscal and monetary policies as the primary means*. The spontaneous effect of the law of value will still have negative consequences, and the country's macro-control and micro-regulation must be used to avoid or alleviate these consequences. Macro-control mainly involves adjusting market activities such as investment and consumption through fiscal, monetary, and other economic means and policies. This also includes making use of the necessary administrative means before, during, and after the process, so as to achieve macro-economic goals such as full employment, price stability, rational structure, and balance of international payments. Micro-regulation is basically the comprehensive use of economic, legal, administrative, and other means to manage the behaviour of microeconomic entities so as to maintain

---

151. Xi Jinping. *Excerpts from Xi Jinping's Discourse on Socialist Cultural Construction*. Central Literature Publishing House, 2017. http://theory.people.com.cn/n1/2017/0619/c148980-29347273.html

normal market competition, promote scientific and technological innovation, develop independent intellectual property rights, promote social harmony, and maintain a healthy ecology. The beneficial results include achieving the comprehensive coordination and sustainable development of the economy, politics, society, culture, and ecology.

While the *market plays a decisive role* in the field of material resources, a more accurate picture is that the short-term allocation of general resources by the market is combined with the direct allocation by the government of special resources, such as geological resources and infrastructure, and with the long-term allocation by the government of numerous general resources. The effectiveness of the *decisive role of the market* is predominantly reflected in the short-term allocation of general resources, driven by the law of value and on the basis of short-term interests. Meanwhile, the effectiveness of the government's allocation of resources is principally demonstrated in the long-term provision of countless general resources, and in the regulation and allocation of special resources such as geological resources, infrastructure, and transportation. In the short-term allocation of general resources, the market thus plays a decisive role. In the long-term allocation of certain general resources, the government realises planning and allocation by combining short-term with long-term interests.

Due to the non-renewable nature of special resources, such as geological resources, the government strengthens the regulation and allocation of these resources by coordinating short-term and long-term interests, local interests, and overall interests. The market-oriented operation of specific production and business projects is not identical to market decisions, because the essence of market decisions is that production and business projects in the area of resources are determined by the microeconomic subjects themselves. In fact, many important projects involving the national economy and the livelihoods of individuals are first planned and decided upon by the government, and then carried out using market-oriented operations. For a time following the reform and opening up, the *decisive role of the market* was implemented in the allocation of resources such as rare earth elements and coal. The result was that the resources were exploited in a destructive and inefficient manner and sold at low prices worldwide. China was taught a grim lesson when mining disasters became frequent even as the *coal bosses* quickly enriched themselves. At present, the country is witnessing the simultaneous phenomena of large-scale overcapacity in the steel and coal industries, high prices for residential housing, and a real estate *bubble*. All of these hazards are related to excessive activity by the market, and the absence of a government response.

In addition to the two points above, the characteristics of the dual, regulatory role of the market and the government need to be analysed from three other aspects.

First, there is a need to examine the roles of the market and the government in allocating resources in areas outside the field of material production, areas such as education, culture, and health. What is needed is an analysis from a third angle. The allocation of general cultural, medical, and health resources can play a decisive role in the market, but in areas such as these, the leading role of the government should be incorporated, universally, with the decisive role of the market. The large-scale development of education and culture provides an important context for economic and social development and acts as a vital carrier of the core socialist value system and its internal values. In these areas, therefore, social benefits should be placed first, and should be combined with economic benefits; accordingly, the share of relevant resource allocation realised through the market should be relatively small. Many projects in education and culture have functions of global and long-term intellectual support, cultural inheritance, cultural cohesion, and cultural orientation that shape economic and social development. Only if the lead role is played by the government can efficient allocation of non-material resources be achieved. General Secretary Xi Jinping has stated that culture has a productive role as well as being an ideological attribute, and no matter how the reform is carried out, the significance of culture cannot be changed, and the position that culture is fundamental cannot be lost.

The second aspect is connected with the relationship between the market and the government in resource allocation. Does resource allocation only involve the relationship between the market and the government? In a nutshell, there are two levels of resource allocation; one is comprised of market and government allocations, and the other of private and public allocations. From the fourth perspective of the relationship between the two types of allocations, the *theory of the decisive role of the market* in socialism with Chinese characteristics is related to the mixed economy with public ownership as the centerpiece. The dominant role of public ownership, with its qualitative and quantitative advantages, is an inherent requirement of the socialist market economy with Chinese characteristics and makes up one of its essential features. *In the socialist economy, unlike the situation in the capitalist system, the role of the state-owned economy is not simply to operate in sectors where private enterprises are unwilling to invest, or to remedy the deficiencies of private enterprises and market mechanisms, but to achieve sustained, stable, and coordinated development of the national economy and to consolidate and improve the socialist system.* As was stated in the Third Plenary Session of the 18th Central Committee of the Communist Party of China, 'We must unswervingly consolidate and develop the public ownership economy, adhere to the dominant position of public ownership, fully develop the leading role of the state-owned economy, and continuously enhance the vitality, control, and influence of the state-owned economy'[152]. If public ownership no longer has a dominant position in the socialist economy, the efficiency of government regulation will be greatly weakened, and the implementation of national economic and social development strategies will be adversely affected. As a result, the country will lack an economic foundation able to ensure the fundamental interests of the people and common prosperity. The kind of reform that advocates selling public schools, enterprises, and hospitals is indicative of neoliberalism.

China has adopted a basic economic system in which public ownership is kept as the mainstay of the economy while diverse forms of ownership are allowed to develop side by side. Compared with the contemporary capitalist economic system, whose mainstay is private ownership, this will better fulfill the internal requirements of the modern market economy and features higher performance and more fairness. Accordingly, we must continue to increase support for state-owned enterprises, especially central enterprises. State-owned enterprises are the lifeblood of the country's economy, and we need to depend on them at critical moments. What the United States and other Western countries are afraid of is the powerful strength of the Communist Party of China. One reason why the Communist Party of China is developing rapidly is that our state-owned enterprises support it, providing financial strength and material and human resources while effectively controlling the national economic lifeline. This is vital for China, and it is necessary to be very clear on this point. The management of state-owned enterprises is not entirely determined by the market; political decisions also have a say. It is irrational to conclude that developing state-owned enterprises is a wrong strategy, and that the only way out lies in *denationalisation.* Centuries of economic practice at home and abroad have shown that when public and state ownership take a dominant position, financial, economic, and fiscal crises, as well as wealth polarisation

---

152. 'Decision of the Central Committee of the Communist Party of China on Several Major Issues of Comprehensively Deepening Reform [N].' *People's Daily*, 2013-11-15.

between rich and poor, will not occur as often as they do under various capitalist models. The crucial difference between socialism and capitalism as a basic economic system is manifested in the social ownership structure of the means of production, that is, in whether the mixed ownership is dominated by public capital or private capital.

It is thus evident that we cannot merely focus on the development of mixed ownership and the non-public economy without also considering the growth of the publicly-owned economy; nor can we simply mention the decisive role of the market in resource allocation without including the positive role of the government. These seemingly reformed views and measures actually misinterpret the spirit of the Third Plenary Session of the Eighteenth Central Committee of the Communist Party of China and of General Secretary Xi Jinping's speech. In terms of economics, the socialist position manifests itself first in a belief in public ownership and the common prosperity created by it. Moreover, the economy determines politics; the economic foundation determines the superstructure; and public ownership is the socialist economic foundation of such elements of the socialist superstructure as the Communist Party being in power. Public ownership is the pillar and main body of the diverse economic foundation of society during the primary stage of socialism.

The third aspect concerns the characteristics of the role of the market and government in distribution. What are these characteristics? This brings us to the fifth element of the analysis. In the area of distribution, the market and government each play a greater role in regulating the multiple distributions of wealth and income. In the initial distribution, first of all, the market plays a greater role in regulating the distribution of wealth and income through the spontaneous operation of the law of value, while the government also regulates, to some degree, the distribution of wealth and income through the formulation and implementation of relevant laws and regulations. Only if this latter function of the government is present, can we genuinely achieve an increase in the proportion of labour income in the initial distribution, effectively safeguard labour rights and interests, and achieve the goals of *limiting high incomes, raising low incomes, and expanding the number of middle-income earners*. Second, in the process of redistribution, the government should play a greater role in correcting and adjusting problems such as the wealth polarisation between rich and poor caused by the initial distribution. The aim should be to promote the growth of citizens' wealth and incomes to keep pace with economic developments. In the past, the decisive role of the market was emphasised in meeting the housing needs of urban residents. As a result, housing prices rose sharply, developers experienced a sudden growth in their wealth, and there were vociferous complaints from the public. Only in recent years has the government actively developed regulations for the housing market, which is obviously for the improvement of people's livelihoods.

5. Deepening Reform Requires Perfecting the Market System

The role of the market is played out through the market system. How can a deepening of reform allow this system to be improved? General Secretary Xi Jinping at one point declared clearly, 'Building a unified and open market system with orderly competition is the basis for the market to play a decisive part in the allocation of resources. We must speed up the formation of a modern market system in which enterprises operate independently, compete fairly, consumers choose freely, consume independently, and goods and factors of production flow freely and can be exchanged on an equal footing. We must focus on removing market barriers and improving the efficiency and fairness of resource allocation'[153]. Therefore, we should assign a fundamental place to establishing a sound market system. To improve this system, we need to do the following.

First, we should improve the factor market system. The market system is an objective organic system composed of market elements. It is an organic whole, interconnected, and mutually conditioned by commodity markets such as consumer goods and production materials, factor markets such as capital, labour, technology, information, and real estate markets, and special trading markets such as futures, auctions, and property rights. Since the reform and opening up, China's commodity market has been fully developed, while the markets for factors such as land, capital, and technology have lagged behind. Consequently, factor prices do not reflect the degree of scarcity or supply-demand relations. Since the Third Plenary Session of the 18th Central Committee, the focus has been on three major areas, developing a unified market for urban and rural construction land, improvements to the financial market system, and advancement of the market-oriented mechanism for scientific and technological innovation. It should be said that these are highly realistic and well-targeted goals. Land, capital, and technology are all important production factors. Improving the market for these factors will surely have a profound impact on transforming the pattern of

---

153. Ibid

economic development, optimising the allocation of resources, promoting fair competition, and building an innovative nation.

Moreover, we should establish fair, open, and transparent market rules, which are the primary prerequisites for fair competition in the market. Only through vigorous action to remove various market barriers can the efficiency of resource allocation be improved. This requires continuing to explore the negative list system, unifying market access, further developing the access management model for foreign investment, facilitating the industrial and commercial registration system, advancing the reform of the domestic trade circulation system, reforming the market supervision system, improving the market exit mechanism, etc. All of these factors play an important role in curbing local protectionism, monopolies, and unfair competition, and aid in the establishment of a society of honesty and trust.

Lastly, we should improve the mechanism whereby prices are mainly determined by the market. The formation of prices by a sound market system is the core mechanism through which the market promotes the optimal allocation of resources. The degree to which prices can flexibly reflect changes in value, scarcity of resources, and changes in supply and demand acts as the main indicator showing whether the market system is sound or not. To improve the market system, the extent of government price-setting must, therefore, be limited. On the one hand, efforts should be made to clarify the scope of government pricing, restricting it mainly to important public utilities, public welfare services, and network-based natural monopolies, while emphasising that government pricing should be more transparent and should be subject to supervision by society. On the other hand, we should restore the commodity attributes of certain special resources, press ahead with price reforms in fields such as water supplies, oil, natural gas, electricity, transportation, and telecommunications, and promote the marketisation and standardisation of prices. Of course, the principle that *the government does not intervene improperly* does not necessarily mean that the government should refrain from intervening. The key consideration is whether intervention is appropriate and likely to benefit the national economy and the livelihoods of citizens.

6. How Can the Government Play a More Effective Role?

Since the Third Plenary Session of the 18th Central Committee of the Communist Party of China, a number of one-sided views of *market decision-making* have been advanced in theoretical circles and among economists. These views hold that the role of the market and the role of the government – activist or not – is determined by the market, that the government is the main obstacle to *decision- making by the market,* that the *central mechanism* for deepening reform should be *the reform of government,* and that governmental reform can be reduced to the *simplification and decentralisation of government.* At the 15th Collective Study Meeting of the Political Bureau of the CPC Central Committee, General Secretary Xi Jinping emphasised, 'On the issue of the role of the market and the role of the government, we should adopt the methodology of dialectics and the doctrine that everything has two sides; both the *invisible hand* and the *visible hand* must be used well'[154]. The decisive role of the market in the allocation of resources, Xi Jinping stressed, cannot 'be used to replace or even deny the governmental role; nor can the role of the government replace or even deny the decisive role of the market in the allocation of resources'[155]. How can issues such as *the way in which the government can play a more effective role,* and adherence to the basic economic system, be understood as *determined by the market*? It is just as inaccurate to place undue emphasis on streamlining the administration and delegating power. Governmental reform should be a systematic project aimed at improving the macro-control system, performing government functions in a universally suitable way, and optimising the government's organisational structure. The core objective of this reform should be to establish a democratic, efficient, and service-oriented government ruled by law. In particular, we should pay attention to the following reforms and paths of development.

First, the macro-control and micro-regulation systems need to be improved. According to a decision of the Third Plenary Session of the 18th Central Committee, China's macro-control structure is to undergo three major changes: (1) For general economic entities, more emphasis is to be placed on the guiding role of national development strategies and planning. In the listing of the major policy tools, *financial policy* is to be replaced by the term *monetary policy.* (2) In view of the difficulties faced by local governments in ensuring the effectiveness of central macroeconomic regulation and control, it is also emphasised that we need to improve the evaluation system, correct the erroneous tendency to evaluate economic performance

---

154. 'Correctly play the role of the market and the role of the government to promote sustainable and healthy economic and social development [N].' *People's Daily*, 2014-05-28. http://www.gov.cn/xinwen/2014-05/27/content_2688228.htm

155. Ibid

simply on the basis of economic growth, and increase the weight of indicators such as resource consumption, environmental damage, ecological benefits, and overcapacity. Further, we must strengthen the constraints on local governments. (3) To ensure the coordinated development of the international economy, the decision stressed that we need to create a mechanism for participating in international macroeconomic policy coordination and for improving the international economic governance structure. As immediate measures, we need to highlight the safety and prices of products such as food and medicines, as well as improving regulations on issues such as housing.

Second, governmental functions need to be fully and correctly performed. Efficient and scientific government regulation is premised on the government performing its functions correctly, and it must adapt to the requirements of recent changes in the macro-control system. For market potential to be better developed, the restriction of certain government powers indeed represents an important step. All economic activities by the government that can be effectively regulated by the market should be eliminated, and the government should not be able to engage in *redundant interventions*. At the same time, the government needs to strengthen its formulation and implementation of development strategies, plans, policies, standards, etc., to reinforce its supervision of market activities, and to consolidate the provision of various public services. In principle, all transactional management services should be purchased from the public through contracts and entrustment etc., with proper competition in place.

Finally, the organisational structure of the government should be optimised. The transformation of functions and their implementation require that the government's organisational structure must be further improved. General Secretary Xi Jinping proposed to 'optimise the setting of government agencies and functional allocation [to] improve the administrative operating mechanism in which decision-making power, executive power, and supervisory power both limit and coordinate with each other, [to] strictly control the size of the government body and the number of leaders in accordance with provisions, [and to] reduce the number of institutions and leadership positions'[156]. China should carry out a reform of its system of major departments as soon as possible and retain no more than twenty constituent departments of the State Council. Some departments that, in the past, were directly administered should also be

---

156. Xi Jinping's notes on the draft decision and draft program on deepening the reform of party and state institutions. https://news.12371. cn/2018/04/11/ARTI1523454152698258.shtml

reduced and streamlined. The practice of various countries known for high management effectiveness should be studied in order to reduce the number of deputy posts and the size of government departments at all levels, and in principle, should be to prohibit the transferring of unofficial personnel. Strict procedures, timetables, and reward and punishment measures should be formulated and implemented, while opposition to bureaucracy and departmental selfishness should be highlighted. Educational activities for the masses should be developed and carried out by governments at all levels.

The views of many famous western economists are also noteworthy. Some years ago, Paul Samuelson advised China not to take sides in the relationship between the market and the government, but instead to remain neutral. In a speech at Tsinghua University in the first half of 2014, Joseph Stiglitz said that the role of the market in China was too big, while that of the government was too small. China also did not collect taxes on private capital gains, and its distribution gap was too large.

7. Complementary Functions of the Market and Government

Are the roles and functions of the market and government characterised by an increase on the side of the market and a reduction on that of the government? The answer is no. The two employ methods and mechanisms of economic regulation with different levels of application, fields, and functions. Briefly stated, the decisive role of the market and the more advantageous role of the government need to be viewed as an organic whole rather than as a diametrically opposed relationship. It is necessary to use the desirable and effective functions of market regulation to counter *government regulatory failure*, and to use the excellent functions of government regulation to correct the *failure of market regulation*. The goal should be to form a *'double-high'* and *'double-strong'* pattern that includes a highly efficient market with stronger functions and a highly efficient government with more powerful functions. Such an outcome will not only bring to bear the beneficial regulatory functions of socialist countries but will also help avert the danger of falling into the neoliberal trap and of encountering financial and economic crises. This is not the *semi-government-controlled economy* that is proposed by Chinese and foreign neoliberal *market-determination theorists*. Neither is it the so-called *modern market economic system* that promotes competitive market mechanisms that do not require state control; nor is it the *market-only* reforms that feature abolishing the necessary government macro-controls and micro-regulation, and that all Keynesians have fiercely attacked.

(Originally published in *Social Sciences in Chinese Universities*, Issue 6, 2014)

Chapter *6*

The Gradual Opening up of China's Domestic Capital Market

1. The Impossible Trinity: Proposal

The Impossible Trinity theory states that under the conditions of an open economy, it is impossible for a country to simultaneously achieve the three macroeconomic goals of independent monetary policy, free capital flow, and exchange rate stability. The theory provides a theoretical basis for countries to set macroeconomic goals in contexts ranging from the gold standard system to the Jamaican system. Practice has demonstrated that the Impossible Trinity actually exists. Its theoretical basis is the Mundell-Fleming model (M-F model)[157], which was formally proposed by Paul Krugman.

The M-F model expands on analysis of the effects of different policies in an open economy, showing whether capital will flow freely and suggesting the impact of different exchange rate regimes on a country's macroeconomy. For a country that implements a fixed exchange rate regime and completely free capital flow, the effect of its central bank adopting an expansionary monetary policy will be to increase the money supply and lower interest rates. Declining interest rates will cause the country's interest rate to be lower than in other countries, causing capital outflows. Capital outflows reduce the domestic money supply, which in turn prevents a further decline in interest rates, but this situation is likely to cause a deficit in the balance of payments. Once this occurs, the central bank must intervene in the foreign exchange market, selling foreign currency assets and buying the national currency until the money supply returns to its original level. Similarly, when a country's central bank adopts a tight monetary policy, the money supply decreases and interest rates tend to rise. Higher interest rates will attract capital inflows, which

---

157. Paul Krugman, 'O-Canada', Slate, October 19, 1999, https://slate.com/business/1999/10/o-canada.html.

will prevent interest rates from rising, but this is likely to cause a surplus in the balance of payments. In order to adjust the imbalance of international payments, the central bank will sell domestic currency and buy foreign exchange until the money supply returns to its original level. This shows that monetary policy has no effect under a fixed exchange rate regime. Countries that implement a floating exchange rate regime will adopt an expansionary monetary policy. Interest rates will fall, and large outflows of capital will cause an exchange rate depreciation. Depreciation of exchange rates will improve the trade balance and stimulate income and employment growth. Similarly, a tight monetary policy will cause an exchange rate appreciation, worsening the trade balance and leading to lower income. It can be seen that under a floating exchange rate regime, monetary policy has a substantial impact on income. The M–F model illustrates the relationship between the free flow of capital, a fixed exchange rate regime, and an independent monetary policy, all three of which cannot be achieved simultaneously. This became the analytical foundation for the Impossible Trinity theory.

Krugman detailed the Impossible Trinity in his book 'The Return of Depression Economics and the 2008 Economic Crisis'. In this work, he was able to chronicle how the complete liquidity of domestic capital, monetary policy independence, and stable exchange rates cannot be achieved at the same time. This theory is set out in graphic form in Figure 6-1.

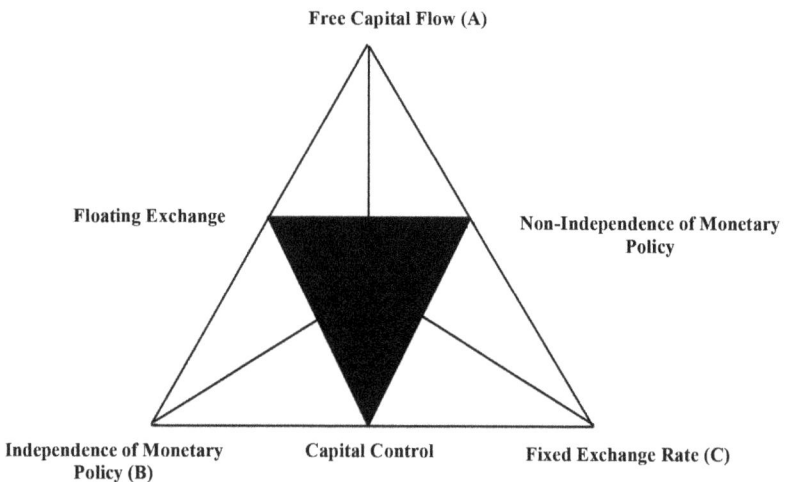

Figure 6-1 'The Impossible Trinity Theory'

The Impossible Trinity refers to A + B + C = 2. When the value of A, B, and C is 1, this means that macroeconomic goals can be achieved. When the value of A, B, and C is 0, this means that macroeconomic goals cannot be achieved. There are three cases, the first of which is (A, B, C) = (1, 1, 0). The economic implication is that a fixed exchange rate system must be abandoned while fully opening capital markets and maintaining monetary policy independence. This combination is mainly found in developed countries such as the United States, the United Kingdom, and Canada. The second case is (A, B, C) = (1, 0, 1). Here, the meaning in economic terms is that if the capital market is completely open and a fixed exchange rate regime is in place, an independent monetary policy cannot be maintained. When a country's economy overheats, and a tight monetary policy is adopted, the high interest rates will attract hot money inflows. This offsets the expected effect of the tightened monetary policy, and vice versa. Instances of this combination are to be found in Hong Kong, China, and Argentina (in 1999). Third, (A, B, C) = (0, 1, 1). The economic significance in this case is that if the stability of the exchange rate and the independence of monetary policy are to be ensured, the free flow of capital has to be abandoned. Free capital flows will cause the amount of funds at home and in the international financial market to change, which in turn will cause constant exchange rate fluctuations. In these circumstances, the implementation of a fixed exchange rate regime cannot be guaranteed; China is in just such a situation. The shortcomings of this particular combination are that capital controls restrict the flow of productive operating capital and monetary investment capital; thus, restrictions on capital for business operations can act as a disincentive to economic development.

In this era of financial monopoly capitalism, the Impossible Trinity has become a classic formulation in international economics, where it has provided a theoretical reference for countries in defining their macroeconomic goals. Meanwhile, this theory also has certain limitations, and scholars at home and abroad have conducted many further discussions on how it might be improved.

2. The Intermediate State, and the Non-corner Solution of the Impossible Trinity Theory

Frankel pointed out that the Impossible Trinity considers extreme cases, that is, completely free flow of capital, complete monetary policy independence, and a fixed exchange rate regime that takes no account of the intermediate situation. He believed that there was insufficient evidence to prove that an intermediate situation could not be considered when choosing a policy portfolio, and that it was possible to consider abandoning half of the monetary policy independence and exchange rate stability, so that half of the exchange rate stability and half of the monetary policy independence could be achieved.[158] Facts have proved that the three elements in the Impossible Trinity are not in a non-reciprocal relationship, and that an intermediate state can exist.

(I) The Intermediate State of the Three Elements

First, there is the possibility of partial capital flows. Capital flows include capital inflows and outflows. A country can allow capital to flow freely without any restrictions, or it can strictly control capital flows between countries, that is, controlling capital outflows and inflows. When capital controls are applied, however, capital cannot be completely stagnant, and some capital flows exist; capital control is thus only partial. The strength of capital mobility depends on the capital controls exercised by a country, and on the profitability of international capital. There are always differences in profits between different countries, so although capital is regulated, there will always be a certain liquidity. Some emerging markets suffer from scarce domestic capital and choose to strictly control capital through limiting capital outflow, while their restrictions on capital inflow are relatively loose. China is a typical example of a country that uses this type of partial capital control.

Second, intermediate states are possible within the exchange rate regime. In addition to the two common exchange rate regimes, the fixed and the floating regimes, many intermediate states may exist. In 1999 the IMF classified exchange rate arrangements into eight groups:[159] exchange arrangements with no separate legal tender, currency board system, other traditional fixed exchange rate peg arrangements, pegged exchange rates within horizontal bands, crawling pegs, exchange rates within crawling bands, managed floating with no predetermined path for the exchange rate, and independent floating. The first two and the last exchange rate regimes are called *corner exchange rate regimes*, and the other five are

---

158. Jeffrey A. Frankel, 'No Single Currency Regime is Right for All Countries or at All Times'[J]. *NBER Working Paper*, (September 1999): 738.

159. International Monetary Fund,. (January 2000). *International Financial Statistics*. Washington: International Monetary Fund.

called *intermediate exchange rate regimes*. On 1 January 1999, there were ninety-two countries that implemented corner exchange rate regimes. Among them, forty-five countries implemented a fixed exchange rate regime, and forty-seven countries implemented a floating exchange rate regime. The other ninety-three countries implemented an intermediate exchange rate regime. For many developing countries that lack developed financial strength, financial markets, and related systems, an intermediate exchange rate regime is a better choice.

Third, there are different levels of weak and strong effectiveness in monetary policy. In an open economy, the independence of monetary policy mainly means that the domestic monetary policy is not affected by the foreign exchange market. However, as the level of economic internationalisation deepens, the independence of a country's monetary policy will weaken, and there will be many factors that affect monetary policies. In addition to foreign exchange market factors, globalisation factors, endogenous currency supply, and currency substitution will also affect monetary policies. Empirical studies have shown that no matter whether a fixed exchange rate regime or a floating exchange rate regime is implemented, the monetary policies of most countries are unable to remain completely independent (Frankel, Schmukler, Servén, 2002)[160]. There are even very special cases where the independence of the monetary policies of countries with floating exchange rates is weaker than that of countries with fixed exchange rates (Hausmann, Gavin, Pages-Sierra, Stein, 1999)[161].

(II) Corner Solution and Non-corner Solution of the Impossible Trinity Model

According to modelling based on the Impossible Trinity, the corner solution and non-corner solution can be derived from a range of situations. The corner solution represents the extreme situation of the three elements, involving two out of three of either (1) the independence of monetary policy, (2) the free flow of capital, or (3) the

---

160. Frankel, Jeffrey A. and Schmukler, Sergio and Servén, Luis, *Global Transmission of Interest Rates: Monetary Independence and Currency Regime* (October 2002). Available at SSRN: https://ssrn.com/abstract=232452

161. Hausmann, Ricardo and Gavin, Michael and Pages-Serra, Carmen and Stein, Ernesto Hugo, Financial Turmoil and Choice of Exchange Rate Regime (January 1999). IDB Working Paper No. 331, Available at SSRN: https://ssrn.com/abstract=1817197 or http://dx.doi.org/10.2139/ssrn.1817197

stability of the exchange rate. The non-corner solution is the intermediate state of the three elements. In other words, it represents
the partial independence of monetary policy, regulated capital flow,
and managed floating. Yi Gang proposes[162] an extended triangular
coordinate system, based on the Impossible Trinity, that provides
a theoretical basis for the *corner solution hypothesis* of the exchange
rate regime. In this paper, x, y, and m are used to represent the stability of the exchange rate regime, monetary policy independence,
and capital liquidity, respectively. Assuming that $x + y + m = 2$, the
Impossible Trinity can be reinterpreted. When the value of x, y, and
m is 1, this means that the macroeconomic goals can be achieved.
When the value of x, y, and m is 0, this means that macroeconomic
goals cannot be achieved. There are three cases: $(x, y, m) = (1, 1, 0)$,
$(x, y, m) = (1, 0, 1)$, $(x, y, m) = (0, 1, 1)$. In the coordinates, Frankel
states that the *half-half* intermediate system,[163] $(x, y, m) = (1/2, 1/2,$
$1)$ is possible. Taking the Impossible Trinity extended by Yi Gang
as a theoretical basis, the monetary policy combination adopted
by China can also be $(1/2, 1/2, 1)$, and the country's future policy
combination will consist of a free capital flow, soft pegged exchange
rate, and semi-independent monetary policy.[164] Shen Guobing and
Shi Jinchuan introduce a variable that affects the choice of exchange
rate regimes in the Impossible Trinity – the borrowing capacity of
local currency in the international financial market (referred to as
the international borrowing capacity of a local currency) – and establish the tetrahedron hypothesis. Shen and Shi believe that there is no
endogeneity between the international borrowing capacity of local
currency and the level of independence or dependence of monetary
policy, the level of exchange rate stability or change, or the level of
capital flow or control. Instead, these are interrelated. Shen and Shi
list all possible combinations of cases and further point out that the
Impossible Trinity model is a special case of the tetrahedron hypothesis.[165] Ma Xinyuan believes that the new variable proposed by Shen
Guobing and Shi Jinchuan, *the international borrowing capacity of the*

162. Yi Gang, Tang Yin. A theoretical basis for the "corner-point solution
hypothesis" of the exchange rate system [J]. *Financial Research*, 2001(8).

163. Ibid

164. Zhang Q, Wang X. The extended "triadic paradox" as a guide for
China's policy mix [J]. *Business Research*, 2004 (17).

165. Shen G. Bing, Shi J. Chuan. The choice of exchange rate regime: the
impossibility triangle and its extension [J]. *World Economy*, 2002 (10).

local currency, has no universal applicability.[166] The addition of the international borrowing capacity of the domestic currency will not expand the trinity into a tetrahedron, so it cannot be generalised. The impact of the *international borrowing capacity of the local currency* on the choice of exchange rate regime should be studied on the basis of the history of changes in the exchange rate regime between the central and peripheral countries. This, in fact, shows indirectly that in addition to the influence of capital flow and monetary policy independence on the choice of exchange rate regime in the Impossible Trinity, there are many other factors that influence the choice of an exchange rate regime. Starting from microeconomic analysis, Chen Zhijun has established a theoretical framework for policy coordination within the framework of the macroeconomics of a new open economy.[167] Through modelling and graphical analysis, he points out that countries with strong economies, such as the United States and the countries of the European Union, have full confidence in their currencies. Thus, they allow their currencies to float; they are confident that the capital flows will be satisfactory, and that independent monetary policies can be implemented. For developing countries, it is difficult to evaluate the welfare of a policy portfolio, so it is impossible to determine which policy combination is the optimal one. Li Cheng and Li Yong (2009) spatialise the Impossible Trinity, incorporating exchange rate regime stability (x), monetary policy independence (y), and capital liquidity (s) as three variables in a three-dimensional coordinate system.[168] The origin is 0 (floating exchange rate, invalid monetary policy, capital control). In the space, there is point F $(1, 0, 1)$ which means that the exchange rate is fixed, and capital can flow freely. Point G $(1, 1, 0)$ means that the exchange rate is fixed, and the monetary policy is independent, while point D $(0, 1, 1)$ signifies a free flow of capital and an independent monetary policy, ΔFGD corresponds to the Impossible Trinity. The plane where ΔFGD is located constitutes the upper bound of a country's choice of policy goals, and there are points between $(0, 1)$ in three coordinates; that is, they are non-corner points. Under the two assumptions that

166. Ma Xinyuan. The Impossible Triangle - An Explanation from a Historical Perspective [J]. *Financial Studies*, 2004 (2).

167. Chen, Zhijun. Reinterpreting the "impossible triangle" in the framework of new open economy macroeconomics [J]. *Journal of Xi'an Jiaotong University*, 2008(11).

168. Li, Cheng, Li, Yong. The non-angular point solution of the "impossible triangle" and the institutional arrangement of China's economic system[J]. *Journal of Xi'an University of Finance and Economics*,2009,22(03):10-16.

capital is an exogenous variable and that a country's exchange rate regime is dominated by the government, the author has established a loss function. The conclusion shows that the minimum value of the comprehensive loss function of exchange rate instability and the loss of monetary policy effectiveness always fall in ΔFGD, which is a non-corner solution. Huang Feiming has established a loan reserve policy framework model. Under the statutory loan reserve policy framework, the monetary authority is able to adjust consumer demand in the total demand by changing the consumer loan reserve ratio, specifically, to affect consumer spending by changing the cost of consumer loans. In this process, there is no need to adjust the money market interest rate, since it will have no impact on the exchange rate, and thus will not affect the changes in net exports. Huang Feiming provides some recommendations on how to implement the statutory loan reserve.[169]

3. China's Options for a Macro-Financial Policy Portfolio

China is faced with two macro-financial policy choices with regard to the Impossible Trinity model: the *extreme system* and the *intermediate system*. Some scholars believe that the intermediate state of each system has its own particular conditions for existence. The intermediate policy system is held to be unstable, and China is urged to adopt an extreme policy system. Another group of scholars (Hernandez and Montiel) believe that a non-corner solution should be chosen for China's macro-financial policy portfolio. They emphasise that after the 1998 financial crisis, the exchange rate regimes of Asian countries did not show a trend toward polarisation.[170]

(I) The Choice of Capital Flow Policy

The Impossible Trinity model and historical experience have proved that it is untenable to insist on capital flows under a fixed exchange rate regime while abandoning an independent monetary

---

169. Huang Feiming. Monetary Policy Independence in an Open Economy: A Theoretical Framework: A Solution to the "Impossible Triangle" of Currency Zones [J]. *International Financial Studies*, 2009(11).

170.   Hernandez, L. & Montiel, P. J. Post–crisis Exchange Rate Policy in Five Asia Countries: Filling the Hollow Middle[J]. *Journal of the Japanese and International Economics*, 2003, 17 (3: p. 336–369.

policy. While ensuring the independence of monetary policy, if capital flows are liberalised, a floating exchange rate regime must accompany it. Capital flow policies can be divided into three types: complete capital control, partial capital control, and capital liberalisation. As mentioned earlier, the strength of capital liquidity depends on a country's capital controls and on the profitability of international capital. There are always differences in profit levels between different countries, so although capital is controlled, there will always be a certain liquidity. This means that there are two options for capital flow policies. One is a partial control of capital flows, and the other is capital liberalisation. Regulation of capital flows can effectively reduce short-term capital speculation, thus helping to maintain the stability of the domestic economy and structural adjustments. There are certain conditions for the opening of a capital account, which should be compatible with the country's financial strength and the degree of soundness of the financial market. At present, countries with capital account liberalisation are mainly developed countries, and developing countries are mainly dominated by capital control.

Scholars in China and abroad have expressed their views on whether China should liberalise its capital account process. Yu Yongding, a member of the Presidium of the Chinese Academy of Social Sciences, has insisted that premature capital account liberalisation would be a subversive mistake on a fundamental issue! Nobel laureate Jean Tirole has pointed out that 'a large amount of capital account liberalisation has brought about speculative foreign exchange transactions and banking crises'.[171] Unregulated capital account opening is unlikely to bring mutual benefits or a win-win result to foreign lenders and domestic borrowers, and in emerging markets will more often than not trigger financial crises. The financial crises that occurred in many emerging markets during the 1980s and 1990s repeatedly proved this point. Without sufficient financial strength and in the absence of regulatory measures, the liberalisation of the capital account process will create opportunities for huge amounts of international capital (especially international speculative capital) to flow in and out of a country. When such inflows and outflows form a *tidal effect*, coming and going like rivers and oceans, and when the capital flow suddenly reverses, a financial crisis will inevitably be triggered. Lang

---

171. Tirole, Jean (21 July 2002). Financial Crises, Liquidity, and the International Monetary System. Princeton University Press. ISBN 9780691099859.

Xianping has also called the liberalisation of capital accounts 'a well-planned conspiracy'.[172] Seeking to pressure Japan to open its financial markets in the 1980s, the United States cited various supposed benefits of the move. In the first place, the U.S. argued that since financial development was conducive to economic development, supervision should be relaxed. Second, the U.S. cited the theory of equilibrium, maintaining that because the United States bought large quantities of goods from Japan, the latter should buy similar quantities from the United States. Third, financial development involves international competitiveness, and the U.S. insisted that Japan open up. With the opening of financial markets, the Japanese economy developed a huge bubble, and the bursting of this bubble caused Japan to be hit by an unprecedented economic downturn.

Another typical example occurred in Thailand. In the late 1980s, Thailand implemented a tightened foreign exchange management system. Then, starting in the early 1990s, it introduced financial reforms and reduced its foreign exchange restrictions on capital account transactions. In 1992, the Thai economy was further opened to foreign investments, which led to a large influx of capital, affecting the real estate industry and the stock market. As a result, a financial crisis erupted in Thailand. As Joseph Stiglitz emphasised, 'The global financial crisis of 2008 suggests that if financial regulation is loosened too quickly, the consequences will be quite devastating. The opening of a capital account contributed to the outbreak of the financial crisis in the United States and the spread of its influences elsewhere'.[173]

Since 2009, when China began to use the RMB for trade settlements, the Chinese government has made capital account liberalisation an important policy of its government and monetary authorities. While attending the 2015 annual meeting of the China Development High-level Forum, Shou Xiaochuan (former Governor of the People's Bank of China from 2002 to 2018) stated that he would make efforts to achieve RMB capital account convertibility in 2015. But what are the benefits of accelerating capital account convertibility in China? There is no pressure on the free flow of capital in China. In recent years, due to the introduction by the U.S. Federal Reserve of a quantitative easing monetary policy, India,

---

172. Lang Xianping. *Lang Xianping says: New Imperialism in China (2)* [M]. Beijing: Oriental Press, 2010.

173. https://web.archive.org/web/20150613170543/http://www.hxw.org.cn/html/article/info7110.html

Brazil, and other countries have experienced serious economic difficulties including capital outflows, currency depreciation, and low economic growth. One of the important reasons why China has avoided such difficulties is that China still retains capital controls. In the process of capital liberalisation, capital flight may occur if the financial market is not sound enough. China's financial market has not yet been improved sufficiently to match the liberalisation of capital accounts, and the free flow of capital across borders cannot improve China's resource allocation. Once a capital account is liberalised, short-term capital flows tend to enter the more liquid and speculative stock and real estate markets, creating stock market and housing bubbles.[174] Martin Wolf, chief economic commentator of the British *Financial Times,* has predicted: 'If the capital account is completely liberalised, the Chinese government will lose control of the most effective leverage of all its economic leverage. If China opens its capital accounts, the situation will be different, that is, any crisis may become more difficult to resolve, and the crisis will have a much greater impact on financial systems in other parts of the world'.[175]

There are also problems of timing in the liberalisation of capital accounts. The timing of China's capital account opening should follow these principles. Before a capital account is liberalised, a current account should first be opened. In the case of a capital account, direct investments should be opened before indirect investments, and long-term investments should be opened before short-term capital flows. Portfolio investments should be opened before the opening of lending, and capital inflows before outflows. The process of capital liberalisation should be gradual in nature. In Japan, current capital account liberalisation began in 1964 and was basically completed thirty-three years later in 1997. The Nobel laureate Robert Mundell, also reminded China to be cautious about capital account liberalisation and RMB convertibility, further suggesting that China should not be anxious for quick success and that it should seek to avoid the consequences of the *1985 Plaza Agreement,* when the United States instigated the continuous appreciation of the yen. As Yu Yongding has pointed out, capital account liberalisation is the last line of defence in China's economic reform. Yu Yongding stated: 'Actually, China's capital accounts, especially long-term capital, are basically open. We have only a few short-term capital flow restrictions, such as the current limit of 50,000 U.S. dollars in RMB exchange. For such

---

174. https://www.guancha.cn/linyifu/2013_08_05_163441.shtml
175. http://www.ftchinese.com/story/001055688

a limit, shall we give up? I think we should not give up'.[176] During the financial crisis, the scale of China's capital flight expanded, and there was an abnormal phenomenon: a large amount of hot money flowed in when it was predicted that the RMB would appreciate. As China continues to liberalise its control over capital accounts, it should therefore be particularly cautious. A full liberalisation of capital flows is still a long way off, and regulatory measures are needed to limit short-term flows of speculative capital. That is to say, China will remain in the state of exercising partial capital controls over non-corner solutions for a long time to come.

(II) The Choice of Exchange Rate Regime

All countries have been faced with diverse choices of exchange rate regime. The fiscal policy of a country under a fixed exchange rate regime is effective, and monetary policy under a floating exchange rate regime is effective as well. It is therefore difficult to define in abstract terms which fiscal policy and monetary policy are most important to determine a country's exchange rate regime. When a capital account is open, full exchange rate marketisation is the most effective option. If a capital account is not open, the country's exchange rate regime will always tend to move to a fixed exchange rate. Therefore, developing countries such as China should choose monetary policy independence and exchange rate stability, while developed countries will choose free capital flow and monetary policy independence (Yi Gang, 2000).[177] The choice of exchange rate regime varies with capital flows. When capital is completely restricted, a country should choose a fixed exchange rate regime. When capital is flowing freely, a country can choose between an intermediate exchange rate regime and a floating exchange rate regime according to the situation. When capital is partially restricted, a country may choose a fixed exchange rate regime, a floating exchange rate regime, or an intermediate exchange rate regime according to specific circumstances. Choosing an exchange rate regime involves weighing the advantages and disadvantages of a fixed exchange rate regime, intermediate exchange rate regime, and floating exchange rate regime. Mundell supported the fixed

---

176. Yu Yongding's Speech at Boyuan Foundation 5th Anniversary Academic Forum (2013)
https://business.sohu.com/20130630/n380273769.shtml
177. Yi Gang. The choice of exchange rate system[J]. *Financial Studies*, 2000(09):46-52.

exchange rate regime by pointing out that it represents a more effective way to fight inflation. However, he added: 'Countries with very unstable monetary and financial conditions (usually the result of banks financing to cover large fiscal deficits) cannot implement a fixed exchange rate. In general, countries with inflation relative to partner countries in their currency zone cannot maintain a fixed exchange rate. In a world without a stable international monetary system, opposition to floating exchange rates does not apply to countries with very large economies. The United States, which is the country with the largest economy, has no unilateral option to implement a fixed exchange rate regime'.[178] The floating exchange rate regime also has certain advantages. It can adjust the balance of payments spontaneously to equilibrate the balance of payments, and it may be beneficial to improve the efficiency of resource allocation without governmental intervention. However, since exchange rate regimes based on the two corners solution require harsh conditions, most of the world's countries currently implement the pegged exchange rate.

At present, China implements a managed floating exchange rate regime based on market supply and demand, with reference to a basket of currencies for adjustment. At the same time, it imposes controls on capital and does not allow for the free exchange of foreign currencies. This shows that China is in an intermediate state exchange rate regime. In the currency reference basket, the U.S. dollar is the mainstay, and when conducting foreign trade, China also needs to pay attention to currencies such as the euro, yen, and British pound. In addition, China has close trading ties with countries along the Belt and Road, and the currencies of these countries should be raised as a basket of currencies. At the same time, the currency weights in the *basket* should not remain unchanged but should be adjusted according to the close relationships between currencies. At present, there is an imbalance between the internal and external elements of the Chinese economy, which is facing internal problems such as overcapacity and excess liquidity. China's external economic environment is complex, and powerful countries are pointing fingers at the changes in the value of the RMB. In this situation, with the choice of the Impossible Trinity as a backdrop, China's goal must be to maintain a relatively stable exchange rate

---

178. The fifth volume of Mondale's economics - exchange rates and optimal currency zones [M]. Xiang Songzuo, Translation. Beijing: China Finance Press, 2003: 43-44.

and to secure an independent monetary policy, at the same time as it abandons the quest for capital liquidity. In fact, the RMB has been slowly appreciating (except for its depreciation in August 2015), which has also altered the effectiveness of other policies. In 2007, the monetary policy implemented by the central bank failed to work. The fundamental reason was that the appreciation of the RMB had attracted a large amount of hot money to flow into China, forming foreign exchange accounts, while at the same time China was restricting capital flows, resulting in the creation of excess liquidity. These issues have also impacted the effectiveness of monetary policy.

(III) The Choices for Monetary Policy

Using the Impossible Trinity, we can theorise on how a fixed exchange rate regime, a free flow of capital, and a non-independent monetary policy might be combined. All analyses, however, have shown that this combination is invalid. Under the conditions of economic opening, if a country chooses to abandon its monetary policy to achieve the goals of a free capital flow and fixed exchange rate regime, it must have sufficient foreign exchange reserves. Conversely, even if a country's total foreign exchange reserves are large, it cannot compete with international hot money. Under the pressure of international hot money, once the central bank exhausts its foreign exchange reserves and still cannot meet the devaluation expectations of international investors or cannot continue to prop up the market, the value of the currency will plummet catastrophically and the fixed exchange rate system will collapse. The devaluation of the Thai baht in 1997 is a typical example. Therefore, a country can either exercise capital controls and a fixed exchange rate regime to ensure the independence of monetary policy, or relax capital flow restrictions, implement a floating exchange rate regime, and keep its monetary policy independent.

Although China aims at an independent monetary policy, there are also cases of limited independence in monetary policies. If, within a free international financial market, a country's exchange rate is attacked by speculators and stable economic development is imperilled, monetary policy will play an important role in minimising the impact of these external shocks on the internal economy. For China, the foreign exchange account has become an important part of the base currency, and the proportion is still rising. In order to hedge foreign exchange payments, the People's Bank of China has implemented a tight monetary policy, increased the reserve ratio, and issued a large number of central bank bills in the financial market. These policies are able to counter the presence of large amounts of foreign exchange, but they also reduce the operating profits of commercial banks and other financial institutions. This further degrades the financing environment of enterprises. It can be seen that the exchange rate regime has a great influence on the currency system. In recent decades, four kinds of conflicts have emerged between China's monetary and exchange rate policies. The first, from 1994 to 1996, was the conflict between a rapid increase in foreign exchange reserves and the need to use monetary policy to combat inflation. The second was the conflict between the rapid decline in the growth of foreign reserves in 1998 and the use of monetary policy to ward off deflation. The third, from 1998 to 2000, was the need to maintain exchange rate stability pitted against the inversion of interest rates in local and foreign currencies. The fourth, beginning in 2002, has been the conflict between the pressures associated with RMB appreciation and the overheating of domestic investment. In choosing a policy portfolio, China could opt to adhere to capital controls and a fixed exchange rate regime in order to maintain monetary policy independence. Or it could relax capital flow restrictions and implement a floating exchange rate regime to maintain monetary policy independence. There is also an intermediate state, which would involve insisting on the effectiveness of monetary policy while maintaining capital controls and pegged exchange rates.

4. Conclusions

Based on the Impossible Trinity, there is a *pendulum effect* involving the free flow of capital, exchange rate stability, and monetary policy. That is, if measures are taken to ensure that one of the three objectives of macroeconomic policies is achieved, the other two can be allowed to *swing* to a certain degree. If we attach great importance to the theoretical and policy recommendations of the four Nobel Prize winners (Mundell, Krugman, Stiglitz, Tirol) and the three overseas returnees (Lin Yifu, Yu Yongding, Lang Xianping), the famous professor Fang Xingqi, and others, the policies that China should adopt at this stage are to ensure the effectiveness of monetary policy and to maintain a degree of swing between the flexibility of the exchange rate regime and the degree of capital flow. Specifically, while ensuring the effectiveness of monetary policy, a managed floating exchange rate regime should be implemented to match the controlled capital flows.

(Originally published in *Journal of Liaoning University (Philosophy and Social Sciences Edition)*, Issue 5, 2015, second author: Sun Yexia)

Chapter 7

The Opening up of China's Economy

China's vision for global governance and the development of society involves building a community with a shared future for humankind and was proposed by the CPC Central Committee with Comrade Xi Jinping at its centre. Unswervingly developing an open world economy, sharing the opportunities and benefits created by opening up, and achieving mutual benefits for win-win results are all part of China's new vision for the opening up of the economy.

* * *

Section I The Strategy of Constructing an Economic Circle Around China

1. Regional Economy Is the Trend of World Economic Development

Openness, integration, and mutual benefits are among the objective trends in the development of the market economy, a development that is meant to transcend ideology and social systems. The development of a regional economy has also drawn people's attention and is reflected in the fact that the growth of world trade volume has been much faster than the growth in value of world output. This indicates that progressively greater quantities of the products that are created worldwide are breaking through the borders of individual countries, developing into a regional economy, economic group, and economic circle, and are becoming a part of economic integration. All these functions require economic cooperation as their common content, and the mutual opening of markets among member states as their shared foundation. From the perspective of developmental trends, the conflicts and contradictions between Asian-Pacific, American, and European circles will, it is presumed, eventually be replaced with cooperation and coordination. The mutual opening of markets between regions will come to form a global opening. Already, the development of the regional economy has combined separate economies into a larger economic zone. In this economic zone, a set of planning structures consisting of treaties, laws, organisations, and institutions, equally binding on all parties, will be established. The advantage of China's regional economy lies in solving the problems of the rational division of labour between regions, finding solutions to the comprehensive development of the regional economy, coordinating the distribution of productive forces through regional planning, and specifically, supplementing and implementing the existing divisions of the three objective economic zones of east, middle, and west.

2. The Circle Model of China's Economic Integration with Foreign Countries and the Economic Circle around China

In order to adapt to the development of the world economy, China should initiate, maintain, and expand an international exchange and division of labour among the member states of the world's regional economic groups. Additionally, it should attempt through any means necessary to place itself in the industrial cooperation system of neighbouring countries and regions. To be specific, China should directly develop economic cooperation in the first circle (China and neighbouring Asian-Pacific countries and regions), the second circle (developed capitalist countries in North America and Europe), and the third circle (South American and African countries). Subsequent action should specifically involve indirect regional economic cooperation; that is, China should, through participation in regional economic groups composed of the countries in the first circle, permeate into countries in the second and the third circles utilising the power of regional economic groups.

China is situated in the middle of an economic growth zone of the crescent-shaped Western Pacific *arc of prosperity*. More importantly, economic cooperation in the Asian-Pacific subregion is beginning to surge. All these factors serve to provide China with a precious opportunity to implement its foreign regional economic and trade integration strategies. In the process of strategically and expediently accelerating the *circle-level* regional integration and opening up, it is imperative for China to implement an array of detailed reforms to the economic system, to the industrial organisation, and to the integration policies. In order to fulfil this strategy, the focus should be on the first circle, with the specific goal of establishing an economic circle around China.

There are three strategies, corresponding to China's current geo-economic strategic position, that can be used progressively to achieve this goal. The first strategy involves coastal circles and border circles. As long as the northwest, southwest, and northeast regions have invigorated their cooperation with surrounding and overseas regions, coupled with a timely focus on promoting regional cooperative circles, such as the South China Economic Circle and Yellow Sea Economic Circle, then China will be able to progress from coastal circles to border circles. This goal has an excellent chance of being achieved satisfactorily. The next strategy is to expand small circles into large circles. It will be especially necessary to implement the strategic step of *promoting large circles with small circles and facilitating small and medium sized circles with large circles*. For example, the Tumen River Economic Circle is a small circle. The Northeast Asia Economic Circle and East Asia Economic Circle are middle circles, and the Pacific Economic Circle, also known as the Asian-Pacific Economic Circle, is a large circle. The third strategy will be to facilitate the move from intangible circles to tangible circles. The former refers to the substantive combination of trade, industry, technology, and other fields between the Chinese economic region and the Asian-Pacific region. The latter refers to the institutional and organisational combination of the Chinese economic region and the Asian-Pacific region. China should start by accelerating the development of various intangible circles and strive to develop multilateral regional cooperation in various fields based on bilateral relations. Simultaneously, the conditions should be created for gradually establishing a variety of tangible economic circles ranging from low-level to high-level.

3. Medium and Long-Term Visions of China's Regional Development

Since China's reform and opening up, regional economic changes have had three characteristics: (1) A gradual separation has occurred between resource-producing regions and those whose economies are based on processing industries. (2) The focus of economic growth has moved northward with the shift of the economic growth mode from light industry (for example, textiles) to heavy industry (as exemplified by chemicals production). (3) The existing regional economic ties that have existed since the 1980s have been broken, and new regions have been in the making. Based on these characteristics and looking ahead to the next twenty years, there is a need for China's economy to be divided into seven economic regions: the Northeast Economic Zone, Beijing-Tianjin-Hebei-Shandong Economic Zone, Yangtze River Delta Economic Zone, South China Coastal Economic Zone, Middle Yangtze River Economic Zone, Middle Yellow River Economic Zone, and Southwest Economic Zone. This proposal is based on the principle that geographically adjacent industrial-intensive areas can support relatively independent industrial systems based on the size of their populations and the scale of market demand. Of course, in the longer view, the financial and trade zones will maintain the current three-pillar pattern of the southern, eastern, and northern economic circles.

In addition, the economic relations between mainland China, Hong Kong, and Taiwan are progressing day by day, and the interdependence of these entities is continually deepening. The relations here have been largely characterised by the flow of capital; and the division of labour between markets and industries and the division of labour within industries is gradually becoming more interdependent. The special phenomenon involved, featuring the effects of economic integration but with no institutional arrangement, is called a *natural economic territory*. This development trend will not only help improve the resource utilisation efficiency of the three economies but will also enable them to discover more common interests. After a division of labour is formed, the economies will be integrated into participating in international competition and into improving their status within the international economy.

The possibility of expanding the economic circle around China to Central and South Asia is also of practical significance for the development of China's western region. The western part of Xinjiang is bordered by Afghanistan, Pakistan, and India, and the northwest and north are bordered by Mongolia, Russia, Kazakhstan, Kyrgyzstan, and Tajikistan. In this region, the major religion is Islam, and about half of the people speak the traditional Turkic languages of Central and Western Asia. Therefore, one of the key factors deciding whether China's economic circle can establish a stable and lasting cooperative relationship with Central Asia in the future is the question of whether Xinjiang's economic and social development potential can be strengthened so as to create a *development pole* with the dual developmental effects of internal cohesion and diffusion, and of whether the Central Asian market can gradually be expanded based on its geographical, economic and cultural advantages, thus extending the northwestern border of China's economic circle. In addition, China's Tibet and parts of Xinjiang are geographically integrated with South Asia. These two autonomous regions can rely on their comparative advantages to join in the internal cooperation of South Asia, forming a Pan-South Asian Economic Circle and gradually becoming one of the world's new poles of economic growth.

(Originally published in *Exploration and Free Views*, Issue 4, 1994)

*   *   *

Section II Theory and Strategy of Comparative Advantage, Competitive Advantage, and Intellectual Property Advantage

International competition and the international division of labour should be based on comparative advantage. This is the traditional view of classical economics. The theory of competitive advantage emerged in the 1990s. However, as time has gone by, the limitations of comparative advantage and competitive advantage have become more and more obvious. Theories more in line with actual requirements need to be developed to explain and guide international competition and national economic development. Intellectual property advantage refers to the cultivation and utilisation of the economic advantage bestowed by independent intellectual property rights, with independent core technologies and renowned brands as the main content. This is the third advantage relative to comparative advantage and competitive advantage. This section does not simply deny the comparative advantage theory and the competitive advantage theory but rather makes the case that the intellectual property advantage theory is a new development related to the former two theories.

1. The Development of Comparative Advantage Theory in China and Its Limitations

For a long time, China's participation in the international division of labour and exchange has been guided by the theory of comparative advantage. That is, the difference between countries in their labour productivity and resource endowments affects the direction of world trade and the gains made from it. Through an international division of labour, both trading parties (even the one with an absolute disadvantage) will gain enhanced benefits. Until now, many scholars and practitioners have emphasised the need for China to make use of its comparative advantages in resources. In reality, it should be obvious that *comparative advantage* has great limitations and is not applicable to China's plans.

With the development of international trade, the theory of comparative advantage has become increasingly ineffective at fully and rationally explaining new phenomena. The specific shortcomings of this theory are as follows. First, various preconditions for comparative advantage theory no longer exist in today's world. Whether discussing a comparative cost theory based on differences in labour productivity or a resource endowment theory based on the supply of production factors, the premise of comparative benefits is that the supply and production conditions of each country cannot be changed, and resources and production factors cannot flow between countries. Only under this assumption can the resources and products with comparative advantages have a monopolistic advantage. However, today's production factors and resources are able to flow between countries at rapid rates. Natural resources can be improved, restored, or replaced by new materials, and improvements to the skills and quality of the workforce can overcome the problem of insufficient labour. Second, the comparative cost mentioned in the comparative advantage theory is used to compare domestic products. It does not necessarily mean that domestic products with relatively low costs will definitely have a competitive advantage in international competition. Third, the comparative advantage theory focuses solely on economic factors, while ignoring non-economic factors and economic security. Fourth, comparative advantage focuses only on static comparative benefits, while ignoring dynamic development advantages. Fifth, the comparative advantage theory unilaterally emphasises the importance of capital and implies that as long as enough capital is accumulated, a mechanism for the development of high-tech industries will automatically be created. The theory ignores an important consideration, the cultivation of information, knowledge, and human capital. These factors are especially significant for innovation in the area of information technology. Sixth, comparative advantage demonstrates that if the market price mechanism is fully utilised under free trade conditions, the optimal allocation of scarce resources on an international scale will be achieved. This concept emphasises the role of the market. As long as the market mechanism works and a scarcity of resources exists, comparative advantage will function objectively. To secure this end, the country's development strategy must also conform to the requirements of the principle of comparative advantage. However, this strategy ignores the role of enterprises as the major players of competition. In fact, modern enterprises can allocate scarce resources through conscious strategic decisions and create artificial, comparative advantages. Analysis of China's situation as a large developing country shows that its comparative advantage in resources consists of nothing more than a large amount of cheap labour and a large number of natural resources, available in relatively small quantities per capita. For China, the choice of an industrial and technological structure that is consistent with the comparative advantage determined by resource endowment amounts to nothing more than vigorously developing labour-intensive, low-skilled industries. If followed, this strategy means that China will fall into a *comparative advantage trap*, because the market demand for labour-intensive products is inelastic. China's future market capacity will be small, market expansion will be difficult, trade frictions will intensify, and the terms of trade will deteriorate. In the context of rapid technological innovation, the comparative advantages of labour-intensive products will eventually cease to exist, and the vigorous development of labour-intensive industries will also lead to leakage of imports and savings. The first of these refers to the need for developing countries to use part of their income to import technology-intensive products from abroad for consumption. The second refers to domestic savings leaking abroad to purchase investment goods because of a lack of domestic investment goods production. It is difficult for such an industrial structure and trade pattern to play a role in driving the development of the domestic economy, and this prevents labour-intensive industries from acting as the leading sector driving industrial upgrades (Yang Shujin, 1983).[179]

(I) The Comparative Advantage in Resource Endowments Lacking Technological and Competitive Advantages Cannot Be Sustained

According to the theory of comparative advantage, China has an almost inexhaustible supply of cheap labour. For China, the development of labour-intensive industries has created a strong competitive advantage in international trade. However, once the differences in productivity are taken into account, the advantage stemming from low wages in the exporting from China of labour-intensive products will not be obvious. It may even be viewed as a disadvantage compared to some other countries. For example, in 1998 the average wage in the United States was 47.8 times that of China. However,

179. Yang Shujin. *Theories and Strategies of Economic Development*. Jiangsu People's Publishing House; 1983.

considering the production factor, the cost in the United States of the labour used to create the same amount of added manufacturing value was only 1.3 times that in China. For Japan, the figures were 29.9 and 1.2. Wages in the Philippines and Bolivia were about four times higher than those in China, but unit labour costs were 30-40% lower. Therefore, taking technological factors into account, there is no advantage for us in developing labour-intensive industries, let alone relying on labour-intensive industries to promote the upgrading of industrial structure and achieve convergence with developed countries.

In actual trade, whether a country's potential comparative advantages can be realised and whether trade profits can be obtained depends on whether a country's products with comparative advantages have a competitive advantage. If there is no competitive advantage, products will be excluded from international exchange, and comparative benefits will not be realised. Comparative advantage represents a comparison with other resources of the country and with the situation in another country. It is not necessarily international competitiveness in terms of price. In addition, it is affected by the international financial system and other non-price factors, such as product quality, performance, style, packaging, transportation costs, brand preference, cultural connotations, after-sales service, and differentiation. Therefore, the competitiveness of products in the international market is determined by both price competitiveness and non-price competitiveness. If developing countries are weak in terms of non-price competitiveness, they will lose their competitive advantage even if they have a comparative advantage in low wages.

(II) Choosing an Industrial Structure Based on Comparative Advantages Will Bring Serious Consequences

It is clear to see that in addition to the limitations of the comparative advantage theory analysed previously, if China's trade and economic development strategies are guided solely by comparative advantages, labour-intensive industries that have comparative advantages may not necessarily enjoy competitive advantages in world trade. If China insists on selecting industries and technological structures based on comparative advantages, vigorously developing labour-intensive industries, and exporting labour-intensive products, a series of consequences will result.

First, the conditions for trade will deteriorate. The development of labour-intensive industries in China based on comparative advantages may lead to a deterioration of the conditions for trade, which can be analysed from the perspective of supply and demand. From the perspective of supply, developing countries participate in the international division of labour based on their existing comparative advantages, and their production lies mainly in the areas of primary and labour-intensive industrial products. As a gradually increasing number of developing countries join the process of globalisation, the supply of labour-intensive products will increase, forming the so-called *Fallacy of Composition*, which will intensify the international competition for sales of such products and worsen the conditions for trade. From the perspective of demand, this is also an important reason for the deterioration of conditions for trade in developing countries. Because of the economic development of each country and the increase in per capita incomes, the demand for labour-intensive products in the international market is decreasing day by day. From the perspective of demand structure, the market for traditional labour and resource-intensive products is becoming increasingly saturated, and the international consumer demand structure and its corresponding investment demand structure are being transformed to a higher level. The labour-intensive products exported by China are less processed, low-tech, and of low quality. Exports of such low and medium-grade, labour-intensive products are bound to encounter shrinking international markets and declining prices. The conditions surrounding trade in high-tech products with developed countries are becoming even more unfavourable. In this regard, Prebisch (1950) and Singh (1950)[180] conducted theoretical and empirical analyses of trade in primary products in the 1950s, while Sakar and Singer (1991)[181] made corresponding analyses of trade in labour-intensive manufactured products in the 1990s.

Considering the deteriorating conditions for trade, many industries that enjoy comparative and competitive advantages are not suitable for China's participation. One example is the textile industry, about which many people express optimism. This is a typical labour-intensive industry, but in the international division of labour, being involved in this industry is not the best choice for China due

---

180. Prebisch, Raul (1950) 'The Economic Development of Latin American and its Principal Problems, New York: United National Problems, April 1950 pp. 9-15 and Singer, H.W. (1950), "The Distribution of Gains between Investing and Borrowing Countries' *American Economic Review*, 1950, Vol. 40, No. 2, pp. 473-485

181. Sarkar and Singer (1991, Sarkar, Prabirjit and Singer, H.W., 'Manufactured Exports of Developing Countries and their Terms of Trade Since 1965', *World Development*, 1991, Vol. 19, No. 4 pp-333-340

to the slow growth of the global market, and because the design and subsequent processing of fabrics, which require a high level of knowledge and sophisticated technologies, are not China's fortes. There are numerous examples of this kind.

Second, labour-intensive products have low demand elasticity, low added value, and are prone to *pauperised growth* in exports. At the same time, the export market for China's labour-intensive products is too concentrated, and the production sites are not evenly distributed. This makes these products extremely vulnerable to the impact of international economic fluctuations. As stated by Todaro (1991), a specialist in the field of developmental economics, third world countries with abundant supplies of unskilled labour are trapped in a stagnant situation that perpetuates *comparative interests* in non-technical, non-productive activities, because they specialise in producing products that make intensive use of unskilled labour, offer poor demand prospects, and suffer from weak worldwide trade conditions. As a result, the growth of capital, an entrepreneurial spirited environment, and enhancement of technical skills in these countries will be restrained.

Third, the discriminatory trade policies that developed countries employ against developing countries have hindered China's labour-intensive products by erecting countless trade barriers, and space for development in the international market is becoming increasingly limited. These factors have put China's export trade in labour-intensive products in a subordinate and disadvantaged position within the international division of labour, with the result that China is at risk of falling into a *comparative advantage trap*. In the current social space, labour-intensive products in which less developed countries have competitive advantages account for only a small portion of the whole. When many less developed countries with similar resource endowments come to carve up the competitive advantages of these products, each country will have fewer types of products. Moreover, and unlike small countries, China, as a vast developing country, cannot possibly achieve sustained and rapid development with a limited number of labour-intensive products. If China ignores the fact that it is a big country, and proceeds to engage in specialised production, it will never have a huge global market. At the same time, the advantages of natural resource endowment that exist in various regions of the country, with large differences between them, will not be fully utilised.

The above analysis shows that it will be difficult for China to accomplish the arduous task of economic development solely by relying on comparative advantages. This brings us to the question: is the theory of comparative advantage obsolete and worthless? The answer is a resounding *no*. Abundant natural resources and low labour costs are favourable conditions for economic development. The development of many now-developed countries was driven initially by industries that had access to rich resource endowments. But if China is satisfied with these factors alone, it will tend to fall into the *comparative advantage trap*. In view of the limitations of traditional comparative advantages, some scholars have maintained that China's competitiveness should be improved on the basis of competitive advantages.

Most scholars, however, believe that comparative advantage and competitive advantage do not exist in an all-or-nothing relationship, but rather, that the two advantages are compatible to a certain extent. The important thing is to find an approach that can transform potential comparative advantage into competitive advantage. An in-depth analysis reveals that this approach is represented by technological innovation. If developing countries attach importance to technological progress, they can prevent the deterioration of trade conditions and promote economic development. Yin Xiangshuo and Xu Jianbin[182] proved through models that if developing countries specialise in producing and exporting low-tech products, their trade conditions will in fact deteriorate in the long run. This will lead to a reduction in their original comparative advantages, making it logical for them to implement a strategy of import substitution and instead to increase domestic production of high-tech products. However, if a market process centred on low-tech products is the only one that exists, it will not improve the trade conditions of developing countries. Nor will it increase the levels of welfare in these countries or narrow the gap with the developed world. If, conversely, developing countries take the opportunity to use government education and technology policies to develop education and improve human capital, while also promoting scientific research and improving technology, they will eventually narrow the gap with developed countries. Moreover, it is advisable for developing countries to implement educational, scientific, and technological policies to promote the development of high-tech industries before trade conditions deteriorate. If developing countries promote technological development from the

---

182. Yin, Xiangshuo, Xu, Jianbin. On the terms of trade, comparative advantage, and technological progress of backward countries [J]. *World Economic Journal*, 2002 (6).

beginning, they may affect world product prices before the conditions for trade deteriorate. In this way, they can hope to prevent a further degradation of their trade conditions, and to narrow the gap with the developed countries.

2. The Development of Competitive Advantage Theory in China and Its Shortcomings

Since the 1980s, Michael Porter has successively published his famous trilogy: *Competitive Strategy* (1980), *Competitive Advantage* (1985), and *National Competitive Advantage* (1990), which proposes and improves upon the theory of competitive advantage. Porter believes that the fundamental reason why a country can prosper is that it has a competitive advantage in the international market. This competitive advantage stems from the competitive advantage of the country's leading industry, and the competitive advantage of the leading industry derives from superior production efficiency due to enterprises employing innovative mechanisms. The national competitive advantage to which Porter refers is the competitive advantage of enterprises and industries, and it includes six factors: production, domestic demand, relevant supporting industries, the strategic structure of enterprises and competition between them, the role of the government, and opportunities (including important inventions, technological breakthroughs, major changes in the factors of production, supply and demand, and other disruptions).

Chinese scholars began introducing Porter's theory of national competitive advantage in the early 1990s, and research in the area reached its peak in the mid-to-late 1990s. Some scholars put comparative advantage and competitive advantage theories in parallel, believing that the comparative advantage theory was outdated and that primacy should be given to the competitive advantage theory. More and more scholars, however, concluded that the relationship between the two could not be severed, and that a path from comparative to competitive advantage should instead be sought. Ultimately, scholars still incline towards competitive advantage, and rarely mention the flaws of competitive advantage theory. In reality, Porter's theory has its own limitations as well, and fails to understand the actual situation in China.

First, many conclusions concerning competitive advantage are not useful for explaining the situations of developing countries. The diamond model is based primarily on the growth processes of developed countries, especially the United States and Japan. Porter believes that the more demanding and advanced the market is, the higher the competitiveness of the industry. In most developing countries, however, the development of many industries is still in its infancy or growth stage, and these industries are unable to meet the challenges and demands of the market. If those challenges and demands are codified by developing countries in the form of laws (such as strict environmental protection laws or product quality laws), then when these countries involve themselves in international competition, their related industrial enterprises will find it difficult to compete with enterprises from developed countries. In the end, they will lose their international competitiveness.

Second, the implicit premise of the theory of competitive advantage is that capital is abundant, and that enterprises can easily obtain advanced technology and management experience. This is not completely consistent with real-world conditions. Capital flows on an international scale are still subject to many restrictions, and some poor countries have limited capital accumulation capabilities. Especially for some developing countries, backward technology and insufficient management experience pose even greater problems. Therefore, a certain degree of monopoly and trade protection is necessary when supporting one's own nascent industries, and free competition will only deal a severe blow to national industries. When analysing Japan's experience, most economists cite the industrial support policy implemented by the Ministry of International Trade and Industry as an important reason for Japan's economic successes, and the fact that the competitive advantage theory ignores this point is obviously a fundamental defect.

Third, the diamond system includes several attributes, and simplified answers tend to obscure some of the most important parts of the question. This reflects the complexity of the factors affecting international competition and national economic development after World War II. There are many aspects affecting a country's economic development, and different countries experience a variety of influential factors. However, to take too many factors into consideration is to go to another extreme, and if all factors regardless of their degree of influence are taken into account, the real key factors will often be obscured. Scientific research involves abstracting laws or other decisive factors from complex phenomena, rather than listing all the factors that may be influential.

Fourth, Porter's analysis does not consider the role of multinational corporations. Numerous examples show clearly that the role of multinational corporations in international trade and the international division of labour cannot be ignored. At the same time, industrial competitive advantages do not always depend entirely on domestic factors.

Fifth, the logic of Porter's model is that a country's competitiveness depends on the competitiveness of its enterprises and industries. Therefore, Porter's analysis starts from the competitive strategies of enterprises. However, he attributes the competitive advantage of enterprises almost completely to the power of the external market and assumes that this power is consistent with the enterprise's market positioning and the ability to build barriers to entry and exit. The external environment of an enterprise is very important, but overemphasising external factors such as domestic markets, related industries, competition, opportunities, and the government while ignoring the company's own factors is also unconvincing.

Especially in the case of China, a multitude of factors are involved in competitive advantage, and it is hard to take account of all these factors within a short period of time. Unless a strategy with appropriate priorities is formulated, the quality of development will be adversely affected. Porter himself has admitted that a country's competitive advantage does not need to incorporate all the key elements; the lack of a handful of these elements will not make seeking and obtaining a competitive advantage impossible. However, Porter fails to explain how a country can develop from having one or two kinds of resources (such as natural resources) to the point where it is equipped with an overall interactive competitive advantage. Further, and as explained, a country needs monopolistic resources if it is to achieve sustainable development and lasting competitiveness. But as analysed earlier, substitutes can often be found for natural resources, and in many cases these resources can be traded between countries, meaning that monopolies are difficult to secure. Meanwhile, a nation's greatest wealth is often one of the intangible resources: knowledge. Owning the advantage of independent intellectual property rights is the key for an enterprise and a country to obtain monopolistic profits.

3. Constructing the Theory and Strategy for an Intellectual Property Advantage

The shortcomings of the theory of comparative advantage have made China realise that as it seeks to promote selective catch-up and the high-efficiency development of its economy, China should not rely solely on the development of industries with comparative advantage. Being satisfied with comparative advantage may also lead to a deterioration in trade conditions and causes it to fall into the comparative advantage trap. A multitude of factors are involved in competitive advantage, and they do not, in sum, correspond to the realistic requirements of developing countries. In the new century, knowledge, brands, and core technologies are playing more important roles than ever. These roles are of great significance for enterprises if they are to participate in world competition, enhance comprehensive national strength, and contribute to maintaining national security. Therefore, it is urgent for emerging countries to cultivate intellectual property advantages, thus making them more competitive. In principle, knowledge and technology have no national boundaries, and less developed countries can imitate or buy advanced technology. For companies and even countries, however, the most advanced technology and renowned brands are often not available. Without a system of independent scientific and technological innovation or a system for developing brands, China can only be controlled by others.

At present, in view of the theoretical and practical shortcomings of comparative advantage and competitive advantage, China should strenuously cultivate and develop the *third advantage*, that is, the *intellectual property advantage*. The intellectual property advantage refers to the economic advantage that results from gradually coming to own independent intellectual property rights, with their main content consisting of independent core technologies and well-established independent brands. This is the third advantage that exists alongside comparative advantage and competitive advantage.

Intellectual property advantage is not completely opposed to comparative advantage and competitive advantage but is both different from and related to them. It cannot be separated from the fundamental elements of comparative advantage and competitive advantage; rather, it amounts to a core national advantage that has its basis in established comparative advantage and competitive advantage. Free from the theoretical shortcomings of general competitive advantage, it features the economic and competitive advantages that are innate to core technologies and prestige brands. Intellectual property advantage should not only be embodied in China's high-tech industrial enterprises; it also needs to be among the attributes of strategically significant industrial sectors, which must progressively master core technologies and develop famous brands based on independent research. A recognised strength of China's strategic industries needs to be their independent development of unique products and processes, and at the same time, their establishment of technical standards based on independent intellectual property rights. Intellectual property advantage should also be reflected in China's traditional national industries and low-end product sectors, including labour-intensive industrial sectors. Independent intellectual property must play a part in creating a national brand with influence in the international arena, and in key low and medium-level technologies.

Comparative advantage is a static advantage determined by a country's resource endowments and transaction conditions, and it is a condition for obtaining competitive advantage, which is the result of a comprehensive ability to transform potential advantages into actual advantages. Comparative advantage, as a potential advantage, can manifest itself as real export competitiveness only when it is transformed into a competitive advantage. To achieve the structural upgrading of China's export products, China must be guided by comprehensive international economic competition and must transform its existing comparative advantages into competitive advantages. The key is to create and cultivate China's own intellectual property advantages.

Only through the advantages of independent intellectual property rights can the competitive advantages of enterprises and industries be established and maintained well into the future. In other words, intellectual property advantages are a necessary condition for lasting high-end competitive advantages. Porter emphasises the importance of high-level human capital and R&D in the first item of the diamond system. In countries with high levels of material capital, companies must hire talents with high human capital, and must emphasise the importance of R&D and new product development. This is a prime requirement and standard if these companies are to use their own comparative advantages and gain competitive advantages in the international market.

In addition, and compared with comparative advantages and competitive advantages, intellectual property advantages more appropriately reflect the character of the times and the requirements of economic development. Comparative and competitive advantages are often measured by import and export value or by net export value. Import and export values, however, do not necessarily represent the true state of international competitiveness, or reflect the industry's role in the domestic industrial structure, industrial upgrade status, and contribution to GDP. This is due to the fact that export and import value are affected by many factors, such as economic fluctuations, the country's foreign policy, and so forth. Similarly, it is not necessarily the export volume that makes a major contribution to GDP; domestic demand is also an important aspect that cannot be ignored. Therefore, some data on comparative advantage and competitive advantage may not reflect the essence of the problem. The role of intellectual property rights in this new era is decisive. Only a suitable technological developmental path can narrow the gap with developed countries and allow the economy to selectively catch up with or outstrip them.

The cultivation of intellectual property advantages involves a comprehensive and long-term effort. Compared with developed countries, there is a big gap between China's advantages and disadvantages in the area of intellectual property rights. This requires us to recognise trends, accelerate development, and formulate a lasting and comprehensive catch-up strategy. What I want to emphasise here is that *intellectual property advantage does not mean high-tech*. It should have different meanings and priorities for different periods, industries, and research institutions. In its short-term strategy, manufacturing industry should focus on *learning by doing*, and thus develop practical technologies. Enterprises should be the foundation of technological innovation, and the country should continue to raise its technological standards. When devising a medium-term strategy, it is necessary to recognise the development trend of the world's industries, and to promote research and development in areas such as biochemistry, electronic technology, and information technology. The state should promote cooperation and coordination while strengthening the protection of intellectual property rights, with multi-system scientific research institutions as the main actors. As for long-term strategies, it is necessary to strengthen basic research, with national and university research institutions as the driving entities, to increase capital and investment in human resources, to improve the quality of citizens, and to create and develop a national scientific and technological innovation system. In addition, all regions and departments must pay attention to creating renowned brands, protecting the original national famous brands, and expanding new famous brands at home and abroad.

China is faced with a new era full of opportunities and challenges and, in the view of our Shanghai-school economists, needs to maximise the dynamic benefits of trade development and better promote the sound adjustment of industrial structure through foreign trade. China must develop and use its core technologies with independent intellectual property rights, while creating international brands with independent intellectual property rights, and using the theory of intellectual property advantage as a strategy to deal with economic globalisation and the development of foreign trade. Moreover, it should base itself on the combination of comparative advantages and competitive advantages in order to vigorously develop national enterprise groups with control over holdings, technologies (especially core technologies), and brands (especially prestige brands). China should prioritise the cultivation and use of intellectual property advantages and establish itself as the *world factory* instead of the world's processing factory. The aim in this case is to rapidly complete the transformation from being a large trading country to being a trading powerhouse. An approach that merely emphasises the protection of domestic and foreign intellectual property rights, and that does not stress the creation of independent intellectual property rights, is not the *roadmap* or philosophy for technological development that China really needs. Nor is a strategy that depends solely on the continuous introduction of foreign capital, technology, and foreign brands, that wallows in openly subservient thinking, and that ignores the double-sided effects of multinational R&D institutions in China while blindly allowing powerful countries to promote *scientific and technological colonialism.*

(Originally published in *Seeking Truth*, Issue 6, 2004, second author: Lian Shu)

* * *

Section III Pursuing Not Only *Made in China*, but Also *the Chinese Standard*

At the recent Central Economic Work Conference, China was urged to continue to improve its independent innovative capabilities and to accelerate the construction of an innovative country. If China is to raise its self-innovation and international competitiveness to the level required, there is an urgent need to create and protect intellectual property in the field of technology. In recent years, China has redoubled its efforts in a variety of areas and has recorded impressive results. Quite a few problems, however, have also surfaced.

First, China is finding it impossible to correctly evaluate and deal with technical barriers to trade, because laws related to intellectual property rights are partly deficient. Due to the accelerated integration of intellectual property rights and technical standards, for example, some forms and fields of intellectual property rights that had not previously attracted attention have now become key points. However, it appears that the existing *Intellectual Property Law* lacks appropriate provisions for dealing with these rights, and that as a result, the corresponding parts of the *Anti-Monopoly Law* and *Anti-Unfair Competition Law* cannot be properly enforced. For instance, there is a lack of practical and effective protection schemes for intellectual property rights in the field of Chinese medicine. In addition, the incomplete, inconsistent, and non-standard nature of existing technical regulations means that the current market access and market supervision systems are not sound enough. This has led to a failure to effectively implement joint intellectual property legal provisions, and in this case, technical barriers to trade cannot be evaluated or dealt with correctly.

Second, there are shortcomings in the institutional environment that is meant to promote the formation of protection mechanisms in the area of technical intellectual property, with this environment revealing many defects as the socialist market economic system has gradually advanced. These flaws are not only reflected in aspects such as the mechanism for the evaluation of scientific and technological achievement that emphasises quantity but disregards quality. They are also found in the lack of clear requirements applying to the patent output of national scientific and technological plans, and in the dislocation of the major players of market economy competition and of the national science and technology plan. Finally, they are also reflected in the lack of technological innovation awareness, the weak basis for scientific research, the lack of a good technological innovation mechanism, the pursuit of profitability, and the decentralised operations of most technological innovation organisations. The overall situation still needs to be improved.

Third, the establishment of a relatively sound system of technical barriers to trade needs to be strengthened. Due to the lack of core independent intellectual property rights, a sizable gap exists between China and developed countries in terms of transforming international standards and advanced foreign standards into domestic standards, and also in the area of participating in and leading the drafting of international standards. Especially in the field of high-tech standardisation, China's influence is small. In addition, the lack of connection between the formulation of certain technical standards on the one hand, and scientific research and production on the other, makes it hard to adapt in time to the needs of the market and to rapid technological development. Further, although standards have been established relating to Intelligent Grouping & Resource Sharing (IGRS), High-Density Digital Laser Disc System (EVD), mobile 3G network mode (TD-SCDMA), a wireless network security protocol (WAPI), and other systems, China remains in an awkward market situation due to the misalignment or inappropriateness of choices by decision makers.

To solve the existing problems, China needs to adopt new ideas and new countermeasures as soon as possible. First, China should learn from the successful experience of foreign intellectual property law protection, and actively improve its relevant legal systems. In order to prevent enterprises and business groups from abusing *Intellectual Property Law*, domestic legislative departments can learn from the successful experiences of the United States, Japan, and the EU in intellectual property protection. For example, there are impressive benefits to be gained by establishing a relatively sound antitrust law, and by improving the institutional construction of intellectual property departments within multinational companies. China must facilitate the formulation of an *Anti-Monopoly Law*, be mindful of the legislative work of the antitrust review in intellectual property licensing to restrict foreign companies' abuse of technical standards and patents in the domestic market and focus on their monopolistic behaviours. Additionally, it is necessary to reform and improve China's technical regulation system and operational mechanism in accordance with scientific methods. For example, a methodical classification of China's current technical laws and regulations must be undertaken to remove the components that violate international practices and do not meet the requirements of the principles of the socialist market economy. Concurrently, and in line with China's security requirements, compulsory standards related to safety, hygiene, health, and environmental protection should be formulated. Relevant laws, technical standards, and inspection systems that are targeted at and aimed to prohibit and restrict related foreign technical products should be formulated and implemented. Meanwhile, products that do not meet technical standards should be rejected.

Second, China should transform the formation mechanism of technical intellectual property rights as soon as possible, putting it on a market track, and speeding up the correction of existing defects in its institutional environment. In addition, enterprises need to raise their awareness of intellectual property rights, especially the protection of technical intellectual property rights. They need to increase technological investment and understand national macro-control policies, as well as the domestic and international development trends of the technology field. Governments at all levels must also earnestly implement the spirit of the Program of Action for the Protection of Intellectual Property Rights (2006–2007). The short-term work and associated measures should lay emphasis on combating piracy and trademark infringement in the commodity trading market, on strengthening the rectification and control of key issues of patent infringement, and on consolidating the protection of intellectual property rights in imports and exports. In the longer term, it is necessary to improve the system of laws and regulations, establish an efficient law enforcement coordination mechanism, improve the level and capabilities of corporate intellectual property protection, give full play to industrial associations and intellectual property intermediary organisations, strengthen publicity, and intensify training.

Third, China should continue to construct a technical trade barrier system, taking the lead from common international practices while also adapting the system to China's actual conditions. China must carefully analyse the situation surrounding areas of existing practice that are deficient or lacking, and selectively concentrate its efforts on creating a compendium of enterprise-level technical standards, industry technical standards, and regional technical standards that have extensive coverage and are of the highest technical level, which serve the national interests to the greatest extent possible. Such standards are urgently needed. Simultaneously, it will be necessary to reform the standardisation system of work management, and to establish a new model for enterprises to serve as major players in formulating the earlier-mentioned technical standards. The objective must be to form enterprise technology alliances that can break through the barriers of foreign intellectual property and technical standards, while encouraging domestic enterprises to apply for patents abroad and to break into the world market. Moreover, it is urgent to participate in international standardisation activities, so as to cultivate talents in this area and to promote the implementation of independent intellectual property rights. China also needs to support the use in industry of patented technologies, thus promoting the formation and development of the independent intellectual property rights of enterprises. The obvious benefit will be to lay a solid micro-foundation for these technologies. It is possible to adopt advanced international standards in numerous areas with little negative impact and in accordance with specific national conditions, whether through adopting these standards in full, partially, or completely adjusting them, or involving both national and international elements so as to satisfy the requirements of enterprises, industries, regions, and the country.

Fourth, key industries such as telecommunications should be highlighted, and it is necessary for the government, industry, and academia to jointly implement the *comprehensive strategy for international standards*. The annual output of mobile phones in China has reached 303 million, accounting for about half of the global production of these items. However, more than 90% of the Chinese character input software installed on mobile phones is imported from abroad. For this reason, hundreds of millions of yuan in patent fees have to be paid each year. The patent fee for each phone amounts to 0.3 U.S. dollars. Moreover, the standards adopted for Chinese character input software and developed by foreign companies mostly adhere to the standards issued by China in 1980. The mandatory Chinese character standards from 2000 have not been implemented. In domestic and foreign business circles, it is observed that *third-class companies sell labour, second-class companies sell products, first-class companies sell patents, and super-first-class companies sell standards*. If a company wants to truly become stronger and larger, it must incorporate international standards into its business strategy. Instead of complacently accepting *Made in China*, the Chinese people should focus on *Created in China*, and according to Chinese standards.

Currently, the average age of international standards is 3.5 years, while the figure for China's existing 21,000 national standards is 10.2 years, and there are 9,500 antiquated national standards that are no longer applicable. In recent years, 60% of China's exports have suffered from direct and potential economic losses of about fifty billion U.S. dollars. One of the reasons is that the antiquated standards are not aligned with new international standards. For example, there is a big gap between the national standards for washing machine noise and similar international standards. This results in about 20% of washing machines in the Chinese market being forced to *delist*. A gratifying message came in October 2006. The State Administration of Radio, Film, and Television issued a self-developed mobile multimedia broadcasting industry standard that included mobile phones and TVs. Although this was not an international standard, the twenty-one core patents covered by it are mostly at world-leading levels. Concurrently, the National Standards Committee stated that it would take three years to solve the problem of obsolete standards in China, and that the country should strive to reach the international advanced level by 2015. In the future, government, industry, and academia should jointly launch activities aimed at competing for international standards based on the technology patents of enterprises, and actively strengthening international recognition and negotiation capabilities. These endeavours will allow China to become a large and strong country in the area of international standards.

(Originally published in *Wen Hui Bao*, December 13, 2006)

* * *

Section IV Strengthen Independent Innovation to Maintain National Industrial Security

In recent years, foreign companies, especially multinational corporations, have changed their investment strategies in China. One of the most prominent changes has seen foreign capital accelerate mergers with and acquisition of leading domestic enterprises, especially large state-owned enterprises. Increasing numbers of cases are to be found in this category, and more than ten key enterprises in China's equipment manufacturing industry have merged. As national enterprises have been acquired by foreign capital, various problems have surfaced. When these key enterprises, prominent firms, and industry leaders with a good momentum of development have been acquired and have come under the control of foreign capital, they have lost their independent innovation rights, high-quality assets, technical strength, brands, and markets. As a result, the technical teams and technical capabilities cultivated through years of independent research and development have been controlled, utilised, and even eliminated by foreign capital. Vast sums in enterprise profits have flowed out, and the brand value of enterprises and their products has suddenly been swallowed up by foreign investors. This has increasingly attracted the attention of senior leaders, economic analysts, and the rest of society.

1. Industrial Leaders Are the Foundation for Building an Innovative Country and the Embodiment of Major National Interests

The attempted acquisition of China's Xuzhou Construction Machinery Group (XCMG) by the Carlyle Group, an American private equity group, is currently in the process of approval, and provides an excellent example. XCMG ranks among the top firms in China's machinery industry in terms of total assets, annual sales, and the market competitiveness of its major products such as crane trucks. XCMG is not only the vanguard of China's construction machinery industry, but also among the leading enterprises in China's entire machinery sector, where its position is very important. In 2006, XCMG ranked first among China's construction machinery enterprises with an operating income of twenty billion yuan. In 2007, the company's planned targets were to realise an operating income of 24.83 billion yuan, representing a year-on-year increase of 22.5%, and a product sales income of 20.52 billion yuan, a year-on-year increase of 17%. At the end of 2010, the company was maintaining its lead position in the domestic industry, was becoming an important participant in the international market, and was achieving the status of a well-known brand. It reached an operating income of fifty billion yuan, sales income of thirty billion yuan, and export earnings of one billion U.S. dollars. These achievements ranked it among the top ten international construction machinery enterprises. So why would such an important state-owned giant be sold to a foreign investor?

In the revised agreement, Carlyle has made major concessions and compromises, turning the acquisition into a joint venture in which XCMG holds a 55% stake and Carlyle a 45% stake. The revised version stipulates that the position of chairperson of the board is to be held by the Chinese side, and the agreement also includes other conditions that seem to be beneficial to China. Despite all these favourable terms, observers still believe that the government departments will not approve this merger.

The crux of the problem has been that XCMG is a landmark enterprise in China's construction machinery industry. What China wants is not the funds supplied by Carlyle for the acquisition, or the advanced technology provided, but the dominance of the development of China's construction machinery industry, the security of China's industry, and the development of China's own internationally famous brand. If XCMG is acquired by a foreign investor, other key enterprises in the same industry or other manufacturing industries will follow its example. If this occurs, then China's entire national industrial base, developed over decades, will be vulnerable to foreign capital and to control by foreign forces. If this pattern continues, China's national industry will become an appendage of foreign capital. Moreover, the equipment manufacturing industry represents a strategic focus for China. It created the foundation for China to break through foreign technological blockades and allowed it to establish a strong military industry. Many of XCMG's products, such as bulldozers, loaders, and tower cranes, have dominated the domestic market and prevented foreign brands from entering. Various foreign products have been squeezed out of the Chinese market by Chinese companies, such as those producing equipment for the concrete machinery industry.

The background story of the XCMG merger and acquisition (M&A) case is that foreign capital has adopted a flanking tactic after proving unable to penetrate China's construction machinery market directly. It has sought to take advantage of China's reforms to state-owned enterprises in order, through acquisitions, to win control of an important area of the country's manufacturing. With this in mind, it has not hesitated to make concessions, and high-ranking officials from the U.S. government have come to China to add to the persuasive effort. The political intentions are self-evident. Carlyle's attempted acquisition of XCMG is actually a strategic step through which foreign capital aims to control and dominate China's construction machinery industry. The clear and present danger is that actions like these may cause a domino effect and destroy the national construction machinery industry entirely. The facts concerning joint ventures between Chinese and foreign companies in the past twenty years have shown that in the mergers and acquisitions of Chinese domestic companies that have occurred, the tactics that buyers have customarily used include dissolving the R&D team of the merged company, wiping out its R&D strength, and destroying the independent Chinese brand. In recent years, cases of foreign mergers and acquisitions, such as those involving China's Nanfu Battery and Wuxi Weifu, have illustrated the true purpose of foreign capital when it sets out to acquire leading Chinese enterprises.

At present, China represents the world's largest national construction development effort, and this situation is expected to continue in the future. If XCMG is acquired by foreign capital, and if China's construction and engineering machinery industry passes to foreign control, then China will have to purchase the heavy machinery used in construction at inflated prices from foreign investors. Only then will it truly see the great harm caused by such foreign acquisitions.

2. To Establish a Risk Prevention Mechanism for Foreign Mergers and Acquisitions to Maintain National Industrial Security

To protect China's interests, it is necessary to pay close attention to foreign M&As, which should be of serious concern to Chinese society. China needs to have a clear understanding of the intentions of foreign capital entities in acquiring China's leading companies. It is wishful thinking to believe that buy-ups by foreign capital will help China achieve greater development. Regardless of whether enterprises acquired by foreign capital are national enterprises or not, Chinese enterprises with good developmental momentum are precisely those enterprises that are able to achieve independent leadership, to focus on independent innovation, and to strive to acquire foreign enterprises, rather than plodding along with domestic joint ventures. The claim that acquisitions by foreign capital do not lead to reduced fiscal tax revenues and employee wages is erroneous, since it ignores the fact that huge profits and the future cash flows of the company will be obtained on a permanent basis by foreign investors. Another adverse effect is that the people who actually control the company will be under looser supervision and may pursue their immediate interests at the expense of the long-term interests of the enterprise. In short, without the development and strengthening of national enterprises, it will be impossible to achieve prosperity quickly either for the country or for the people. I, and my colleagues, call on the government to take immediate measures to ensure that due importance is attached to national industrial security, that the government effectively strengthens its protection of national industries, and that they establish a risk prevention mechanism for foreign mergers and acquisitions.

For these reasons, my colleagues and I believe that Carlyle's attempted acquisition of XCMG does not comply with the relevant provisions of national industrial policy and would damage the security of China's industry. Therefore, the arguments advanced in support of Carlyle's acquisition of XCMG are unfounded. The departments of the State Council should defend national interests and disapprove of mergers like this.[183]

Additionally, the government must promptly discard the idea that *absorbing foreign strategic investors* can offer the primary means for large, state-owned enterprises to restructure, and should delete investment attraction from the government's list of assessment indicators. It must be emphasised that the reform of large state-owned enterprises should mainly use domestic resources to solve financial problems and should achieve technological progress through outward-bound mergers and acquisitions, independent research and development, and the introduction of new technology.

Furthermore, Carlyle, in this case, tried to take advantage of the local government's eagerness to attract new investments, and drew up a huge, non-binding investment attraction plan. Advanced as a

---

183. https://www.reuters.com/article/carlyle-xugong-idUSSHA323138 20080722

bidding condition, this provided a reason for selling state-owned enterprises. Lessons should be learned from this, and procedures and detailed rules for the sale of state-owned assets as part of the reform of state-owned enterprises (SOE) should be formulated as soon as possible. The transaction supervision system should be improved as well.

Moreover, and as a matter of urgency, China should establish a national strategic interest management mechanism. It should include the drawing up of a list of industries and enterprises that must be controlled by the state, removing the eligibility of these enterprises for restructuring, and establishing a case monitoring and early warning mechanism for foreign mergers and acquisitions in China that involve domestic enterprises. This mechanism should encompass a wide variety of activities, including conducting a broad range of consultations utilising experts in the respective fields, improving the strict system charged with reviewing government agencies, and implementing institutionalised public opinion surveys and public monitoring.

Lastly, China should step up its efforts to reformulate and improve the *Anti-Unfair Competition Law*, the *Anti-Monopoly Law,* and other relevant legislation so as to ensure the security of China's industry.

(Originally published in *China Reform News*, April 5, 2007, second author: Li Bingyan)

*   *   *

Section V Build a Community with a Shared Future for Humankind, and Lead the Healthy Development of Economic Globalisation

In today's world, material wealth continues to accumulate, science and technology are advancing day by day, and human civilisation has developed to an unprecedented level. Conversely, there are constant regional conflicts, the gap between rich and poor is reaching a critical level, problems of terrorism and refugees are prominent, and the world is faced with increasing uncertainty. How should China address these issues and what measures should it take? From the 2016 Hangzhou Summit of G20 Leaders and the Lima Summit of APEC Leaders to the 2017 Davos World Economic Forum and the Belt and Road International Cooperation Summit Forum, President Xi Jinping has offered profound answers with a grand historical vision, visionary ideas, innovative thoughts, and new strategies. He has provided a complete and systematic Chinese plan for leading the healthy development of economic globalisation.

1. China's Vision of Building a Community with a Shared Future for Humankind

To build a community with a shared future for humankind is the Chinese vision, put forward by the CPC Central Committee, with Comrade Xi Jinping at its core, for global governance and the further development of human society. This vision conforms to today's trends, fully embodies the sense of responsibility to provide mutual assistance and shows the way forward for promoting human welfare and the maintenance of world peace.

In the first half of the 20th century, the most urgent desire of humanity, which had suffered the catastrophes of two world wars, was to make peace. In the 1950s and 1960s the most powerful longing of colonial peoples was to achieve national independence. After the end of the Cold War, the most ardent demands of all parties were to expand cooperation and to develop together. Peace and development can be said to be the common aspirations of all humankind. *China must listen to the voices of the people, carry the historical torch, and continue to march forward courageously on the marathon track of peace and development.* To establish a fair and reasonable international order, a series of recognised principles have been formulated in modern times to further the evolution of state relations. One example is the principle of equality and sovereignty among countries that found expression in the *Peace of Westphalia*,[184] which was drawn up more than 360 years ago. Similar examples include the spirit of international humanitarianism established by the *Geneva Convention*, the basic principles for handling international relations and maintaining world peace and security established by the *Charter of the United Nations* more than seventy years ago, the Five Principles of Peaceful Coexistence advocated more than sixty years ago by the Bandung Conference, and forty years ago, the United Nations General Assembly's declaration and program of action on establishing a new international economic order.

To pass on the torch of peace from generation to generation, to maintain the driving force of development, and to make civilisation shine brightly is what people of all countries have expected and what politicians

---

184. https://en.wikipedia.org/wiki/Peace_of_Westphalia

of this generation should do. China's solution has been to build a community with a shared future for humankind, to achieve a win-win status, and to partake of the common benefits. The destiny of humankind should be in the hands of all the world's people, and it is these same people who should govern global affairs worldwide. World security should be maintained by all countries; international rules should be formulated jointly by every country; and the benefits of development should be shared by all people. The community of a shared future for humankind is the development and sublimation of a community of ethnic groups, interests, and regions. It focuses on the sustainable development of human civilisation and the establishment of a new civilised order. It goes beyond the narrow vision of a nation or a state and reflects the ruling ideas and values of the Communist Party of China.

2. Adhere to the Chinese Concept of Win-Win Cooperation

Every country has its own national interests, and its first priority is to run its own affairs well. However, other countries also have the right to develop themselves, and they too must safeguard their own interests. Therefore, each country should safeguard its own interests through embracing a broader vision, and they should not harm the interests of others. As President Xi Jinping has said, 'We must unswervingly develop an open world economy, share opportunities and benefits in opening up, and achieve mutual benefits with win-win results'[185]. We should adhere to the concept of win-win cooperation and actively build a new type of international relations centred on win-win cooperation. We must insist that all countries, big or small, strong or weak, rich or poor, take the lead in pursuing a new path of dialogue instead of speaking in confrontational terms. We must urge them to pursue partnerships rather than alliances and must emphasise that we need to balance justice with benefits, standing together regardless of the situation. The concept of win-win cooperation transcends the boundaries of race, culture, country, and ideology, and provides a new perspective for solving the practical problems facing human beings and for thinking about the future development of humankind. It offers a rational and feasible plan. The concept of win-win cooperation advocates that we

185. Xi Jinping, 'Sharing the responsibility of the times and promoting global development' Keynote speech at the opening ceremony of the World Economic Forum Annual Meeting 2017, January 17, 2017. http://www. xinhuanet.com/world/2017-01/18/c_1120331545.htm

must unswervingly develop an open world economy, share opportunities and benefits in opening up, and achieve mutual benefits and
win-win results. China must make greater efforts to promote global
interconnections so that all countries can achieve linked growth and
move towards common prosperity. China needs to unswervingly
develop global trade and investment, promote investment and trade
liberalisation, facilitate opening up, and oppose protectionism in a
clear-cut manner. 'Protectionism can be compared to enclosing your-
self in a dark room, where you seem to have avoided being battered
by the wind and rain, but in doing so, you are meanwhile cut off
from the sun and the air. The trade war can only hurt both sides',[186]
President Xi Jinping remarked in his keynote speech at the opening ceremony of the World Economic Forum in 2017. The concept of
win-win cooperation is a good way to counter actions that go against
the trend of globalisation, and it acts as a guide for the promotion of
a fairer and more reasonable global governance.

In the vast ocean of the world economy, it is impossible to cut off
the flow between countries of capital, technology, products, and
people. It is against the trend of the times to let the ocean of the
world economy retreat to small lakes and rivers. Economic globalisation has made the global village incrementally smaller, and
social information has made the world progressively flatter. Different countries and regions already have common interests, and they
stand together through thick and thin. The outdated zero-sum game
must be discarded because the winner-take-all idea does not reflect
the aspirations of the world's peoples. History has shown that brute
force and self-interest are not the ways for human beings to coexist,
and military violence cannot establish a better world. It is the common aspiration of the people of all countries to promote the building
of a community of a shared future with lasting peace and common
prosperity. The Chinese concept of win-win cooperation absorbs the
wisdom and essence of Chinese traditional culture and internalises
it into new values; in this, it conforms to the trend of the times characterised by peace and development and demonstrates our vision
and foresight.

3. Promote the Chinese Spirit of Reform and Innovation

At the present time, the fundamental problem facing the world economy is insufficient growth momentum. Therefore, the most urgent

---

186. https://america.cgtn.com/2017/01/17/full-text-of-xi-jinping-
keynote-at-the-world-economic-forum

task is to lead the world economy out of danger and onto the track of healthy and sustainable development. How can China provide impetus for world economic development? President Xi Jinping answered: 'Through reform and innovation'. He has stated: 'Innovation is the primary force guiding development. Unlike the previous industrial revolutions, the fourth industrial revolution is unfolding at an exponential rather than linear pace. We need to relentlessly pursue innovation. Only with the courage to innovate and reform can we remove bottlenecks blocking global growth and development'.[187]

Over the past forty years, China has overcome difficulties encountered in its progress through *reform and opening up*, has bravely removed institutional obstacles to development, and has recorded remarkable achievements in liberating and developing productive forces. From rural reform to urban reform, from economic restructuring to structural reform in all aspects, from invigorating the domestic economy to opening up to the outside world in all respects, a series of reforms and innovative practices have provided a valuable Chinese experience those developing countries can use to advance their economies and lift themselves out of poverty. China is committed to promoting innovation through reform and opening up, leading reform and opening up by innovation, and stimulating sustained and sound economic and social development. Taking institutional innovation as the core, China will accelerate the building of a new system for developing an open and innovative economy. It will foster and develop new forms of industry and trade, with a focus on business innovation. China must use technological innovation as the driving force to accelerate the transformation of the economic development pattern, and to inject strong innovative impetus into the world economy while promoting the development of new domestic drivers.

In a keynote speech at the World Economic Forum in Davos at the beginning of 2017, President Xi Jinping declared: 'We must innovate developmental concepts, go beyond the debate regarding fiscal stimulus or monetary easing, and establish a comprehensive approach to address both symptoms and root causes. We must innovate policy measures and promote structural reforms to create space for growth and increase momentum. We must innovate growth methods and seize the opportunities brought by the new round of industrial revolution and digital economy, so as to cope with the coming challenges from climate change and population aging and resolve the impact of informatisation and automation on employment. In the process

---

187. Ibid

of cultivating new industries, new formats, and new models, we should focus on creating new employment opportunities, so that people from all over the world can regain confidence and hope'.[188] Through an abundance of practices, China has accumulated considerable experience, and the successful path China has taken breeds the spirit of China. President Xi Jinping's important speech focused on the overall development of humankind and sought to realise the greatest common interests of all parties, thus representing an important plan provided by China for world development. It articulates valuable experiences undergone during China's successful development and demonstrates the Chinese spirit of reform and innovation.

4. Advocate an Open and Inclusive Chinese Style

The deliciousness of soup lies in the harmony of different tastes. Diversity is the basic characteristic of human civilisation. History has repeatedly proven that openness brings progress, and seclusion leads to backwardness. Different civilisations should learn from one another's strengths and make progress together, so that exchanges and mutual learning between civilisations can become the driving force for the advancement of human society, and the bond for maintaining world peace.

China's development from a poor and weak country to the second largest economy in the world has not relied on foreign expansion, colonialism, or power politics, but more importantly, on the hard work of its people. China does not seek to stand alone or to dominate but is committed to the common development of all countries in the world. China seeks to realise the common interests of all humankind and to share the fruits of human civilisation and progress. The more China develops, the more beneficial this will be to world peace and progress. The appearance of an increasingly prosperous and powerful China on the international arena is not only conducive to safeguarding the interests of the Chinese people, but also to enhancing the common well-being of people from all countries. Since the founding of the People's Republic of China, China has been committed to solving its own problems while providing assistance to developing countries without putting forward any requirements with regard to politics. China will continue to provide assistance to foreign countries within its capacity. Since the outbreak of the international financial crisis, China's contribution to world economic

---

188. Ibid

growth has averaged over 30% annually. In the next five years, China will import eight trillion U.S. dollars of goods and absorb 600 billion U.S. dollars of foreign investment. China's total foreign investment will reach 750 billion U.S. dollars, and outbound tourism will reach 700 million. This will bring more opportunities for the development of all countries in the world. China's development has benefited from interaction with the international community, and China is willing to contribute its experience of development to all countries worldwide. The Chinese people are well aware of the hardships of achieving national prosperity and rejuvenation, so they have a great esteem for all the achievements people have recorded globally. It is an earnest hope of China that the lives of people all across the world will continue to improve. China will not nurse jealousy against the countries that prosper or complain about the countries that achieve prosperity by enjoying the fruits of China's development. China will continue to pursue an open and inclusive policy, will share its development opportunities with other countries in the world, and will welcome all other countries to participate in China's progress. President Xi Jinping in his important speeches on many international occasions has won high praise from many countries.

5. Using Chinese Wisdom to Improve Global Governance

Global governance refers to the formulation of a series of binding international rules to regulate the behaviour of various countries and maintain a normal international political and economic order. The existing global governance system was formed under the leadership of developed countries after World War II. It has reasonable and legitimate aspects, as well as others that are imperfect and inappropriate. Since the Communist Party of China's 18th National Congress, China has appeared on the international stage as a defender and reformer of the existing international order. China has done its best to achieve the greatest possible common benefits and win-win results. On the theoretical level, China has enriched its understanding of global governance, and has further developed its positions in this area. On a practical level, China regards global governance as an important issue for participating in multilateral diplomacy and proposes its characteristic Chinese solutions.

From a global viewpoint, China has integrated its own interests with those of the rest of the world, and while safeguarding its own interests, has promoted the common prosperity and progress of all countries. China has taken an active part in the reform of global

governance. It has maintained its posture as a reasonable and cour-
teous major country and has cultivated an international image of
moderation and confidence. For example, in the face of the global
environmental crisis, China maintains that humankind should follow the principle of harmony between humanity and nature and
pursue sustainable development. China actively advocates a green,
low-carbon, sustainable mode of production and way of life. It continues to blaze a trail of civilised development that features increased
production, prosperity, and sound environmental practices. In addition, China is committed to making economic globalisation more
dynamic, inclusive, and sustainable. China supports the establishment of an open, inclusive, transparent, and non-discriminatory
multilateral trading system, and it advocates for the establishment of
fair and equitable new international political and economic orders.
On the basis of its integration into the existing international order,
China has actively promoted the reform and improvement of global
governance. China's positive attitude towards global governance
will help the world's countries to set a clear direction, build consensus and enhance confidence.

6. China's Efforts to Advance Belt and Road Construction

The Belt and Road Initiative (or BRI) proposed by President Xi Jinping embraces the heritage of the ancient Silk Road and sets out to
improve upon it. In line with the requirements of the times and the
aspiration of all countries to speed up development, China is committed to extensive consultation, joint contributions, and shared
benefits. China is committed to connecting with relevant countries to
advance development, achieve mutual benefits, and realise win-win
results through opening up and cooperation. In the current international situation, where economic globalisation has encountered
resistance, the construction of the BRI has become an important
public asset provided by China to the world. It is a major initiative through which China aims to lead the healthy development of
economic globalisation in this new era, and represents a concrete,
practical step in pursuing the goal of achieving win-win cooperation
among all countries.

Connectivity is an important aspect and measure of the BRI. If
the Belt and Road construction is likened to two wings of the world
economy, then connectivity is the bloodline and meridian of these
two wings. The connectivity of the BRI is not just about building
roads and bridges or linking single lines or planes. It is also about

coordinating efforts in five areas, namely policy communication, infrastructure connectivity, free (without tariffs) trade, financing, and people-to-people connectivity. This is an all-dimensional, networked connectivity. It is an open and inclusive system full of vitality and popular wisdom.

In order to promote the construction of the BRI, China has established the Silk Road Fund, has initiated the establishment of the Asian Infrastructure Investment Bank, and has promoted the establishment of the BRICS New Development Bank, with the aim of supporting the common development of all countries. Conscious that the old zero-sum thinking is not conducive to safeguarding and developing the universal interests of humanity, China has always believed that only when the world develops well can China prosper, and that if China develops well, then the world will be better. As President Xi Jinping said in his speech at the opening ceremony of the Belt and Road International Cooperation Summit Forum in May 2017, 'Over the past four years, more than 100 countries and international organisations around the world have supported and participated in the construction of the Belt and Road. China has signed cooperation agreements with more than forty countries and international organisations and has conducted institutionalised capacity cooperation with more than thirty countries'.[189] It can thus be said that although the Belt and Road Initiative originated in China, its fruits have benefited the world.

(Originally published in *Southern Entrepreneur*, Issue 9, 2017, second author: Zhu Bingyuan)

---

189. http://www.xinhuanet.com/2017-05/14/c_1120969677.htm

Index

About The Author

Cheng Enfu was born in Shanghai, China in 1950. He is an academician of the Chinese Academy of Social Sciences (CASS) and a member of the Presidium of the CASS Academic Divisions, Director of the Center for Economic and Social Development at the CASS, Vice Director and Chief Professor of the Academic Committee of the University of Chinese Academy of Social Sciences, and former President of the CASS Academy of Marxism. He is also a distinguished professor of the Center for Innovation of Marxism at Northwestern Polytechnical University and a chair professor at Shandong University.

He is a member of the Education, Science, Culture and Public Health Committee of the Thirteenth National People's Congress. He edits two international journals published in the UK: *International Critical Thought* and *World Review of Political Economy,* and two Chinese journals: *China Journal of Political Economy* and *Journal of Economics of Shanghai School.* He is Chair of the World Association for Political Economy, the Chinese Association for Political Economy, and the China Society for Foreign Economics. He is President of the World Culture Forum and the China Forum on Innovation of Marxism. He is also an international member of the Japan Society of Political Economy, an honorary professor at Saint Petersburg University and the Moscow University of Finance and Law, and Director of the Institute of the Economics of Shanghai School at the Shanghai University of Finance and Economics. He has published more than 600 papers and 40 books in 10 countries including the US, Russia, Japan, Italy, India, Vietnam, etc. He gave explanations at a collective study session of the CPC Politburo, and reported on theoretical issues at symposiums hosted by two General Secretaries of the CPC Central Committee.

www.ingramcontent.com/pod-product-compliance
Lightning Source LLC
Chambersburg PA
CBHW050558270326
41926CB00012B/2106